Advances in Macroeconomic Theory

This is IEA conference volume no. 133

Advances in
Macroeconomic Theory

Edited by

Jacques Drèze
CORE, Université Catholique de Louvain
Belgium

in association with
International Economic Association

First published 2001 by
PALGRAVE
Houndmills, Basingstoke, Hampshire RG21 6XS and
175 Fifth Avenue, New York, N. Y. 10010
Companies and representatives throughout the world

PALGRAVE is the new global academic imprint of
St. Martin's Press LLC Scholarly and Reference Division and
Palgrave Publishers Ltd (formerly Macmillan Press Ltd).

ISBN 0–333–77353–5

This book is printed on paper suitable for recycling and made from fully managed and sustained forest sources.

A catalogue record for this book is available from the British Library.

Library of Congress Cataloging-in-Publication Data
International Economic Association. World Congress (12th : Buenos Aires, Argentina)
        Advances in macroeconomic theory / edited by Jacques Drèze.
        v. cm. — (I.E.A. conference volume ; 133–)
        "Volume 1 of the proceedings of the IEA Congress held in Buenos Aires, Argentina : congress editor, Jacques Drèze."
        "Palgrave in association with International Economic Association."
        Papers from the Twelfth World Congress of the International Economic Association (IEA), held in Buenos Aires on August 23–17, 1999, at the invitation of of the Asociacion Argentina de Economia Politica (AAEP). The congress was dedicated to the memory of the late Michael Bruno, President of the IEA 1992–95.
        Includes bibliographical references and index.
        ISBN 0–333–77353–5
        1. Macroeconomics—Congresses. I. Drèze, Jacques H. II. Bruno, Michael. III. Title. IV. Series.

        HB172.5 .I567 199
        339—dc21
                                                        2001021195

10   9   8   7   6   5   4   3   2   1
10   09 08 07 06 05 04 03 02 01

Printed in Great Britain by Antony Rowe Ltd, Chippenham, Wiltshire

Contents

The International Economic Association

A non-profit organization with purely scientific aims, the International Economic Association (IEA) was founded in 1950. It is a federation of some 60 national economic associations in all parts of the world. Its basic purpose is the development of economics as an intellectual discipline, recognizing a variety of problems, systems and values in the world and taking note of methodological diversities.

The IEA has, since its creation, sought to fulfil that purpose by promoting mutual understanding among economists through the organization of scientific meetings and common research programmes, and by means of publications on problems of fundamental as well as current importance. Deriving from its long concern to assure professional contacts between East and West and North and South, the IEA pays special attention to issues of economies in systemic transition and in the course of development. During its 50 years of existence, it has organized more than a hundred round-table conferences for specialists on topics ranging from fundamental theories to methods and tools of analysis and major problems of the present-day world. Participation in round tables is at the invitation of a specialist programme committee, but 12 triennial World Congresses have regularly attracted the participation of individual economists from all over the world.

The Association is governed by a Council, comprising representatives of all member associations, and by a 15-member Executive Committee which is elected by the Council. The Executive Committee (1999–2002) at the time of the Buenos Aires Congress was:

President:	Professor Robert Solow, USA
Vice-President:	Professor Vittorio Corbo, Chile
Treasurer:	Professor Jacob Frenkel, Israel
Past President:	Professor Jacques Drèze, Belgium
Other members:	Professor Bina Agarwal, India
	Professor Maria Augusztinovics, Hungary
	Professor Eliana Cardoso, World Bank
	Professor Gene Grossman, USA
	Professor Seppo Honkapohja, Finland
	Professor Valery Makarov, Russia
	Professor Andreu Mas Colell, Spain
	Professor Mustapha Nabli, Tunisia
	Professor Adrian Pagan, Australia

Professor Hans Werner Sinn, Germany
Professor Kotaro Suzumura, Japan

Secretary-General: Professor Jean-Paul Fitoussi, France
General Editor: Professor Michael Kaser, UK

Sir Austin Robinson was an active Adviser on the publication of IEA Conference proceedings from 1954 until his final short illness in 1993. The Association has also been fortunate in having secured many outstanding economists to serve as President: Gottfried Haberler (1950–53), Howard S. Ellis (1953–56), Erik Lindahl (1956–59), E.A.G. Robinson (1959–62), Ugo Papi (1962–65), Paul A. Samuelson (1965–68), Erik Lundberg (1968–71), Fritz Machlup (1971–74), Edmund Malinvaud (1974–77), Shigeto Tsuru (1977–80), Victor L. Urquidi (1980–83), Kenneth J. Arrow (1983–86), Amartya Sen (1986–89), Anthony B. Atkinson (1989–1992), Michael Bruno (1992–95) and Jacques Drèze (1995–99).

The activities of the Association are mainly funded from the subscriptions of members and grants from a number of organizations, including continuing support from UNESCO, through the International Social Science Council. Specific support from the latter was received for the Buenos Aires Congress under its Project R4/CAR.

Acknowledgements

The Twelfth World Congress of the International Economic Association (IEA) was held in Buenos Aires on 23–27 August 1999, at the invitation of the Asociación Argentina de Economía Política (AAEP). The IEA is deeply grateful to the AAEP for its willingness to host the congress, and above all for superbly handling the local arrangements. The 1260 registered participants undoubtedly feel equally grateful.

The congress was dedicated to the memory of the late Michael Bruno, President of the IEA, 1992–95, as a tribute to his valuable contributions to economics, and in particular to the IEA.

The Organizing Committee consisted of Enrique Bour, president, Rolf Mantel, vice-president, Victor Beker, executive secretary, Marcela Cristini, Maria Echart, Marcos Gallacher and Javier Ortiz. It is very sad that Rolf Mantel died prematurely in February 1999. He had been a productive researcher and an influential member of the Latin American scientific community. He was an exceptionally fine person. The IEA joins Mrs Mantel and Rolf's numerous friends in treasuring his memory.

Special thanks go to Enrique Bour, former AAEP President, who shouldered much responsibility as president of the Organizing Committee. He showed exceptional dedication, ability and congeniality.

Financial support towards the local organization came first from Banco Central de la Republica Argentina, soon complemented by Banco de la Nación Argentina, Banco de la Provincia de Buenos Aires, Banco Hipotecario, Ministerio de Relaciónes Exteriores, Comercio Internacional y Culto, Secretaría de Industria, Comercio y Miniera and Secretaría de Programación Económica y Regional. Their support is gratefully acknowledged.

The logistics of the congress were handled with competence by the staff of Maria Graziani y Asociados of Buenos Aires and by IEA administrative assistants Marie David and Véronique de Labarre.

The scientific programme included two series of invited lectures, one on 'Macroeconomics' organized by Jacques Drèze (Université Catholique de Louvain) and one on 'Inequality' organized by Richard Freeman (Harvard University and London School of Economics). These lectures appear in the present Proceedings volume and in Volume 2. The rest of the programme comprised 310 contributed papers, selected from a still larger number of submissions by a 30-member Programme Committee ably and diligently chaired by David de la Croix (Université Catholique de Louvain). From these, important papers dealing with Latin American issues constitute Volume 3, edited by Enrique Bour, Daniel Heymann and Fernando Navajas.

Maureen Hadfield and Michael Kaser supervised the editorial process. The IEA expresses its gratitude to all participants in their efforts for both programme and publication.

Some hundred authors of invited papers, in particular authors from emerging countries, received travel grants to Buenos Aires. These grants were funded by the World Bank, the World Bank Institute, the Inter-American Development Bank, the Asian Development Bank and the European Investment Bank. Their support is gratefully acknowledged.

The main credit for the success of the congress goes to the authors of invited lectures and contributed papers. They supplied a rich intellectual material, incompletely but representatively covered in these three volumes.

List of Contributors

Michael Adler, Columbia University, New York, USA.
Ricardo Caballero, Massachusetts Institute of Technology, Cambridge, Mass., USA.
Stephen G. Cecchetti, Ohio State University, Columbus, Ohio, and Federal Reserve Bank of New York, USA.
Vittorio Corbo, Universidad Catholica de Chile, Santiago, Chile.
David de la Croix, IRES Université Catholique de Louvain, Louvain-la-Neuve, Belgium.
Jean-Pierrre Danthine, Université de Lausanne, Switzerland.
John B. Donaldson, Columbia University, New York, USA.
Jacques Drèze, CORE, Université Catholique de Louvain, Louvain-la-Neuve, Belgium.
William Easterly, The World Bank, Washington DC, USA.
Richard Freeman, Harvard University, Cambridge, Mass., USA, and London School of Economics and Political Science, UK.
Bruce Greenwald, Columbia University, New York, USA.
Erica L. Groshen, Bank for International Settlements, Basle, Switzerland, and Federal Reserve Bank of New York, USA.
Mohamad Hammour, DELTA-ENS, Paris, France.
Seppo Honkapohja, University of Helsinki, Finland.
Roumeen Islam, The World Bank, Washington DC, USA.
Francis Kramarz, Centre de Recherche en Economie et Statistique, INSEE, Paris, France.
Adrian Pagan, Australian National University, Canberra, Australia.
Danny Quah, London School of Economics and Political Science, UK.
Carlos Rodriguez, CEMA University, Buenos Aires, Argentina.
Robert M. Solow, Massachusetts Institute of Technology, Cambridge, Mass., USA.
Joseph E. Stiglitz, Stanford University, Stanford, Cal., USA.
John Taylor, Stanford University, Stanford, Cal., USA.

List of Abbreviations and Acronyms

AAEP	Asociación Argentina de Economía Política
AR	auto-regression
ARCH	autoregressive conditional heteroskedasticy
BHPS	British Household Panel Study
CEPR	Centre for Economic Policy Research
CIA	cash-in-advance
CNRS	Conseil National de la Recherche Scientifique
CORE	Center for Operations Research and Econometrics
CPI	consumer price index
CPS	Current Population Survey
CREST	Centre de Recheches en Économie et Statistique
DADS	Déclarations Annuelles de Données Sociales
DELTA	Departement et Laboratoire d'Économie Theorique et Appliquée (joint research unit of the CNRS, EHESS and ENS)
DGP	data generating process
DMMO	Déclarations de Mouvement de Main d'Oeuvre
DNA	deoxyribonucleic acid
EC	European Commission
EC12	European Community, 1986 membership
ECB	European Central Bank
ECLAC	UN Economic Commission for Latin America and the Caribbean
EGARCH	exponential generalized ARCH
EHESS	École des Hautes Études en Sciences Sociales
EM	emerging market
EMBI	emerging markets bond index
ENS	École Normale Supérieure
ESOP	employee stock-ownership programme
Fed	Federal Reserve Board
FOMC	Federal Open Market Committee
FRB	Federal Reserve Board
FTC	Federal Trade Commission
G-7	Group of Seven
GDP	gross domestic product
GE	general equilibrium
IEA	International Economic Association
i.i.d.	independently and identically distributed
ILO	International Labour Organisation
IMF	International Monetary Fund

INSEE	Institut National de la Statistique et des Études Économiques
IPR	intellectual property rights
IRES	Institut de Recherches Économiques et Sociales
IT	information technology
K/L	capital:labour ratio
LDC	less developed country
LFS	Labour Force Survey (France)
M&A	merger and acquisition
Mercosur	Southern Cone Common Market
MIT	Massachusetts Institute of Technology
MSR	money supply rules
NBER	National Bureau of Economic Research
n.i.d.	normally independently distributed
PAYG	pay-as-you-go
P/E	price/earnings
PFMC	pension fund management company
PPP	purchasing power parity
PSID	Panel Study of Income Dynamics
R&D	research and development
RBC	real business cycle
RE	rational expectations
REE	RE equilibrium
S&P	Standard and Poor's
SEM	simultaneous equation model
SETAR	self-exciting threshold autoregression
SMIC	salaire minimum interprofessional de croissance
SVAR	structural VAR
TMCM	Taylor's multicountry model
TQM	total quality management
UK	United Kingdom
UNESCO	United Nations Educational, Scientific and Cultural Organization
US(A)	United States of America
VAR	vector auto-regression
VECM	vector error correction model
VMA	vector moving average
WGET	Walrasian general equilibrium theory
WPI	wholesale price index

1
Introduction: Advances and Challenges in Macroeconomics

Jacques Drèze
Université Catholique de Louvain, Belgium

This volume collects the 16 invited lectures on macroeconomics delivered at the Twelfth World Congress of the International Economic Association in Buenos Aires, 23–27 August 1999. Responsibility for issuing the invitations and suggesting topics rested with me, so I am fully accountable for selection bias. Authors knew that they were addressing a general audience. They were urged to cover a broad topic rather than a sharp contribution, and to present their own views rather than a balanced survey. The typical lecture summarized, with a minimum of technicality, the main conclusions of the author's research over a decade or more in some broad area of relevance to macroeconomics. Beyond the value of the individual lectures, this volume offers a selective but largely spread-out picture of ongoing research in macroeconomics. I first summarize the lectures (section 1.1), then offer some speculative conclusions of my own on the state of the discipline (section 1.2).

1.1 Advances in macroeconomics

1.1.1 Growth and fluctuations

Robert Solow (Chapter 2) reminds us that the neoclassical growth model was initially designed (in particular by himself) to study long-run equilibrium. He then expresses surprise that the same basic model is used nowadays to study short-run fluctuations, labelled 'real business cycles' (RBC). With the benign wit to which he has accustomed his readers, Solow discusses how this diversion came about. He stresses the role assigned to prices in bringing about equilibrium, and voices reservations about the ability of prices to adjust fully at business cycle frequencies. Extending Keynesian ideas in the direction of microeconomic foundations, while adding market imperfections to RBCs, is conducive to some convergence. A more ambitious programme calls for developing a macroeconomic theory of the middle run, a programme to the definition of which Solow contributes a few thoughts of his own.

1

Among his suggestions for characterizing short-run equilibria and understanding the occasional persistence of under-utilization of resources (the Depression of the 1930s, European unemployment over the last quarter-century, Japan in the 1990s), Solow also lists (with muted conviction) the possibility of multiple equilibria reflecting coordination failures. That possibility is developed in my own lecture (Chapter 3), as an implication of market incompleteness. Under downward real rigidity of some (not all) wages and prices, there typically exists a continuum of supply-constrained equilibria, where the extent of supply rationing reflects history (path dependency) and expectations of future developments, including future supply rationing. I first explain how incomplete markets introduce volatility in aggregate demand, especially investment, leading to alternative equilibria under price and wage rigidities. Next, I review how uncertainty with incomplete markets justifies second-best real wage rigidities, forces firms to cover fixed costs at all demand realizations (with associated downward price rigidities) and leads risk-averse firms to behave as if they faced kinked demand curves. Under-utilization of labour and of fixed capacities come in.

The existence of a continuum of supply-constrained equilibria is established in two theorems. The emergence of supply-constrained equilibria (how they come about) is accounted for by a tâtonnement process in prices and quantities allowing for downward rigidity of some prices and wages along the adjustment. The process converges to supply-constrained equilibria.

Turning to policy, I note that coordination failures not only magnify the consequences of price–wage rigidities but are also endowed with persistence, and subject to continuous recurrence. This suggests sustainable policies of demand stabilization (for instance through counter-cyclical investments with adequate social returns), and policies addressed to by-pass the wage–price rigidities linked to incomplete markets (for instance through cyclically adjusted labour taxes or financial innovation).

An assessment by insiders of the accomplishments to date of real business cycle theory (RBC) is offered by Jean-Pierre Danthine and John Donaldson (Chapter 4). The RBC ongoing research programme aims at identifying empirically the market imperfections that have clear macroeconomic significance. This search is largely guided by the shortcomings of simpler formulations in matching data, the so-called 'puzzles'. The authors review stylized facts relating to labour markets, prominent among which is the 'employment variability puzzle', to which several answers have been investigated (contracts, efficiency wages, but also labour–time indivisibility). Other facts, relating to productivity or unemployment, permit some discrimination, but inconclusively so, regret the authors. Turning to money, the negative impact of an unanticipated increase of money supply on nominal interest rates is treated as a stylized fact, explained only in part by sluggish adjustments in prices and/or portfolios. Regarding the celebrated 'equity premium puzzle', the authors refer to models of habit formation, also considered by de la Croix (Chapter 13), and to their own research on 'peso-effects' and factor share variability. They also refer to presumed imperfections, such as imperfect competition or expectational errors; and to recent models combining several imperfections, a feature that seems required to account for some of the empirical evidence within the postulated framework. The authors' conclusions on which combination of market imperfections may survive in a convincing new macroeconomic paradigm are guarded – we are not yet there, but (unlike Solow (Chapter 2) or Pagan (Chapter 11)) they are confident that the path is right.

1.1.2 Money, finance and inflation

John Taylor (Chapter 5) writes about an approach to macroeconomic policy evaluation (labelled the 'new normative macroeconomics') which uses dynamic stochastic policy models, policy rules (including 'Taylor rules') and policy trade-offs. 'A policy rule is a description of how the instruments of policy should be changed in response to observable events' (p. 83). The distinctive feature of this avenue of policy evaluation research is that it permits a simple formulation of rational expectations: agents know the rule followed by monetary authorities. Alternative rules are then compared on the basis of simulations of their steady-state stochastic implications. The author reports on extensive simulations, within alternative macro-models, of a few interest-rate setting rules (differing as to the numerical coefficients assigned to deviations of inflation and output from target values). Performance is assessed, both in terms of summary measures and with reference to specific policy questions. Current attention is focused on the trade-off between inflation variability and output variability. This line of research is presented as compatible with alternative underlying theoretical specifications (though typically embodying some nominal frictions and a specific monetary transmission mechanism, the interest channel), and as susceptible of implementation through a variety of econometric specifications.

Bruce Greenwald (Chapter 6), also building on joint work with Joseph Stiglitz, sees in a specific imperfection of financial markets a distinct source of aggregate fluctuations. The argument is simple. The inside information of a firm's management creates an asymmetry relative to investors, which limits the scope for equity financing and assigns a role to the firm's net wealth. Output decisions made under uncertainty about selling prices will respond positively to net worth. The income effect (for firms) of price increases exacerbates fluctuations. Because net worth evolves with retained earnings, a persistence mechanism emerges. Also transfers of wealth from households to firms (for instance due to income effects of lower interest rates) become expansionary.

The same reasoning applies to banks, a special case of firms with output taking the form of loans. The net worth of banks, evolving with earnings linked to interest rate differentials, becomes a determinant of the supply of loans. Transfers of wealth from depositors to banks are expansionary. Also, the net worth of banks is influenced by asset prices, which defines yet another channel of monetary transmission. The chapter ends on an application to small open economies.

Increased use of inflation targeting in the conduct of monetary policy stresses the importance of understanding inflation, the issue addressed by Stephen Cecchetti and Erica Groshen (Chapter 7). The first problem is to measure trend inflation. Statistical and theoretical arguments concur to favour the use of *trimmed means* (averages of individual price changes omitting the tails of the distribution). The second problem is to estimate both future inflation and the (lagged) impact of monetary policy (interest rates) on inflation. Path dependency and non-linearities are unavoidable sources of imprecision. The third problem is to set an optimal inflation target, balancing negative 'sand effects' and positive 'grease effects'. Inflation introduces rising uncertainty and distortions in relative prices (sand); but moderate inflation mitigates the impact of downward nominal rigidities (grease). There exist statistical procedures to distinguish the two empirically – namely, the distinction between symmetrical, intra-market relative price movements (sand) and asymmetrical, inter-market movements. The authors suggest a target of 2.5 per cent for CPI inflation, or a band of 0–2 per cent for bias-adjusted inflation. The target could be adjusted negatively to the rate of productivity growth and positively to the stability of monetary policy.

1.1.3   Labour markets

Part III of this volume, devoted to labour markets, opens with the provocative lecture of Richard Freeman (Chapter 8) on 'the relation between economic institutions and outcomes'. Labour market institutions and social policies differ markedly across such countries as the US, Japan, Scandinavia, Germany and Italy. Freeman asks, and answers, three questions: (i) Do these different institutions and policies affect economic outcomes? They have identifiable large effects on distribution, but modest hard-to-uncover effects on efficiency. (ii) Can institutional differences persist in a global economy? Yes. (iii) Has the current lead candidate for peak economy, the US, found the right institutions for the twenty-first century? Too soon to tell.

Evidence that institutions do affect distribution comes from the lower dispersion of wages and benefits associated with unionization or collective bargaining, confirmed by the changes in dispersion for workers moving between union and non-union jobs; it also comes from cross-country comparisons, confirmed by the changes in dispersion following regime changes.

The set of modest or inconclusive results on efficiency implications includes the following: profit-sharing raises productivity by 3–4 per cent; two-thirds of unionized firms are more productive than non-unionized firms, but not enough to absorb the extra costs linked to unionization; minimum wages have at most modest effects on employment; employment protection laws do not affect employment but result in longer spells of both job tenure and unemployment; cross-country comparisons have led to different rankings of institutions in the 1970s, 1980s and 1990s. As for current trends, they reveal divergence across countries of the rates of unionization and collective bargaining coverage; the convergence of incomes per capita is unrelated to labour market institutions.

Finally Freeman notes that several candidates for peak overall performance among capitalist economies have replaced each other at short intervals. The US candidacy today, almost entirely based on employment performance in the 1990s, and easily challenged on the inequality front, needs confirmation through a few more years of full employment accompanied by reduction in poverty.

Freeman advances two hypotheses as potential explanations of the strong impact on distribution, weak impact on efficiency; namely: (i) there exist rents to the joint use of factors of production and the division of these rents matters little to efficiency; (ii) no matter how rents are appropriated, capital and labour will reach an efficient outcome through non-wage bargains (Coase Theorem).

It is an unplanned but fortunate coincidence that the other two lectures in Part III have bearing on these two hypotheses. In a set of recent papers, Ricardo Caballero and Mohamad Hammour have investigated the implications of *specificity* in production: 'a factor is specific with respect to a production arrangement ... when it would lose part of its value if used outside this arrangement' (Chapter 9, p. 173). Specificity generates precisely the kind of (quasi-) rents listed by Freeman as a possible explanation of his findings. Caballero and Hammour do, however, reach substantially different conclusions about the relevance of labour market institutions for efficiency.

'Institutional arrangements are mechanisms that help address the problems that arise from the need to cooperate' (Chapter 9, p. 175). Cooperation gives rise to specificity, hence to division and possibly to appropriation of rents – with implications for both distribution and efficiency. 'A poor institutional environment *discourages cooperation* between factors of production. In equilibrium, this results in *under-employment, market-segmentation* and *technological exclusion* of the "appropriating" factor' (Chapter 9, p. 177). A factor is 'appropriating' when it captures a larger share of the rents than warranted by its *ex ante* terms of trade. Caballero and Hammour apply these ideas to an interpretation of French unemployment, 1975–95. They identify an 'institutional push' in favour of labour, starting in 1968 and culminating in 1981. The appropriation of rents by labour resulted in rising wages and a declining profit rate. From 1983 on, trends are reversed, because newly invested capital is no longer 'appropriated'. The authors conclude 'that institutions are the main culprit behind persistent unemployment in Europe' (Chapter 9, p. 182).

Turning to technological restructuring, Caballero and Hammour first argue that 'a poor institutional environment results in *sclerosis* – the inefficient survival of low-productivity jobs. Moreover, it causes the restructuring process to be *unbalanced*; given the level of creation, destruction is excessively high' (Chapter 9, p. 191). Accordingly, the destruction process during recessions is not conducive to significant restructuring. They find confirmation of their theory in the observation that merger waves are concentrated in periods of rising, not declining, stock-market valuation. The limited restructuring during recessions is imputed to financial market imperfections, of the kind also stressed by Greenwald (Chapter 6) and Easterly, Islam and Stiglitz (Chapter 17).

Francis Kramarz (Chapter 10) surveys the results of recent empirical research on (nominal) wage rigidities in the United States and Europe. The survey bears on a dozen studies, and Kramarz finds that results vary between countries, time periods, data sources, categories of workers or even econometric techniques. Accordingly, the evidence of nominal wage rigidities might appear mixed, were it not for the consistent finding that inflation matters: distributions of wage changes in years of high inflation strongly differ from those observed in years of low inflation, with higher spikes at zero in the latter. A corroborating finding from France is that 60 per cent of nominal pay cuts in a given firm either come from a lower annual bonus or reflect a change in working conditions. From this, and the survey evidence collected by Bewley to the effect that employers are extremely reluctant to cut pay, Kramarz concludes: 'I believe that evidence of wage rigidity exists, or to be more specific, firms appear to prefer to cut employment rather than cut wages in a downturn' (Chapter 10, p. 215).

Two studies of firm-level data for France in the 1990s suggest that firms control their wage bills through entry and exit, with little adjustment in the pay of stayers, especially low-skilled stayers. In particular, wage bill contractions bear disproportionately on entry. Kramarz concludes that firms find ways of circumventing wage rigidities, as hypothesized by Freeman.

1.1.4 Econometrics

Econometric research of significance to macroeconomics has advanced along several lines in the recent past. One line concerns the analysis of richer bases of microeconomic data, as illustrated in the lectures of Cecchetti and Groshen, Freeman or Kramarz. Macroeconometrics has also evolved significantly, as growing attention was paid to the time-series nature of aggregate data. Adrian Pagan (Chapter 11) reviews developments along that second line. His lecture is organized around the distinction between the complementary steps of *summarizing* the data and *interpreting* the data, a distinction of which he stresses the logical as well as methodological importance.

Statistical fit is the guideline for summarizing data. Economic reasoning enters only to guide the choice of data series to be investigated. The early focus on first and second moments has been enriched significantly by the computation of auto-correlation functions. For univariate series, simple linear parametric models, like first and second order auto-regression, often provide parsimonious representations with suitable dynamics. Hetero-skedasticity can be added, for instance to account for 'clustering of volatility'. Vector auto-regression provides a natural extension to multivariate series, leading also to study impulse responses and co-integration. In both cases, the contribution of non-linear extensions remains uncertain.

Turning to interpretation, Pagan concentrates mostly on the multivariate models, which occupy centre stage in macroeconometric research. He reviews successively structural vector auto-regressions (SVAR), simultaneous equations (SEM) and calibrated models. The popularity of SVAR is linked to the view that fluctuations are driven by shocks. Economic theory then bears on the properties of the error terms (shocks), in particular their covariances and propagation. Because many SVAR models are exactly identified, the distinction between summary and interpretation is blurred, possibly resulting in invalid interpretations. These models have their own limitations for policy analysis, which explains why institutions concerned with policy formation still rely extensively on SEMs, now typically incorporating rational expectations.

Pagan divides his discussion of calibrated models into academic models and policy models. The specification of academic calibrated models is typically derived from the behaviour of optimizing agents. A weakness of the approach concerns the verification of how well the models fit the data – an issue on which Pagan offers several suggestions. Calibrated policy models typically come on a larger scale, but share many features with the academic variety. It is sometimes possible to use a small-scale approximation of a large model to check the empirical validity of the latter.

1.1.5 Dynamics

Part V, devoted to dynamics, contains two chapters (two more suffered from late withdrawals). Honkapohja (Chapter 12) treats the important topic of learning dynamics, successively under complete and incomplete learning. The distinction is that in the former case, but not in the latter, there is convergence to a rational expectations equilibrium. Which case obtains depends upon properties of both the economic model and the learning rule followed by the agents. Alternative specifications entail rich dynamic possibilities, which are illustrated by Honkapohja for a simple overlapping generations model with a continuum of agents and a positive production externality: each agent's productivity increases with aggregate labour input. Agents form expectations (about next period's aggregate labour input) on the basis of past data. An instance of complete learning is obtained if each forecast is given by the updated mean of past observations, a simple illustration of 'econometric learning'. Under suitable specifications, there exist three Pareto-ranked steady-state equilibria – low (L), intermediate (U) and high (H), with (L) and (H) locally stable under the assumed learning rule and (U) unstable. The stable equilibrium (L) is an instance of coordination failure. Policies can be devised to move the economy from (L) to (H) – but there also exist misguided policies with the opposite effect.

In order to illustrate the richer dynamics permitted by incomplete learning, Honkapohja introduces productivity shocks in the same model, and considers a learning rule corresponding to adaptive expectations. These specifications introduce the possibility of endogenous fluctuations: for 'small' shocks, (L) and (H) remain locally stable; for larger shocks, there exist positive probabilities of transition from the (L) neighbourhood to the (H) neighbourhood and vice versa (endogenous fluctuations). Honkapohja concludes with a discussion of the choice by agents of the parameter defining the adaptive-expectations learning rule and introduces the concept of (Nash-)equilibrium in learning rules. Overall, learning equilibria are viewed as more appealing than exogenously postulated rational expectations.

David de la Croix (Chapter 13) reviews some macroeconomic implications of alternative dynamic specifications of preferences. A central objective is to generate more persistent propagation mechanisms in real business cycle models, where the standard specification rests on inter-temporal preferences that are additively separable and stationary. A first generalization, labelled 'personal capital' by de la Croix, introduces lagged consumption as an argument of instantaneous consumption preferences. This increases the propensity to smooth consumption, a welcome feature given the 'excess smoothness puzzle' in standard RBC models; it requires adjustments to portfolios, increasing the volatility of asset returns, and to savings, increasing the volatility of investment. A second generalization, labelled 'social capital', introduces lagged *aggregate* consumption as an argument of individual preferences. This leads to a 'consumption externality', which could be corrected by taxes and/or additional provision of public goods. A third generalization, labelled 'family capital', introduces parents' consumption as an argument of children's preferences, in an overlapping generations framework. Under specific assumptions, this feature opens the door to rich dynamics: oscillations, a poverty trap and a decline scenario.

Turning to the supply of effort, de la Croix and his co-authors have introduced a worker's past wages in the effort supply functions of an efficiency wage model, thereby obtaining the high variability of employment and low variability of wages which standard RBC models fail to reproduce. They have similarly introduced to advantage the wages and past wages of peers.

1.1.6 Development

Both Vittorio Corbo of Chile and Carlos Rodriguez of Argentina draw from their Latin-American experience clear conclusions about economic policies conducive to stability and growth. Both have witnessed, perhaps more vividly in Latin America than elsewhere, the radical reorientation of thinking about development. In the words of Corbo,

> the old import-substitution-cum-government-intervention model of the 1950s and 1960s, with a weak concern for macroeconomic stability, has been replaced by a model where restoring and maintaining macroeconomic stability is a central element and where the role of markets and government have been radically changed ... to ensure macroeconomic stability, to provide a regulatory and institutional infrastructure for the development of a competitive market economy, and to improve the supply of public goods, especially social services for the poorest groups in the population (ch. 14, p. 286).

Restoring and maintaining macroeconomic stability is the theme developed by Rodriguez (Chapter 15). He starts from the observation that macroeconomic imbalances – current or prospective – result in substantial and costly country-risk premia. Controlling fiscal deficits and inflation, both current and prospective, is essential to reduce the country-risk premia – there is no other way. In particular, nominal devaluations in the presence of unsustainable fiscal deficits are useless and counterproductive. Successful stabilization need *not* be contractionary, because it reduces the country premia hence real interest rates. But the premia of individual countries are contaminated by those of comparable countries (contagion effect) and by financial developments worldwide.

In Latin America, financial instability has resulted in 'dollarization', the use of the US dollar instead of the local currency. The phenomenon has not receded as inflation abated, and Rodriguez regards it as irreversible. He notes that dollarization deprives the central bank of its role as lender of last resort. The extreme form of dollarization calls for the central bank to behave like a currency board, as has been the case in Argentina since 1991. The function of lender of last resort was restored there through credit lines with foreign banks. Currency boards are not a panacea – certainly not a substitute for fiscal discipline. But they enable a country to break out of the vicious circle of inadequate tax collection under high inflation, as was the case for Argentina. Still, Rodriguez argues that a monetary union with the United States would entail additional benefits to both countries.

Corbo (Chapter 14) regards stabilization and trade opening as the first phase of policy reform; he looks at the next deeper phase of stepping up growth and improving the access of the poor to social services; he then returns to new issues of macroeconomic management. Endogenous growth theory stresses the role of infrastructure. Insufficient investment during the years of macroeconomic instability and limited funding opportunities suggest concentrating public investment on public services for the poor (such as health care and education) while encouraging private provision of other public goods (such as toll roads and airports). This calls for developing a suitable regulatory framework, starting with improved training of regulators. It also calls for eliminating unnecessary drains on public budgets: Corbo singles out pension reform as a significant instance.

Corbo finds that much remains to be done towards improving the quality of education and equality of opportunities. Information is scanty, an argument in favour of decentralization. There is resistance to change, though some specific avenues of promising reform can be defined. Broadly similar remarks apply to health services.

Corbo's discussion of new issues of macroeconomic management complements that of Rodriguez. On the choice of an exchange-rate regime, he sees flexible exchange rates as the remaining alternative to a fully credible fixed-rate system of the currency board family. Under the latter option, the exchange rate provides the nominal anchor. Under the former, inflation targeting through an interest rate instrument is gaining favour also in Latin America; but the single instrument does not permit adjoining either an exchange-rate target, or a (generally desirable) current-account target; hence, the central bank may face a trade-off between conflicting objectives.

Danny Quah (Chapter 16) reports on cross-country growth comparisons, a relatively recent concern on which research has been stimulated by availability of better and richer data, in particular the Penn World Tables assembled by Summers and Heston. In a simple non-stochastic, neoclassical growth model, each individual country converges to its own steady-state growth path. For a cross-section of countries, these paths are not identical; neither are the initial positions relative to the growth paths. The cross-section therefore shows considerable diversity, and the underlying structure has important implications for empirical analysis.

Quah devotes his attention to technology (productivity), first as a factor contributing to an explanation of the large cross-sectional variation of performance across countries, second to enquire about the process governing its dissemination between countries. He ends with an open question: which theoretical considerations will validate his empirical finding that patterns of trade (who trades with whom) are relevant to the clustering of countries into subgroups characterized by a common path of technological evolution?

William Easterly, Roumeen Islam and Joseph Stiglitz (Chapter 17) treat short-term fluctuations under the heading 'volatility'. A first assertion (empirically documented elsewhere) is that volatility of output growth is more pronounced in developing than in developed countries: the former are both more exposed to, and less able to cope with, volatility. The central tenet is that volatility is associated with (shocks are intensified by) short-run dynamic adjustments triggered by wealth or cash-flow effects on financial intermediaries; these dynamic adjustments are described as dominating the short-run behaviour of economies where institutional safeguards are weak. As also explained by Greenwald (Chapter 6), the direct implication of negative wealth or liquidity shocks affecting financial intermediaries is a contraction in the supply of credit, curtailing investment and transmitting the shock to the rest of the economy. A chain of liquidity shocks may cause systemic bankruptcies. Credit rationing has wealth and liquidity implications for firms, leading them to contract output and employment. Liquidity constraints on governments help explain the surprising observation that developing countries tend to conduct pro-cyclical fiscal policies, in contrast to developed countries.

Another example of perverse short-run adjustments concerns wages. Real wages are reported to be more flexible in developing than in developed countries. But the income effects of wage adjustments have destabilizing consequences for aggregate demand, and these may dominate the substitution effects. It is the authors' conviction that incorporating these dynamic effects will produce macroeconomic paradigms general enough to encompass the specificity of different sets of countries.

1.2 Challenges in macroeconomics

So much for the trees. What about the forest? The diversity of the material covered in this book invites the search for common threads. I offer a few very personal suggestions, with the warning that they emanate from someone who approached macroeconomics from a general equilibrium background.[1]

Definition. I start from the definition of macroeconomics in the *Lectures on Macroeconomics* by Olivier Blanchard and Stanley Fischer (1989, p. 27): 'dynamic general equilibrium under uncertainty, with incomplete (and possibly imperfect) markets'. That definition combines concisely five important features. My subjective count reveals that, *on average*, between three and four of these features play a significant role in the lectures below. I surmise that all authors in this volume implicitly or explicitly accept such a definition.

The definition is unquestionably demanding. 'Dynamic ... under-uncertainty' means that agents must solve sequential decision problems under uncertainty. The analytical complexity of these problems is well known, calling for numerical solutions. This is clearly a dimension along which microeconomic research is important to the advancement of macroeconomics.[2] 'General equilibrium ... with incomplete markets' raises conceptual difficulties: with what decision criteria should firms be endowed? What should be assumed about the coordination of individual expectations? And so on. There are also technical difficulties: even for simplified equilibrium concepts, existence theory is more demanding than with complete markets (degree theory instead of fixed points); cardinality and stability of equilibria largely remain to be studied, especially for monetary economies; and so on.

The definition makes no reference to *macro* as such. I understand macroeconomics to be concerned with aggregate quantities (output, employment, inflation).[3] Beyond the challenge of developing a suitable general equilibrium theory lies the further challenge of extracting from it some *condensed operational model(s)* of the interaction among a few key aggregate variables.

Methodology.   All the lectures in this volume deal with market economies and somewhere in the back – or in the front – of the minds of all authors lies the theory of first-best efficient competitive equilibria in real economies, i.e. Walrasian general equilibrium theory (WGET). I regard as a unifying thread that most, perhaps all, authors are concerned with *specific departures from that theoretical model, departures which have significant macroeconomic implications*.[4] Diversity comes from the methodological path along which the investigation is conducted and from the nature of the market imperfections selected for investigation.

Aside from those lectures which bear upon a specific topic (Chapters 7, 8, 10 and 11) or which proceed from a reduced form (Chapters 5 and 15), I see two methodological options at work, namely: (i) start from the first-best theory, and introduce imperfections as needed to accommodate facts (Chapters 4, 13, 14 and 16); or (ii) start from specific departures from the first-best model, and investigate their macroeconomic implications (Chapters 3, 6, 9, 12 and 17).[5] To illustrate, Danthine and Donaldson (Chapter 4) state (in an unpublished abstract) that the RBC research programme is 'meant to identify and incorporate into dynamic general equilibrium models those market imperfections which are most relevant for macroeconomic theory and policy'. This is almost exactly the definition of my category (i). In contrast, Honkapohja (Chapter 12) starts from incomplete markets (today's young do not trade today with tomorrow's young), recognizes that agents' expectations (which substitute for price information) must be based upon learning, and obtains unexpectedly rich dynamics – a clear illustration of my category (ii). Similarly, I note that incomplete markets breed price rigidities and demand volatility, and obtain unexpectedly ubiquitous coordination failure equilibria.

I feel inclined to contrast the methodological stances of my categories (i) and (ii) by labelling them respectively (i) top-down and (ii) bottom-up. Both approaches face the same central difficulty: how to cope with a *multiplicity of imperfections*.

Imperfections. I identify three themes as recurring: *imperfect information, incomplete markets* and the *role of institutions*. These appear significantly in respectively seven, five and four lectures (out of ten candidates). Information and incomplete markets are linked, since the latter automatically raise the issue of what substitute exists for the missing price information. The role of expectations is rooted in these information problems. Note also that some institutions (e.g. contracts) are developed to generate information or to address problems arising from market incompleteness.[6] The search for macroeconomic implications of such imperfections is a welcome recent development, mostly conducted in bottom-up fashion.[7] (A likely explanation is that my three themes concern interactions among heterogeneous agents, a source of conceptual as well as technical difficulties in the RBC top-down methodology.)

Of course, many other imperfections appear below, and more generally in macroeconomic research: externalities, increasing returns, market power, and so on. Going from Walrasian general equilibrium theory to an *encompassing framework* in which all these imperfections can be fitted requires revisions of the three basic ingredients of WGET: the primitives of the model, the assumptions about primitives and the equilibrium concept. In as much as possible, one would like to trace imperfections back to the primitives, but there is some unavoidable compromise in drawing the line. Thus, in standard WGET, a set of firms is introduced among the primitives, whereas the births and deaths of firms result from an economic process. Similarly, the gathering and transmission of information is a process with an economic dimension, as stressed by Quah (Chapter 16); but authors like Radner (1982) start, understandably, from an exogenous information structure. Which markets exist and which do not, given some transactions technology, is an economic problem on which little progress has been made to date – and similarly for institutions.

It should be added that condensed operational macro-models, and especially their reduced forms, typically proceed from *derived imperfections*, like price–wage rigidities. This is methodologically justified, so long as a framework exists within which these imperfections can be derived from more basic considerations.

Encompassing framework. The reason why WGET provides a ubiquitous reference, also for macroeconomics, is the strength and generality of the two welfare theorems. Because an equilibrium is an optimum, and every optimum can be sustained as an equilibrium after lump-sum transfers, we may reduce the problem of achieving an optimum to the simpler one of implementing an equilibrium. But the primitives, assumptions and equilibrium concept of WGET are special. When we modify the model, either in search of modifications that reconcile predictions with observations (top-down), or because we identify directly some modifications as relevant (bottom-up), *the welfare theorems no longer hold.* For instance, without markets for trading contingently on future events, efficient risk-sharing does not result from decentralized market transactions. In what sense can the modified model still be useful as a reference benchmark for macroeconomics? The key step is to define, and hopefully characterize, *'constrained Pareto optima'*: allocations that are Pareto optimal relative to the set of allocations that remain feasible in the modified model. The important result concerning economies with incomplete markets is not that the set of feasible allocations generically fails to contain first-best optima. It is that *equilibrium allocations generically fail to be constrained Pareto optima*, even for permissive concepts of equilibria (such as those assuming perfect foresight, as in Magill and Shafer (1991).

A sensible programme then combines a positive side – studying the equilibrium allocations of a suitably modified general equilibrium model and verifying their empirical validity – and a normative side – finding ways of improving upon these equilibria to attain a constrained Pareto optimum. That programme might be viewed as an abstract description of ongoing research efforts in macroeconomics, as seen by a general equilibrium theorist.

The task of defining sensible equilibria, and of characterizing constrained Pareto optima, is demanding enough for imperfections introduced one by one. Dealing *simultaneously* with *several imperfections* will occupy theorists for a while. Some obvious extensions of WGET are at hand or in sight: infinite horizons with overlapping generations, money, increasing returns, equilibria with monopolistic competition, auctions, bargaining or quantity constraints. It remains to handle them simultaneously. The hard core probably consists of the trilogy identified above: imperfect information and incomplete markets, two themes actively pursued; and the role of institutions, which remains more elusive.

Condensed operational models. Turning to condensed operational models, the lectures noted below suggest a need for versatility, to accommodate diversity (between developed and developing countries, between economies with different institutions, between short run and more persistent fluctuations, etc.). The current practice concentrates on three markets: output, labour and money; and models their imperfections on a derived basis (like nominal rigidities). It seems clear that money is giving way to 'money and assets'. The distinction between skilled and unskilled labour may or may not have staying power. Dynamics but also versatility invite explicit attention to the stock of physical capital. One could easily end up with, say, five markets. There is another important route towards versatility, namely initial conditions. These concern stocks (physical capital, the unemployed with attention to distributions of duration), but also properties of the temporary equilibrium inherited from yesterday: the extent of resource under-utilization, the extent to which relative prices may be out of line, trend inflation, and possibly more.

Initial conditions for static models come as a by-product of dynamic models. Condensed dynamic models, more or less operational, are the subject matter of a flourishing industry. Often the 'condensation' is more extreme than macro-theorists would wish. In that industry, as elsewhere in macroeconomics, we are limited by our technical abilities, while technical requirements limit entry. The interplay of statics and dynamics in the search for condensed operational models has a distinguished history that is far from closed.

The scope for developing versatile condensed models is wide. The merits of versatile models is that they obviate the need to introduce multiple imperfections at once; it is enough that the model structure allows for the multiplicity. The selection of relevant imperfections will then come in part from the assumed characteristics of an economy (e.g. its labour market institutions), in part from the initial conditions – to be endogenized by dynamics.

Broad challenges surround both the extension of the general reference framework for macroeconomics and the development of more versatile condensed operational models. I invite users of this volume to reflect on these broad challenges as they read individual chapters.

Notes

1. For a different, but not divergent perspective, see Blanchard (2000).
2. In (Chapter 3, p.35), I refer to the work of Dixit and Pindyck (1994) on *Investment under Uncertainty*, which offers a nice illustration.
3. Blanchard (2000, fn. 2) concentrates on 'macroeconomics as the study of fluctuations, mundane ... or sustained'.
4. Blanchard (2000) similarly writes: 'much of the current work is focused on the role of imperfections'.
5. My references do not include Solow (Chapter 2), who might fancy to be classified under (i) in the long run, under (ii) in the short (and probably also the medium) run.
6. See also Caballero and Hammour (Chapter 9, section 9.2.1).
7. Mostly – not invariably, witness the interest of the RBC school in efficiency wages, which arise from an information asymmetry (Chapters 4 and 12).

References

Blanchard O. (2000) 'What Do We Know about Macroeconomics that Fisher and Wicksell Did Not?', NBER Working Paper no. 7550.

Blanchard, O. and Fischer, S. (1989) *Lectures on Macroeconomics* (Cambridge, MASS: MIT Press).

Dixit, A. K. and Pindyck, R. S. (1994) *Investment under Undertainty* (Princeton, NJ: Princeton University Press)

Magill, M. and Shafer, W. (1991) 'Incomplete Markets', ch. 30 in Hildenbrand, W. and Sonnenschein, H. (eds) *Handbook of Mathematical Economics*, vol. IV (Amsterdam: North-Holland), pp. 1524–614.

Radner, R. (1982) 'Equilibrium under Uncertainty', ch. 20 in Arrow, K.J. and Intriligator, M.D. (eds), *Handbook of Mathematical Economics*, vol. II (Amsterdam: North-Holland), pp. 923–1006.

Part I
The General Framework

2

From Neoclassical Growth Theory to New Classical Macroeconomics

Robert M. Solow
Massachusetts Institute of Technology, USA

The puzzle I want to discuss – at least it seems to me to be a puzzle, though part of the puzzle is why it does not seem to be a puzzle to many of my younger colleagues – is this. More than forty years ago, I – and many others, especially Trevor Swan and James Tobin – worked out what has since come to be called neoclassical growth theory. It may not be clear exactly what we or I – I had better speak for myself – thought growth theory applied to, what it was trying to describe. We may have to talk more about that later. But it was clear from the very beginning what I thought it did not apply to, namely short-run fluctuations in aggregate output and employment, what used to be called the business cycle and is now often called that again. In those days I thought growth theory was about the supply side of the economy, whereas the business cycle was mostly to be analysed in terms of changes in aggregate demand.

The puzzle I spoke of a moment ago now arises: if you pick up an article today with the words 'business cycle' in the title, there is a fairly high probability that its basic theoretical orientation will be what is called 'real business cycle theory' and the underlying model will be ... a slightly dressed up version of the neoclassical growth model. The question I want to circle around is: how did that happen? I am not at all concerned with who wrote what when; my interest is in the formal assumptions or the informal background presumptions or perhaps the judgements of fact that encouraged this transformation of a theory *without* business cycles into a theory *of* business cycles.

There are several stages to this story, and I want to follow them all because each stage represents an implicit choice about what is the best way to think about macroeconomics. Students brought up in a particular tradition often do not even see that a choice has been made. By the way, I am emphatically not suggesting that these choices are matters of taste, like the choice of what to have for breakfast. Some ways of doing macroeconomics are better than others, at least for particular classes of problem. We may not know for sure what the best currently available way happens to be; but

19

when we choose we are consulting arguable criteria like empirical plausibility, analytical power and practical utility, not an essentially undiscussable preference for brown bread over white bread.

2.1   The Harrod-Domar problem

I want to start the story one stage before neoclassical growth theory, that is, with the Harrod-Domar model. Roy Harrod and Evsey Domar were by no means identical thinkers. They both concluded, however, that any equilibrium growth path would have to satisfy a certain condition: $sv = n + m$. The product of the fraction of aggregate output saved and the reciprocal of the capital–output ratio would have to equal the sum of the rate of growth of the working population and the rate of labour-augmenting ('Harrod-neutral') technical progress. If that were not so, smooth growth could not possibly persist.

But both Harrod and Domar treated those four key numbers as independent parameters. They did seem to represent quite separate aspects of the economic system: the psychological and sociological propensity to save, technologically determined capital intensity, the demography and sociology of the labour force, and the rate of innovation. In that case, however, the odds that four independent parameters would satisfy the Harrod-Domar condition must be negligibly small, and steady-state growth a virtual impossibility.

Of course the way out of this box – and history suggests looking for a way out – is that one or more of those parameters could be an endogenous variable. That is not far-fetched; after all, there is precedent for regarding any or all of them as economic variables: saving behaviour, capital intensity, technical progress, even population growth. That is only half the battle, however. In order to make a theory of growth rather than a theory of disaster, there had better be good economic reason for believing that the variable parameter is likely to adjust in the right direction to satisfy the Harrod-Domar condition.

2.2   The neoclassical response and prices

As everyone knows, the earliest neoclassical growth model chose capital intensity as the primary adjustable parameter. (Some of the others, especially the saving rate, also figured in the literature from the beginning.) Now comes the point I am really aiming to emphasize. Why might capital intensity actually do the job? One striking thing about the Harrod-Domar model is that it made no serious connection with the price mechanism. The path of the neoclassical model, on the other hand, can quite naturally be supported by a corresponding path for prices, the relevant ones being the real wage and the real interest rate. So the transition from Harrod-

Domar to the neoclassical growth model did two things. It introduced enough flexibility to make steady-state growth something other than an anomaly, and it at least allowed for the possibility that price-guided adjustment might make steady-state growth a robust outcome. Later elaboration, especially the introduction of a representative immortal consumer who maximizes a time-additive utility over an infinite horizon, only made the price-mechanism more important and made further demands on its flawless operation.

2.3 Prices and quantities in the short run

Now leave growth aside for a while, and think about short-run macroeconomics, and fluctuations in output and employment. For a while the dominant framework for thinking about the short run was roughly 'Keynesian'. I use that label for convenience; I have absolutely no interest in 'what Keynes really meant'. To be more specific, the framework I mean is what is sometimes called 'American Keynesianism' as taught to many thousands of students by Paul Samuelson's textbook and a long line of followers.

One way of characterizing this framework is to say that it regarded *quantities* – such as real consumption and investment, and employment – as the rapidly adjusting endogenous variables of the economy, and *prices* – especially relative prices – as slowly adjusting. If you had asked a pre-Keynesian economist a canonical question – what would happen if there were a sudden, unexpected increase in the desire to save – the answer would have run primarily in terms of induced changes in interest rates and perhaps some other prices, with a fall in the interest rate reducing saving and increasing investment so that shifts in production and employment can then react to move the economy to a new equilibrium with less consumption and more investment, but of course with full employment.

After Keynes the answer would have focused more on the likelihood that the initial fall in consumer spending might lead immediately to lower sales, lower profits, lower investment, lower employment, less income generally, and very likely further induced reductions in consumption and investment. Things would probably get worse before they got better. Prices might react slowly and even perversely: for example, unemployment and excess capacity might induce reductions in nominal wages and prices, but if prices fell faster than wages, the real wage could stay unchanged or even rise. It is not important, except to theorists, whether we are looking at some new sort of equilibrium or just an intolerably slow return to full employment.

This sort of model involved an unconventional dichotomy. Part of the time, maybe but not necessarily most of the time, economy-wide production and employment are limited by aggregate demand; there is excess supply of labour and productive capacity. Part of the time, the immediate limitation to current production and employment comes from the supply side. There is excess demand for output. (It goes without saying that, on a sector-by-sector basis, some parts of the economy will be demand-limited while simultaneously other parts will be supply-limited. There have been attempts to model this kind of situation; and the important recent empirical work of Davis and Haltiwanger documents its existence within US manufacturing. But that is a digression.) The thing to keep in mind is that this dichotomy violates the standard, almost defining, neoclassical presumption that sector by sector, and therefore as a whole, the economy is usually at the intersection of demand and supply curves, kept there by the prompt equilibrating movement of prices.

This way of looking at short-run macroeconomics was hotly opposed, even during the time when it was the majority view. Naturally some of the hostility to it was ideological in origin, because the Keynesian type of model justified some kinds of government intervention in the economy. I am not now concerned with that sort of thing. Another source of heated opposition within the economics profession arose mainly from resistance to the downgrading of the role of prices in the short-run macrodynamic story told in the Keynesian style. That is what I want to concentrate on. (No doubt the ideological and analytical issues get mixed up on both sides in individual instances, maybe even typically; but that comes under the heading of 'human, all too human'.) I believe that the subtext of the tremendous academic fuss about 'microfoundations' for macroeconomics was really all about the market-clearing function of prices. There were always at least informal microfoundations for Keynesian models, just the wrong sort of micro-foundations.

2.4   Another neoclassical reponse – real business cycles

In much the same way that one reaction to Harrod-Domar was the elaboration of the neoclassical growth model, one reaction to Keynesian ideas was a reassertion of some sort of short-run neoclassical macro-model. There did not seem to be one readily available, however. Straightforward insistence on Walrasian general equilibrium did not seem like a promising approach to macroeconomics. Anyhow, in view of a natural affinity between short-run macroeconomics and dynamics – the business cycle, after all – and perhaps also an aesthetic impulse to avoid any sharp split between short-run and long-run modelling strategies, the reaction took the form of an adaptation of – guess what – the neoclassical growth model.

The prototypical real-business-cycle model goes like this. There is a single, immortal household – a representative consumer – that earns wages from supplying labour; it also owns the single price-taking firm, so the household receives the net income of the firm. The household takes present and future wage rates and present and future dividends as given, and formulates an optimal infinite-horizon consumption-saving (and possibly labour-saving) plan. The whole sequence of wages and prices matters to the household and affects the timing of its consumption and labour supply.

The firm looks at the same prices, and maximizes current profit by employing labour, renting capital and producing and selling output. In the simplest models of this kind, the firm needs only to maximize period by period. In the ordinary way, an equilibrium is a sequence of inter-temporal prices and wage rates that make the decisions of household and firm consistent with each other. This is nothing but the neoclassical growth model. It would make no fundamental difference to its operation if the household followed some simple behavioural rules of thumb, such as saving a fixed fraction of its income, supplying labour inelastically, and so on, and then it would be exactly like the prototypical neoclassical growth model.

The embellishment of an additive-intertemporal-utility-maximizing household makes some difference to the usual interpretation of the model. It is easy to see that the competitive equilibrium actually solves a technocratic maximization problem. The equilibrium consumption path is the one that a would-be planner would choose to maximize the household's inter-temporal utility, constrained only by initial conditions, the technology for producing output from labour and capital, and the usual accounting identities. Under ideal conditions, the productive side of the economy carries out the household's desired programme (as if guided by an Invisible Hand, one might say).

In other words, the competitive equilibrium path solves exactly the problem Frank Ramsey solved in 1928. The only difference is that Ramsey thought of himself as solving a problem of inter-temporal maximization of social welfare. What Ramsey formulated as a normative problem of welfare economics has been transformed by real-business-cycle theory into a problem of positive economics. The central model of today's macroeconomics assumes that the economy you see is actually tracing out, before your very eyes, the path that maximizes infinite-horizon social welfare as seen from the point of view of the representative consumer-producer.

Where is the business cycle in all of this? I have described the model as if it were exact and deterministic. In that case there might be no business cycle, though there might be fluctuations. The theory actually imagines that the model economy is disturbed from time to time by unforeseeable shocks to the technology and to the household's tastes. Then a more elaborate dynamic-programming apparatus is required, but the general idea is the same. The economy adapts as well as it possibly can to those shocks, always trying to optimize – this time in terms of expected value – on behalf of the representative consumer.

There is thus nothing pathological or remediable about observed fluctuations. Unforeseeable disturbances are by definition unforeseen; after one of them has happened, the economy is already making optimal adjustments, given its technology and the inter-temporal preferences of its single inhabitant or identical inhabitants. There is no role for macroeconomic policy in this world. If the government is better at foreseeing shocks or assembling information than the private sector, it should of course share its knowledge. Otherwise the best it can do is to perform its necessary functions in the most regular, predictable way, so as not to add unnecessary variance to the environment.

This does not strike an observer as a wholly plausible description of a modern capitalist economy, so I should emphasize in fairness that it is merely the crudest version of real-business-cycle theory. A lot has been added to that basic structure, but the prototype is useful precisely because it leaves the basic structure visible. The point I want to make is one I mentioned earlier: an important intellectual function of this model is to restore price-mediated market clearing to the centre of the stage, in contrast to macro-models that downplay the role of the price system. In this it is like the earlier versions of neoclassical growth theory, only more so.

I mean the phrase 'even more so' in two senses, one important and the other trivial. The trivial point is that neoclassical growth theory, at least as I understand it, rests on the relatively weak proposition that there is a calculable sequence of prices – real wage and interest rate – that will support the convergent trajectory and the steady state to which it converges. (There is some vague handwaving about possible market imperfections.) The real-business-cycle use of the model provides it with an institutional framework – consumer optimization, perfect competition, perfect foresight or rational expectations, and insists on it minute by minute.

2.5   Short and long run

The important difference is that neoclassical growth theory is explicitly only meant to hold in the long run, whatever that may mean, whereas real-business-cycle theory is explicitly meant to hold on the business-cycle time scale, which must mean quarter-by-quarter. Criteria such as empirical plausibility and practical utility, as applied to these stories, must apply with respect to different sets of facts and different social purposes.

What does it mean to say that a growth model is only supposed to apply in the long run? After all, a decade is made up of 40 quarters. Is it logically possible to be a Keynesian in the short run and a neoclassical in the long run, or is that something like claiming to believe that the sun revolves around the earth in the short run but the earth revolves around the sun in the long run? (Keep in mind that there is an alternative analogy from science: everyone agrees that Newtonian physics is perfectly adequate at low velocities, but relativistic physics is right and Newtonian physics is wrong at high velocities. Presumably that means that relativistic physics would be accurate at low velocities, too, but would just give the same answers as Newtonian physics.)

I propose to report what I now think about this question. Naturally I tend to extrapolate backwards and presume that I held the same view 45 years ago. In fact I think I did, but that hardly matters now.

2.6 The function of growth theory

We have an intuitively reasonable aggregative concept of 'potential GDP', characterized by reasonably full employment, reasonably full use of capacity. It is not completely independent of prices as long as there is more than one variable factor of production or more than one producible good. But we have various empirical ways of estimating potential GDP or deviations from it, and we do not think of it as being terribly sensitive to minor variations in prices. However, there can be wide and significant gaps between alternative estimates of potential GDP at crucial times.

Sometimes the economy operates below potential for non-trivial intervals of time, and sometimes it operates above potential. Here is where measurement methods can matter: I happen to think that the standard Hodrick-Prescott filter tends to understate potential GDP today in Germany, say, by enough to give bad signals to monetary policy in Europe. Any reasonable measure, however, would lead to the following broad statement: if you measure the total (cumulative not annual) growth of a modern industrial economy over an interval of, say, 20 years, it is very large compared with the size of observed deviations from potential. For example, an economy growing at 2 per cent a year will grow by almost 50 per cent in 20 years. Except at the bottom of bad recessions or the top of unsustainable booms, the deviation from potential GDP is usually considerably less than 10 per cent.

The conclusion to be drawn from this observation is that the track of such an economy over, say, 20–50-year intervals is reasonably approximated by the track of potential GDP. My notion is that growth theory is the attempt to model the track of potential GDP on the 20–50-year time scale. In doing this one uses the appropriate average rates of saving and investment, population growth, technological progress, and whatever else matters. The role of the price system, *in conjunction with prevailing economic institutions and prevailing macroeconomic policies*, is to ward off very large deviations of actual from potential GDP. One would not want to use a growth model to track an economy in deep depression or in a runaway boom.

An alternative answer to the same question is to say that the function of a growth model is to track the path of an economy that just happens never to stray from full use of its potential. You could imagine, for instance, a planning board that successfully carries out the instructions: 'Invest *x* per cent of GDP, and maintain full employment and full capacity utilization all the time.' You could go one step further and instruct the planning board to maximize the standard sort of inter-temporal social welfare function defined on the stream of consumption *per capita*. Then we are back to the Ramsey problem pure and simple.

Of course there are no planning boards any more, certainly not successful ones. So the likeliest field of application for aggregative growth models is the one that I mentioned first: the description and analysis of the average behaviour of an economy over a long-enough period that business cycles can be seen as minor deviations.

This way of looking at it casts an interesting light on the real-business-cycle model. One possible interpretation is the planning board again. In the face of unanticipated shocks, the board is to manage the economy so as to maximize the forward-looking expected value of a standard inter-temporal social welfare function. The stumbling-block in my mind is whether this construction can hope to describe the quarter-by-quarter or year-by-year behaviour of a fluctuating market economy, like yours or mine. If we think that the price system can do the job required by the neoclassical growth model – to keep the economy from straying too far from the path of potential GDP – should we also believe that it can keep the economy always near an optimal path, on the much shorter time scale required by the real-business-cycle model?

2.7   Convergence

That seems to me to be asking too much. So I am inclined to be more Keynesian in the short run, more neoclassical in the longer run. But there is more to be said, from both points of view. The short-run Keynesian model certainly needs to allow more scope for wages and prices to do their thing. Just as the crudest C + I + G model gave way to highly elaborated versions of IS–LM, so the rather loosely attached supply side needs something deeper than rigid nominal wages, a short-run production function and the real-balance effect. That would move it a little closer to the real-business-cycle way of thinking, but only part of the way.

The other side of the fence has been getting much more academic attention. The simpler sort of RBC model that I have been using for expository purposes has had little or no empirical success, even with a very undemanding notion of 'empirical success'. As a result, some of the freer spirits in the RBC school have begun to loosen up the basic framework by allowing for 'imperfections' in the labour market, in the goods market, and even in the capital market. The model then sounds better and fits the data better. This is not surprising: these imperfections were chosen by intelligent economists to make the model work better; and anyway we all think we know that the world is full of such imperfections.

The more interesting consequence is – or might be – a bit of convergence. Some of those imperfections, especially but not only in the labour market, play an important role in Keynesian models, and will lead in that direction. Correspondingly, when more price-mediated adjustments are introduced into a generally Keynesian model, the result is bound to look a little more like a model of the RBC persuasion. I do not want to make too much of this. My guess is that for a while macroeconomics will continue to be more like the Balkans than like the Elysian Fields. Why? For several reasons: a bit of ideology here, a bit of testosterone there, plus the very great difficulty of getting decisive empirical tests from a handful of highly correlated but still noisy time series.

2.8 Short and long runs again

This brings me back to a question already touched on, but only briefly. You will have gathered some of the reasons why my own preferred stance in macroeconomics is to be a sort of eclectic Keynesian in the short run and a sort of eclectic neoclassical in the long run. The question is whether that is merely a self-contradictory daydream. I gave two analogies earlier, neither of which seems quite right. Obviously you cannot be a Ptolemaic astronomer in the short run and a Copernican in the long run, not logically. Obviously you can be Newtonian at low velocities and Einsteinian at high velocities; every physicist does just that. But the second case is easy to understand even if, like me, you know zero about physics. Relativity is believed to be true at every velocity, but at low velocity it gives answers that are so indistinguishably close to Newton's as not to be worth the trouble.

The case of macroeconomics is not exactly analogous. Maybe there is a unified theory that is valid in every run; but I do not pretend to know what it is. A convinced RBC theorist must believe that the Ramsey model *is* that overarching theory; but that seems wholly implausible. Presumably what is wanted is a model in which, given enough time and enough tranquillity, the price system allocates resources, surely not efficiently, but well enough to hold deviations from potential GDP within reasonable limits. Over shorter intervals, and more disturbed intervals, however, quantities move faster than prices, and income-driven processes may dominate price-driven corrections. If I am right, such a theory would look more Keynesian if you watched it on a short time scale, more neoclassical if you watched it on a long time scale.

Actually, lapse of time, mere length of run, may not be the only factor that governs which approximation is better. The size of a disturbance may be more important in determining whether price or quantity reactions dominate macro-behaviour. Even RBC theorists have tended to treat the Great Depression of the 1930s as *sui generis*, or at least as not representing an optimal adjustment to some unspecified shock. The case of Japan in the 1990s may be another example of an economy that was allowed to sink too far (as well as too long) to be rescued by normal processes, or normal policies for that matter. If I am on the right track, construction of macro-models with varying and endogenous speeds of adjustment belongs high on the agenda of current macroeconomic theory. The idea of a 'corridor' within which the economy behaves stably, but outside which the rules are different, was floated by Axel Leijonhufvud years ago, but did not catch on.

It may well be that formal unification of short-run and long-run macro-economics is not going to happen because it is in practice impossible. The precise nature of the connections between short and long run may depend too much on changeable beliefs and expectations of differently placed agents in the economy. It is not a step forward to assume away the heterogeneity of agents and endow the one that remains with model-based rational expectations. (I would agree strongly, however, that one of the defining characteristics of a longer-run equilibrium is that the expectations on which behaviour is based should not be blatantly contradicted by the observed outcome.) In the end, there may be no practicable alternative to living with the uncomfortable dualism of short and long run, all the while looking for little ways to stitch them together. Maybe this is the macro-economics of the medium run.

One unifying thread is certainly the evolution of the capital stock. We have always realized that investment is a source of both current demand and future supply. This is surely one important route by which short-run fluctuations have an effect on the medium-run or even the long-run path of potential output. Reciprocally, the relation between potential output and current demand is one determinant of investment spending. So there is just the sort of dynamic interaction of demand and supply that is needed to knit together the Keynesian short run and the neoclassical long run, if only it can be worked out, as Jacques Drèze has suggested.

The last notion I want to introduce, or question I want to raise, has to do with the idea of multiple equilibria. We all know that Keynes claimed to have provided a theory of unemployment equilibrium. That was the significance of the 'General' in *The General Theory*: an equilibrium in which the labour market cleared was supposed to be only one among a continuum of equilibrium possibilities. Most of us think that Keynes was unable to make good on that claim. He lacked the analytical equipment that is required to do the job. Today, however, we have been there and done that. Starting with John Bryant's simple 1983 mechanism and branching out from there, a whole variety of models has been created with two key properties: they can exhibit multiple equilibria, and those equilibrium configurations can be Pareto ranked. In the macroeconomically most interesting models, equilibria with more output are better than those with less.

The generic characterization of such models is that they are about 'coordination failures'. Many of them are important elaborations of an ancient scenario: universally held pessimistic expectations lead to defensive decisions that sum to a bad low-level outcome and confirm the expectations that brought it about in the first place. If all agents had started with optimistic expectations, all would have made aggressive decisions – about production, employment, and so on – and the resulting good aggregate outcome would have confirmed the expectations that brought it about in the first place. Any such model needs a 'story line' to explain why the ordinary price mechanism cannot be relied upon to coordinate agents' agreement on the socially (and eventually individually) desirable decisions. It is worth emphasizing that this requires attention to out-of-equilibrium behaviour. Russell Cooper has categorized most such stories as 'macroeconomic complementarities'. Real-business-cycle theory and related stories eliminate these possibilities by writing a script in which the economy solves a nice convex optimization problem.

All this is interesting, no doubt, but why bring it up now? What I have in mind is too vague to be called a conjecture, but might perhaps be dignified with the label of a thought. Another way that the macroeconomic short and long runs might be stitched together is to allow that, on the business-cycle time scale, the coordination-failure sort of scenario is the relevant one. It may even be that the longer it lasts and the worse it is, the harder it is to break out of. Ordinarily, however, through learning or policy intervention or institutional innovation or maybe even sometimes with the help of the insights of economists, coordination occurs. If it is successful, the economy behaves more like a neoclassical growth model, at least until another major shock generates another coordination failure.

One difficulty with all accounts resting on the availability of several equilibria is that it is hard to imagine what would constitute an empirical test of the underlying model. Maybe the secret of getting more agreement about macroeconomics is to make use of observational material that goes beyond the prices and quantities recorded in the national accounts.

3
On the Macroeconomics of Uncertainty and Incomplete Markets*

Jacques Drèze
CORE, Université Catholique de Louvain, Belgium

3.1 Macroeconomics, uncertainty and incomplete markets

As a full-time academic, I have led a rather uneventful life. Yet, I have engaged in two venturesome explorations. On my 65th birthday, my wife and I took off in our 42-ft sloop and sailed around the world. Also, I have explored some macroeconomic issues. That second venture proved more hazardous, more demanding and rather less rewarding than the first.

My interest in macroeconomics arose in the late 1970s, as the recession lingered on. Over the following decade, I travelled across the spectrum of theoretical, econometric and policy studies (cf. Drèze (1991)). The European policy debate convinced me that the main stumbling block on the road to effective policies came from the shortcomings of macroeconomic theory, in particular, the relative neglect of the demand side. I thus decided to concentrate on theoretical research, an orientation visible in this address, which articulates semi-formally the main themes which have haunted me lately. But I wish to stress at the outset the practical and policy-based motivation behind sometimes abstract theorizing.

There is a distinctly European flavour to my concerns. Let me bring out some salient facts. Figure 3.1 displays the evolution of unemployment and capacity utilization in EC12 over the period 1973–93. The striped area corresponds to the waste of non-storable resources (labour and capacity) over the period 1974–89. The idleness of both labour and capital suggests that more output was at hand, if only the idle resources could be mobilized.

Another indication of the waste of resources is provided by output, whose growth rate displays substantial volatility. Table 3.1 splits the period

---

* Presidential Address to the XIIth World Congress of the International Economic Association.

Figure 3.1 Under-utilization of productive factors in the European Economic Community

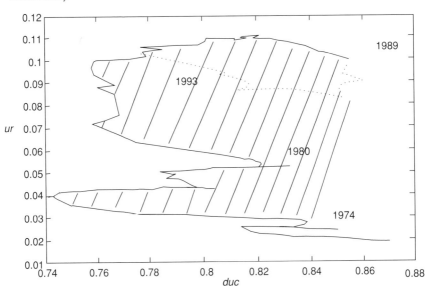

1976–95 into sub-periods of 5 years each. For Europe, though not for the US, the table reveals differentials of 1.5 per cent among successive averages, that is, of 7.5 per cent among overall growth for successive sub-periods. Yet 3 per cent annual growth was within reach throughout. Volatility, with persistence of underactivity over several years, is part of the picture to be understood. So is the Europe–US contrast.

Table 3.1 GNP growth, real average rates, 1976–95

	1976–80	1981–85	1986–90	1991–95
EC12	3	1.5	2.9	1.3
US	3	2.7	2.5	2.3
Japan	4.4	3.8	4.5	1.4
Belgium	3	.8	3	1.4
France	3.1	1.5	3.2	1.1
Italy	4.8	1.6	3	2.5
Netherlands	2.6	1	3.1	1.8
Spain	2.6	1	3.1	1.8
UK	1.8	2.5	3.4	1.2
West Germany	3.3	1.2	3.4	1.9

Figure 3.2a   Growth rate of real GDP, EC12, 1971–94

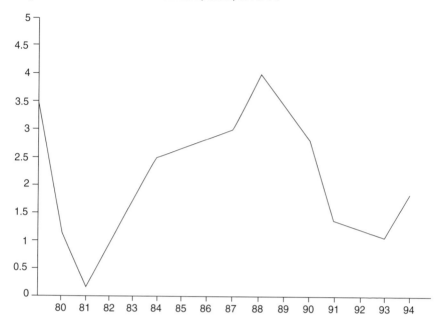

Figure 3.2b   Growth rate of real investment, EC12, 1971–94

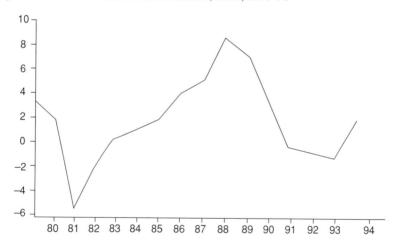

Figure 3.2 brings out the role of investment in that volatility. It displays the growth rates of output and investment in EC12, 1980–94. It confirms the simultaneity of the output and investment cycles[1] and the volatility of

investment (the scale of the bottom panel is four times the scale of the upper panel).

Uncertainty and incomplete markets belong intimately in a realistic treatment of most economic problems. Macroeconomics is no exception. Uncertainty means that the economic environment tomorrow is not known today. At best, there exists a *set* of alternative, mutually exclusive, states of the environment, one and only one of which will materialize. This reflects our uncertainties about fundamentals – such as tastes, resources and technology – but also about developments beyond the purely economic sphere: Will Mercosur lead to a monetary union? Will agreement on pollution charges come about? Will confidence in the monetary institutions of South-East Asia be restored?

Complete markets are an idealization under which it is imagined that agents can trade all commodities (goods and services) contingently on future states of the environment. That is, hedging opportunities are unlimited. Instead markets are incomplete when consumers save more, as they did in 1990, but firms do not know whether they intend to retire sooner, to pay more taxes or to consume more. Markets are incomplete when firms do not know how future consumption will be allocated between tourism in Latin America, housing or gadgets. Markets are incomplete when workers do not know on what terms they might find alternative employment, should their firm be downsized. Markets are incomplete when currently inactive or unborn agents are concerned, as with forest management. And so on.

Figure 3.3 depicts the structure of this chapter. I shall outline two implications of market incompleteness: volatility of demand, especially investment; then wage and price rigidities. These are microeconomic issues, so land is in sight and navigation is easy. Afterwards, I shall turn to macro-economic considerations.

3.2   Incomplete markets breed demand volatility

At a point in time, economic agents observe some, but not all, aspects of the economic environment. Their information is asymmetric. Based on what they observe, they hold expectations about future states and associated economic developments. Economists are seldom unanimous, to say the least, so expectations are bound to be multivalued. Information is asymmetric, so expectations are heterogeneous. All this is fully consistent with rationality.

Current observations and expectations determine the market behaviour of agents. Because the information of individual agents is not fully observable, revisions of expectations may be triggered by new information not previously recognized as significant – as when publication of the monthly trade statistics caused a minor panic on Wall Street in November 1987. Such phenomena generate volatility of expectations, hence of market

Figure 3.3   Outline of the chapter

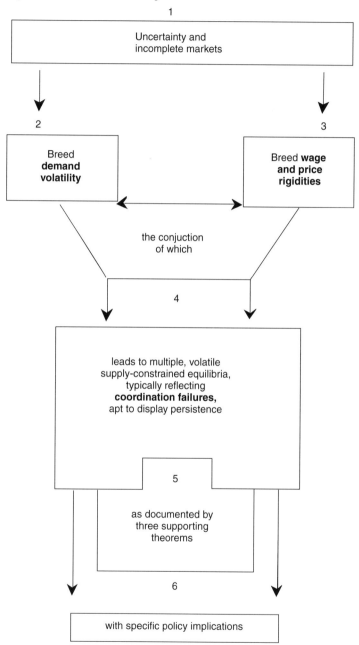

behaviour, relative to observed data – relative to 'fundamentals', some would say.[2]

Let me spell out two specific illustrations of how future uncertainties breed volatility. Uncertainty about future incomes (more variance at unchanged mean) reduces consumption and increases savings, under the generally accepted condition of (endogenously) diminishing absolute risk aversion (cf. Drèze and Modigliani (1972)). A parallel result concerning investment appears in the book of Dixit and Pindyck (1994) on *Investment under Uncertainty*, which extends and integrates several earlier contributions, like Bernanke (1983) or McDonald and Siegel (1986). An irreversible investment should be undertaken, not whenever the net present value of the associated profit stream is positive (as often taught), but when that value is higher than the value of an option to carry out the same investment at a later date – possibly with more information. But the option value increases with the uncertainty about future cost or demand conditions. So, greater uncertainty encourages postponement and reduces current investment demand.

Thus, the equilibrium of savings and investment will be upset by a *change in the uncertainty* perceived by economic agents. A fundamental macroeconomic relation is thus recurrently perturbed.

The insistence by Dixit and Pindyck that investments should be timed optimally also implies that a small displacement in time will usually have a second-order effect on utility or profits, at equilibrium. An event entailing a small incentive for households or firms to postpone investment could thus lead to a significant reduction of aggregate investment demand, with macroeconomic consequences of the first order. This is a sort of 'menu costs' argument in reverse. It contributes to our understanding of the volatility of investment (as illustrated in Figure 3.2b).

A clear example of increased uncertainty is provided by the Gulf War of 1990. When the conflict erupted, taxpayers realized that in some way they would foot a bill, of unknown severity. So, consumption expenditures, especially for durables, were curtailed. Investment, by households as well as business firms, had better be postponed pending more information about how long and costly the war might be. In the US, gross capital formation fell by 9 per cent in 1990–91, while real private consumption deviated from its 3 per cent trend growth and declined slightly. Unemployment rose by 2 percentage points, at unchanged real wages, with inflation staying on trend.

The foregoing rests on uncertainty, without explicit reference to incomplete markets. The idealization of complete markets would attenuate both the volatility of market behaviour and its consequences. First, complete markets would bring out the circumstances leading to revisions of behaviour, eliminating surprises and improving common information. Second, contingent markets cleared *ex ante* would permit immediate equilibrium when an event occurs. Otherwise, the adjustment evolves in real time, with temporary disequilibrium along the process. (Of course, the reasoning assumes universal *ex ante* clearing, an idealization that would be infinitely costly to implement!)

3.3 Incomplete markets breed wage and price rigidities

Because weather forecasts span only a few days, risk-averse sailors embarking on long passages base their schedules on statistical regularities, which impose rigidities. When the absence of markets prevents agents from hedging price variations, it may be second-best efficient to limit price variations in the first place.[3] The second-best efficiency defines an optimal trade-off between *ex post* allocative efficiency, which requires price flexibility, and *ex ante* risk-sharing efficiency, which is enhanced by bounded price flexibility, under incomplete markets. The gains in *ex ante* risk-sharing efficiency originate in the fact that, under incomplete markets, the degree of risk aversion varies across agents, often in a systematic way; for instance, it is higher for workers or consumers than for firms. Reconciling the two goals is sometimes possible in the framework of long-term contracts.

A transparent example is provided by mortgage loans, for which standard contracts stipulate a fixed nominal interest rate, not adjusted to future variations of nominal rates. In this way, the borrower is insured against these variations. In principle (i.e. the savings-and-loans disaster in the US notwithstanding), lenders are in a better position to bear the risk of interest rate variations, because they have better access to hedging on financial markets and because their equity is held by investors with diversified portfolios.[4]

I may mention in passing that a similar argument applies to country loans. Emerging countries are more sensitive to risk than such lenders as rich countries, multilateral institutions or large banks. The practice in the seventies of issuing loans at variable rates was an inefficient risk-sharing arrangement, which left the borrowers exposed when interest rates sky-rocketed in the late seventies and early eighties. There remains scope for corrective action today; see Drèze (1999d).

How does this reasoning explain wage rigidities in the face of unemployment? We know from the literature on implicit labour contracts[5] that employment in a firm facing cost or demand uncertainties is efficient provided the marginal value product of labour matches in all states its opportunity cost, which is equal to market wages under full employment, to reservation wages otherwise. The spread between the two can be substantial, perhaps 40 to 50 per cent.[6] Instead, wages should fluctuate less than marginal value products, to provide income insurance to risk-averse workers. If the firm were risk neutral, wages should be constant across macroeconomic fluctuations. This is the same idea as fixed nominal rates in mortgage contracts. But many workers are not covered by long-term contracts. Some are employed under temporary contracts. Some will enter the market tomorrow (as in the case of today's students) or re-enter it (as in the case of workers temporarily withdrawn from work or threatened with dismissal). These workers-to-be bear the uncertainties surrounding future labour-market conditions.[7]

In states unfavourable to labour, market clearing tomorrow might call for wages falling to reservation levels and 'voluntary' unemployment. In other states, competitive wages might result in low profitability or inflationary pressures. Containing wage flexibility through downward rigidity in low-wage states and incremental labour or income taxes in states more favourable to labour, enhances risk-sharing efficiency for prospective job seekers.

The argument for second-best wage rigidities cum unemployment benefits is spelled out in Drèze and Gollier (1993).[8] It provides an explanation of downward real-wage rigidities complementary to other theories, like efficiency wages, union bargaining or insider power, but more sharply focused on macroeconomic fluctuations.[9]

In practice, downward wage rigidity at the low end of the scale is implemented through unemployment benefits and minimum wages, which are themselves downward rigid, either in nominal terms (in the US) or in real terms (in Europe). These legalize a form of social consensus, often seen as redistributive, but also interpretable as a form of *ex ante* insurance.[10] Higher in the scale, downward wage rigidity for new recruits inherits whatever rigidity prevails for workers under contract, because wage discrimination by hiring date (two-tier contracts) is notoriously unpopular and seldom practised.[11] The implicit-contracts argument thus operates indirectly also for new recruits.[12]

Regarding downward price rigidity in the face of unused capacity, there is an argument to which I assign significance, even though my analytical work on this topic is still in progress. The standard explanation of this phenomenon is imperfect competition, see, for example, Bénassy (1995). (More on this below.) An alternative, or complementary explanation relates to incomplete markets. Excess capacity means capacity, hence prior investment, hence fixed costs and more often than not, debt service. Fixed costs and debt service must be covered under all states of the environment, if the firm is to survive. And firm survival matters, due to the costs of bankruptcies and reorganizations. Under complete markets, it would suffice to cover fixed costs on average: profits could be transferred *ex ante* from good states to bad states through financial transactions. It would then be possible to price at marginal cost in all states: the profits earned when operating at full capacity could be used to cover fixed charges in all states (through contingent transfers). This is the stochastic analogue of peak-load pricing: prices equal to marginal costs at all times, fixed costs covered entirely from the mark-up at peak times.

Under incomplete markets, it is *not* possible to transfer profits freely across alternative states, so fixed charges must be covered *in each state* from the receipts in *that* state. Hence prices in each state must exceed marginal cost by a mark-up sufficient to cover fixed charges.[13] Broadly speaking, this means average cost pricing, hence downward price rigidity below capacity.[14]

Adding imperfect competition, I record that firms setting prices so as to equate marginal costs and marginal revenues are often uncertain about the price elasticity of the demand for their products. Greenwald and Stiglitz (1989) argue that price adjustments may be riskier than output adjustments. Under any kind of menu costs leading to finite price adjustments, uncertainty about the demand elasticity leads risk-averse firms to behave as if they faced a kinked demand curve (see Drèze (1979b)). This feature is interpretable as an incomplete markets phenomenon.[15] It provides an additional rationale for demand kinks, distinct from the traditional argument in terms of reactions by competitors (Sweezy (1939)) and from the search-theoretic argument developed by Stiglitz (1984). The kink leads directly to price rigidity.

An important side implication of average-cost pricing – whether due to constant returns or to fixed costs – concerns the reaction of output and employment to demand shocks. Under diminishing returns and market-clearing output prices, demand shocks affect the price level at unchanged output and employment under rigid real wages, but affect output and employment under rigid nominal wages; see Grandmont (1989). Under average-cost pricing with non-increasing average cost, demand shocks affect output and employment in both cases. The mix of firms operating under diminishing returns on the one hand, constant or increasing returns on the other hand, is thus relevant to the operating characteristics of real economies. There are always some quantity effects when the latter firms matter, as they do in reality.

3.4   From volatility and rigidities to coordination failures

With experienced sailors, serious mishaps result only from the conjunction of several problems – like a dragging anchor compounded by a wind shift near a lee shore. I wish to bring together wage–price rigidities and aggregate-demand volatility, expecting some mishaps from the conjunction. My task is more conveniently carried out after a digression, which provisionally ignores the price rigidities.

With incomplete markets, an economy goes through a sequence of temporary equilibria, in the terminology of Hicks (1936) and Grandmont (1974, 1977, 1982, 1988). At a point in time, economic agents make some idiosyncratic observations, hold expectations about future states of the economy and define accordingly their supply or demand schedules for trading on spot markets. Spot markets concern contemporaneous goods and services, and assets; they are complemented by a few markets for futures and options on the same.

The supplies and demands of individual agents are brought into agreement through some adjustment process. Hopefully, an equilibrium exists and is obtained as rest point of a stable adjustment process.

When new information arrives, individual expectations are revised. Spot markets are reopened. The adjustment process starts all over again, and a new temporary equilibrium is reached. The path followed by the economy through time is a sequence of temporary equilibria (see Grandmont (1982, 1988) for a survey of properties).

There is one idealized case where the sequence is always well defined and Pareto efficient. It is a special case of what Radner (1972) calls 'equilibrium of plans, prices and price expectations in a sequence of markets'. Two very strong assumptions are needed, sequentially complete markets and perfect foresight. The first assumption (not used by Radner) states that, although markets are incomplete, they permit agents at any date to transfer wealth across all the events at the following date; that is, markets are 'one-period ahead complete', and will be so again in the future. The second assumption (used by Radner) asserts that, at any point in time, price expectations for all markets to be opened in the future are single valued, common to all agents, and such that the transactions planned by the agents will clear these markets.[16]

Under these very strong assumptions, the sequence of temporary equilibria implements an equilibrium with complete markets. Hence, Arrow-Debreu existence theorems carry over, as do stability theorems for Walrasian tâtonnement. But the coordination of plans and price expectations in the absence of markets is a dark mystery, even darkened by the possibility of multiple equilibria.[17] Yet, for all I can tell, this is also the model underlying 'new classical macroeconomics'.

Relaxing somewhat my two precious assumptions can open the door to multiple sequences of equilibria. As stressed by Keynes, all agents hold expectations about each other's expectations, now and later. There results an interdependence conducive to multiple, equally consistent equilibria: formal examples are easy to construct. Today, other sources of multiplicity are being discovered left and right. Some are surveyed in a classic paper by Cooper and John (1988), stressing strategic complementaries and spillovers. A standard source is monopolistic competition; see Dixon and Rankin (1995). Woodford (1991) derives multiplicity from kinked demand curves. A parallel literature studies multiple paths, chaos and endogenous cycles in aggregated dynamic models (see Benhabib and Farmer (1997)).

It is common practice in that literature to associate multiplicity with 'self-fulfilling expectations': when there exist multiple equilibria, it is enough that all agents expect one of them to come about, and their expectations will be realized. Again, the coordination of expectations without markets is a dark mystery.

When equilibria are multiple but some are in a sense better than others, the possibility of a coordination failure arises. An inferior equilibrium may obtain, that could only give way to a superior one through a coordinated modification of the plans, or expectations, of some or all agents. A clear-cut concept of 'better' is Pareto ranking, which requires special assumptions; macroeconomists are usually satisfied with ranking of such aggregates as output or employment.[18]

So, by coordination failure I refer to equilibria for which there exist superior feasible alternatives. A stronger concept refers to existence of a superior alternative implementable through a well-defined feasible policy.

Sailors often follow roundabout courses, such as going from Panama to San Francisco by way of Hawaii. My digression places me in a position to sail downwind through the core argument of this address. I extend step by step the reasoning of my digression to price rigidities and supply constraints.[19]

I start again from asymmetrically informed agents addressing to the market supply and demand schedules reflecting their expectations. The equilibrium concept and adjustment process are no longer Walrasian tâtonnement, as some prices are, say, downward rigid. When a price is downward rigid, quantity constraints come in to ration excess supply – workers are unemployed or capacities unused. Following van der Laan (1982, 1984), I define a 'supply-constrained equilibrium' by:

- a vector of prices for all commodities, consistent with *a priori* given bounds on some prices
- a set of vectors of quantity constraints, one for each agent,[20] limiting the supply of commodities with downward-rigid prices
- a set of optimizing choices by all agents, compatible with these signals, such that all markets clear.[21]

Hopefully again, such an equilibrium exists and can be obtained as rest point of a stable adjustment process. My first and third theorems below address these two issues.

As new information arrives, the process restarts, taking the economy through a sequence of supply-constrained equilibria, that is of temporary equilibria with supply rationing.

Individual agents rationally anticipate such a sequence, so their expectations concern quantity constraints on par with prices. The expectations are idiosyncratic, if only because the constraints are idiosyncratic. In the idealized model, existence and stability followed from Walrasian theory. I extend these results to price rigidities and idiosyncratic expectations of quantity constraints in three theorems. Now, incomplete markets introduce conceptual and technical complications, like defining decision criteria for business firms or using degree theory to prove existence. To avoid these, I retain provisionally the repugnant assumptions of sequentially complete markets and perfect price foresight. But I use these assumptions to establish the existence of multiple equilibria and coordination failures *even in that idealized case*; thus not at all to conclude that an equilibrium is an optimum. It is my conjecture, backed by one elementary example, that a formal treatment of incomplete markets and imperfect foresight will reinforce my conclusions.[22] What I offer today is barely sufficient to bring out some specific implications of uncertainty and incomplete markets for macroeconomics – barely sufficient, like when you sneak into the lagoon of a Polynesian atoll with half-a-foot clearance under your keel.

The next step in my digression was to consider multiple sequences of temporary equilibria, and coordination failures. Supply-constrained equilibria are natural candidates for coordination failures, due to the aggregate demand externality. Relaxation of the constraints on one commodity leads through income effects to relax the constraints on other commodities. As a firm hires more workers, the demand for output increases somewhere, leading to more hirings, and conversely. A multiplier operates. My second theorem asserts existence of a continuum of supply-constrained equilibria, sometimes Pareto ranked, hence of coordination failures.

These equilibria are associated with alternative levels of supply constraints inherited from the past or expected to prevail in the future. The selection of a specific equilibrium depends in particular upon the unobserved state of information of the agents. Regarding tomorrow's equilibrium, multiplicity and volatility are two sides of the same coin. When resources are under-utilized, there typically exist other equilibria at less restrictive levels of current and future constraints but still compatible with the fundamentals of the economy (physical assets and technology, demand and supply behaviour) and with the price rigidities. In such a case, there is a coordination failure, and the issue of devising a corrective policy arises. The policy might aim at lifting today's constraints or at raising expectations about tomorrow's constraints. Multiplicity says that feasible alternatives exist – neither more nor less.

This is my own interpretation of the flourishing literature on multiple equilibria, sunspots, animal spirits, self-fulfilling expectations, endogenous business cycles and the like, to which I am adding a chapter on incomplete markets and price rigidities.

The link from volatility to under-utilization of resources and persistence has a static and a dynamic aspect. First, availability of inputs sets an upper limit to output, but there is no lower limit, so that volatility manifests itself as under-utilization (or else as inflationary pressure). Once the under-utilization is there, it will persist as a coordination failure until conditions change. Second, under-utilization is apt to *generate* persistence, for three identifiable reasons: lower activity today reinforces the expectation of low activity tomorrow; low investment today contracts supply possibilities tomorrow; low activity today influences adversely financial positions tomorrow.[23]

The picture is thus complete, and may be summarized as follows:

Given that some prices are downward rigid, we observe supply-constrained equilibria, where the extent of rationing is linked to history (path dependency) and to idiosyncratic unobserved expectations about future quantity constraints. These equilibria and associated expectations are multiple and volatile. They typically reflect coordination failures, and they are subject to persistence.

This is not the alpha and omega of macroeconomics. It is a tentative presentation of an intriguing and probably useful emerging chapter. My analytical results require extension and generalization. The feedbacks, whereby potential coordination failures exacerbate volatility and rigidities, deserve explicit analysis. My treatment undoubtedly neglects many macroeconomic implications of uncertainty and incomplete markets that others will bring out. Also, it badly needs extension to expectation formation and learning.

3.5 Three theorems

On ocean passages, no landmarks are in sight, and sailors rely on celestial or satellite navigation. They share faith in abstract calculations with mathematical economists. My core argument is backed by three theorems. Two bear on existence, the third bears on dynamic adjustment. They are proved for real economies extending over time under uncertainty and defined by the same primitives as in Arrow-Debreu. The real nature of the model is an obvious limitation, given my interest in nominal as well as real rigidities. I have satisfied myself that all three theorems extend naturally to suitably defined monetary economies,[24] as confirmed by research in progress with Jean-Jacques Herings (1998). Otherwise, the framework is general and flexible.

My distinctive modelling assumption is an *a priori* given partition of commodities into two groups. Commodities in group I have flexible prices, their supplies or demands are never subject to quantity rationing.

Commodities in group II have fixed prices in the existence theorems, downward rigid prices in the stability theorem.[25]

Think about group II as including labour services, in particular unskilled labour, and goods which are produced from facilities entailing fixed costs. Think about the latter prices as equal to marginal cost plus a mark-up. The mark-up is precisely the price of the input 'capacity'. Thus, the price rigidities concern non-storable inputs, for which recurrent under-utilization is empirically documented. The exogenous partition and bounds on prices are not a fully general specification, but one that has proved usefully tractable.

The equilibrium concept is always the supply-constrained equilibrium, as defined above.

Now for the first theorem. Take as given the partition into group I and group II commodities, with group I non-empty; and take as given the prices of group II commodities, positive but arbitrary. Consider then an exogenous set of supply constraints for the group II commodities, that is, one vector for each agent. Again these vectors are strictly positive, but otherwise arbitrary.

Theorem 1: Under standard assumptions, there exists a supply-constrained equilibrium, with the group II prices as given, and with supply constraints for group II commodities at least as severe as stipulated by the exogenous vectors.[26]

Think about these exogenous vectors as representing constraints inherited from the past or expected in the future. There always exists a supply-constrained equilibrium where these constraints, whatever they may be, are validated, possibly with room to spare. The result holds if the rigid prices are compatible with a competitive equilibrium and again if they are not. In either case, markets for flex-price commodities clear through prices. Nothing is said by the theorem about how the flexible prices adjust to the supply rationing – but they do.[27]

The generality of the result may surprise. Let me guide your intuition. The challenge, in the fix-price case, is to eliminate excess demand for those commodities whose prices might be too low relative to other fixed prices. Income effects see to that. Real incomes can be depressed both by constraining the supply of other group II commodities or by adjusting the prices of group I commodities. After all, that is also the logic of fighting demand-pull inflation through tight fiscal policies or high interest rates. Tightening the income constraints generates the supply-constrained equilibria, with a multiplier process at work.[28]

Supply-constrained equilibria are thus pervasive. That does not make them arbitrary. Demand is never constrained, so that all the standard equilibrium conditions associated with the demand side are satisfied. Broadly speaking, the supply constraints affect the levels of income and income expectations of households, the levels of demand and demand expectations of firms. In an aggregated macro-model, which ignores micro-level substitutions or complementarities, there is a one-dimensional continuum of equilibria, indexed by the perceived aggregate wealth of the households, a macroeconomic determinant of aggregate demand and activity.[29]

The first theorem does not establish multiplicity.[30] Additional assumptions see to that. Thus theorem 3.1 (ii) in Herings and Drèze (1998) reads as follows:[31]

Theorem 2.1: Under standard assumptions plus differentiability of the supply and demand functions of individual agents, there exists a connected set (i.e. continuum) of different supply-constrained equilibria – except for a null set of initial endowments (i.e. generically in initial endowments).[32]

Actually, when the rigid prices are compatible with a competitive equilibrium, a stronger result follows from an assumption of extended substitutability, that is, the net demand for any commodity does not increase when the prices and/or supply possibilities of other commodities are decreased.[33] The stronger result is:

Theorem 2.2: Under standard assumptions plus differentiability and extended substitutability, when the fixed prices for group II commodities are compatible with a competitive equilibrium, there exists a continuum of supply-constrained equilibria, ranging from the competitive equilibrium to an arbitrarily small supply of the fix-price commodities.[34]

The conclusion entails Pareto-ranked equilibria, that is, coordination failures. When the rigid prices are incompatible with a competitive equilibrium, the continuum of equilibria is still there; but the Pareto reference is lacking, pending further research.

It remains to explain how supply-constrained equilibria come about. When new information arrives, an economy does not find itself automatically at a supply-constrained equilibrium. Some adjustment process, bringing about orderly rationing of supplies and no rationing of demands, is necessary to that end. I now describe such a process, thereby completing the picture sketched so far. It is an extension to downward price rigidities and supply rationing of the Walrasian tâtonnement process, which operates through prices alone. A significant first result is reported in Drèze (1999a), following the earlier contribution in Drèze (1991b), also extended in Herings *et al.* (1999). It is in the spirit of the existence theorem stated above, which it complements naturally, though with a less general specification.

There are again two groups of commodities, group I with flexible prices and group II with prices downward rigid *along the process* (thus, lower bounds are defined sequentially). My published paper concerns a real exchange economy, where resources are supplied inelastically to the market (they cannot be consumed directly, as with specialized labour and capacities). But the extension to production and elastic supply of resources should prove straightforward.[35] Participants in the exchange receive two kinds of signals: prices for all commodities, and quantity constraints on the supply of group II commodities.[36] The process starts from arbitrary vectors of prices and supply constraints, say inherited from yesterday's allocation and today's revised expectations; these signals define the constrained budget sets of the agents. These agents express effective demands, the aggregation of which defines market excess demands. Prices of group I commodities adjust up or down, proportionately to excess demands, as under Walrasian tâtonnement. Supply constraints for group II commodities adjust up or down, proportionately to excess demands. These constraints are bounded below by zero and above by unconstrained supply. In case of excess demand at unconstrained supply, prices of group II commodities adjust upward. That is, prices of group II commodities are not raised until all possible quantity adjustments have been performed. This reflects the idea that 'quantities move faster than prices', as suggested by Keynes (1936) and Leijonhufvud (1968).

These adjustment rules for the signals, and the reactions of the agents expressing the effective demands corresponding to the prevailing signals, define together a tâtonnement process in continuous time.[37]

Theorem 3: Under standard assumptions, plus differentiability and extended substitutability, the process is quasi stable, that is, any limit point of a trajectory is a rest point of the process; and every limit point of a trajectory is a supply-constrained equilibrium.

This is theorem 4.1 in Drèze (1999a). It provides a simple answer to the question: how do supply-constrained equilibria come about – for instance after a (positive or negative) shock to expectations? Answer: through progressive adjustments of prices and quantities, as stipulated by the process.

It helps intuition to visualize how the process operates in an economy with given labour supply and productive capacities. Firms hire or fire labour as needed to satisfy effective demand. At full use of capacities, prices (i.e. mark-ups) are raised as needed to choke off excess demands. Similarly, wages are raised for types of labour in excess demand. All along, the markets for goods and services with flexible prices are progressively brought to clear through prices.

One advantage of this dynamic model over the static one underlying the existence theorems is that the initial quantity constraints for some goods are raised along the adjustment. That is, initially pessimistic expectations can be revised upward in the light of market observations. The multiplier process works up and down – though with an asymmetry: it can be stronger downward than upward, but never the other way around.

3.6   Landfall: some policy conclusions

Landfall after an ocean crossing is always exciting, relieving, and conducive to reflection upon the lessons of the passage. I draw three lessons from this lecture: (i) we should take coordination failures seriously; (ii) we should try to obviate demand volatility; (iii) we should try to by-pass wage–price rigidities.

First, *we should at all times be aware of the possibility of under-utilization of resources*, labour and production capacities, *reflecting coordination failures*, sustained by price rigidities, as distinct from incorrect prices. This is where I depart from the work of the 1970s, centred on price distortions. We tend to think about real rigidities as keeping prices and wages at levels inconsistent with attainment of a first-best allocation, mostly due to market power. The consequences of these distortions are then viewed as proportional to the distance at which prices stand from market-clearing levels, and to elasticities of supply and/or demand. Under coordination failures, the price distortion may be modest – in the limit inexistent – yet the inefficiencies sustained by the rigid prices may be substantial, according to the theorems. *Coordination problems magnify the consequences of price rigidities.*

The possibility of coordination failure is always there. It may not be easy to detect, as the under-utilization may be partly or wholly due to other causes, including wrong prices, including also the need to adjust progressively to major shocks such as oil price hikes, a war, a major political transition or a currency crisis. There is thus an identification problem, of which again we should be aware, and we should rely on econometric models detailed enough to recognize that problem and progress towards its resolution. I note with interest that some recent macroeconometric work by Henri Sneessens and his associates[38] concludes with multiple equilibria and path dependency, suggesting an empirical extension of the theory.

The dual of the identification problem is that we cannot infer from the observation of unemployment or excess capacities that prices are wrong – more worries for econometricians and policy makers.

Second, my coordination failures operate through the aggregate demand externality. So, *we should at all times be aware of the importance of the demand side* – a timely warning to European theorists and policy makers. Let me at once dispel a possible misconception. There is no immediate link from the recognition of the aggregate-demand externality to Keynesian fiscal or monetary stimulation. The nagging problem with coordination failures is their potential recurrence. If overcome today, they may reappear tomorrow, should expectations so dictate. Debt-financed fiscal stimulation may need to be repeated over and over again, leading to unsustainable debt accumulation. As for monetary stimulation, interest rates may be right at a coordination failure. And there is a natural limit to successive reductions of nominal interest rates, namely zero; beyond that limit, expected inflation must take over to sustain negative real rates; current obsession with price stability does not favour that route. In coping with demand volatility, *the challenge is to define repeatedly sustainable policies*, the only policies apt to maintain longer-run expectations at levels compatible with full employment today. This much we have learned definitively from the rational expectations revolution.

The recurring threat of coordination failures suggests attempting to maintain continuously a slight demand pressure, while forestalling inflationary tendencies through a dynamic supply response.[39] Returning to a question raised at the outset, I have wondered whether the recent US performance might be due, in part, to greater immunity from coordination failures, owing precisely to the demand pressure resulting from a low savings rate, permitted by the current account deficit, and accompanied with low inflation pressure, permitted by the stagnation of real wages. European economies in contrast might be more exposed to coordination failures, due no doubt to more entrenched rigidities, also due to the uncertainties surrounding European integration. You cannot possibly pursue a project of such ambition without creating institutional uncertainties – but you should attempt to minimize these. There is a lesson here for Mercosur.

One natural way of guaranteeing that demand-stimulation policies are sustainable is to concentrate them on investments with adequate social returns – not on digging holes and filling them again! The challenge is to identify investment projects that remain justified across the vagaries of private investment and its timing. Six years ago, a group of French and Belgian economists, convened by Edmond Malinvaud and myself,[40] outlined a 'European initiative for growth and employment' in which we advocated additional investments in low-income housing, urban renewal, urban transportation and trans-European networks of transportation and communication. These seem to meet precisely the requirement of positive long-run social returns, little affected by short-run information flows.[41] Promoting these at times when other private investments are temporarily curtailed is an effective way of coping with volatility and even with persistent deficiency of aggregate demand. An operational proposal for housing is detailed in Drèze, Durré and Sneessens (1998). But the full long-run implications of the proposal remain to be investigated.

Third, I have established a solid *link between price–wage rigidities and coordination failures*, within a very general model and without special assumptions other than the obvious market incompleteness.

We must ask ourselves whether and how flexibility contributes to overcome coordination failures. Stiglitz (1999) argues that abrupt changes in relative prices, especially wages, have been destabilizing during the recent

East Asia crisis. Drèze (1997) contains simple RBC-type examples where wage flexibility has no effect on employment, and my discussion there leads to the conclusion:

> I thus see three cogent reasons why organised labour would resist the idea of fighting coordination-failure unemployment through wage flexibility:
> (i)   uncertain effectiveness, *specific* to the context of coordination failures;
> (ii) inefficient risk sharing, *compounded* by the volatility of employment associated with coordination failures;
> (iii) adverse redistributive transfers, *compounded* by the potential recurrence of coordination failures.

I have adduced above specific reasons why incomplete markets breed rigidities. We should address these reasons squarely. To begin with wages, the objective is to retain the merits of bounded flexibility of net earnings for *ex ante* risk-sharing efficiency, while restoring flexibility of wage costs to firms. This can in principle be attempted by adjusting to circumstances the substantial wedge (40 per cent or more) between net earnings and wage costs. Labour taxes, mainly social insurance contributions, could vary as a function of the level of unemployment – with low contributions when unemployment is high and conversely. See Drèze (1993) for a specific proposal. An altogether different alternative, equally worthy of attention, would proceed through a basic income obviating the need for downward wage rigidity; see for example Atkinson (1995).[42]

Regarding prices, I have stressed the problem of maintaining firm solvency in the face of unfavourable demand conditions when fixed charges are substantial – leading to some kind of average-cost pricing, whereas efficiency would call for marginal-cost pricing. Cyclically adjusted labour taxes would reduce labour costs in recessions, hence contributing to downward price flexibility there. I have also wondered whether more efficient financial arrangements could increase price flexibility, a theme already explored inventively by Greenwald and Stiglitz (1990, 1993) and authors concerned with the credit channel of monetary transmission.

Equity financing does not impose debt service in all states. Thus, promoting access to equity financing by small and medium firms should be on the agenda. But equity financing raises the issue of control, and carries a puzzling equity premium. New forms of bonds could be devised, namely cyclically indexed bonds which call for lower repayments under unfavourable macroeconomic conditions, against higher repayments when they are favourable.[43] Creating assets indexed on macroeconomic aggregates, as advocated on independent grounds by Shiller (1993) or Drèze (1999b, section 5), could yield the unexpected dividend of facilitating marginal-cost pricing.[44] There is thus scope for targeted policy intervention both on the demand volatility front and on the wage–price rigidities front. What is more, there is scope for operating on both fronts simultaneously. In the 'European initiative' proposal referred to above, we advocated targeted investments, and we advocated promoting these through temporary, counter-cyclical labour-tax cuts. We were thus outlining precisely the combination of policies which emerges from my discussion today. With six years of hindsight, I marvel at how closely a collective policy proposal could anticipate the conclusions of theoretical research still in the making. I now realize that the research outlined here was not only motivated by policy issues, as announced at the outset. It was also inspired by the policy discussions. This illustrates the benefits from interaction between policy concerns and theoretical research. I regard that interaction as crucial for the long-term programme of integrating micro- and macroeconomics into a unified discipline.

Notes

1. Standard correlation .9 in Real Business Cycles calibrations.
2. I avoid the words 'sunspots' and 'animal spirits', because the information at stake is genuine, even if its significance is not fully recognized.
3. This was also the motivation behind my early work on equilibria with price rigidities, Drèze (1975).
4. More recently, a variety of contracts, differing as to initial rates and scope for future revisions, have been offered. Borrowers are free to choose their preferred combination of expected rates and variability of future rates, on the basis of their own constraints and risk aversion. This enhances overall market efficiency. Note that it all happens in the framework of long-term contracts.
5. See Baily (1974), Gordon (1974), Azariadis (1975), the informal introduction in Drèze (1979a) or the survey by Rosen (1985); individual labour contracts are introduced in Drèze (1989b) and general equilibrium with incomplete markets and labour contracts is treated in Drèze (1989a).
6. Granting that the disutility of being unemployed typically exceeds the disutility of working, unemployment benefits provide an approximate measure of reservation wages.
7. We hardly ever see future or contingent labour contracts (whereby for instance a first-year law student signs up with a Brussels law firm four years ahead contingently on graduating and not marrying a foreigner ...).
8. See also Bean (1984).
9. Efficiency wage theories argue that wages may not adjust to changes in labour supply, but leave them free to adjust to other circumstances. Insiders are assumed insensitive to unemployment. Instead, unions are assumed concerned with the unemployed as well; see Oswald (1985) or Pencavel (1985).
10. See Drèze (1999b).
11. This is in violation of second-best efficiency; see Drèze and Gollier (1993, section 4). On the rationale for absence of wage discrimination, see Drèze (1986, section

2.3.3), Bewley (1998) or the 'hiring scenario' of the insiders–outsiders theory, e.g. Lindbeck and Snower (1988) or Lindbeck (1993, p. 41).

12. The incremental labour or income taxes recommended by the second-best analysis in states particularly favourable to labour are seldom implemented. This feature need not detain us, as my interest focuses on downward rigidities.

13. For instance, Hall (1987) reports mark-ups of 50 per cent in more than half the industries he studies, and Bils (1987) concludes that mark-ups are 'very countercyclical'.

14. Technically, incomplete markets turn an *ex ante* convex technology into an *ex post* non-convex one – with well-known associated difficulties. The rationale for average-cost pricing under fixed costs in competitive environments is presented in Dehez and Drèze (1988).

15. Firms cannot quote prices contingent on demand *elasticity*, which is not observable.

16. Because Radner (1972) does not assume sequentially complete markets, he only obtains existence of a 'pseudo equilibrium' which need not be Pareto efficient; see also Radner (1982, section 5.4).

17. See Hahn (1999), Chichilnisky (1999b) or Drèze (1999c, section 6 and appendix).

18. The presumption is that such aggregates could be translated into Pareto ranking through suitable transfers; but suitable transfers are not always identified, seldom implementable and never fully implemented.

19. The seminal paper on this topic is Grandmont and Laroque (1976).

20. You may be unemployed whereas your neighbour is not.

21. Technically, van der Laan also imposes that at least one (unspecified) commodity be free from quantity constraints; the property holds trivially when at least one commodity is free from price rigidity.

22. See footnote 29.

23. This in particular hardens tomorrow's price rigidities, as suggested in section 3.3 above.

24. Suitably defined: there is lack of unanimous agreement about modelling money in general equilibrium; I favour the approach developed in Drèze and Polemarchakis (1998, 2001).

25. I am satisfied that existence holds under downward rigidities, as confirmed by research in progress with Jean-Jacques Herings.

26. This is theorem 3.2 in Drèze (1997), building upon Dehez and Drèze (1984).

27. For instance you would expect lower real-estate values in regions of high unemployment.

28. Technically, the fixed prices of some number n of fix-price commodities freezes $n - 1$ relative prices; but the specification allows for n quantity constraints, leaving one degree of freedom towards accommodating the exogenous supply constraints. That degree of freedom corresponds to the relative price of group I and group II commodities.

29. In a two-period model with S states and $J < S$ assets, there is an $(S - J + 1)$-dimensional continuum of equilibria, revealing that indeterminacy increases directly with the degree of market incompleteness $(S - J)$.

30. Jean-Jacques Herings and I (see the appendix of Drèze (1997) and section 4 of Herings and Drèze (1998)) have produced examples where the rigid prices are compatible with competitive equilibria, yet all supply-constrained equilibria constrain to zero the supply of the fix-price commodities. (One worker is sick, or one machine breaks, and the whole manufacturing sector comes to a standstill!)

These examples are extreme, but they proved helpful in identifying sufficient conditions for a more realistic structure of equilibria.
31. The proof relies on a fixed-point theorem due to Felix Browder (not Brouwer!) (1960) published in *Summae Brassiliensis Matematicae* and extended to correspondences by Mas-Colell (1974).
32. If there is a hidden rock in the middle of a bay, generically you can sail anywhere – but prudent sailors do not. Unlike that case, the genericity in theorem 2.1 is innocuous.
33. This is equivalent to gross substitutability plus non-inferiority.
34. This is theorem 3.1 (iii) in Herings and Drèze (1998). A similar result, proved by John Roberts (1987, 1989), for the special case of homothetic consumer preferences and constant-returns production, provided the inspiration for Drèze (1997).
35. The result also holds in a monetary economy, with a mixture of real and nominal downward rigidities.
36. The paper is written for the case of proportional rationing, germane to inelastic supply, but the result should hold for any allocation of the constraints among the agents defined by Lipschitz-continuous functions; see also Drèze (1991b) for a very general, discrete specification.
37. The process is defined by a system of differential equations with discontinuous right-hand sides; appropriate techniques are described in Champsaur *et al.* (1977); the complications associated with discontinuities led me to analyse first the special case of fixed supplies.
38. Cf. Lubrano *et al.* (1996), Shadman-Mehta and Sneessens (1997).
39. This was the parting theme of my late friend William Vickrey (1993), and I am pleased to help keep his concern alive.
40. See Drèze and Malinvaud *et al.* (1994).
41. In particular, megacities raise problems that will be with us for many years.
42. This link with macroeconomic stability should inspire the advocates of basic income. ...
43. In Belgium, some mortgage contracts stipulate postponement of repayments of the principal if the borrower becomes unemployed, and loans indexed on the gross operating surplus of not-for-profit firms are being considered.
44. Translating that idea to the firm level no doubt raises issues of moral hazard and observability. Similar difficulties would arise if loans were indexed on prices charged by firms – an otherwise attractive idea, since it would be equivalent, for pricing purposes, to blowing up demand elasticities.

References

Atkinson, A.B. (1995) *Public Economics in Action* (Oxford: Clarendon).
Azariadis, C. (1975) 'Implicit Contracts and Underemployment Equilibria', *Journal of Political Economy*, vol. 83, no. 6, pp. 1183–202.
Baily, M. (1974) 'Wages and Employment under Uncertain Demand', *Review of Economic Studies*, vol. 41, no.1, pp. 37–50.
Bean, C. (1984) 'Optimal Wage Bargains', *Economica*, vol. 51, pp. 141–49.
Bénassy, J.P. (1995) (ed.) *Macroeconomics and Imperfect Competition* (Aldershot: Edward Elgar).
Benhabib, J. and Farmer, R.E.A. (1997) 'Indeterminacy and Sunspots in Macroeconomics', mimeo, New York University, New York.

Bernanke, B.S. (1983) 'Irreversibility, Uncertainty and Cyclical Investment', *Quarterly Journal of Economics*, vol. 98, pp. 85–106.

Bewley, T. (1998) 'Why Not Cut Pay?', *European Economic Review*, vol. 42, no. 3–5, pp. 459–90.

Bils, M. (1987) 'The Cyclical Behavior of Marginal Costs and Prices', *American Economic Review*, vol. 77, pp. 838–55.

Browder, F.E. (1960) 'On Continuity of Fixed Points under Deformations of Continuous Mappings', *Summa Brasiliensis Mathematicae*, vol. 4, pp. 183–91.

Champsaur, P., Drèze, J.H. and Henry, C. (1977) 'Stability Theorems with Economic Applications', *Econometrica*, vol. 45, pp. 273–94.

Chichilnisky, G. (1999a) (ed.) *Markets, Information, and Uncertainty: Essays in Economic Theory in Honour of K.J. Arrow* (Cambridge: Cambridge University Press).

Chichilnisky, G. (1999b) 'Existence and Optimality of a General Equilibrim with Endogenous Uncertainty', ch. 5 in Chichilnisky (1999a).

Cooper, R. and John, A. (1988) 'Coordinating Coordination Failures in Keynesian Models', *Quarterly Journal of Economics*, vol. 103, pp. 441–63.

Dehez, P. and Drèze, J.H. (1984) 'On Supply-Constrained Equilibria', *Journal of Economic Theory*, vol. 33, no.1, pp. 172–82; reprinted as ch. 3 in Drèze (1991a).

Dehez, P. and Drèze, J.H. (1988) 'Competitive Equilibria with Quantity-Taking Producers and Increasing Returns to Scale', *Journal of Mathematical Economics*, vol. 17, pp. 209–30; reprinted as ch. 4 in Drèze (1991a).

Dixit, A.K. and Pindyck, R.S. (1994) *Investment under Uncertainty* (Princeton, NJ: Princeton University Press).

Dixon, H.D. and Rankin, N. (1995) *The New Macroeconomics: Imperfect Markets and Policy Effectiveness* (Cambridge: Cambridge University Press).

Drèze, J.H. (1974) (ed.) *Allocation under Uncertainty: Equilibrium and Optimality* (London: Macmillan).

Drèze, J.H. (1975) 'Existence of an Exchange Equilibrium under Price Rigidities', *International Economic Review*, vol. 16, no. 2, pp. 301–20; reprinted as ch. 2 in Drèze (1991a).

Drèze, J.H. (1979a) 'Human Capital and Risk Bearing', *Geneva Papers on Risk and Insurance*, vol. 12, pp. 5–22; reprinted as ch. 17 in Drèze (1987).

Drèze, J.H. (1979b) 'Demand Estimation, Risk Aversion and Sticky Prices', *Economics Letters*, vol. 4, pp. 1–6; reprinted as ch. 7 in Drèze (1987).

Drèze, J.H. (1986) 'Work Sharing: Some Theory and Recent European Experience', *Economic Policy*, vol. 1, no. 3, pp. 561–619; reprinted as ch.17 in Drèze (1991a).

Drèze, J.H. (1987) *Essays on Economic Decisions under Uncertainty* (Cambridge: Cambridge University Press).

Drèze, J.H. (1989a), *Labour Management, Contracts and Capital Markets, A General Equilibrium Approach* (Oxford: Blackwell).

Drèze, J.H. (1989b) 'The Role of Securities and Labour Contracts in the Optimal Allocation of Risk Bearing', ch. 3 in Loubergé, H. (ed.) *Risk, Information and Insurance. Essays in the Memory of Karl H. Borch* (Dordrecht: Kluwer); reprinted as ch. 11 in Drèze (1991a).

Drèze, J.H. (1991a) *Underemployment Equilibria: Essays in Theory, Econometrics and Policy* (Cambridge: Cambridge University Press).

Drèze, J.H. (1991b) 'Stability of a Keynesian Adjustment Process', ch. 9 in Barnett, W., Cornet, B., d'Aspremont, C., Jaskold Gabszevicz, J. and Mas-Colell, A. (eds) *Equilibrium Theory and Applications* (Cambridge: Cambridge University Press); reprinted as ch.10 in Drèze (1991a).

Drèze, J.H. (1993) 'Can Varying Social Insurance Contributions Improve Labour Market Efficiency?', ch. 8 in Atkinson, A.B. (ed.) *Alternatives to Capitalism: The Economics of Partnership* (London: Macmillan).

Drèze, J.H. (1997) 'Walras-Keynes Equilibria, Coordination and Macroeconomics', *European Economic Review*, vol. 41, pp. 1735–62.

Drèze, J.H. (1999a) 'On the Dynamics of Supply-constrained Equilibria' in Herings, P.J.J., van der Laan, G. and Talman, A.J.J. (eds) *Theory of Markets* (Amsterdam: North-Holland), pp. 7–25.

Drèze, J.H. (1999b) 'Jobs and Economic Security in the 21st Century' in Löffer, H. and Streissler, E.W. (eds) *Sozialpolitik und Ökologieprobleme der Zukunft* (Vienna: Österreichische Akademie der Wissenschaften), pp. 65–96.

Drèze, J.H. (1999c) 'The Formulation of Uncertainty: Prices and States', ch. 3 in Chichilnisky (1999a).

Drèze, J.H. (1999d) 'Public Economics, Public Projects and their Funding', *Asian Development Review*, vol. 15, pp. 1–17.

Drèze, J.H., Durré, A. and Sneessens, H. (1998) 'Investment Stimulation, with the Example of Housing', *Cahiers BEI*, vol. 3, no. 1, pp. 99–114.

Drèze, J.H. and Gollier, C. (1993) 'Risk Sharing on the Labour Market and Second-Best Wage Rigidities', *European Economic Review*, vol. 37, pp. 1457–82.

Drèze, J.H. and Malinvaud, E. with De Grauwe, P., Gevers, L., Italianer, A., Lefebvre, O., Marchand, M., Sneessens, H., Steinherr, A., and Champsaur, P., Charpin, J.-M., Fitoussi, J.-P. and Laroque G. (1994) 'Growth and Employment: The Scope for a European Initiative', *European Economy, Reports and Studies*, vol. 1, pp. 75–106; French text 'Croissance et emploi: l'ambition d'une initiative européenne', *Revue de l'OFCE*, vol. 49 (1994), pp. 247–88.

Drèze, J.H. and Modigliani, F. (1972) 'Consumption Decisions under Uncertainty', *Journal of Economic Theory*, vol. 5, no. 3, pp. 308–35.

Drèze, J.H. and Polemarchakis, H. (1998) 'Money and Monetary Policy in General Equilibrium', ch. 4 in Kirman, A.P. and Gérard-Varet, L.A. (eds) *Economics Beyond the Millennium* (Oxford: Clarendon).

Drèze, J.H. and Polemarchakis, H. (2001) 'Intertemporal General Equilibrium and Monetary Policy', forthcoming in Leijonhufvud, A. (ed.) *Monetary Theory as a Basis for Monetary Policy* (Basingstoke: Palgrave).

Gordon, D.F. (1974) 'A Neo-Classical Theory of Keynesian Unemployment', *Economic Inquiry*, vol. 12, pp. 431–59.

Grandmont, J.M. (1974) 'On the Short-Run Equilibrium in a Monetary Economy' ch. 12 in Drèze (1974).

Grandmont, J.M. (1977) 'Temporary General Equilibrium', *Econometrica*, vol. 45, pp. 535–72.

Grandmont, J.M. (1982) 'Temporary General Equilibrium Theory', ch.19 in Arrow, K.J. and Intriligator, M.D. (eds) *Handbook of Mathematical Economics* (Amsterdam: North-Holland).

Grandmont, J.M. (1988) (ed.) *Temporary Equilibrium: Selected Readings* (San Diego: Academic Press).

Grandmont, J.M. (1989) 'Keynesian Issues and Economic Theory', *Scandinavian Journal of Economics*, vol. 91, pp. 265–93.

Grandmont, J.M. and Laroque, G. (1976) 'On Keynesian Temporary Equilibria', *Review of Economic Studies*, vol. 43, pp. 53–67.

Greenwald, B.C. and Stiglitz, J.E. (1989) 'Toward a Theory of Rigidities', *American Economic Review*, vol. 79, no. 2, pp. 364–69.

Greenwald, B.C. and Stiglitz, J.E. (1990) 'Asymmetric Information and the New Theory of the Firm: Financial Constraints and Risk Behavior', *American Economic Review*, vol. 80, no. 2, pp. 160–65.

Greenwald, B.C. and Stiglitz, J.E. (1993) 'Financial Market Imperfections and Business Cycles', *Quarterly Journal of Economics*, vol. 108, pp. 77–114.

Hahn, F.H. (1999) 'A Remark on Incomplete Market Equilibrium', ch. 4 in Chichilnisky (1999a).

Hall, R.E. (1987) 'The Relation Between Price and Marginal Cost in US Industry', *Journal of Political Economy*, vol. 96, pp. 921–47.

Herings, P.J.J. and Drèze, J.H. (1998) 'Continua of Underemployment Equilibria', Discussion Paper no. 9805, CenTER Tilburg, and Discussion Paper no. 9845, CORE, Louvain-la-Neuve.

Herings, P.J.J., van der Laan, G. and Talman, D. (1999) 'Price-Quantity Adjustment in a Keynesian Economy', in Herings, P.J.J., van der Laan, G. and Talman, D. (eds) *The Theory of Markets* (Amsterdam: North-Holland), pp. 27–57.

Hicks, J.R. (1936) *Value and Capital* (Oxford: Clarendon).

Keynes, J.M. (1936) *The General Theory of Employment, Interest and Money* (London: Macmillan).

Leijonhufvud, A. (1968) *On Keynesian Economics and the Economics of Keynes* (Oxford: Oxford University Press).

Lindbeck, A. (1993) *Unemployment and Macroeconomics* (Cambridge, Mass.: MIT Press).

Lindbeck, A. and Snower, D. (1988) *The Insider–Outsider Theory of Employment and Unemployment* (Cambridge, MASS: MIT Press).

Lubrano, M., Shadman-Mehta, F. and Sneessens, H. (1996) 'Real Wages, Quantity Constraints and Equilibrium Unemployment: Belgium, 1955–1998', *Empirical Economics*, vol. 21, pp. 427–57.

Mas-Colell, A. (1974) 'A Note on a Theorem of F. Browder', *Mathematical Programming*, vol. 6, pp. 229–33.

McDonald, R. and Siegel, D. (1986) 'The Value of Waiting to Invest', *Quarterly Journal of Economics*, vol. 101, pp. 707–28.

Oswald, A. (1985) 'The Economic Theory of Trade Unions: An Introductory Survey', *Scandinavian Journal of Economics*, vol. 82, no. 2, pp. 160–93.

Pencavel, J. (1985) 'Wages and Employment and Trade Unionism: Microeconomic Models and Macroeconomic Applications', *Scandinavian Journal of Economics*, vol. 82, no. 2, pp. 197–225.

Radner, R. (1972) 'Existence of Equilibrium of Plans, Prices and Price Expectations in a Sequence of Markets', *Econometrica*, vol. 40, pp. 289–303.

Radner, R. (1982) 'Equilibrium under Uncertainty', ch. 20 in Arrow, K.J. and Intriligator, M.D. (eds) *Handbook of Mathematical Economics* (Amsterdam: North-Holland).

Roberts, J. (1987) 'An Equilibrium Model with Involuntary Unemployment at Flexible, Competitive Prices and Wages', *American Economic Review*, vol. 77, pp. 856–74.

Roberts, J. (1989) 'Equilibrium without Market Clearing', ch. 6 in Cornet, B. and Tulkens, H. (eds) *Contributions to Operations Research and Economics* (Cambridge, MASS: MIT Press).

Rosen, S. (1985) 'Implicit Contracts: A Survey', *Journal of Economic Literature*, vol. 23, no. 3, pp. 1144–75.

Shadman-Mehta, F. and Sneessens, H. (1997) 'Demand-Supply Interactions and Unemployment Dynamics: Is There Path Dependency? The Case of Belgium, 1955–1994', paper presented at the CEPR Conference on Unemployment Persistence, Vigo.

Shiller, R.J. (1993) *Macro Markets: Creating Institutions for Managing Society's Largest Risks* (Oxford: Clarendon).

Stiglitz, J.E. (1984) 'Price Rigidities and Market Structure', *American Economic Review*, vol. 74, pp. 350–55.

Stiglitz, J.E. (1999) 'Toward a General Theory of Wage and Price Rigidities and Economic Fluctuations', *American Economic Review*, vol. 89, no. 2, pp. 75–80.

Sweezy, P. (1939) 'Demand under Conditions of Oligopoly', *Journal of Political Economy*, vol. 47, pp. 568–73.

Van der Laan, G. (1982) 'Simplicial Approximation of Unemployment Equilibria', *Journal of Mathematical Economics*, vol. 9, pp. 83–97.

Van der Laan, G. (1984) 'Supply-Constrained Fixed Price Equilibria in Monetary Economies', *Journal of Mathematical Economics*, vol. 13, no. 2, pp. 171–87.

Vickrey, W. (1993) 'Today's Task for Economists', *American Economic Review*, vol. 83, pp. 1–10.

Woodford, M. (1991) 'Self-Fulfilling Expectations and Fluctuations in Aggregate Demand', ch. 20 in Mankiw, N.G. and Romer, D. (eds) *New Keynesian Economics*, vol. 2 (Cambridge, MASS: MIT Press).

4
Macroeconomic Frictions: What Have We Learned from the Real Business Cycle Research Programme?

Jean-Pierre Danthine
University of Lausanne, Switzerland and CEPR
and
John B. Donaldson
Columbia University, New York, USA

4.1 Two quick answers to the question at hand ...

Two extreme, definitive, answers to the question posed in the title and one more murky and incomplete can be contemplated. The first holds that we have learned nothing from the Real Business Cycle (RBC) programme on the subject of frictions simply because it has nothing to teach us: the RBC programme is the wrong research programme, a mistaken detour in our attempt to understand short-run macroeconomic phenomena. One stated reason for such a view, phrased by Bob Solow in this volume, is that the underlying neoclassical growth model was designed to be a model for the long run, a time horizon at which one may hold that all the necessary price and wage adjustments have been made. It is thus not an appropriate model for studying short-run phenomena, fluctuations occurring at quarterly frequencies, a time horizon where, to the contrary, the flex wage and price hypothesis must be *a priori* ruled out.

At the other extreme of the spectrum, there is another definitive answer, one naturally arising from a narrow, yet frequent, interpretation of the RBC programme. In that restrictive view, within which the RBC approach is often confined (see most recent macro textbooks, e.g. Burda and Wyplosz (1997)), the RBC programme would have taught us that most macro phenomena can be understood with the help of a perfect market frictionless model, a close cousin of the neoclassical stochastic growth model. If one accepts this claim, what we would have learned from the RBC programme is that the world is frictionless! Moreover, we would have learned that business cycles are real: real productivity shocks, as opposed to monetary shocks or preference shocks (animal spirits or information shocks) are the dominant source of business cycle fluctuations. Real business cycle theorists would, in a sense, have established the triumph of new classical macroeconomics and the futility of macroeconomic stabilization policies.

4.2 ... with which we cannot be satisfied

The basis for these claims is the fact that key business cycle facts appear to be 'surprisingly' well accounted for by the moneyless neoclassical growth model with technology shocks. Table 4.1 illustrates the dimensions along which this claim is usually made. It compares the standard deviations, and correlations with output, of output itself, consumption, investment, employment, and productivity for the US economy and for the model economy. The artificial economy here is the neoclassical stochastic growth model enriched with preferences over leisure as well as consumption. It is meant to represent an economy in dynamic competitive equilibrium. This decentralized interpretation is possible thanks to the use of the first welfare theorem (Prescott and Lucas (1972)). In this world, the representative agent optimizes along two margins, the choice between labour and leisure on the one hand, and between consumption and savings and investment on the other. There are no frictions, markets are perfectly Walrasian, and the equilibrium is a Pareto optimum. The illustrated properties correspond to those of a fully calibrated model; that is, the model is parametrized so as to respect a number of important long-run regularities and relevant information found in parallel studies (see Cooley (1997)).

An alternative way to evaluate the basic model's performance consists of comparing the output generated by the model with its real world counterparts. This is done in Figure 4.1, which shows the results of inputting estimated Solow residuals over the period 1948 to 1996 into the artificial

Table 4.1 Business cycle stylized facts for the US economy and for the extended neoclassical growth model

Series	Quarterly US time series (55.3–84.1)			Artificial economy (neoclassical growth model)		
	(a)	(b)	(c)	(a)	(b)	(c)
Output	1.76	1.00	1.00	1.30	1.00	1.00
Consumption	1.29	0.73	0.85	0.42	0.32	0.89
Investment	8.60	4.89	0.92	4.24	3.26	0.99
Capital stock	0.63	0.36	0.04	0.36	0.28	0.06
Hours	1.66	0.94	0.76	0.70	0.54	0.98
Productivity	1.18	0.67	0.42	0.68	0.52	0.98

Standard deviation in per cent (*a*); relative standard deviation (*b*); and correlations with output (*c*). All statistics detrended with the Hodrick-Prescott filter.
Source: Hansen (1985).

Figure 4.1   Actual vs. model-generated data – Solow residuals estimated by King and Rebelo (1999)

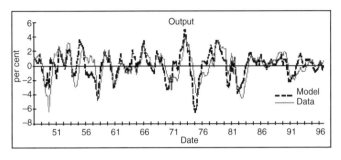

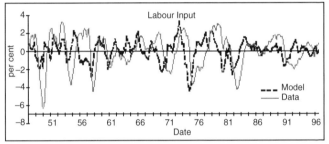

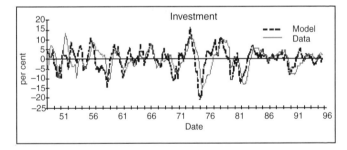

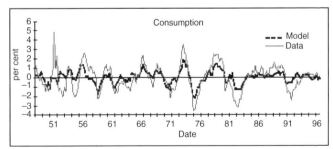

Note: Sample period: 1947:2 – 1996:4. All variables are detrended using the Hodrick-Prescott filter.

Source: King and Rebelo (1999), Figure 7.

economy model. The latter acts as a propagation mechanism transforming these 'productivity' shocks into time series for the major macro-aggregates. The fit with the data is close, with a correlation between the two output curves (first panel) of 0.79.

There are several reasons why we are not satisfied with the above view, suggesting as it does that all that can be said has been said in business cycle theory. The first resides in the fact that the list of standard deviations and correlations contained in Table 4.1 lacks scope. In the language we shall use in a moment, the congruence between model and reality, when limited to the stylized facts of Table 4.1, is not sufficient to give us confidence in the appropriateness of the underlying model. This assertion is confirmed by the fact that, at this level of observation, the expanded neoclassical growth model and a variety of other, very different, models with strongly diverging policy implications are observationally equivalent. Thus, Table 4.2 provides similar data for two alternative models. The first (panel A) is a wage contracting model proposed by Dow (1995). The only amendment proposed to the neoclassical growth model is that firms and workers have to agree on a wage one period in advance, before knowing the realization of the exogenous productivity shock. The second (panel B) is a model with efficiency wages of the shirking type. In this model, proposed by Danthine and Donaldson (1995), there are three types of workers: the young, the old with experience and the old without experience. The overall level of unemployment is 13 per cent; unemployment among the young is 23 per cent. This equilibrium is not a Pareto optimum. It is it is hard to imagine a model more at variance with the original RBC model. Yet in terms of the basic data of Table 4.1, it replicates the stylized facts of the US economy better.

Another reason to question the success of the benchmark RBC model is provided by the many 'puzzles' that have been uncovered by various authors since the inception of this research programme. These puzzles are typically stylized facts outside the list of Table 4.1 which falsify the simple model or one of its extension in a robust way. A number of these puzzles are discussed in what follows.

A third and final reason to contest the position associated with the pure real business cycle school is linked with the interpretation of Solow residuals as productivity shocks. A summary of this line of criticism is to say that 'too much is stuffed into the black box' which we term Solow residuals. One reason to suspect that the role attributed to Solow residuals is excessive is the observation, first made by Hall (1990), that these residuals are in fact correlated with some demand-side variables and that it is thus unwarranted to interpret them as *exogenous* productivity shocks. Another, more intuitive, expression of the same idea is the oft-expressed opinion that Solow residuals are implausibly large and variable, and moreover that they are often negative, an observation which is hard to rationalize, for example

Table 4.2   Business cycle properties of two non-Walrasian models

Variable	Panel A: Wage-contracting model[a]		Panel B: Shirking model		Panel C: Indivisible labour model	
	(a)	(c)	(a)	(c)	(a)	(c)
Output	1.76	1.00	1.74	1.00	1.79	1.00
Consumption	0.42	0.62	1.23	0.99	0.54	0.88
Investment	6.38	0.95	3.32	0.99	5.76	0.99
Capital stock	0.31	−0.05	0.30	0.04	0.49	0.07
Hours, of which	1.85	0.85	1.70	0.98	1.34	0.98
Old experienced			2.17	0.71		
Old inexperienced			8.16	0.03		
Young			2.17	0.95		
Productivity	0.90	0.17	0.29	0.24	0.54	0.88

Standard deviation in percent (a); and correlations with output (c)
Panel A. Wages set in advance 'Contracts (II)' model in Dow (1995)
Panel B. Danthine and Donaldson (1995)
Panel C. Hansen (1985): Indivisible labour model.

Summers (1986). The flip side of the same criticism is the observation that the simple RBC model constitutes a weak propagation mechanism. In several respects what one gets out – the characteristics of the output process – is very similar to what one feeds in – the Solow residuals. This is particularly true of the degree of persistence of the output process (see Cogley and Nason (1995)).

In this perspective, model enrichments that help strengthen the propagation mechanism are particularly welcome. One can think of introducing increasing returns to scale and/or imperfect competition, two properties that tend to enhance the propagation mechanism and that we will discuss later on. Similarly, models with a credit multiplier and several models with non-Walrasian labour markets such as the Dow and the Danthine and Donaldson models of Table 4.2 have a stronger propagation mechanism as well. One must realize, however, that neither credit-multiplier nor non-Walrasian models provide effective guidance as to how to correct for the estimation of productivity shocks from Solow residuals. In fact, all models built on the standard aggregate production function are equally subverted by the doubtful identification of Solow residuals with exogenous productivity shocks. On the contrary, models with variable factor utilization come with instructions as to how to go from Solow residuals to productivity shocks. And they are quite successful in doing that. King and Rebelo (1999), for example, show that the twin assumptions of indivisible labour (detailed below) and variable capital utilization perform extremely well in terms of the criteria of Table 4.1. And this performance is achieved with much smaller estimated productivity shocks (see Figure 4.2 for a comparison of Solow residuals with the productivity shocks estimated with the King-Rebelo model). These (estimated) productivity shocks are more frequently positive and they are uncorrelated with demand-side variables. Yet, King and Rebelo's economy, while not frictionless because of the indivisible labour assumption, is in fact a high-substitution economy; another margin of substitutability rather than an extra friction has been added: within a quarter, firms can adjust the intensity with which they use their capital stock.

Before leaving this subject, it is useful to comment on the interpretation of technology shocks. In business cycle models as well as in growth theory, we have come to associate Solow residuals with changes in the stock of knowledge, which over time make it possible to produce more output at unchanged input levels. In this narrow sense, negative residuals, implying a decrease in the stock of knowledge, are indeed difficult to justify. Hansen and Prescott (1993), however, propose that we should adopt a broader view of what underlies the output variations left unexplained by changes in factor usage. Without questioning the necessity to account as well for possible changes in factor utilization rates, as Burnside, Eichenbaum and Rebelo (1993), Finn (1995) and King and Rebelo (1999) and others do, they argue that the relationship between inputs and output is also affected by changes in the legal and regulatory system of a country and in the non-traded, and thus non-measured, factors of production. They argue

> that the reason for the huge difference [in productivity] between United States and India must be that India has been less successful than the United States in setting up economic institutions conducive to development.

Figure 4.2   Model productivity (–) and empirical Solow residual u–c/s (···)

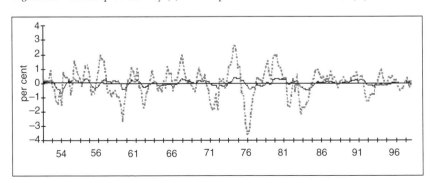

Source: King and Rebelo (1999), Figure 14.

And, that when

> pollution rights are not traded and the government imposes constraints
> on firms with regard to the amount of pollution, this represents a tech-
> nology shock, since the amount of output that can be produced from
> given quantities of market inputs changes.

4.3   The RBC research programme as a mechanism for identifying critical frictions

In the preceding section, we sought to explain why we could not consider
as definitive the frictionless view of the world promoted by a straightforward interpretation of the benchmark RBC model. In so doing, we have
been confronted with the fact that not all amendments to the basic model
will necessarily lead to the introduction of market frictions. We now want
to make precise the process by which such enrichments should be guided.
In our view, the distinguishing feature of the RBC programme is not some
prior insistence on the predominance of technology shocks, or the religious
belief that labour and product markets always clear. Rather it is the view
that the workhorse model for modern macroeconomics will be a dynamic
stochastic general equilibrium model of one form or another, together with
the experimental view of model-building proposed by Lucas (1980). In
Lucas's words,

> one of the functions of theoretical economics is to provide fully articu-
> lated, artificial economic systems that can serve as laboratories in which
> policies that would be prohibitively expensive to experiment with in
> actual economies can be tested out at much lower cost. ... We need to
> test models as useful imitations of reality by subjecting them to shocks
> for which we are fairly certain how actual economies, or part of
> economies, would react. The more dimensions on which the model
> mimics the answers actual economies give to simple questions, the more
> we trust its answers to harder questions.

The key word in the quoted text is the word 'trust'. Models are our experimental tools, our laboratories. In order to trust the answers a model would
provide to hard policy questions, we need to be confident in the model
itself. How do we build such confidence? Lucas's introductory sentence
provides one direction: test models by subjecting them to shocks for which
we are fairly certain how actual economies would react. We can, however,
take a broader stance on this issue. We will more easily trust models which
to a larger extent share the general properties of the data. In that view,
much of what is known as 'calibration' is part of a 'confidence building'
exercise. We know actual economies appear to follow balanced growth

paths, with important ratios remaining approximately constant over the long run. These ratios are identified, for example, with the Kaldor facts (Kaldor (1957)). Similarly, Lucas (1977) identified a set of properties generally associated with business cycles. He stressed that these regularities are independent of time and places and, as such, could reasonably be viewed as defining the business cycle. The quantification of these regularities constitutes the basis for the standard deviations and correlations found in Table 4.1 and we are naturally more confident in models with the ability to match these stylized facts.

But, as already suggested, congruence between model and reality should not be limited to the stylized facts of Table 4.1. They are not sufficient to give us confidence in the ability of the model to answer hard economic policy questions. It is thus natural to go beyond them. The most frequently travelled avenues consist in, first, comparing impulse response functions and, second, looking at conditional as well as non-contemporaneous correlations. It is important, however, to remember here that models are abstractions, and that they cannot conform to reality on each and every dimension. We believe the key to success consists of isolating what we will call 'critical facts'. By facts, we mean characteristics of real economies known with some degree of confidence. By critical, we mean that these facts should be important enough to justify being featured in a good macro-model. There is a good deal of subjectivity in this process which is at the heart of model selection. It depends on the question being addressed, since the latter conditions the characteristics which we would insist that the model possesses.

In the rest of this chapter, we illustrate how this approach may be used, and has been used, to guide the development of the theory and we discuss to what extent present trends indicate the need to enrich the basic model with macroeconomic frictions. We are not far from accepting the view that the RBC research programme is, in fact, an organized research programme precisely aimed at deciding *which particular friction* must necessarily be included in the modelling process. The guiding principle is the capacity of the model, with or without this friction, to explain critical facts. Parsimony requires that only those frictions which prove *necessary* in this sense should find their way into the final dynamic stochastic model that we will use as our benchmark representation of the macroeconomy.

4.4   Labour markets

It is natural, if we think of justifying frictions, to start by focusing on the labour market. In the short history of the RBC literature, one significant fact stands out for the role it has played in the process we want to illustrate. It is the observation that the standard deviation of hours is approximately the same as the standard deviation of output, an observation labelled early on as the employment volatility puzzle. This fact is well documented for the United States; somewhat less so for other countries where the measured ratios (SD(n)/SD(y)) range from 0.50 for Italy to 1.34 for South Africa (Danthine and Donaldson (1993)).

Taking this observation as a fact, nevertheless, we can certainly use the adjective 'significant' because it falsifies the neoclassical growth model which could replicate it only if one hypothesizes an implausibly high willingness to substitute labour and leisure across time periods (indeed, the model of Table 4.1 exhibits a ratio SD(n)/SD(y) = 0.54). It is critical as well because it questions the benchmark model precisely in a dimension where one would expect it *a priori* to be the most vulnerable: that is, in the maintained assumption of clearing (Walrasian) labour markets. For this reason, it provides definite support to proponents of non-Walrasian labour market formulations. Indeed both the shirking and the contracting models of Table 4.2 pass the employment volatility test. Note that not all non-Walrasian formulations do; see for example Danthine and Donaldson (1990).

It is also the case, however, that the employment productivity puzzle can be equally well resolved by adopting another (non-Keynesian) friction, the indivisible labour supply hypothesis to which we now turn (Hansen (1985), Rogerson (1988)). This hypothesis states that agents cannot continuously vary their supply of working hours: that is, they cannot adjust the length of their working day. In effect, they may work full time or not at all (for reasons due to supply – costs of going to work – or demand – such as fixed costs associated with labour management). This implies that all changes in hours will be done along the extensive margin, that the individual intertemporal elasticity of substitution regarding leisure is immaterial – despite the fact that the aggregate elasticity of substitution is infinite – and, because of the latter fact, that the quantity of labour employed is exclusively determined by the demand side of the market (a Keynesian property). The literature has tended to prefer the indivisible labour hypothesis to the various non-Walrasian formulations that have been proposed, probably for reasons of parsimony. This preference may be not be robust, however, to the necessity of replicating other critical facts.

One such possible critical fact is related to the co-variation of real wages or productivity with output. Since Dunlop (1938) and Tarshis (1938), it has been taken as a fact that real wages are close to a-cyclical. This observation is significant because it falsifies the indivisible labour model which needs to be rescued by the adjunction of demand shocks. Christiano and Eichenbaum (1992) propose the introduction of government spending shocks while Hansen and Wright (1992) model shocks to the home production function. In both instances, demand shocks are an adjunction worth mentioning from the perspective of the narrow interpretation of the RBC model (business cycles are not real). This observation also provides support to models where wage adjustments are sluggish, be it because of contracts

(Dow (1995), Boldrin and Horvath (1995), or efficiency wage considerations. Again, both models of Table 4.2 pass this test. So would a gift exchange model with sluggish reference wage, such as proposed for instance by Collard and de la Croix (2000) or the model of section 4.3 in Danthine and Donaldson (1990). On this score, we are confronted with the question of whether this discriminating information is indeed a fact. Contrary to the Dunlop-Tarshis observation, studies on longitudinal micro-data appear to indicate that real wages are in fact quite strongly pro-cyclical, a property obscured by a composition bias: the aggregate statistics are constructed in a way that gives more weight to low-skill workers during expansions than during recessions (Solon, Barsky and Parker (1994); see also Liu (1999)). In the case of models with homogeneous labour, where the composition bias cannot be modelled, these results thus seem to favour underlying mechanisms generating pro-cyclical real wages.

Another natural source of critical facts would seem to be found in the unemployment statistics. In most of the RBC literature, the emphasis so far has been on employment rather than unemployment although this has begun to change as more information on the latter becomes available from micro-data. In particular, it appears that unemployment and the unemployment rate result from the interaction of a number of factors, some cyclical and some operating at lower frequencies. First, the rate of unemployment appears to be largely age dependent (the rate being much higher for young persons who are assembling skill sets and exploring career possibilities) with the consequence that long-term trends in the unemployment rate, especially in the US, are principally driven by changes in the age distribution of the population (Shimer (1998)). This is accompanied by both cyclical variation in the labour force participation rate, as well as its long-term downward trend (Rogerson (1998)), phenomena that have not yet been fully understood and modelled. The net effect of these forces, at the aggregate level, is for unemployment to vary, proportionately, more than employment and for these series not to be perfectly negatively correlated (Hechler (1995)). On this score, efficiency wage models appear to dominate the indivisible labour formulation.

Other independent 'critical facts' on unemployment are hard to come by, however, except in terms of flows. The latter are usable only if one adopts a search-matching type modelling for the labour market. Only now are models beginning to address these issues – see Merz (1995), Andolfatto and Gomme (1996) or Gomes, Greenwood and Rebelo (1997), among several others. While attractive, we do not want to postulate that this is the only promising approach for aggregate general equilibrium macromodelling.

The replication of other micro stylized facts will require models that are considerably more disaggregated than those currently in use. For example, there is persistent wage inequality within and between skill levels. Hansen (1993) explores the relative cyclical variability of quality adjusted versus unadjusted hours and finds the quality adjusted measure only slightly less variable. The current state of the art has not dealt with these issues and it is not fully clear at this point that they will be significant for macro-related questions.

In conclusion, we are not yet ready to decide which friction should be part of the right, parsimonious, description of the labour market in dynamic stochastic general equilibrium models. There is an abundance of observationally equivalent candidates and we are short of discriminating, significant, facts. This is disappointing. Focusing on the labour market seemed a sure recipe for identifying 'necessary' frictions! In this domain, one is forced to accept the view that, at this point, theory is ahead of (significant) business cycle facts (Prescott (1986)).

4.5   Money

As opposed to the shortage of significant facts guiding the modelling of labour markets, the extension of the RBC literature to the realm of monetary economics provides a perfect example of a discriminating experiment exactly aligned on the recommendation of Lucas. The simple experiment for which we know with some confidence how actual economies would react is an unanticipated increase in the money supply. Indeed, there appears to be a consensus that such a monetary shock is normally followed by a fall in nominal interest rate. Christiano, Eichenbaum and Evans (1998) would even argue that the consensus is broader and also bears on the real effects of such an increase in the money supply – increase in output, increase in employment – and on the resulting behaviour of prices – quasi-stability. On the latter dimensions, however, the consensus is more fragile (see Uhlig (1999)). For this reason we limit ourselves to the implications of the first part of the proposition.

The interest rate impact of an unanticipated increase in money is a significant fact because it points clearly towards the necessity of introducing nominal frictions into the model. Indeed it falsifies the standard RBC model with money introduced via a cash-in-advance (CIA) constraint (Cooley and Hansen (1989, 1995)). In this model, the main effect of an unanticipated increase in money is to feed inflationary expectations leading to an increase in the inflationary premium and thus a rise in the nominal interest rate.

Two frictions have been suggested to improve model performance: cost of adjusting prices and cost of adjusting portfolios. The former, generally labelled menu costs, may be introduced either in the form of a direct cost-of-adjustment function or via imposing the constraint that only a fraction of (possibly randomly chosen) firms are allowed to modify their prices in the current quarter (e.g. Calvo (1983)). Obviously, the model context here must be one where firms set prices, that is, where competition is imperfect. The alternative is to stipulate the existence of costs to adjusting portfolios. Again a cost-of-adjustment function may be imposed which penalizes a quick rebalancing of portfolios by individuals. Alternatively, and interestingly, a financial intermediation sector may be introduced. Monetary policy then takes the form of open market operations. The direct effect of a monetary injection falls on commercial banks, and is entirely transmitted to firms' borrowing conditions because households are precluded from adjusting their portfolios during the period. The latter models are known under the label of 'limited participation model of money' (Lucas (1990), Fuerst (1992)).

There may be other solutions to this puzzle. The fact that the main contenders strongly point towards the introduction of meaningful frictions is significant from the perspective of the question with which we began. So is the conclusion of Christiano, Eichenbaum and Evans (1997) that nominal rigidities of the two types contemplated above will not be enough and that they will have to be complemented with other 'real' frictions.

4.6 Financial puzzles

A successful macroeconomic model should be able to explain not only the basic business cycle regularities, but the stylized facts of the financial markets as well. One reason for this is that financial returns provide sharp observations on the inter-temporal rates of substitution which are at the heart of modern explanations for business cycle fluctuations. Important financial observations include the historical mean equity (market index) and risk-free returns and their differences (the equity premium), their respective volatilities (return standard deviations) and their time series correlation structure. While, as we have noted, progress along the business cycle dimensions has been quite substantial, success in replicating these basic financial regularities has been more circumscribed. Prominent instances of the latter are the equity premium puzzle (Mehra and Prescott (1985), Kocherlakota (1996)), and the risk-free rate puzzle (Weil (1989)). In the international arena, the quantity and price variability anomalies (Backus, Kehoe and Kydland (1992, 1995), Hess and Shin (1997)) may as well be related to capital market imperfections as yet not modelled in the RBC setting.

The majority of the relevant financial studies has been undertaken in the context of exchange models which, by construction, cannot simultaneously reconcile financial and business cycle regularities. These studies are nevertheless useful because a mechanism which cannot replicate the financial stylized facts in an exchange setting will be unsuccessful in a production setting as well, as the latter has an even more restricted set of feasible time paths of consumption.[1] Telmer (1993), Heaton and Lucas (1995 a,b) and others explore an initial suggestion by Mehra and Prescott (1985) that incomplete markets constructs may be more successful. Endogenous frictions arising from missing markets are also potentially important for understanding business cycles. When agents are unable to ensure perfectly their income streams, as is the case in such models, individual consumption growth need no longer closely resemble per capita consumption growth, allowing the former to vary more positively with stock returns, and thus generating a larger premium. Unfortunately, these studies have achieved little progress thus far, chiefly because the presence of only one security (e.g. a bond) allows the agents to smooth their consumption quite successfully via a dynamic trading strategy.

Another avenue for model improvement has been habit formation, a type of friction not commonly featured in macro-models; see, e.g. Constantinides (1990) and, more recently, Campbell and Cochrane (1999). The latter, in particular, is able to explain a wide range of financial phenomena by postulating a 'habit' that moves slowly and non-linearly in response to consumption changes. While effective in an exchange setting, it is not clear, however, that this mechanism will be equally successful when placed in a business cycle production context.[2]

Danthine and Donaldson (1999 a,b), in a full production setting, directly address both financial and macroeconomic stylized facts from two distinctly different perspectives. In the first, 'peso' effects with little impact on the macro side have significant implications for asset pricing, in particular giving rise to low risk-free rates. This allows for a replication of both the business cycle facts and the mean levels of security returns.[3] The second study focuses on the impact of the observed highly persistent variability in factor shares. This share variability results in an extra risk factor for equity owners. Adding this distribution risk to the customary systematic risk factors achieves the desired objectives across the full range of real and financial phenomena. A promising alternative route, with an equally active interaction between the real and financial sides of the economy, can be found in the credit multiplier literature (see Gertler (1988) for an overview). More recently Eisfeldt (1999) analyses a dynamic model where the liquidity of risky assets varies endogenously and this property magnifies the effects of productivity shocks. These considerations have yet to be incorporated into a business cycle model, however.

These anomalies and their resolution are obviously significant for finance. But they may reveal shortcomings relevant for macroeconomics as well. If, for instance, habit formation turns out to be the most robust solution to the equity premium puzzle, the modelling of preferences in macro-models will have to be modified accordingly. On the other hand, the international capital market frictions, which may prove necessary to explain the puzzles of international finance may or may not have implications for closed economy macroeconomics.

4.7 Two significant presumptions and their implications

In a recent article using a VAR methodology, Gali (1999) claims that identified positive technology shocks have a negative effect on employment. This observation is in stark contrast with the impact of such shocks in the standard RBC model, where, of course, they stimulate employment. Gali's explanation is that firms are demand-constrained as they would be in a world of imperfect competition with nominal rigidities (temporarily fixed prices). King and Rebelo (1999) suggest that this observation could also be accounted for in a multi-sector model where produced outputs are complements. This possibility notwithstanding, the observation is significant because it reinforces the plausibility of an important friction and because it clearly falsifies the pure technology-driven business cycle model. It does not deserve the status of fact yet, however, as it as not been confirmed in other studies using alternative identification procedures.

Many economists would argue that a wave of consumer pessimism is likely to result in an economic recession. We do not know the extent to which there is a consensus on this view and, indeed, the discussion in the *American Economic Review* of 1993 as to the causes of the US recession of 1991 leads us to doubt that there may be one (Blanchard (1993), Hall (1993), Hansen and Prescott (1993)). This doubt notwithstanding, Danthine, Donaldson and Johnsen (1998) test the reaction of the benchmark model to such a shock, proceeding as follows. They identify consumer pessimism with a change in growth expectations from a regime with a zero probability of a long period of stagnation to one where this probability is positive although very small and not realized in the relevant sample. In the real business cycle model (a version of the indivisible labour model modified to allow for such expectations), such a shock leads to a boom in investment, a natural consequence of the precautionary increase in savings, and to an increase in employment, an equally natural consequence of the precautionary increase in labour supply. Figure 4.3 traces these changes, which have long-lasting consequences when expectations do not revert to their initial level. All in all, the increase in investment makes up for the shortfall in consumption, and the increased use of factors (fixed capital and increased labour) result in an increase in output. This demonstration is troubling. It relies on an assumption of perfect coordination between savings and investment, and on a complete ability of the labour market to adjust in the short run to an increase in labour supply (hence the observed decrease of real wages). At the minimum, the conviction that this is not the way the real economy would actually react to a fall in consumer confidence would lead us to advocate introducing real rigidity in wage adjustments,

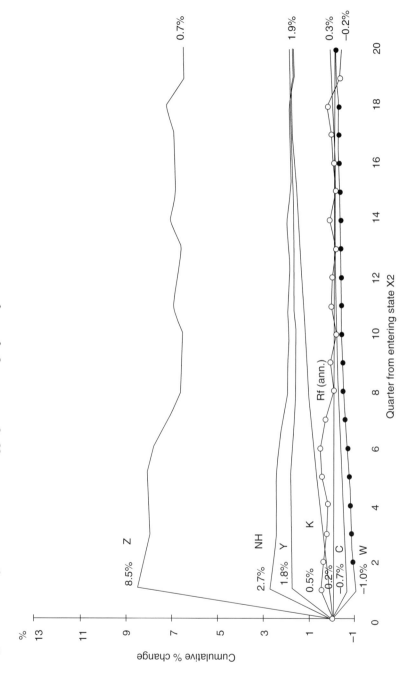

Figure 4.3 Changes in macroeconomic aggregates following a pure expectations shift

i.e. some real friction on the labour market. With this modification, the increase in labour supply would provoke an increase in unemployment, likely to weaken further consumer confidence, and output could not increase without a rise in factor utilization. This is interesting because such an amendment goes in the direction of those suggested as likely in the previous section.

4.8 Conclusion: towards a new neoclassical synthesis?

The facts and presumptions discussed so far have led quite naturally to an increasing fraction of the RBC literature being devoted to dynamic GE models combining different frictions. We would like to complete our discussion by briefly describing two current research directions proceeding in the spirit of the preceding sections. One of these focuses on models combining nominal rigidities with imperfect competition, often combined with increasing returns to scale in production and possibly complemented with an assumption of sluggish wage adjustment. Goodfriend and King (1997) snatch the promising 'new neo-classical synthesis' label and use it for a version of such a model but without the latter feature. How confident are we in this class of models? Very much so if we judge by the fact that these models are starting to be used to provide answers to 'hard' policy questions about the proper conduct of monetary policy. See for instance Clarida, Gali and Gertler (1999), who use it to support a policy of inflation targeting, and Goodfriend and King (1997) who advocate a policy of near-zero inflation aiming to produce a constant path for the average price-cost mark-up. On the other hand, they have not yet passed the traditional tests for confidence building such as those proposed in Table 4.1. In the words of King and Rebelo (1999), 'this research has not yet produced a business cycle model that performs at the same level as the RBC workhorse'. King and Watson (1996) also argue such a model cannot explain the observation that high nominal or real rates predict low output two to four quarters in the future, the 'inverted leading indicator' property.

Cooley and Quadrini (1999 a, b) propose an interesting alternative based on the limited participation model of money – with an operative liquidity effect – and on a search formulation for the labour market – where endogenous creation and destruction of jobs can occur in response to both aggregate and firm level shocks. They also use their model to answer 'hard' questions arguing that the optimal monetary policy should be pro-cyclical in the face of real shocks. Table 4.3 shows that their model accounts well for some basic, traditional, stylized facts of the business cycle. More research is needed to tally the relative merits of these two alternative strategies.

This chapter has reviewed work in progress. We are 'en route', and we believe we have taken the right path. If the current state of short-run

Table 4.3 Business cycle properties of the matching cum limited participation
model

Standard deviations	Artificial economy	US economy
Output	1.63	1.60
Hours	0.46	0.22
Employment	0.94	0.99
Job creation/employment	2.16	4.62
Job destruction/employment	2.23	6.81
Price index	1.72	1.44
Inflation	0.91	0.56
Correlations		
Inflation/stock returns	−0.38	−0.15
Money growth/stock returns	0.19	0.16

Source: Model economy B ($\alpha_u = 0.1$; $\eta = 0.01$; both monetary and real shocks) in Cooley and
Quadrini (1999a), see this source for details.

macroeconomics may not be as close to a consensus as the label 'new neoclassical synthesis' chosen by Goodfriend and King may suggest, we are
nevertheless getting closer and less ideological, and it looks increasingly
likely that the resulting consensus will be a friction-filled dynamic stochastic general equilibrium model. The excitement of part of the profession is
also palpable in the increasing willingness to use these new models to
answer 'hard policy questions'.

Notes

1. The classic equity premium article of Mehra and Prescott (1985) was also cast in
   an exchange setting.
2. Taking a completely different tack, Bansal and Coleman (1996) achieve a very
   substantial reduction in the risk-free rate (and thus an increase in the premium)
   by postulating an implicit transactions function for T-bills. Their results are
   achieved in a monetary exchange economy.
3. This approach can be interpreted as a small departure from pure rational expectations; for a more comprehensive exploration of the asset pricing implications of
   deviations from the rational expectations hypothesis, see Kurz and Motolese
   (1999), though once again only in an exchange setting.

References

Andolfatto, D. and Gomme, P. (1996) 'Unemployment Insurance and Labour-Market
   Activity in Canada', *Carnegie-Rochester Series on Public Policy*, vol. 44, pp. 47–82.
Backus, D.K., Kehoe, P.J. and Kydland, F.E. (1992) 'International Real Business
   Cycles', *Journal of Political Economy*, vol. 100, pp. 745–75.

Backus, D.K., Kehoe, P.J. and Kydland, F.E. (1995) 'International Business Cycles: Theory and evidence', ch. 11 in T. Cooley (ed.) *Frontiers of Business Cycle Research* (Princeton, NJ: Princeton University Press).

Bansal, R. and Coleman II, W.J. (1996) 'A Monetary Explanation of the Equity Premium, Term Premium, and Risk-Free Rate Puzzles', *Journal of Political Economy*, vol. 104, pp. 1135–71.

Blanchard, O. (1993) 'Consumption and the Recession of 1990–91', *American Economic Review*, vol. 83, pp. 270–74.

Boldrin, M. and Horvath, M. (1995) 'Labour Contracts and the Business Cycle', *Journal of Political Economy*, vol. 103, pp. 972–1004.

Burda, M. and Wyplosz, C. (1997) *Macroeconomics: A European Text*, 2nd edn (Oxford: Oxford University Press).

Burnside, C., Eichenbaum, M. and Rebelo, S. (1993) 'Labour Hoarding and the Business Cycle', *Journal of Political Economy*, vol. 101, pp. 245–73.

Calvo, G.A. (1983) 'Staggered Prices in a Utility-Maximising Framework', *Journal of Monetary Economics*, vol. 12, pp. 383–98.

Campbell, J.Y. and Cochrane, J.H. (1999) 'By Force of Habit: A Consumption-Based Explanation of Aggregate Stock Behaviour', *Journal of Political Economy*, vol. 107, pp. 205–51.

Christiano, L.J. and Eichenbaum, M. (1992) 'Current Real Business Cycle Theories and Aggregate Labor Market Fluctuations', *American Economic Review*, vol. 82, pp. 430–50.

Christiano, L.J., Eichenbaum, M. and Evans, C.L. (1997) 'Sticky Prices and Limited Participation Models of Money: A Comparison', *European Economic Review*, vol. 41, pp. 1201–49.

Christiano, L.J., Eichenbaum, M. and Evans, C.L. (1998) 'Monetary Policy Shocks: What Have We Learned and to What End?' mimeo, Northwestern University.

Clarida, R., Gali, J. and Gertler, M. (1999) 'The Science of Monetary Policy: A New Keynesian Perspective', *Journal of Economic Literature*, vol. 37, pp. 1661–707.

Cogley, T. and Nason, J.M. (1995) 'Output Dynamics in Real-Business-Cycle Models', *American Economic Review*, vol. 85, pp. 492–511.

Collard, F. and de la Croix, D. (2000) 'Gift Exchange and the Business Cycle: the Fair Wage Strikes Back', *Review of Economic Dynamics*, vol. 3, pp. 166–93.

Constantinides, G.M. (1990) 'Habit Formation: A Resolution of the Equity Premium Puzzle', *Journal of Political Economy*, vol. 98, pp. 519–43.

Cooley, T.F. (1997) 'Calibrated Models', *Oxford Review of Economic Policy*, vol. 13, no. 3, pp. 55–69.

Cooley, T.F. and Hansen, G. (1989) 'The Inflation Tax in a Real Business Cycle Model', *American Economic Review*, vol. 79, pp. 733–47.

Cooley, T.F. and Hansen, G.D. (1995) 'Money and the Business Cycle', ch. 7 in Cooley, T. (ed.) *Frontiers of Business Cycle Research* (Princeton, NJ: Princeton University Press).

Cooley, T.F. and Quadrini, V. (1999a) 'A Neoclassical Model of the Phillips Curve Relation', *Journal of Monetary Economics*, vol. 44, pp. 165–93.

Cooley, T.F. and Quadrini, V. (1999b) 'How the Fed Should React: Optimal Monetary Policy in a Philips Curve World', mimeo, Rochester University.

Danthine, J.P. and Donaldson, J. (1990) 'Efficiency Wages and the Real Business Cycles', *European Economic Review*, vol. 34, pp. 1275–301.

Danthine, J.P. and Donaldson, J. (1993) 'Methodological and Empirical Issues in Business Cycle Theory', *European Economic Review*, vol. 37, pp. 1–35.

Danthine, J.P. and Donaldson, J. (1995) 'Non Walrasian Economies', ch. 8 in Cooley, T. (ed.) *Frontiers of Business Cycle Research* (Princeton, NJ: Princeton University Press).

Danthine, J.P. and Donaldson, J. (1999) 'Non-falsified Expectations and Asset Pricing: The Power of the Peso', *Economics Journal*, vol. 109, pp. 607–35.

Danthine, J.P. and Donaldson, J. (1999) 'Labour Relations and Asset Returns', mimeo, University of Lausanne.

Danthine, J.P., Donaldson, J. and Johnsen, J. (1998) 'Productivity Growth, Consumer Confidence and the Business Cycle', *European Economics Review*, vol. 42, pp. 113–41.

Dow, J.P. (1995) 'Real Business Cycles and Labour Markets with Imperfectly Flexible Wages', *European Economics Review*, vol. 39, pp. 1683–96.

Dunlop, J. (1938) 'The Movement of Real and Money Wage Rates', *Economics Journal*, vol. 48, pp. 413–34.

Eisfeldt, A. (1999) 'Endogenous Liquidity in Asset Markets', Working Paper, University of Chicago Department of Economics.

Finn, M. (1995) 'Variance Properties of Solow's Productivity Residuals and Their Cyclical Implications', *Journal of Economics Dynamics and Control*, vol. 19, pp. 1249–81.

Fuerst, T. (1992) 'Liquidity Loanable Funds and Real Activity', *Journal of Monetary Economics*, vol. 29, pp. 3–24.

Gali, J. (1999) 'Technology, Employment and the Business Cycle: Do Technology Shocks Explain Aggregate Fluctuations?', *American Economics Review*, vol. 89, no. 1, pp. 249–71.

Gertler, M. (1998) 'Financial Structure and Aggregate Economics Activity: An Overview', *Journal of Money, Credit and Banking*, vol. 20, pp. 559–88.

Gomes, J., Greenwood, J. and Rebelo, S. (1997) 'Equilibrium Unemployment', mimeo, University of Rochester.

Goodfriend, M. and King, R. (1997) 'The New Neo-Classical Synthesis and the Role of Monetary Policy', *NBER Macroeconomics Annual*, 1997, pp. 231–83.

Hall, R.E. (1990) 'Invariance Properties of Solow's Productivity Residuals', in Diamond, P. (ed.) *Growth/ Productivity/ Unemployment: Essays to Celebrate Bob Solow's Birthday* (Cambridge, MASS: MIT Press).

Hall, R.E. (1993) 'Macro Theory and the Recession of 1990–91', *American Economic Review*, vol. 83, pp. 275–79.

Hansen, G. (1985) 'Indivisible Labour and the Business Cycle', *Journal of Monetary Economics*, vol. 16, pp. 309–27.

Hansen, G.D. (1993) 'The Cyclical and Secular Behaviour of the Labour Input: Comparing Efficiency Units and Hours Worked', *Journal of Applied Econometrics*, vol. 8, pp. 71–80.

Hansen, G.D. and Prescott, E.C. (1993) 'Did Technology Shocks Cause the 1990–91 Recession?' *American Economic Review*, vol. 83, pp. 280–86.

Hansen, G.D. and Wright, R. (1992) 'The Labor Market in Real Business Cycle Theory', *Federal Reserve Bank of Minneapolis Quarterly Review*, vol. 16. pp. 2–12.

Heaton, J. and Lucas, D. (1995a) 'Evaluating the Effects of Incomplete Markets on Risk Sharing and Asset Pricing', Working Paper, Northwestern University.

Heaton, J. and Lucas, D. (1995b) 'The Importance of Investor Heterogeneity and Financial Market Imperfections for the Behavior of Asset Prices', *Carnegie-Rochester Series on Public Policy*, vol. 42, pp. 1–32.

Hechler, N. (1995) 'RBC Theory and the Labour Market', PhD dissertation, University of Lausanne.

Hess, G.D. and Shin, K. (1997) 'International and Intranational Business Cycles,' *Oxford Review of Economic Policy*, vol. 13, no. 3, pp. 93–109.

Kaldor, N. (1957) 'A Model of Economic Growth', *Economic Journal*, vol. 67, pp. 59–62.

King, R.G. and Rebelo, S. (1999) 'Resuscitating Real Business Cycles', in Woodford, M. and Taylor, J. (eds) *Handbook of Macroeconomics*, vol. IB (Amsterdam: Elsevier Science).

King, R.G. and Watson, M. (1996) 'Money, Prices, Interest Rates and the Business Cycle', *Review of Economics and Statistics*, vol. 78, no. 1, pp. 35–53.

Kocherlakota, N. (1996) 'The Equity Premium: It's Still a Puzzle', *Journal of Economic Literature*, vol. 34, pp. 42–71.

Kurz, M., and Motolese, M. (1999) 'Endogenous Uncertainty and Market Volatility', Working paper, Stanford University Department of Economics.

Liu, H. (1999) 'A Cross-Country Comparison of the Cyclicity of Real Wages', mimeo, National University of Singapore.

Lucas, R.E., Jr (1977) 'Understanding Business Cycles', *Carnegie-Rochester Conference on Public Policy*, vol. 5, pp. 7–29, reprinted in *Studies in Business-Cycles Theory* (Cambridge, MASS: MIT Press), pp. 215–39.

Lucas, R.E., Jr (1980) 'Methods and Problems in Business Cycle Theory', *Journal of Money, Credit and Banking*, vol. 12, pp. 696–715, reprinted in *Studies in Business-Cycles Theory* (Cambridge, MASS: MIT Press, 1982), pp. 271–96.

Lucas, R.E. Jr. (1990) 'Liquidity and Interest Rates', *Journal of Economic Theory*, vol. 50, pp. 237–64.

Mehra, R. and Prescott, E.C. (1985) 'The Equity Premium: A Puzzle, *Journal of Monetary Economics*, vol. 15, pp. 145–61.

Merz, M. (1995) 'Search in the Labour Market and the Real Business Cycle', *Journal of Monetary Economics*, vol. 36, pp. 269–300.

Prescott, E.C. (1986) 'Theory Ahead of Business Cycle Measurement', *Federal Reserve Bank of Minneapolis Quarterly Review*, vol. 10 (Fall), pp. 9–22.

Prescott, E.C. and Lucas, R.E. (1972) 'A Note on Price Systems in Infinite Dimensional Space', *International Economic Review*, vol. 13, no. 2, pp. 416–22.

Rogerson, R. (1988) 'Indivisible Labour, Lotteries, and Equilibrium', *Journal of Monetary Economics*, vol. 21, pp. 3–16.

Rogerson, R. (1998) 'Comment', *NBER Macroeconomics Annual*, vol. 13, pp. 61–67.

Shimer, R (1998) 'Why is the U.S. Unemployment Rate So Much Lower?' *NBER Macroeconomics Annual, 1998*, vol. 13, pp. 11–61.

Solon, G., Barsky, R. and Parker, J. (1994) 'Measuring the Cyclicity of Real Wages: How Important is the Composition Bias?', *Quarterly Journal of Economics*, vol. 109, no. 1, pp. 1–26.

Summers, L. (1986) 'Some Skeptical Observations on Real Business Cycle Theory', *Federal Reserve Bank of Minneapolis Quarterly Review*, vol. 10 (Fall), pp. 23–6.

Tarshis, L. (1938) 'Changes in Real and Money Wage Rates', *Economic Journal*, vol. 49, pp. 150–54.

Telmer, C. (1993) 'Asset Pricing Puzzles and Incomplete Markets', *Journal of Finance*, vol. 48, pp. 1803–32.

Uhlig, H. (1999) 'What are the Effects of Monetary Policy? Results from an Agnostic Identification Procedure', CEPR Working Paper no. 2137.

Weil, P. (1989) 'The Equity Premium Puzzle and the Risk-Free Rate Puzzle', *Journal of Monetary Economics*, vol. 24, pp. 401–21.

Part II
Money and Finance

5
How the Rational Expectations Revolution has Changed Macroeconomic Policy Research*

John Taylor
Stanford University, USA

The rational expectations hypothesis is by far the most common expectations assumption used in macroeconomic research today. This hypothesis, which simply states that people's expectations are the same as the forecasts of the model being used to describe those people, was first put forth and used in models of competitive product markets by John Muth in the 1960s. But it was not until the early 1970s that Robert Lucas (1972, 1976) incorporated the rational expectations assumption into macroeconomics and showed how to make it operational mathematically. The 'rational expectations revolution' is now as old as the Keynesian revolution was when Robert Lucas first brought rational expectations to macroeconomics.

This rational expectations revolution has led to many different schools of macroeconomic research. The new classical economics school, the real business cycle school, the new Keynesian economics school, the new political macroeconomics school, and more recently the new neoclassical synthesis (Goodfriend and King (1997)) can all be traced to the introduction of rational expectations into macroeconomics in the early 1970s (see the discussion by Snowden and Vane (1999), pp. 30–50).

In this chapter I address a question that I am frequently asked by students and by 'non-macroeconomist' colleagues, and that I suspect may be on many people's minds. The question goes like this: 'We know that many different schools of thought have evolved from the rational expectations revolution, but has mainstream policy research in macroeconomics really changed much as a result?' The term 'mainstream' focuses the question on the research methods that are used in practice by macroeconomists – whether they are at universities, research institutions or policy agencies –

---

* I am grateful to Jacques Drèze for helpful comments on an earlier draft.

when they work on actual policy issues; perhaps the phrase 'practical core' of policy evaluation research in macroeconomics would be a better description than 'mainstream'.

My answer to this question is an unqualified 'yes' and my purpose is to explain why. It would be surprising if mainstream macroeconomics had not changed much since the rational expectations revolution of 30 years ago. After all, mainstream macroeconomics changed greatly in the three decades after the Keynesian revolution. Path-breaking work by Hansen, Samuelson, Klein, Tobin, Friedman, Modigliani and Solow immediately comes to mind. Yet the question indicates a common scepticism about the practical implications of the rational expectations revolution, so my 'yes' answer must be accompanied by a serious rationale.

I try to show here that if one takes a careful look at what is going on in macroeconomic policy evaluation today, one sees that there is an identifiable and different approach that can be accurately called the 'new normative macroeconomics'. New normative macroeconomic research is challenging both from a theoretical and empirical viewpoint; it is already doing some good in practice. The research does not fall within any one of the schools of macroeconomics; rather, it uses elements from just about all the schools. For this reason, I think it is more productive to look at individual models and ideas rather than at groupings of models into schools of thought. As I hope will become clear in this lecture, the models and concepts that characterize the new normative macroeconomics represent one of the most active and exciting areas of macroeconomics today, but they were not even part of the vocabulary of macroeconomics before the 1970s. This suggests that the rational expectations revolution has significantly enriched mainstream policy research macroeconomics.

The new normative macroeconomic research can be divided into three areas: (i) policy models, (ii) policy rules, and (iii) policy trade-offs. This chapter considers each of these three areas in that order.

5.1 The policy models: systems of stochastic expectational difference equations

Because people's expectations of future policy affect their current decisions and because the rational expectations hypothesis assumes that people's expectations of the future are equal to the model's mathematical conditional expectations, dynamic macroeconomic models with rational expectations must entail difference or differential equations in which both past and future differences or differentials appear. In the case of discrete time, a typical rational expectations model therefore can be written in the form:

$$f_i\left(y_t, y_{t-1}, \ldots, y_{t-p}, E_t y_{t+1}, \ldots, E_t y_{t+q}, a_i, x_t\right) = u_{it} \tag{1}$$

for $i = 1, ..., n$ where y_t is an n-dimensional vector of endogenous variables at time t, x_t is a vector of exogenous variables at time t, u_{it} is a vector of stochastic shocks at time t, and a_i is a parameter vector.

The simplest rational expectations model in the form of (1) is a single linear equation ($i = 1$) with one lead ($q = 1$) and no lags ($p = 0$). This case arises for the well-known Cagan money demand model (see Sargent (1987) for an exposition) in which the expected lead is the one-period-ahead price level. In many applications, the system of equation (1) is linear, as when it arises as a system of first order conditions for a linear quadratic optimization model. However, non-linear versions of equation (1) arise frequently in policy evaluation research.

Many models now used for practical policy evaluation have the form of equation (1). Examples include a large multicountry rational expectations model that I developed explicitly for policy evaluation (Taylor (1993b)), and the smaller optimizing single-economy models of Rotemberg and Woodford (1999) and McCallum and Nelson (1999) also developed for policy research. Such rational expectations models are now regularly used at central banks, including the FRB/US model used at the Federal Reserve Board (see Brayton, Levin, Tryon and Williams (1997)); smaller models – Fuhrer/Moore and money supply rules (MSR) models used for special policy evaluation tasks at the Fed (see Fuhrer and Moore (1997) and Orphanides and Wieland (1997)); models used at the Bank of England (see Batini and Haldane (1999)), the Riksbank, the Bank of Canada, the Reserve Bank of New Zealand, and many others.

5.1.1 Similarities and differences

That all these policy evaluation models are in the form of (1), with lead terms as well as lagged terms, demonstrates clearly how the rational expectations assumption is part of mainstream policy evaluation research in macroeconomics. There are other similarities. All of these models have some kind of rigidity – usually a version of staggered price and wage setting – to explain the impact of changes in monetary policy on the economy, and are therefore capable of being used for practical policy analysis. The monetary transmission mechanism is also similar in all these models; it works through a financial market price view, rather than through a credit view.

There are also differences between the models. Some of the models are very large, some are open economy, and some are closed economy. The models also differ in the degree of forward looking or the number of rigidities that are incorporated.

There is also a difference between the models in the degree to which they explicitly incorporate optimizing behaviour. For example, most of the disaggregated investment, consumption, and wage and price setting equations in the Taylor (1993b) multicountry model have forward-looking terms that can be motivated by a representative agent's or firm's intertemporal optimization problem. However, the model itself does not explicitly describe that optimization. The smaller single economy models of Rotemberg and Woodford (1999) and McCallum and Nelson (1999) are more explicit about the representative firms or individuals maximizing utility. One of the reasons for this difference is the complexity of designing and fitting a multicountry model to the data. Given the way that the models are used in practice, however, this distinction may not be as important as it seems. For example, the equations with expectations terms in the Taylor (1993b) model are of the same general form as the reduced form equations that emerge from the Rotemberg and Woodford (1999) optimization problem. Since the parameters of the equations of the Rotemberg and Woodford model are fixed functions of the parameters of the utility function, they do not change when policy changes. But neither do the parameters of the equations in the Taylor (1993b) model.

5.1.2 Solution methods

A solution to equation (1) is a stochastic process for y_t. Obtaining such a solution in a rational expectations difference equation system is much more difficult than in a simple backward-looking difference equation system with no expectations variables. This difficulty makes policy evaluation in macroeconomics difficult to teach and requires much more expertise at central banks and other policy agencies than had been required for conventional models. This complexity is also one of the reasons why rational expectations methods are not yet part of most undergraduate textbooks in macroeconomics.

Many papers have been written on algorithms for obtaining solutions to systems like equation (1). In the case where $f_i(.)$ is linear, Blanchard and Kahn (1980) showed how to get the solution to the deterministic part of equation (1) by finding the eigenvalues and eigenvectors of the system. Under certain conditions, the model has a unique solution. Many macroeconomists have proposed algorithms to solve equation (1) in the non-linear case (see Taylor and Uhlig (1990) for a review). The simple iterative method of Fair and Taylor (1983) has the advantage of being very easy to use even in the linear case, but less efficient than other methods (see Judd (1998)). Brian Madigan at the Federal Reserve Board has developed a very fast algorithm to solve such models. I have found that the iterative methods work very well in teaching advanced undergraduates and beginning graduate students. They are easy to programme within existing user-friendly computer programmes such as Eviews. I also use iterative methods to solve my own rather large-scale multicountry rational expectations model (Taylor (1993b).

I think more emphasis on solving and applying expectational difference equations should be placed in the economics curriculum. Many graduate students come to economics knowing how to solve difference and differential equations, but expectational difference equations such as (1) are not yet standard and require time and effort to learn well. It is difficult to understand, let alone do, modern macro policy research without an understanding of how these expectational stochastic difference equations work.

5.2 Which is the best policy rule? A common way to pose normative policy questions

The most noticeable characteristic of the new normative macroeconomic policy research is the use of policy rules as an analytically and empirically tractable way to study monetary and fiscal policy decisions. A policy rule is a description of how the instruments of policy should be changed in response to observable events. This focus on policy rules is what justifies the term 'normative'. The ultimate purpose of the research is to give policy advice on how macroeconomic policy *should* be conducted. The policy advice of researchers becomes, for example, 'Our research shows that policy rule A works well'. (The word 'normative' is used to contrast policy research that focuses on 'what should be' with positive policy research that endeavours to 'explain why' a policy is chosen.)

To be sure, the study of macroeconomic policy issues through policy rules began before the rational expectations assumption was introduced to macroeconomics (see work by Friedman (1948) and A.W. Phillips (1954), for example). Policy rules have appealed to researchers interested in applying engineering control methods to macroeconomics.

But the introduction of the rational expectations assumption into macroeconomics significantly increased the advantages of using policy rules as a way to evaluate policy. With the rational expectations assumption, people's expectations of policy have a great impact on changes in the policy instruments. Hence, in order to evaluate the impact of policy, one must state what that future policy will be in different contingencies. Such a contingency plan is nothing more than a policy rule. One might say that the use of policy rules in structural models is a constructive way to deal with the Lucas critique.

The use of policy rules in macroeconomic policy research has increased greatly in the 1990s and represents a great change in mainstream policy evaluation research. There is much interest in the use of policy rules as guidelines for policy decisions and the staffs of central banks use policy rules actively in their research. The starting point for most research on policy rules is that the central bank has a long-run target for the rate of inflation. The task of monetary policy is to keep inflation close to the target without causing large fluctuations in real output or employment. Alternative monetary policies are characterized by monetary policy rules that stipulate how the instruments of policy (usually the short-term interest rate) react to observed variables in the economy.

5.2.1   The timeless method for evaluating policy rules

How are policy rules typically evaluated? The method can be described as a series of steps. First, take a candidate policy rule and substitute the rule into the model in equation (1). Second, solve the model using one of the rational expectations solution methods. Third, study the properties of the stochastic steady-state distribution of the variables (such as inflation, real output, unemployment). Fourth, choose a policy rule that gives the most satisfactory performance; here one uses, implicitly or explicitly, the expected value of the period (instantaneous) loss function across the steady state (stationary) distribution. Fifth, check the results for robustness by using other models.

Observe the special nature of the optimization in this description. Policy rules are being evaluated according to the properties of the *steady-state stochastic distributions*. This can be justified using a multiperiod loss function with an infinite horizon with no discounting. But the key point is that the research method views the policy rule as being used for all time. Stationary means that the same distribution occurs at all points in time. Michael Woodford uses the adjective 'timeless' to refer to this type of policy evaluation because of its stationary character. The timelessness or stationarity is needed in order to evaluate the policy in a rational expectations setting and also to reduce the problems of time inconsistency which would arise if one optimized taking some initial conditions as given.

There are many examples of this type of policy evaluation research. McCallum (1999) provides a useful review of the research on policy rules through 1998. Let me discuss some more recent research, starting with a research project on robustness of policy rules which nicely illustrates how the timeless policy evaluation method works. I then discuss some particular applications to policy.

5.2.2   A comparative study with robustness implications

This project is discussed in detail in a recently published conference volume (Taylor (1999)). This summary of the study is drawn directly from my introduction to that volume. The researchers who participated in the project investigated alternative *monetary* policy rules using different models as described earlier. The following models were used: (1) the Ball (1999) Model, (2) the Batini and Haldane (1999) Model, (3) the McCallum and Nelson (1999) Model, (4) the Rudebusch and Svensson (1999a) Model, (5) the Rotemberg and Woodford (1999) Model, (6) the Fuhrer and Moore (1997) Model, (7) the MSR used at the Federal Reserve, (8) the large FRB/US model used at the Federal Reserve, and (9) my multicountry model (Taylor (1993b)), labelled TMCM in the tables. For more details on these models, see the references below or the conference volume itself.

It is important to note, given the purpose of this chapter, that two of the models in this list are not rational expectations models. The Ball (1999) model is a small, calibrated model and the Rudebusch and Svensson (1999a) model is an estimated time series model. I think it is useful to compare the results of such models with the formal rational expectations models; both these and the rational expectations models are approximations of reality. For small changes in policy away from current policy, the non-rational expectations models may be very good approximations. Note, however, that the method of policy evaluation with the non-rational expectations models is identical to that of the rational expectations models: stochastically simulating policy rules and observing what happens.

Five different policy rules of the form

$$i_t = g_\pi \pi_t + g_y y_t + \rho i_{t-1} \tag{2}$$

were examined in the study. In equation (2) the left-hand side variable i is the nominal interest rate, while π is the inflation rate and y is real GDP measured as a deviation from potential GDP. The coefficients defining the five policy rules are:

	g_π	g_y	ρ
Rule I	1.5	0.5	0.0
Rule II	1.5	1.0	0.0
Rule III	3.0	0.8	1.0
Rule IV	1.2	1.0	1.0
Rule V	1.2	.06	1.3

Rule I is a simple rule that I proposed in 1992. Rule II is like Rule I except that it has a coefficient of 1.0 rather than 0.5 on real output. For policy Rules III, IV, and V the interest rate reacts to the lagged interest rate, while for Rules I and II it does not. Rule V is a rule proposed by Rotemberg and Woodford (1999). This rule places a very small weight on real output and a very high weight on the lagged interest rate. These policy rules do not exhaust all possible policy rules, of course, but they represent some of the areas of disagreement about policy rules.

How are these policy rules evaluated with the models? The typical method is to insert one of the policy rules (that is, equation (2) with the parameters specified) into a model, which has the form of equation (1) stated above. The rule then becomes one of the equations of the model and the model can then be solved using the methods discussed earlier. From the stochastic process for the endogenous variables one can then see how different rules affect the stochastic behaviour of the variables of interest such as inflation or real output. One can either examine the realizations of stochastic simulations or compute statistics that summarize these realizations. Tables 5.1 and 5.2

report the results of the simulation or analytical computations of the standard deviations of inflation and output. Consider first a comparison of Rule I and Rule II. Table 1 shows the standard deviations of the inflation rate and of real output for Rule I and Rule II. These standard deviations are obtained either from the simulations of the models or from the calculated variance covariance matrix of y_t. The table also shows the rank order for each rule in each model for both inflation and output variability. The sum of the ranks is a better way to compare the rules because of arbitrary differences in the model variances.

For all the models, Rule IV results in a lower variance of output compared with Rule III. But for six of the nine models Rule IV gives a higher variance of inflation. Apparently there is a trade-off between the variance of inflation and output, a point that I come back to later in the chapter.

Now compare Rules III, IV and V. According to the results in Table 5.2, Rule III is most robust if inflation fluctuations are the sole measure of performance: it ranks first in terms of inflation variability for all but one

Table 5.1 Comparative performance of Rules I and II

| | Standard deviation of: | | | |
	Inflation	Output	Inflation rank	Output rank
		Rule I		
Ball	1.85	1.62	1	2
Batini-Haldane	1.38	1.05	1	2
McCallum-Nelson	1.96	1.12	2	2
Rudebusch-Svensson	3.46	2.25	1	2
Rotemberg-Woodford	2.71	1.97	2	2
Fuhrer-Moore	2.63	2.68	1	2
MSR	0.70	0.99	1	2
FRB	1.86	2.92	1	2
TMCM	2.58	2.89	2	2
Rank sum	–	–	12	18
		Rule II		
Ball	2.01	1.36	2	1
Batini-Haldane	1.46	0.92	2	1
McCallum-Nelson	1.93	1.10	1	1
Rudebusch-Svensson	3.52	1.98	2	1
Rotemberg-Woodford	2.60	1.34	1	1
Fuhrer-Moore	2.84	2.32	2	1
MSR	0.73	0.87	2	1
FRB/US	2.02	2.21	2	1
TMCM	2.36	2.55	1	1
Rank sum	–	–	15	9

Source: Taylor (1999b).

model for which there is a clear ordering. For output, Rule IV ranks best, which reflects its relatively high response to output. However, regardless of the objective function weights, Rule V has the worst performance for these three policy rules, ranking first for only one model (the Rotemberg-Woodford model) in the case of output. Comparing these three rules with the rules that do not respond to the lagged interest rate (Rules I and II) in Table 5.1 shows that the lagged interest rate rules do not dominate rules without a lagged interest rate.

Table 5.2 Comparative performance of Rules III, IV and V

| | | Standard deviation of | | |
	Inflation	Output	Inflation rank	Output rank
		Rule III		
Ball	2.27	23.06	1	2
Haldane-Batini	0.94	1.84	1	2
McCallum-Nelson	1.09	1.03	1	1
Rudebusch-Svensson	∞	∞	1	1
Rotemberg-Woodford	0.81	2.69	2	2
Fuhrer-Moore	1.60	5.15	1	2
MSR	0.29	1.07	1	2
FRB/US	1.37	2.77	1	2
TMCM	1.68	2.70	1	2
Rank sum	–	–	10	16
		Rule IV		
Ball	2.56	2.10	2	1
Batini-Haldane	1.56	0.86	2	1
McCallum/Nelson	1.19	1.08	2	2
Rudebusch-Svensson	∞	∞	1	1
Rotemberg-Woodford	1.35	1.65	3	1
Fuhrer-Moore	2.17	2.85	2	1
MSR	0.44	0.64	3	1
FRB/US	1.56	1.62	3	1
TMCM	1.79	1.95	2	1
Rank sum	–	–	20	10
		Rule V		
Ball	∞	∞	3	3
Batini-Haldane	∞	∞	3	3
McCallum-Nelson	1.31	1.12	3	3
Rudebusch-Svensson	∞	∞	1	1
Rotemberg-Woodford	0.62	3.67	1	3
Fuhrer-Moore	7.13	21.2	3	3
MSR	0.41	1.95	2	3
FRB	1.55	6.32	2	3
TMCM	2.06	4.31	3	3
Rank sum	–	–	21	25

Source: Taylor (1999b).

Table 5.2 also indicates a key reason why rules that react to lagged interest rates work well in some models and poorly in others, in comparison with the rules without lagged interest rates. As stated above, two of the models (Ball (1999) and Rudebush-Svensson (1999a)) that give very poor performance for the lagged interest rate rules are non-rational expectations models. However, the rules exploit people's forward-looking behaviour: if a small increase in the interest rate does not bring inflation down, then people expect the central bank to raise interest rates by a larger amount in the future. In a model without rational expectations, it is impossible to capture this forward-looking behaviour. Because Rule V has a lagged interest rate coefficient greater than one, it greatly exploits these expectations effects; this is why it does not work so well in non-rational expectations models. Again these results underscore the importance of rational expectations ideas for policy evaluation research.

5.2.3   Recent applications

Now let me consider a few of the many recent applications of the research to specific practical policy questions.

Research on the zero interest rate bound

Mervyn King (1999), now the deputy governor of the Bank of England, has used policy rules of the form of equation (2) to examine the important problem of the zero lower bound for nominal interest rates. He simulated a rational expectations model and determined the likelihood that the interest rate will hit zero. He concludes that the probability is very low, assuming that policy does not deviate from a good policy rule for too long. Fuhrer and Madigan (1997) and Orphanides and Wieland (1997) obtained similar results by simulating policy rules in models like (1). Orphanides and Wieland (1999) find the danger of hitting the lower bound calls for choosing a slightly higher inflation target.

Inflation forecast based rules

Svensson (2000) and Batini and Haldane (1999) examine a whole host of policy rules that can be used for inflation by targeting central banks. Some of these bring the forecast of inflation into the policy rule and are therefore called 'inflation forecast based rules'. For example, the forecast of inflation rather than the actual inflation and actual output might appear in equation (2). Thus far, there is no agreement about whether including a forecast of inflation can improve economic performance, though is it clear that a forecast of inflation that is too far out can cause stability problems.

Should central banks react slowly?

Woodford (1999) uses policy rules to examine the rationale for the sluggishness of changes in interest rates by central banks. Many observers of central bank reactions note that the interest rate seems to react with a lag, as would occur if a lagged dependent variable appeared in the policy rule. There is some dispute about whether that lagged term might represent serial correlation rather than slow adjustment in empirical work. In any case, Woodford presents simulations of some models that show that such slow responses may be optimal.

The role of the exchange rate

Much of the research has focused on economies that have a large domestic sector, such as the United States, and may not be completely relevant for small and very open economies. Ball's (1999) small open economy model study shows that it is useful for central banks to react to the exchange rate as well as to inflation and real GDP in equation (2).

5.3   Policy trade-offs: a focus on variances rather than means

In the years before the beginning of the rational expectations revolution, Milton Friedman and Edmund Phelps threw into doubt the idea of a long-run Phillips curve trade-off between inflation and output or unemployment. Expectations were at the heart of the Friedman-Phelps critique of the Phillips curve trade-off, and it was an attempt to explain the Phillips curve correlations that motivated Robert Lucas to bring rational expectations into macroeconomics in his celebrated paper on 'Expectations and the Neutrality of Money' (Lucas (1972)).

However, along with the rational expectations assumption, Lucas also brought a perfectly flexible price assumption into his model, and together these two assumptions nullified a trade-off between inflation and unemployment, even in the short run, that could represent a meaningful choice for policy makers. Monetary policy was ineffective, as shown by Thomas Sargent and Neil Wallace (1975), who used a simplified model that incorporated Lucas's basic assumptions.

However, if there is some degree of price or wage stickiness, as is assumed in the mainstream models used for policy evaluation today, then there is still a trade-off facing policy makers, even if expectations are rational. But how can this trade-off be described, analysed and estimated? The nature of the trade-off is not between the levels of inflation and output, but between the variability of inflation and the variability of output (Taylor (1979)). Such a trade-off naturally arises in any model in which there is price stickiness and stochastic shocks, which of course is true of virtually all models used for policy evaluation today. This kind of trade-off even occurs in models without rational expectations.

The trade-off is typically represented as a curve in a diagram with the variance (or standard deviation) of inflation around some target inflation rate on the horizontal axis, and the variance (or standard deviation) of real output or unemployment around the natural rate on the vertical axis. Of course in a given policy problem, there may be many other variables of concern, such as the interest rate or the exchange rate, and it is possible to create a trade-off between any two of these variables. However, since the level of the natural rate of unemployment or potential output cannot be affected by monetary policy, these levels should not be in the loss function. The focus of variances makes it clear that the policy problems related to inflation and unemployment are mainly about economic fluctuations rather than economic growth.

A simple example to illustrate the calculation of a variability trade-off is the following model:

$$\pi_t = \pi_{t-1} + by_{t-1} + \varepsilon_t \tag{3}$$

$$y_t = -g\pi_t \tag{4}$$

The first equation is a standard expectations-augmented Phillips curve and the second equation is a shorthand description of macro policy. The negative relationship between inflation and real output in equation (4) combines aggregate demand and a monetary policy rule in which the interest rate is increased (reducing real output) when inflation rises. Different policies can be represented by different choices of the parameter g. For simplicity, I have assumed that there are no demand shocks in equation (4).

A trade-off between the variance of y and the variance of π can be obtained by substituting equation (4) into equation (3); this results in a first-order stochastic difference equation in π_t from which one can find the steady-state variance of inflation. The steady state variance of output is then obtained from (4). Now as one varies the policy parameter g one traces out different combinations of the variance of inflation and the variance of real output. An increase in the parameter g represents a less accommodative policy. Higher values of g reduce the variance of inflation, but increase the variance of real output. Although this derivation is for a very simple model, it illustrates the nature of the trade-off that arises in most of these models with sticky prices and wages and stochastic shocks. Erceg, Henderson and Levin (2000) provide a careful analysis of the nature of this trade-off in more complex models. For other simple expositions of the output–inflation variability trade-off see Walsh (1998), Bullard (1998), and Dittmar, Gavin and Kydland (1999).

5.3.1   How stable is the output-inflation variability trade-off?

The Friedman-Phelps criticism of the original Phillips curve was that it was not stable, and therefore could not be relied on for policy analysis. In fact large shifts in that curve occurred over time as the inflation rate rose and then fell in the 1970s and 1980s. The variability trade-off – viewed as an alternative to the original Phillips curve – would not be of much use for policy research if it also shifted around a lot. Before reviewing how this trade-off is used in policy evaluation research it is important to examine its stability over time.

Comparing estimates of the variability curve in different time periods is a rough way to get a feel for the extent of such shifts. Figure 5.1 suggests a fair degree of stability. It shows several estimates of the variability trade-off for the US estimated at different points in time by different researchers.

Figure 5.1   Comparison of different estimates of inflation-output variability trade-off curves from 1979 to 1999

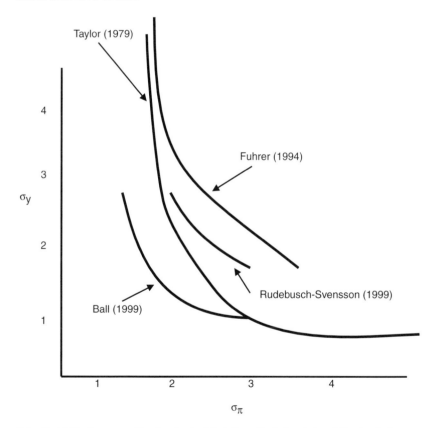

Notes: Variability is measured by the standard deviation of inflation (σ_π) and the standard deviation of output as a deviation from trend (σ_y). Although the curves in Figure 5.1 are not exactly the same, the differences seem to be well within the estimation errors of the models. Any shifts in the parameters of the models used to estimate the curves are not large enough to have significantly shifted the curves. In fact, the curves estimated with data into the 1990s seem to be spread around the curve estimated in the 1970s.

One of the curves (Taylor (1979)) was estimated using data through the mid-1970s. The other three were independently estimated in the 1990s using data from the 1980s and 1990s as well. These other curves are found in papers by Fuhrer (1994), Rudebusch and Svensson (1999a), and Ball (1999).

5.3.2   Policy applications of the variability trade-off

A brief overview of recent policy evaluation research using this variability trade-off illustrates how it is used in practice.

Money versus the interest rate as the instrument

Rudebusch and Svensson (1999b) have used the trade-off to show how money targeting could lead to a deterioration of macroeconomic performance compared with inflation targeting using an interest rate rule. They do this by deriving a variability trade-off for their model and then showing how monetary targeting is inefficient, leading to a point to the right and above the curve.

Price level versus inflation targeting

Mervyn King (1999) showed how a big decrease in inflation variability might be achieved with only a small increase in output variability by using a policy in which the price level is given some small weight. He shows this by computing a trade-off curve and then showing how the movement along the curve entails big rightward movements and only small downward movements. Dittmar, Gavin and Kydland (1999) reach a similar conclusion using a variability trade-off, though their characterization of price level targeting is different from King's.

Optimal inflation forecast target

Batini and Haldane (1999) and Levin, Wieland and Williams (1999) use the variability trade-off to show how increasing the horizon in an inflation forecast targeting procedure for the central bank has the effect of reducing output variability and increasing inflation variability. They show that the horizon for the forecast should not be too long if forecasts are used in policy rules.

The curvature of the variability trade-off

Batini (1999) estimates trade-off curves for the UK and finds that curvature is very sharp, indicating that the same policy would probably be chosen for a wide variation of the weights on inflation and output. However, King

(1999) emphasizes that the estimates of curvature are very uncertain, and some research on the standard errors of these curves would be worthwhile.

The possibility that the output inflation variability trade-off curve has a sharp turn is very important, because it suggests that the big debates about how large the coefficient on output should be in a policy rule are not so important in fact. If the curve has a sharp turn then there are sharply increasing opportunity costs of reducing either inflation variability or output variability.

5.4   Conclusion

Like any assumption, the rational expectations assumption is a simplifying one, and its success depends both on its plausibility and its predictive accuracy. Clearly, the assumption works better in some situations than in others. And like any other simplifying assumption, researchers are constantly trying to improve on it. Attempts to modify rational expectations to account for learning, for example, are as old as the rational expectations assumption itself: see Evans and Honkapohja (1999). Recent work has endeavoured to find ways to preserve the endogeneity of the rational expectations assumption while relaxing some of the more unrealistic aspects of the assumption (see Kurz and Mototese (1999)).

However, thinking of the 'rational expectations revolution' solely in terms of a technical expectations hypothesis runs the risk of missing many of the truly enriching effects that rational expectations research has had on macroeconomics since the early 1970s. In this respect the rational expectations revolution is like the Keynesian revolution: The 'aggregate expenditures multiplier' discovered by Richard Kahn and put forth by Keynes in his *General Theory* was a technical idea. It in turn spurred interest in empirical work on consumption and investment, analysis of difference equations, econometric models, computer algorithms, and innovations in teaching such as Samuelson's Keynesian cross-diagram. Though an integral part of Keynes's theory, the Keynesian multiplier is not a good way to describe the overall impact of the 'Keynesian revolution'.

So, too, it would be misleading to describe the overall impact of the rational expectations revolution solely by the rational expectations assumption itself. One also must include the many empirical policy models with expectational difference equations, such as the ones mentioned in this chapter, as well as the large volume of research on policy rules and policy variability trade-offs. I have argued here that these policy models, policy rules and policy trade-offs represent a whole 'new normative macroeconomics' that includes ideas from many different schools of thought, but which nonetheless quite identifiable and different from the macroeconomics that existed prior to the 1970s.

References

Ball, L. (1999) 'Policy Rules for Open Economies', in Taylor, J.B. (ed.) *Monetary Policy Rules* (Chicago: University of Chicago Press), pp. 127–56.

Batini, N. (1999) 'The Shape of Stochastic-Simulation Generated Taylor Curves', unpublished paper, Bank of England.

Batini, N. and Haldane, A.G. (1999) 'Forward-Looking Rules for Monetary Policy', in Taylor, J.B. (ed.) *Monetary Policy Rules* (Chicago: University of Chicago Press), pp. 157–201.

Blanchard, O.J. and Kahn, C.M. (1980) 'The Solution of Linear Difference Equations under Rational Expectations', *Econometrica*, vol. 48, pp. 1305–11.

Brayton, F., Levin, A., Tryon, R.C. and Williams, J.C. (1997) 'The Evolution of Macro Models at the Federal Reserve Board', in McCallum, B. and Plosser, C. (eds) *Carnegie-Rochester Conference Series on Public Policy*, vol. 47 (Amsterdam: North Holland, Elsevier Science), pp. 43–81.

Bryant, R., Hooper, P. and Mann, C. (1993) *Evaluating Policy Regimes: New Empirical Research in Empirical Macroeconomics* (Washington, DC: Brookings Institution).

Bullard, J. (1998) 'Trading Tradeoffs', *National Economic Trends* (St Louis: Federal Reserve Bank of St Louis) December.

Clarida, R., Gali, J., and Gertler, M. (1999) 'The Science of Monetary Policy: A New Keynesian Perspective', *Journal of Economic Literature*, vol. 37 (4), pp. 1661–707.

Dittmar, R., Gavin, W.T. and Kydland, F.E. (1999) 'The Inflation–Output Variability Tradeoff and Price Level Targets', *Review* (St Louis: Federal Reserve Bank of St Louis) January–February.

Erceg, C.J., Henderson, D.W. and Levin, A.T. (2000) 'Optimal Monetary Policy with Staggered Wage and Price Contracts', *Journal of Monetary Economics*, vol. 46, pp. 281–313.

Evans, G.W. and Honkapohja, S. (1999) 'Learning Dynamics', in Taylor, J.B. and Woodford, M. (eds) *Handbook of Macroeconomics* (Amsterdam: North Holland), pp. 449–542.

Fair, R.C. and Taylor, J.B. (1983) 'Solution and Maximum Likelihood Estimation of Non Linear Rational Expectations Models', *Econometrica*, vol. 51, pp. 1169–85.

Friedman, M. (1948) 'A Monetary and Fiscal Framework for Economic Stability', *American Economic Review*, vol. 38, pp. 245–64.

Fuhrer, J.C. (1994) 'Optimal Monetary Policy and the Sacrifice Ratio', in Fuhrer, J.C. (ed.) *Goals, Guidelines and Constraints Facing Monetary Policymakers* (Boston: Federal Reserve Bank of Boston).

Fuhrer, J.C. and Madigan, B.F. (1997) 'Monetary Policy When Interest Rates are Bounded at Zero', *Review of Economics and Statistics*, vol. 79, pp. 573–85.

Fuhrer, J.C. and Moore, G.R. (1997) 'Inflation Persistence', *Quarterly Journal of Economics*, vol. 110, pp. 127–59.

Goodfriend, M. and King, R. (1997) 'The New Neoclassical Synthesis and the Role of Monetary Policy', in Bernanke, B. and Rotemberg, J. (eds) *Macroeconomics Annual 1997* (Cambridge, Mass: MIT Press), pp. 231–82.

Judd, K.W. (1998) *Numerical Methods in Economics* (Cambridge, Mass: MIT Press).

King, M. (1999) 'Challenges Facing Monetary Policy: New and Old', paper presented at Federal Reserve Bank of Kansas City Conference, Jackson Hole, August 1999.

King, R.G. and Wolman, A.L. (1999) 'What Should the Monetary Authority Do When Prices are Sticky?' in Taylor, J.B. (ed.) *Monetary Policy Rules* (Chicago: University of Chicago Press), pp. 349–404.

Kurz, M. and Mototese, M. (1999) 'Endogenous Uncertainty and Market Volatility', Working Paper, Stanford University (May).

Levin, A., Wieland, V. and Williams, J.C. (1999) 'Robustness of Simple Monetary Policy Rules under Model Uncertainty', in Taylor, J.B. (ed.) *Monetary Policy Rules* (Chicago: University of Chicago Press), pp. 263–318.

Lucas, R.E., Jr (1972) 'Expectations and the Neutrality of Money', *Journal of Economic Theory*, vol. 4 (April), pp. 103–24.

Lucas, R.E., Jr (1976) 'Econometric Policy Evaluation: A Critique', *Carnegie-Rochester Conference Series on Public Policy* (Amsterdam: North-Holland).

McCallum, B.T. (1999) 'Issues in the Design of Monetary Policy Rules', in Taylor, J.B. and Woodford, M. (eds) *Handbook of Macroeconomics* (Amsterdam: North Holland), pp. 1483–530.

McCallum, B.T. and Nelson, E. (1999) 'Performance of Operational Policy Rules in an Estimated Semiclassical Structural Model', in Taylor, J.B. (ed.) *Monetary Policy Rules* (Chicago: University of Chicago Press), pp. 15–56.

Orphanides, A. and Wieland, V. (1997) 'Price Stability and Monetary Policy Effectiveness when Nominal Interest Rates are Bounded by Zero', Working Paper, Board of Governors of the Federal Reserve System.

Orphanides, A. and Wieland, V. (1999) 'Price Stability and Monetary Policy Effectiveness when Nominal Interest Rates are Bounded at Zero', Working Paper, Federal Reserve Board.

Phillips, A.W. (1954) 'Stabilization Policies in a Closed Economy', *Economic Journal*, vol. 64, pp. 290–323.

Rotemberg, J.J. and Woodford, M. (1999) 'Interest Rate Rules in an Estimated Sticky Price Model', in Taylor, J.B. (ed.) *Monetary Policy Rules* (Chicago: University of Chicago Press), pp. 57–126.

Rudebusch, G.D. and Svensson, L.E.O (1999a) 'Policy Rules for Inflation Targetting', in Taylor, J.B. (ed.) *Monetary Policy Rules* (Chicago: University of Chicago Press), pp. 203–62.

Rudebusch, G.D. and Svensson, L.E.O. (1999b) 'Eurosystem Monetary Targetting: Lessons from U.S. Data', mimeo, Federal Reserve Bank of San Francisco.

Sargent, T.J. (1987) *Macroeconomic Theory*, 2nd edn (New York: Academic).

Sargent, T. and Wallace, N. (1975) '"Rational" Expectations, the Optimal Monetary Instrument and the Optimal Money Supply Rule', *Journal of Political Economy*, vol. 83, pp. 241–54.

Snowden, B. and Vane, H. (1999) *Conversations with Leading Economists: Interpreting Modern Macroeconomics* (Cheltenham: Edward Elgar).

Svensson, L.E.O. (2000) 'Open-Economy Inflation Targeting', *Journal of International Economics*, vol. 50, no. 1, pp. 155–83.

Taylor, J.B. (1979) 'Estimation and Control of a Macroeconomic Model with Rational Expectations', *Econometrica*, vol. 47, pp. 1267–86.

Taylor, J.B. (1993a) 'Discretion Versus Policy Rules in Practice', *Carnegie-Rochester Conference Series on Public Policy*, vol. 39, pp. 195–214.

Taylor, J.B. (1993b) *Macroeconomic Policy in a World Economy: From Econometric Design to Practical Operation* (New York: W.W. Norton).

Taylor, J.B. (1999a) 'A Historical Analysis of Monetary Policy Rules', in Taylor, J.B. (ed.) *Monetary Policy Rules* (Chicago: University of Chicago Press), pp. 319–47.

Taylor, J.B. (1999b) 'Introduction', in Taylor, J.B. (ed.) *Monetary Policy Rules* (Chicago: University of Chicago Press).

Taylor, J.B. (1999c) 'Staggered Price and Wage Setting in Macroeconomics', in Taylor, J.B. and Woodford, M. (eds) *Handbook of Macroeconomics* (Amsterdam: Elsevier, North Holland), pp. 1009–50.

Taylor, J.B. and Uhlig, H. (1990) 'Solving Nonlinear Stochastic Growth Models: A Comparison of Alternative Solution Methods', *Journal of Business and Economic Statistics*, vol. 8, no. 1, pp. 1–17.

Walsh, C.E. (1998) 'The New Output-Inflation Tradeoff', *Economic Letters* (San Francisco: Federal Reserve Bank of San Francisco), 6 February.

Woodford, M. (1999) 'Optimal Monetary Policy Inertia', mimeo, Princeton University, Princeton, NJ.

6
Monetary Policy in an Imperfect Information World*

Bruce Greenwald and Michael Adler
Columbia University, New York, USA

The widespread development of models of imperfect information has provided a wealth of new perspectives for investigating the impact of monetary policy on both long-term economic growth and cyclical fluctuations.[1] This body of work describes a number of new theoretical mechanisms which may affect the role of monetary policy. Indeed, a complete enumeration of the potential monetary effects in question is beyond the scope of any single paper of manageable length, and this chapter does not attempt to provide such a summary. Instead it analyses monetary policy in the context of a single particular model. Nevertheless, the focused model presented in this chapter has broad implications which capture many of the general features of the new imperfect-information-based monetary models, particularly the ways in which they differ from traditional classical and Keynesian alternatives. Monetary policy in this model does have consistent real effects on output, but it operates as much by reducing business risk and by redistributing resources to the business sector as it does by stimulating aggregate demand through interest rate reductions. Moreover, these effects do not depend on many of the familiar price-rigidity and closed-economy features which drive other models of monetary policy effectiveness. Thus, in addition to characterizing the likely role of monetary policy in a world of imperfect information and rigidities, the model is intended to help identify the critical assumptions upon which that role depends. For this purpose, the model of the paper has four fundamental features which distinguish it from other common variants of the imperfect-information/rigidities approach.

First, it is explicitly dynamic in nature. Business cycles in the model arise because the model responds to external shocks in a way that intensifies rather

---

* This chapter arises from work done jointly with Joseph Stiglitz, and thanks are due to him and to Jacques Drèze for valuable comments. Any errors are, of course, the responsibility of the authors.

than attenuates a shock's immediate impact, although there are dynamic forces which over time tend to restore full employment. The model is not, therefore, one in which the economy generates cycles by shifting among many (or a continuum of) eligible equilibria, some with greater and some with less unemployment. The justifications for this are two fold. First, business cycles appear empirically to be characterized by regular sequences of changes in output, employment, profitability and firm balance sheets. Recovery seems historically to have followed recessions with a certain inevitability, even if unemployment has persisted for long periods, as in the 1930s. For the purposes of comparison to the available data, therefore, a model which provides a description of dynamic changes has certain advantages over a model of multiple equilibria with no clearly specified pathway among them. Second, variations in long-term growth rates, being dynamic phenomena, call for dynamic explanations. They also appear empirically to be significantly affected by short-term economic fluctuations. An explicitly dynamic monetary model has the advantage of providing a framework for analysing the connections involved.

The second feature of the model is that it incorporates an international sector. Monetary interactions are taken into account. The model, therefore, describes the impact of monetary policy in a 'small' open economy.

Third, the model contains a reasonably explicit institutional specification of the behaviour of firms and banks. This has the unfortunate effect of reducing the generality of the model's implications. However, there are significant offsetting advantages. First, empirical evidence suggests that the impact of monetary policy varies from economy to economy. One strong possibility is that these variations are related to variations in institutional structure. Thus, investigating the impact of institutional structures explicitly provides some guidance as to which institutional differences are important. Incorporation of explicit institutional structures into the model also means that the model provides a context for evaluating the consequences of alternative specifications of institutional behaviour. Information transmission, especially if less than perfect, depends critically on institutional realities. Thus, attention to these structures is central to the study of the consequences of informational imperfections. Finally, the actual institutional assumptions made are reasonably general and easily altered. As a result, they should not unreasonably limit the applicability of the model.

The fourth special aspect of the model is that it allows complete price flexibility. This does not mean that the model has no rigidities. Imperfect information generally restricts trading opportunities and thus quantity rigidities are intrinsic to these models. However, allowing explicit price rigidity may obscure more about the likely impact of imperfect information than it illuminates. Prices serve two functions. They determine the marginal incentives governing economic behaviour which is the traditional route by which they are assumed to affect output and employment levels. But, in addition, prices determine the distribution of income and purchasing power; largely a function of inframarginal prices. In many imperfect information models with price rigidity it is not clear whether the critical impact of the rigidities are related to marginal prices and incentives or to inframarginal prices and the distribution of income.

The distinction between these two effects is a significant one for at least three reasons. First, marginal prices are likely in practice to be far more flexible than inframarginal prices. For example, it is well documented that in times of low employment demand, unions are quite flexible in making concessions at the margin on hours and working conditions. At the same time they are generally inflexible with regard to base wage levels. Thus, the importance in practice of a model whose implications depend on marginal rigidities may be quite different from that of a model driven by inframarginal ones. Second, for policy purposes, if marginal rigidities are significant then there are policy approaches that can be tailored towards inducing price and wage flexibility at the margins without attempting to interfere with inframarginal wages and the overall distribution of income. However, if under-employment is related to the distribution of income (i.e. inframarginal wages) then such policies will have little impact.[2] For the latter case, effective policy interventions will require changes in the distribution of income which may be much harder to achieve. Third, nominal price rigidities in inflationary environments are difficult to justify. However, rigidities in the distribution of income may still persist as average wage and loan rates are adjusted upward to account for anticipated inflation. By allowing full price flexibility, our model effectively eliminates marginal rigidities. However, income distribution rigidities, due to the information-related breakdowns of markets for transferring wealth (and income), are fundamental to the model. Thus, the implications our model, which include the possibility of extended periods of underemployment, do not depend on marginal price rigidities.

This chapter consists, beyond this introduction, of three sections and a brief conclusion. The first section introduces the nature of imperfect information and its impact on the behaviour of firms. Section two extends this analysis to banking institutions and, in this context, describes the impact of monetary policy on those institutions and, through them, on non-financial firms. Finally, section three embeds this institutional structure of banks and firms in a global economic context to focus on the likely effects of monetary intervention in an open economy.

6.1   The impact of imperfect information on firms

The basic assumption which differentiates the present model from classical alternatives is that a firm's decision-makers (i.e. managements) know more about their firm's prospects than external investors. As a result when these decision-makers attempt to sell additional common stock to outside investors at any established market price, those outside investors should be properly sceptical of the bargain they are being offered. If the true value per share of the firm exceeds its market price, then managements will be reluctant to sell additional shares at that price. In contrast, if the prospective value per share of the firm is less than its market price, then management, aware of this discrepancy to an extent that external investors are not, will be eager to sell additional shares.[3] However, investors presumably know of this tendency and will react negatively to any attempt to sell additional shares, leading to a drop in the company's stock market value when new equity issues are announced. This reaction will, in turn, constitute a significant disincentive to new share issues by management and, in the extreme, may lead the market for newly issued equity to dry up completely. Empirical evidence supports the existence and significance of these effects. First, new equity (stock) sales are only a small fraction both of equity financing (which is dominated by retained earnings) and overall financing, including debt, even for jurisdictions and times for which tax considerations are minimal.[4] Second, equity issue announcements have well-documented adverse impacts on company stock prices.[5] For simplicity, we will assume that firm sales of new shares (equity issues) are not possible.[6]

This means that increases in a firm's base of equity capital (on which paid-out returns are discretionary) must come from reinvested earnings and the accumulation of equity is a dynamic process which depends importantly on past profitability. Formally, this can be described by assuming that

$$e_{t+1} = \text{period } t + 1 \text{ firm equity} = \pi_{t+1} - d_{t+1} + e_t \tag{1}$$

where

π_{t+1} = firm profits (after debt and other factor payments) in period $t + 1$;

and

d_{t+1} = period $t + 1$ dividends.

We will assume that profits are generated from a constant-returns-to-scale production process using only a labour input which must be hired, paid and put to work one period before output is available for sale. Formally this means that

$$\pi_{t+1} = p_{t+1} \, (k\ell_t) - w_t\ell_t - r_t \, (w_t \, \ell_t - e_t) \tag{2}$$

where
p_{t+1} = Price of output realized in period $t + 1$
  k = production constant, which without loss of generality may be
        taken to be one,
  ℓ_t = amount of labour hired in period t,
  w_t = wage in period t,
  r_t = return on debts contracted to support production in period t.

The expression $(w_t \ell_t - e_t)$ is the amount of borrowing that a firm must do in period t to pay its wage bill at that time.

Two aspects of this structure ought to be noted. First, the basic process involves investing resources in fixed amounts at fixed and known costs or, in the case of the debt financing, with a promise (supported by sanctions) of a fixed payment. The return which subsequently materializes depends on a future price whose level is uncertain when production decisions are made. The consequences of variations in this price, which embody the risk incurred by the firm, are entirely absorbed by the firm's stock of equity.[7] Thus, it is the firm's willingness to bear this risk that will determine the level of production (in this case reflected in ℓ_t). It should be clear that this risk-bearing structure will carry over into far more complex models with, for example, several periods of staggered labour inputs required to produce output.

Second, we will assume that the level of dividends, d_t, is based on prior commitments which cannot be lightly given up. This corresponds closely with both received practical wisdom concerning dividends and the theoretical implications of adverse selection in financial decisions as applied to dividends (considering them as negative equity issues). For expositional simplicity, therefore, we will simply assume that dividends are zero; formally that, $d_t = 0$ for all t. Then the evolution of firm equity levels will depend entirely on the evolution of profits.

The next step in the model is to specify how the firm determines its desired level of production and, hence, risk. In contrast to the classical model we will assume that instead of maximizing expected profits, the firm maximizes the expected utility of the terminal value of its equity. Formally, firms select ℓ_t to

$$max\ E\ [u(e_{t+1})] \qquad (3)$$

subject to the equity evolution constraints (1) and (2).

In the imperfect information literature there are a number of models giving rise to such an objective function which, it should be noted, only makes sense if new equity cannot be raised by selling shares.

The one that applies most directly is that of Leland and Pyle (1977). They consider the case of an owner-entrepreneur who maximizes the expected utility of his own end-of-period wealth. In this case, adverse selection forces the entrepreneur to hold a disproportionate share of his wealth in the stock of his own company (otherwise investors would be sceptical of the firm's value and bid down the price of shares actually sold). Thus, the entrepreneur maximizes the expected utility of the sum of his other wealth – assumed for convenience to be invested in risk-free assets and the market portfolio – and the terminal value of his fraction of the company. Alternatively, we could consider a professional manager who acts as the agent of outside stockholders. If that manager faces a linear incentive schedule which depends on the end-of-period equity position of the firm, he will maximize the objective function of equation (3), with the incentive function as an added constraint.[8] Another agency model which gives rise to an objective function like that of equation (3) is one in which the entrenched position of existing management enables them to expropriate a fraction of the net equity value of the firm. This then becomes part of the manager's wealth. Assuming their other holdings are riskless they will maximize the utility of their end-of-period wealth by maximizing a function like that of equation (3). Finally, if a firm's managers maximize expected profits less an expected cost of bankruptcy which rises with the level of firm activity (in this simple case ℓ_t), then their behaviour is entirely equivalent to that involved in maximizing the objective function of equation (3).[9]

Firm behaviour under these circumstances can be summarized relatively simply. The combination of rigidities (embodied in the equity sales constraint) and uncertainty (embodied in the firm's objective function) leads to a firm supply function, which depends not just on expected prices, wages, interest rates and price uncertainty, as it would in a conventional model, but also on the firm's beginning-of-period equity position. Formally, if we chose units so that k in the production function is unity, then

$$q_{t+1} = \ell_t = F(p_{t+1}^E, \sigma_p^2, w_t, r_t; e_t) \equiv \text{output in period } t+1 \qquad (4)$$

where p_{t+1}^E is the expected level of $t+1$ prices, σ_p^2 is the uncertainty in that price level, and F is a labour demand function which depends positively on p_{t+1}^E and e_t and negatively on σ_p^2, w_t and r_t. If the utility function of equation (3) is characterized by constant relative risk aversion, then equation (4) is linear in e_t so that

$$q_{t+1} = \ell_t = f(p_{t+1}^E, \sigma_p^2, w_t, r_t)(e_t) \qquad (4a)$$

Several points about the behaviour of such a firm are worth noting. First, and most importantly, output depends on the equity position of the firm as perceived by its managers. Moreover, the magnitude of this effect is far from trivial. With constant relative risk aversion, the elasticity of output with respect to firm equity is one. Since the equity positions of firms vary significantly over the business cycle (especially if anticipated future retained earnings are taken into account),[10] this effect alone (which does not exist in conventional models) provides an explanation for significant output fluctuations.

Second, the impact of the risk variable (σ_p^2) may be greatly intensified in this model. There is a widely but informally held view that variations in risk are unlikely to be a significant factor in aggregate output fluctuations. This argument grants that variations in business risk will indeed affect a firm's cost of capital as the increased risk is passed along to investors. However, since interest rate variations do not appear empirically to have a strong impact on firm activity levels, risk-related variations in the cost of capital are also unlikely to have a significant impact. The key point about the present model is that imperfect information undermines the market for sharing risks with new investors via new equity sales. Increased risk stays with the firm's current owners whose only means of limiting risk is to adjust its level of output.

Consider the effect of a demand shock which leads to a lower than expected price realization, p_{t+1}, and perhaps also to an upward revision in the firm's estimate of σ_p^2. The loss associated with this low price comes out of the firm's equity. With perfect information, this loss of firm 'wealth' has no effect on its ability to bear risk. The firm simply sells new equity to the very consumers who benefit from lower prices and carries on with its usual production plan. Any perceived increase in environmental uncertainty could be absorbed by increasing firm equity levels and reducing the debt burden associated with any particular level of production. Thus, increases in uncertainty are indeed attenuated by established risk-sharing mechanism. In our world of imperfect information, however, adverse selection in the equity markets eliminates these options. Not only can higher perceived risk no longer be absorbed by higher firm equity levels, the loss of equity from a low price realization cannot be made good by new equity sales. Thus, the only response available to the firm for reducing future demand risk is to reduce output.

A third important characteristic of the model arises from the role of equity levels in determining output. This gives rise to persistent cyclical changes in production. Again consider the impact of a sudden reduction in equity levels (due for example to an unusually low output price realization) in the context of equations (1) and (2). If output is to remain at its existing level the loss must be made good and this can only be done by internal equity accumulation[11] which depends, in turn, on future prices and profits. However, because the immediate response of the firm is to reduce output, profits in the future will be lower than they would otherwise be, when and if higher price outcomes subsequently materialize, and the return to pre-shock levels of output may be extended over relatively long periods of time.

The role of government policy interventions in this environment is more complicated than either classical or traditional Keynesian prescriptions. Lower real wages and interest rates will, as in those other models, stimulate output. However, fully anticipated expansionary fiscal policy will not have the usual expansionary Keynesian effect. If fiscal policy does not alter the distribution of equity between firms and households (to the benefit of firms), it will not generate increases in output, except for the classical effects of increased goods demand on interest rates and capital accumulation. This may be a reassuring implication of the model, given the very mixed empirical record of fiscal policy interventions.

A more important channel of policy impact in the model is through the uncertainty variable. Government policies that provide firms with guaranteed or quasi-guaranteed returns, as in wartime or in connection with certain kinds of public works projects, should be a powerful expansionary force.[12] For the same reasons, inconsistent and unpredictable government interventions (e.g. those which lead to high and varying inflation rates) which create uncertainty will have a significant contractionary effect.

Unexpected policy changes, which generate unusually high price level realizations, will transfer equity from households to firms with a consequent expansionary impact on the economy as a whole. However, this is not a 'trick' that ought to be consistently effective. And, if firm equity is heavily invested in financial assets (e.g. the stock of other firms or commercial real estate as in Japan), the resulting impact on financial markets (either an unusual boom or a collapse) may have a highly destabilizing effect on firm equity levels, and hence, output.

6.2   Banks and monetary policy

In a world of imperfect information, financial institutions play a critical role. In this model, banks will be representative financial institutions. They will be assumed to collect deposits from customers and lend the proceeds of those deposits, their own equity and other borrowed funds to firms. They may also invest in or borrow from a general loan market. For simplicity, we will assume that banks borrow and lend in this market (which is also available to other firms and households) at a common rate of interest.

The mechanisms by which banks make loans to firms will not be modelled in detail. Asymmetric information between banks and borrower firms may limit borrowing just as it limits equity sales by firms and may lead to credit rationing.[13] However, we will ignore these issues for the moment. Banks will be assumed to be firms, like other firms, controlled by agent/managers who maximize the expected utility of the bank's end-of-period equity position. Like other firms, banks will be assumed to be unable to sell equity in financial markets. Thus, banks too must accumulate equity over time through retained earnings. A bank is essentially a firm whose output consists of loans to non-financial firms on which it receives an uncertain return at the beginning of the next period, r^D_{t+1}, per dollar loaned at the beginning of the period. The bank's inputs are deposits, whose level and interest rate we will assume for the moment are determined by the monetary authority, and borrowings from the general loan market. Formally, a typical bank is assumed to maximize

$$E[u(e^B_{t+1})] \tag{5}$$

where

$$e^B_{t+1} = r^D_{t+1} D_t - r^o_t (D_t - M_t - e^B_t) - r^m_t M_t + e^B_t \tag{6}$$

$$\equiv \text{Bank equity at the end of period } t.$$

In equations (5) and (6),
   $D_t \equiv$ loans made in period t,
   $M_t \equiv$ bank deposits in period t,
   $e^B_t \equiv$ bank equity in period t,
   $r^M_t \equiv$ rate of interest on bank deposits in period t,
   $r^o_t \equiv$ rate of interest on other borrowed funds in period t.

Under these circumstances, the bank's behaviour can be described by a loan supply function that, broadly speaking, depends on the expected return on loans, r^{DE}_{t+1}, the uncertainty of that return, σ^2_R, the costs of borrowings and deposits, r^o and r^m respectively, and the bank's equity position. This can be written formally as

$$D_t = G(r^{DE}_{t+1}, \sigma^2_R, r^o_t; W^B_t)$$

where

$$W^B_t = (1 + r^o_t)e^B_t + (r^o_t - r^m_t)M_t \tag{7}$$

is a bank 'wealth' variable, since the bank actually acquires equity in two ways. The first is the accumulation over time described by equation (6) in which bank equity can grow only from bank profits. There is, however, a second source of bank wealth as long as the monetary authorities mandate interest rates on deposits below the rate prevailing in the market for general borrowings. This is captured by the second term in equation (7) which describes the component of bank profits due to the subsidy provided by the monetary authorities whose value is known at the beginning of period t.

   Monetary policy in the model operates through three channels, only two of which are characteristic of traditional models. The first and more familiar is the impact of monetary policy on asset market equilibrium and through the asset market equilibrium on the borrowing rate, r_t^0. The second effect of monetary policy is through its impact on the market uncertainty variables (σ_R^2, and σ_p^2). Predictable, stable and transparent monetary policies which reduce the uncertainties faced by firms and banks will stimulate economic activity and, for the reasons discussed above in connection with firm behaviour, market failures due to imperfect information may greatly enhance these effects.

It is the third channel, however, which is particular to the imperfect information model. Restrictions on deposit interest rates allow the monetary authorities to transfer wealth from depositors (households and firms) to banks when they expand the money supply. In the extreme case where deposits pay no interest and monetary expansions become a permanent part of the future money supply, the discounted present value of this subsidy in perpetuity is equal to the value of the money supply itself:

$$r_t^0 M_t / r_t^0 = M_t$$

Moreover, this effect is quite different and certainly more powerful than the traditional wealth effects associated with monetary policy. First, it does not depend on any form of illusion since what is involved is a real transfer of wealth from depositors to banks. Second, the wealth transferred is not merely an addition to the total wealth of the economy, it represents an addition to the equity base of banks. To understand the difference in impact consider the effect of an expansion of the money supply of $50 billion (assume this represents a 10 per cent increase). The addition to the wealth of the overall economy of a country like the United States would be trivial and, in classical theory, this gain in wealth should affect only household demand. However, the addition to bank equity will be far more significant, since bank equity, even including the implied value of monetary subsidies, is a far smaller number than total wealth. In addition, the likely impact of an increase in bank equity on lending and thus on economic activity is likely (dollar for dollar) to be far greater than the impact of wealth additions on household demand.

In what follows we will make one further simplifying assumption. We will assume that banks and non-financial firms are for informational purposes fully integrated. Under these circumstances bank and firm wealth will be fully interchangeable and the firm supply function of equation (4) will be driven by a single economy-wide equity level; formally that

$$e_t = (e_t^F + e_t^B)\,(1 + r_t^0) + (r_t^0 - r_t^m)M_t \tag{8}$$

where e_t^F refers to the equity level of non-financial firms. This aggregate equity level will be driven over time by both bank and non-bank profits and depends directly on monetary policy.

The justification beyond simplicity for this assumption is twofold. First, in many economies, banks and industrial firms are in fact integrated into common groups. The common equity assumption should apply directly to these important economies (e.g. Japan). Second, in many other economies banks and industrial firms do share information closely in the context of long-term relationships. Banks provide both equity capital and close supervision (including broad memberships) in these situations. The assumption of common information may more accurately describe these situations than the opposite assumption of complete separation. Common information and shared equity between banks and client firms is, therefore, a useful representative case.

The consequences for policy of less than complete information are qualitatively easy to describe. In general, uneven distributions of equity both among firms and between firms and banks attenuates the impact of equity additions. With decreasing returns large equity additions will have smaller effects on output than small equity additions. Hence uneven additions to equity will have smaller output effects than even distributions. Similarly, if banks are not perfectly integrated with firms then bank equity additions will have smaller effects (in general) than firm equity additions, and monetary policy which increases bank equity will be less potent than under a situation of shared equity. One further point should, however, be noted. Firms hold deposits in banks and, thus, monetary policy transfers resources from firms to banks as well as from households to banks. If banks and firms are fully integrated, then the firm-to-bank transfers will not affect output. However, if they are not fully integrated, firm-to-bank transfers will have a negative impact on firm output. This will certainly attenuate and perhaps even reverse the household-to-bank transfer effects of monetary policy.[14]

One final channel of monetary policy which operates through the equity level of the firm-banking sector may be particularly important whenever either firms or banks directly hold significant financial assets.[15] Then, the composite price, p_{t+1}, whose realization determines the business sector's equity level will include the prices of financial assets. If monetary policy significantly affects these asset prices, then it will affect business equity by that means also. And, a collapse in financial/asset prices, like that experienced in Japan (whether generated by monetary policy or not), may have a powerful contractionary effect.

6.3 Monetary policy in a global environment

So far we have been considering only the partial equilibrium consequences of monetary policy based on the implicit assumptions that monetary policy can affect not only the real money supply (and hence business sector equity) but also the level of interest rates, r_t^0, and, through them, overall economic stability. In a closed economy with imperfect information, these assumptions are familiar ones.[16] However, for a small open economy in an integrated global environment, they are more problematical.

In a global context, the markets which must clear in equilibrium are those for output, labour, borrowing, domestic money and foreign exchange. We will assume that the first of these clears automatically. Output which is not sold domestically can be sold internationally at a given world price. The output market equilibrium requires that

$$p_t = x_t \, p_t^w \text{ for all } t \tag{9}$$

where p_t is the realized price of domestic output in period t, x_t is the exchange rate in period t and p_t^w is the world price of output in period t.[17] If domestic demand exceeds domestic production then the necessary output will be imported from abroad. In either case, for this small open economy, domestic prices will be determined by the world price level and the exchange rate, or, in slightly different terms, the real exchange rate will be fixed. An advantage of this assumption is it eliminates the possibility of monetary policy operating through its impact on real exchange rates (the Mundell-Fleming effect), which, in turn, depends on significant price rigidities affecting marginal demand and output decisions. The fact that removal of this possibility does not eliminate the impact of monetary policy illustrates one of the significant aspects of the imperfect information model.

Next, in order to simplify the analysis as far as possible, we will assume that labour is perfectly elastically supplied at a given real wage; formally that

$$w_t = \bar{w} p_t \text{ for all } t. \tag{10}$$

This has three consequences. First, macroeconomic fluctuations will be entirely reflected in employment changes rather than output changes which tend to maximize output fluctuations by eliminating any counter-vailing changes in wages. Second, unemployment will not formally be an issue in the model, although it could clearly be incorporated by including efficiency wage considerations. Instead we can simply regard output fluctu-ations and the associated employment changes as representing the full range of observed cyclical phenomena. Third, because declining wages in low output periods tend to stimulate future output and profits, the length of cycles with these fixed wages will be extended as firm and bank equity accumulates more slowly than it otherwise would.

Of the remaining three markets, one is redundant. If international payments are in balance and money supply equals money demand, then borrowing will equal lending (including foreign borrowing and lending). Similarly, if firm borrowing and lending are in balance and money supply equals money demand, then the balance of payments will be in equilibrium. The two clearing equations which we will consider explicitly are those for money and foreign exchange. The money market will be assumed to be in equilibrium when the money supply is equal to a money demand of the usual sort. Formally, this means that

$$M_t = p_t L(r_t^o, \ell_t) \tag{11}$$

where L is a liquidity preference function of the usual kind depending positively on productive activity and negatively on alternative interest rates (since r_t^m is fixed exogenously it has been suppressed in the equation).

With no restrictions on international borrowing and lending and static expectations concerning exchange rates, equilibrium in the balance of payments requires that:

$$r_t^o = r_t^w \tag{12}$$

where r_t^w is the world interest rate.[18]

Conventional wisdom under these circumstances is that monetary policy will have no effect. However, substitution from equations (9), (10) and (12) into the money demand equation and the basic output supply function yields the following relationships that characterize the impact of monetary policy. They are

$$M_t = p_t L(r_t^w, \ell_t) \tag{13}$$

and

$$q_{t+1} = \ell_t = F(p_t \, \overline{w}, r_t^w, e_t) \tag{14}$$

where the arguments of F relating to expected future price and price uncertainty have been dropped for notational convenience and business sector equity is determined by

$$e_t = (p_t \, q_t - w_{t-1} \, \ell_{t-1}) - r_{t-1}^o(w_{t-1} \, \ell_{t-1} - e_{t-1}) + (r_{t-1}^o - r_{t-1}^m) \, M_{t-1} + e_{t-1} \tag{15}$$

In this situation, an increase in the money supply can affect output in two ways. First, it adds to business sector equity through the penultimate 'seignorage' term on the right-hand side of equation (15).[19] Second, if the increase in the money supply is unexpected, leading to unexpectedly high levels of p_t, then e_t will be higher than expected with an expansionary effect on output.

Admittedly if the price level adjusts completely and instantaneously to changes in the money supply and money supply decisions are properly anticipated, then money will be neutral and monetary policy will have no real effect (since real 'seignorage' will be independent of monetary policy). However, the requirement that prices adjust in this way both goes far beyond the requirement that prices be flexible and is inconsistent with recorded empirical data. With less than immediate and full adjustment in prices to money supply changes, there will be a solution to equations (13) and (14) in which a greater money supply, even if fully anticipated, will lead to a higher level of employment and output. This occurs despite the fact that prices are assumed to adjust fully and flexibly to clear the goods market (or markets) both domestically and internationally (which in this simple case merely requires that the real exchange rate not vary). The critical effect in this small open economy is the impact of monetary-policy-induced transfers on the *supply* of output (through its impact on business sector equity).

Several points are worth making about this equilibrium. First any immediate policy effects are reinforced by the impact of the policy regime involved on price uncertainty. Also to the extent that financial market conditions affect firm equity levels directly through firm holdings of financial assets, the impact of monetary policy on financial markets equilibria will amplify the basic output effects described by equations (13)–(15).

If real interest rates and real exchange rates are not fully determined by global interactions, then several factors become important. These include the usual effects of higher interest rates and exchange rates on aggregate demand – negative and positive respectively – but also the effect of these changes on firm equity positions. Since the business sector (including banks) is invariably a net debtor, higher interest rates transfer resources from firms to households and have a negative effect on firm equity and output. If business sector debts are held by foreigners and denominated in foreign currency, then an increase in the exchange rate (a currency devaluation) will transfer equity from the business sector to these foreigners which will go some way towards offsetting the expansionary impact of higher exchange rates on net exports. This may in part represent a rationale for recommending restrictive monetary policies in the face of the kinds of hidden devaluation crises experienced in Asia and Latin America – since higher domestic interest rates may attract foreign capital and, in the process, reduce downward pressure on the value of the currency. However, it should be noted that such a monetary policy also undermines business sector equity positions directly as higher interest rates transfer resources to both domestic and foreign lenders. On balance, therefore, it should be pursued cautiously or not at all.

One final point must be made. Financial deregulation which removes controls on bank deposit interest rates – so that r_t^o equals r_t^m after adjusting for the value of transaction-related deposit services – may undermine the effectiveness of monetary policy. If the 'seignorage' effect in equation (15) is the primary source of the immediate impact of monetary policy, then removing it will greatly reduce the weight of that policy. This may well account for the widely but informally remarked upon 'fact' that in the United States, the same monetary policy effects on output have required increasingly large variations in interest rates and monetary controls. The real impact of monetary policy may have been largely undermined by financial deregulation and along with it the ability of the Federal Reserve Board to mismanage the economy. If this is so, then the apparent recent successes of American monetary policy may have more to do with the underlying stability of the economy than to active management by the monetary authorities.

6.4 Conclusion

The foregoing analysis represents, it must be emphasized, the implications of one very simple model. However, they are both sufficiently at variance with standard monetary policy analyses and consistent with observed phenomena that attention to information imperfections and related rigidities should form some part of future policy discussion.

Notes

1. See Drèze, Ch. 3 in this volume, for a valuable model and summary of these developments.
2. A practical example arose in the early 1990s in the United States. The administration proposed a targeted investment tax credit focused only on new investment in order to maximize investment incentives per dollar of tax relief. In practice, the business community preferred lower average corporate tax rates which were embodied in the final legislation and for whatever reason led to continued high levels of business investment.
3. This assumes that in so far as management serves the interests of shareholders, it serves those of current shareholders, not prospective shareholders.
4. See Mayer (1990).
5. See Asquith and Mullins (1986) among others.
6. What applies here to equity issues also applies to more general risk-sharing arrangements. If an informed party wants to share a risk at an established price with an uninformed partner, that price is likely to be disadvantageous to prospective partners.
7. Among other things this means that the model as specified implicitly rules out complete futures markets.

8. Strictly speaking the manager's reward may depend on the external equity market value of the firm not its internal equity position. But, in a rational expectations world, the best way for the manager to maximize a function of the former is to maximize a function of the latter.
9. See Greenwald and Stiglitz (1993).
10. If e_t is taken to be a certainty equivalent associated with a firm balance sheet consisting of relatively risky assets (inventory and plant and equipment) and relatively fixed liabilities (debt), then the widely observed variations in firm balance sheets (i.e. unintended inventory accumulation) associated with business cycles will embody still further reductions in e_t.
11. It should be noted here that empirically firms do not appear to sell significant amounts of equity in the downward phases of recessions. Cyclical balance sheet improvements are related largely to operating decisions to cut production (inventories) and investment.
12. This effect should be much more pronounced than in a classical model where risks are efficiently distributed by financial markets.
13. See Stiglitz and Weiss (1981).
14. I am grateful to Jacques Drèze for pointing this out.
15. This may arise either directly or partially through interests in financial assets used as collateral for loans.
16. For a full discussion of the closed economy situation see, for example, Greenwald and Stiglitz (1993).
17. This is most easily thought of as holding for a single universal commodity, but it applies equally for all tradable goods. For non-tradable goods, there is a market clearing condition of the usual sort. However, including such a sector complicates the analysis without affecting its basic qualitative implications. See Greenwald (1999) for a model including both traded and non-traded goods.
18. This will not strictly be true unless worldwide lenders are risk neutral. But, a similar relationship with world interest rates and the local currency 'beta' determining local interest rates will hold.
19. If an increase in the money supply redness the interest rate, it might seen that the sign of $d(r_t^0 M_t)/dM_t$ would be ambiguous. However, as the business sector is unvariably a net debtor, a decline in the interest rate will leave it unambiguously better off.

References

Asquith, P. and Mullins, D. (1986) 'Equity Issues and Stock Price Dilution', *Journal of Financial Economics*, vol. 13, pp. 296–320.

Greenwald, B.C. (1999), 'International Adjustment in the Face of Imperfect Financial Markets', in Pleskovic, B. and Stiglitz, J. (eds) *Annual World Bank Conference on Development Economics, 1998* (Washington, DC: World Bank), pp. 273–89.

Greenwald, B.C. and Stiglitz, J.E. (1993) 'Financial Market Imperfections and Business Cycles', *Quarterly Journal of Economics*, vol. 108, pp. 77–114.

Leland, H.E. and Pyle, D.H. (1977) 'Information Asymmetrics, Financial Structure and Financial Intermediation', *Journal of Finance*, vol. 32, pp. 371–87.

Mayer, C.P. (1990) 'Financial Systems, Corporate Finance and Economic Development', in Hubbard, R.G. (ed.) *Asymmetric Information, Corporate Finance and Investment*, pp. 216–40 (Chicago: University of Chicago Press).

Stiglitz, J.E. and Weiss, A. (1981) 'Credit Rationing in Markets with Imperfect Information', *American Economic Review*, vol. 71, pp. 393–410.

7
Understanding Inflation: Implications for Monetary Policy*

Stephen G. Cecchetti
Ohio State University
and
Erica L. Groshen
Federal Reserve Bank of New York

7.1 Introduction

If prices and wages were perfectly flexible, monetary policy would be irrelevant. But casual observation suggests both that nominal prices and wages are at least somewhat rigid and that monetary policy has real effects. Economists' understanding of the nature of these rigidities has improved in recent years. At the same time, policy makers have begun to incorporate economists' theoretical and empirical findings in their institutions and actions. This chapter explores the ways in which our empirical understanding of nominal rigidities informs three key dimensions of the conduct of monetary policy: how we measure core inflation, how we control inflation, and how we choose inflation targets.

The overriding theme of our analysis is that an understanding of the nature of shocks and rigidities is crucial for the conduct of a sound monetary policy. Shocks and rigidities vary along a number of dimensions. Efficient inflation measurement, optimal inflation goals, and the effective execution of policy will all vary depending on these aspects of an economy's structure.

To be specific, shocks can be predominantly real, affecting relative prices, or primarily nominal, moving the general price level. They may also be big

* This paper was written while Cecchetti was Director of Research of the Federal Reserve Bank of New York, as well as Professor of Economics, Ohio State University, and Research Associate, National Bureau of Economic Research. Groshen is Assistant Vice President in the Domestic Research Function of the Federal Reserve Bank of New York. We are grateful to Jacques Drèze for asking us to organize our thoughts on this topic, to Roisin O'Sullivan and Palle Andersen for comments, to Valerie LaPorte for editorial assistance and to Nathaniel Baum-Snow for research assistance.

or small, and they may be frequent or rare. Different economies are susceptible to very different types of shocks. For example, a country like the United States or a region like the European Monetary Union primarily faces small background shocks. Alternatively, Australia, a country heavily dependent on its exports of raw materials, and Norway, an oil-producing country, are more prone to occasional large shocks.

Similarly, there are several key differences in rigidities. Some nominal rigidities are symmetrical, affecting both upward and downward movements, while others exhibit more stickiness downward. In addition, rigidities can vary in their degree. For example, if symmetric wage and price stickiness is a result of costly adjustment (menu costs), then economies that have recently experienced high inflation may have implemented price- and wage-change technologies that make individual changes less costly, resulting in more frequent adjustments and a lower level of symmetric stickiness. Downward rigidity will also vary across countries, depending, for example, on wage-setting practices.

With this in mind, we begin our analysis by noting the diversity of approaches to the conduct of monetary policy around the world. Countries vary substantially in their choice of regime. Some target inflation explicitly, others target money, and still others attempt to fix their exchange rates. Not surprisingly, their macroeconomic circumstances and outcomes have varied dramatically as well. These divergences raise questions about how various types of nominal rigidity affect each aspect of monetary policy. In particular, what evidence do we have of the existence of specific rigidities, and what is the implication for the conduct of monetary policy?

The first monetary policy issue we address concerns the measurement of core, or trend, inflation. Rigidities cause inflation-induced price adjustments to occur asynchronously, an effect that introduces biases into the usual measures of price changes and lowers the signal-to-noise ratio in such measures. Recent research has advanced our understanding of these issues and offers some intriguing alternatives (such as medians and trimmed means) to the common average index.

Second, the nature and extent of rigidities creates potentially variable lags in the monetary policy transmission mechanism, complicating the policy maker's job. The execution of policy requires forecasts of the variables of interest – normally output and inflation – plus a quantitative estimate of the impact of policy changes. In addition to obscuring the level of trend inflation, nominal rigidities make price and wage adjustments dependent on the actual pattern of shocks hitting the economy, introducing considerable uncertainty into inflation forecasts, and complicating the measurement of the impact of policy substantially. Recent research illuminates the nature of this challenge and suggests how we might formulate policy in the face of this uncertainty.

Third, the nature of shocks and rigidities affects the level of inflation that monetary policy makers should target. Our chapter looks at two combinations of shocks and rigidities and their contrasting implications for optimal targets. Symmetric rigidities with nominal shocks imply that optimal inflation should be close to zero. Downward rigidities with real shocks imply that zero inflation is too low a target.

We conclude our analysis by considering some implications of recent theoretical and empirical research on wage and price rigidity for the implementation of monetary policy. First, we suggest ways in which the inflation trend can be more accurately measured, and second, we address the question of how best to select an inflation target.

7.2   Conduct of monetary policy

The decade of the 1990s has seen a convergence in the goals and methods used for the conduct of monetary policy around the world. A number of forces have driven this development. First, during the high inflation of the 1970s and 1980s, many countries saw prices rise well in excess of 50 per cent per year for extended periods.[1] This experience led to a clear consensus that even moderate levels of inflation damage real growth and that low inflation must therefore be a primary objective of monetary policy. Casual observation suggests that low-inflation countries experience higher growth rates, and so there are strong incentives to devise ways in which to keep inflation low.[2]

Second, evidence indicates that, in most countries, short-run money demand functions are unstable and thus meaningful measures of money, such as M3, are very difficult to control. As a result, monetary targeting alone is no longer viewed as a viable strategy for stabilizing prices. Finally, excessive exchange-rate volatility is seen as damaging. The discussion about the appropriate exchange-rate regime is clearly ongoing, but a shrinking cohort of countries organize their policy framework with the goal of reducing or eliminating fluctuations in the value of their currency relative to that of some anchor country. Since these anchor countries typically have low inflation, this strategy calls for maintaining similarly low rates.

As consensus has grown on these issues, many countries have redesigned their central banks and, for the most part, achieved remarkable reductions in inflation.[3] A survey of 77 countries reported in Morandé and Schmidt-Hebbel (1999) divides countries into three groups on the basis of their monetary policy regime: exchange rate targeting, monetary targeting, or inflation targeting. The recent trend favours explicit or implicit inflation targeting. At least ten countries or central banks now set explicit inflation targets that clearly dominate any other targets or objectives. These countries are New Zealand, which in 1988 became the first industrialized country to adopt an explicit 'hard' inflation target; Canada, Chile and

Israel, which adopted inflation targeting in 1991; the United Kingdom, which moved to explicit inflation targets in 1992; and Australia and Sweden, which changed their policy frameworks in 1993; the Czech Republic and Spain which adopted targets in 1994 and 1995, respectively; and the European Central Bank, which announced a target in 1999. Morandé and Schmidt-Hebbel (1999) list a total of 45 countries that, over the past decade, have adopted some form of inflation target: 12 industrialized, 12 transitional and 21 developing.[4] Similarly, many other countries have changed their monetary regimes to target monetary aggregates or exchange rates with the goal of creating a credible low inflation policy.[5]

Regardless of the specific target a country chooses for implementing monetary policy, central banks face a number of practical difficulties in maintaining low levels of inflation. Inflation-targeting countries must specify an index to target, set a level for the target, decide whether to state the target as a band (for example, between 0 and 2 per cent) or as a point, and choose the number of quarters or years over which the target will be averaged. Similar choices must be made by countries that target money or exchange rates. These practical decisions are best based on a solid theoretical and empirical understanding of the processes underlying inflation. Fortunately, in recent years, economic research has shed considerable light on these processes. The next three sections of this chapter survey what we now know about core inflation measurement, inflation control, and the choice of an optimal long-term inflation level.

7.3   Core inflation measurement

Before policy makers can hope to control inflation, they must measure it; preferably on a timely basis.[6] This is a difficult task that has attracted substantial attention among both academic and central bank economists.[7] One of the primary difficulties associated with the measurement of inflation is the presence of considerable amounts of transitory noise.[8] That is, monthly or quarterly inflation readings can differ significantly from the longer-term trend in inflation. A few numbers provide some perspective. Over the past 15 years, the standard deviation of (annualized) monthly changes in the US Consumer Price Index (CPI) has been 2.2 percentage points. Meanwhile, the 12-month changes have had a standard deviation that is half that value, or 1.1 percentage points; and the 36-month moving average has had a standard deviation of only 0.8. Clearly the monthly changes in consumer prices provide only limited information about the trend.

The experience of the first half of 1999 provides an excellent example of how noisy and confusing monthly CPI movements can be. The monthly readings varied between 0 (there was no change from April to May) and nearly 9 per cent (from March to April) at an annual rate. All the while, the trend was very likely somewhere between 2 and 3 per cent per year. Although this example is surely extreme, it points out a serious practical problem. How far do monthly or quarterly aggregate price indexes have to move away from the perceived trend in inflation before policy makers change their view of the trend? Put another way, when and how should monetary policy makers respond to what look initially like short-term inflation changes?

To address these issues, we first need to identify the sources of this noise. Once we have this information, we can start to find ways of reducing the noise in our measured indexes. Experience suggests that transitory moves in price indexes are often attributable to clearly discernible events. We can distinguish among three different types of transitory CPI noise. These are summarized in Table 7.1, and we now describe them further.

First, inflationary price changes are not uniform. That is, different prices adjust at different times because nominal price adjustment is costly and adjustment costs differ across products. Prices which are costly to change (such as rents) will be more rigid, that is they will change less often, but by larger increments when they do. This variation leads to divergent inflation measures across products and time even if the trend is unchanged.

Second, relative price changes (reflecting real shocks) can temporarily affect measures of inflation even if they are not associated with a nominal shock. Some sectors may be affected more rapidly than others because they are directly exposed, or because they have more flexible prices. In addition,

Table 7.1   Three sources of noise in inflation measurement

	Shock	Rigidity	Noise
Asynchronous price changes	Nominal, aggregate price movements	Symmetric wage/ price rigidity	Flexible price sectors adjust first, rigid sectors lag
Incomplete adjustment to real shocks	Real relative wage/price shock	Symmetric wage/ price rigidity	Flexible price sectors adjust first, rigid sectors lag; or sectors directly affected adjust first, others lag
		Downward wage/ price rigidity	Positive changes occur first, negative ones lag
Flaws in seasonal adjustment	Change in timing of seasonal events	Symmetric timing rigidity	Seasonal adjustment itself yields sectoral changes that are temporarily over- or under-stated

if prices are rigid downwards, then upward price movements will occur before the compensating downward adjustments. Broad-based resource shocks, such as variation in petroleum prices, will have widely divergent effects on the prices of different consumer goods, and these do not all occur simultaneously. Exchange-rate shifts also affect prices differently; the prices of imported and import-competing goods are much more likely to change quickly than the prices of non-traded goods and services. Moreover, the size and timing of real shocks differ across sectors, leading to heterogeneous price changes.

Finally, because the CPI is measured on a monthly basis, inexact seasonal adjustment can also add noise to inflation measures. Firms with high costs of adjustment will limit the frequency with which they change prices. When these adjustments are coordinated among firms within a sector, they produce recurrent patterns. In order to reveal movements in the trend, statistical agencies use various adjustment techniques to remove normal seasonal fluctuations from the monthly numbers. However, these techniques are not foolproof. In particular, minor changes in the timing of price adjustments – say, a decision by apparel manufacturers to change the prices of summer clothes in February rather than March one year – can confound seasonal adjustment. In that case, February would record a jump in inflation matched by a corresponding drop in March.

These observations suggest that prices from different sectors of the economy will contain different amounts of information about inflation trends. There is considerable variation both in the importance of shocks and in the degree of nominal rigidity. Some industries are more prone to large relative price movements than others and some product prices are easier to change. Measuring the inflation trend requires that we sort out the real shocks from the nominal ones on an economy-wide basis, taking account of these potentially large cross-sectional differences.

A common strategy used to estimate core inflation is systematically to remove certain components of the price indexes. In the United States, it is standard to remove food and energy prices, both of which appear substantially more volatile than prices of other goods and services. The rationale is that short-term movements in these prices stem from rapid adjustment to frequent real shocks that are often reversed, and so they contain substantially less information about the long-term trend.

Returning to the experience of early 1999, we can see the benefits of excluding food and energy prices when trying to gauge the inflation trend. The highest reading of the CPI excluding food and energy is again from March to April, but the increase is estimated at just 4.75 per cent (at an annual rate). The lowest reading is from January to February, and is slightly below 0.7 per cent at an annual rate. By excluding food and energy, the range of inflation readings over this brief five-month period is reduced by more than half, from nearly 9 per cent to just over 4 per cent.

Still, the strategy of excluding food and energy relies on two arbitrary assumptions: that food and energy prices never contain information about the inflation trend, and that other prices always do. Neither of these assumptions is likely to be true. An alternative approach would be to look to economic theory for guidance on how we might construct measures of trend or core inflation. This strategy, adopted in a series of papers by Bryan and Cecchetti,[9] is based on the observation that the economy is, roughly speaking, composed of two groups of price setters. The first have flexible prices in the sense that they set their prices every period in response to realized changes in the economy. Common examples include producers of fruits, vegetables and motor fuel. The second group of price setters, by contrast, set prices infrequently, and face potentially high costs of readjustment. For example, we are thinking about those who set prices for housing rentals, restaurant meals or magazines at the news-stand.[10] New Keynesian macroeconomic theory focuses on this second group in building models in which, as a result of sticky prices and *menu costs*, purely nominal disturbances have potentially long-lived real effects. The first group, the realization-based price setters, have the potential to create noise in standard price indexes. Because they can change their prices quickly and often, these firms have little reason to care about long-term trends in aggregate inflation. In sectors where prices are costly to change, price setters cannot correct mistakes quickly, and so the paths of their prices are much smoother. Prices set by these expectations-based price setters contain information about the trend that is not present in the flexible prices of the first group.

To give some indication of the relative volatility of different prices, we have computed some simple standard deviations from monthly component price indexes. Looking at the period since 1985, we find that the highest variation is in the prices of fuel oil (for home heating), motor fuel (for cars), and fruits and vegetables. The standard deviation of monthly changes in inflation in these commodities (measured at an annual rate) ranges from 23 per cent for the foodstuffs to 45 per cent for fuel oil. This is between 10 and 20 times the standard deviation in the overall CPI. At the other end of the spectrum are 'food away from home' (restaurant meals) and shelter (which largely measures housing rental costs, or the rental equivalent value of home ownership) – the only two significant components with less volatility than the overall CPI.

These observations have led to the development of a new set of price measures that combine existing price data differently. The logic, as described in Bryan and Cecchetti (1994), is straightforward. Each firm in the economy adjusts prices, taking into account anticipated future developments. Following an initial adjustment, previously unanticipated shocks hit the economy. These real shocks create the desire for relative price adjustments. Only some firms experience shocks that are large enough to make immediate adjustment worthwhile. As a result, the observed change in the aggregate price level will depend on the shape of the distribution of the desired adjustments. In particular, if this distribution is skewed (as often seems to be the case in practice), then the aggregate price level will move up or down temporarily. Once every firm adjusts its prices this transitory movement in the aggregate index disappears.[11]

The proposed solution to the problem of noise created by infrequent and asynchronous adjustment (in the absence of downward price rigidity) is to use alternative statistical procedures for combining the disaggregated inflation information. The standard methodology for computing the aggregate CPI is to construct a weighted average of price data, in which the weights are based on expenditure surveys. But the sample mean is only one potential estimate of the central tendency of a distribution. An alternative is to use the (weighted) median of the component inflation data, as well as measures called *trimmed means*.[12] Trimmed means are a generalization of the concept of a median. A sample of data is first ordered, as it is in the construction of the median, and then some percentage of the highest and lowest observations are eliminated while the remainder are averaged. For example, if one has 100 sample data points, then the computation of a 15 per cent trimmed mean involves averaging the 70 observations in the centre of the distribution.[13]

Trimmed means are a natural solution to the difficulties created by nominal rigidities. In contrast to the average CPI excluding food and energy (which assumes that all noise comes from two sectors), the trimmed mean assumes that any extreme change is probably noise, no matter what sector it comes from. That is, the trimmed mean focuses on the centre of the distribution to tell us what the trend is doing. As noted above, when firms face costs of price adjustment, and the desired price changes are skewed, then the aggregate price index will contain transitory movements reflecting the fact that only price setters who wish to make large moves will find it worthwhile paying the cost. Substitution of a trimmed mean or the median for the sample average will reduce this source of noise and improve the signal policymakers need.

To see the difference this can make, we return to a comparison of the median CPI with the all-items CPI and the CPI excluding food and energy. Looking at the median in the first few months of 1999, we see that the lowest reading is 1.3 per cent from February to March, and the highest reading is 3.6 per cent, from March to April, both at an annual rate. Thus, the range for the all-items CPI is nearly 9 per cent, for the CPI excluding food and energy, it is 4 per cent, and for the median it is 2.3 per cent. Moreover, the standard deviation in monthly inflation for the past 15 years is 2.1 per cent for the all-item CPI, 1.4 per cent for the CPI excluding food and energy, and 1.3 per cent for the median (again, all values are at an annual rate). We will simply note that it is possible to improve on this last measure by choosing the trimmed mean that minimizes monthly variation.

An inflation-targeting regime needs both an appropriate, transparent target and timely information about the trend in that measure. The research cited above suggests that trimmed means provide superior timely measures of trend inflation. However, the public is unfamiliar with this measure. Thus, adoption of a trimmed mean might not offer the transparency desirable in an inflation goal. If so, how can these findings be incorporated into an inflation targeting regime? We offer two possibilities. The first is to have the measure produced, announced and explained by a statistical agency independent of the central bank. This role for a disinterested party should alleviate most concerns and increase understanding of the rationale for the unfamiliar measure. Alternatively, a central bank could maintain an average CPI target, but rely on the trimmed mean as the best short-run monitoring device for tracking trends. Since the advantage of the trimmed mean lies in its lower sensitivity to noise, while preserving the trend (as captured in long-run averages), this tack is theoretically sound. In either case, transparency and sound monetary policy both dictate the need for an extensive study of the dynamic and long-run relationship between the trimmed mean and average CPI in their country. Then, the central bank must be prepared to explain policy decisions in light of both measures.

Many central banks now compute a number of alternative estimates of core inflation, including medians and trimmed means. Álvarez and de los Llanos Matea (1999) cite numerous examples. We note here several interesting empirical regularities. First, for the dozen or so countries for which we have seen data, the median significantly reduces high-frequency noise. Secondly, we note that for countries other than the United States, the median appears to be systematically below the mean. The reason for this second finding is that, outside the United States, cross-section distributions of long-run price changes are positively skewed. This could suggest greater downward rigidities in those countries, but a fuller explanation of the finding will require further research.

7.4 Inflation control

It is generally agreed that all central banks should strive to reduce inflation and keep it at low levels. While the measurement of inflation poses substantial challenges, these seem minor in comparison with the difficulties of controlling inflation.

Inflation control can be thought of as a fairly technical problem in which the policy maker uses an instrument such as an interest rate to meet an inflation (or output growth) objective.[14] To carry out such a task, the policy makers must have a substantial amount of information. Most importantly, the policy maker needs to know what will happen to the objective (inflation) in the absence of any policy action, as well as what the impact of any particular action on the objective will be. Thus, inflation control requires forecasts of inflation and estimates of the response of inflation to changes in interest rates. Neither of these is straightforward to obtain. Forecasting inflation is a daunting task. For example, over the past decade, the standard deviation of forecast errors in professional forecasters' predictions of US inflation one year ahead has been about 1 full percentage point, implying a 90 per cent confidence band of about 3 percentage points. Over this same period, inflation has averaged only about 3 per cent. Nothing seems to forecast inflation very well, except inflation's own history.[15] Indeed, the relationship between price inflation and any potential indicator – such as wages, unemployment or commodity prices – is very unstable. Theory provides us with a reason for the difficulty of forecasting: when monetary policy regimes change, the relationship among various quantities in the economy shift as well, rendering prior statistical regularities unreliable.

From here the problem only gets worse. Not only is it difficult to forecast inflation, but our ability to predict the effect of monetary policy actions on inflation (and output) is very limited. A number of researchers have estimated the response of prices to interest rate movements in many countries. The first difficulty is in getting the estimates to display the proper sign. Most of us have a fairly firm belief that increases in interest rates are consistent with monetary contractions and should eventually drive inflation down. Unfortunately, it is more difficult than one would think to obtain this empirical result in standard models.[16] Then, beyond the difficulty of obtaining the proper sign, lie the issues of precision and statistical significance. For example, using a simple four-variable model (encompassing output, aggregate prices, commodity prices and the federal funds rate), one can estimate that a 100 basis point increase in interest rates will drive inflation down by about one-half of one percentage point after three years. But two standard deviation bands on this estimate go from approximately plus 1 per cent to –1.75 per cent.[17]

Why is it so difficult to estimate the effects of monetary policy actions? The answer is both that the economy responds to different shocks in different ways, and that the economy's response depends on history, so the same shock will prompt different reactions at different times. Textbook discussions treat the transmission mechanism as invariant to the path by which the economy has arrived at its current state. This is surely not true. Consider for a minute the implications of costly price adjustment. A large monetary shock will lead all firms to adjust and thus could result in smaller real effects than a small nominal shock that causes incomplete adjustment. The path of such shocks matters as well. Standard tools for estimating the economy's response to monetary policy actions are ill-suited to capturing the non-linear responses that theoretical models suggest should be pervasive. As the literature makes clear, linear approximations do not work well.

Rigidities obscure both trend inflation and the impact of policy actions from the policy maker's view.

Policy is made every day, and so despairing over our lack of knowledge and the inadequacies of our models is pointless. Instead, the most productive course is to take seriously the need to make policy in an uncertain and unstable environment. The imprecision of our knowledge must be built into the fundamentals of our policy-making procedures.

7.5   The optimal rate of inflation

Higher prices or faster inflation can diminish involuntary, disequilibrium unemployment. ... The economy is in perpetual ... disequilibrium even when it has settled into a stochastic macro-equilibrium. ... [When wages are rigid downward] price inflation ... is a neutral method of making arbitrary money wage paths conform to the realities of productivity growth.

James Tobin, 'Inflation and Unemployment', American Economic Association Presidential Address (1972)

[Higher, more variable inflation causes: a] reduction in the capacity of the price system to guide economic activity; distortions in relative prices because of the introduction of greater friction, as it were, in all markets; and very likely, a higher recorded rate of unemployment.

Milton Friedman, 'Inflation and Unemployment', Nobel Lecture (1977)

Who is right? Widespread reductions in core inflation and the growing use of explicit or implicit inflation targets by central banks make this question particularly relevant. Is the most economically efficient level of price changes zero, as Friedman suggests, or something greater than zero, as Tobin implies? The answer depends both on the structural rigidities in the economy and on the type of shocks the economy faces. But while the effectiveness of monetary policy depends on the nature of nominal rigidities, and the task of the policy maker is to respond to external shocks, not all rigidities and not all shocks are created the same. Differences in the types of shocks to which a country is prone and the types of rigidities built into that country's wage- and price-setting institutions will influence the optimal low-inflation goal.

Both the resolution of the controversy between Friedman and Tobin and the implications of this controversy for the choice of an optimal inflation target depend on the extent to which shocks are real or nominal, predominantly big or small; and the degree to which prices and wages are more rigid downward than up, and more or less sticky. A substantial amount of research has been devoted to these issues.[18] Tobin's argument has been called the *grease effect*: a certain amount of inflation benefits economic performance in labour and product markets by allowing greater wage and price flexibility in the face of presumed downward rigidities. Maintaining the metaphor of the economy as a geared machine, we use the term 'sand' to refer to Friedman's characterization of the effects of inflation: in this view, inflation interferes with the transmission of price signals, disrupting the smooth operation of the economy. We now turn to a discussion of each of these effects, which we summarize in Table 7.2.

7.5.1 How inflation impairs economic efficiency: sand

The case for an optimal inflation level of zero (or lower) is based on the belief that the grease effects of inflation are small while the sand effects are big. In a world where wage and price rigidities cause asynchronous adjustment to shocks, inflation results in inefficient idiosyncratic price or wage adjustments and relative price distortions. This is the Friedman *sand*.[19] The rigidities involved are symmetrical in that the costs of equal-sized upward or downward movements (in response to a change in the aggregate price level) are the same.

There are several reasons why firms might adjust differently to the same nominal shock, causing relative prices to vary. These include forecast disagreement, due to uncertainty;[20] menu costs that result in episodic rather than continuous adjustment (such as negotiating, advertising and design costs);[21] factors that make it difficult for consumers to comparison-shop (such as hard-to-gauge quality differences);[22] and contractual obligations such as collective bargaining agreements or leases. Asynchronous adjustment means that aggregate price movements are not transmitted instantaneously or

Table 7.2 Comparisons of inflation's grease and sand effects in the labour market

	Sand	Grease
Rigidities	Symmetric: menu costs; forecast disagreement (uncertainty); timing rigidities	Asymmetric: downward nominal rigidity (money illusion, nominal contracts, fairness)
Shocks	Nominal, aggregate price movements	Real relative wage/price shocks
Inflation's welfare effects	Disruptive – distorts relative wages and prices, misdirecting resources	Beneficial – speeds wage and price adjustments, redirecting resources quickly
Limits on welfare effects	None or cost of indexation	Size of real shocks
Price or wage differentials affected	Intra-market (within products/ skill-groups, across companies)	Inter-market (across products, inputs or skill groups)

uniformly, so market participants confuse adjustment lags or errors with real shocks. This misunderstanding has two effects. First, and most obviously, pricing errors result in resource misallocations. The second effect arises because people anticipate that resource misallocations will occur. The potential for arbitrary relative price movements creates risk that will lead firms to purchase insurance of various forms. For example, a firm may choose to build a smaller factory in order to guard against the possibility of variable profit streams. There is evidence that higher levels of inflation are associated with increases in this type of risk.[23]

We can conclude that asynchronous price and wage adjustment in the presence of inflation creates two complementary problems. First, it makes it difficult for policy makers to measure inflation accurately and expeditiously; second, it misleads economic agents. In the labour market, unintended wage changes alter firms' wages relative to the market and can produce unnecessary layoffs, workforce dissatisfaction, or resignations. These wage changes can also impose additional costs by compelling firms to improve information or increase the frequency of adjustments.

The conclusion at this point is clear. If all shocks were nominal and rigidities were symmetrical, then the optimal level of inflation would be zero. In this environment, any positive level of inflation would disrupt price signals, and the higher the inflation the worse the disruptions. These costs could be mitigated by indexing or by policies aimed at improving forecasts; but these solutions themselves would redirect resources from more productive uses. Deflation would have identical effects, leading us to conclude that price stability would be most efficient.[24]

7.5.2   How inflation overcomes rigidities: grease

If shocks are predominantly real, creating a desire for firms and workers to adjust relative prices and wages, and nominal wages and prices are more rigid downward than upward, then the conclusion changes dramatically. In this case, prices, and therefore resource allocations, adjust slowly and inefficiently to shocks, and small amounts of inflation provide the means for the necessary adjustment by reducing real product prices or workers' real pay without a cut in the corresponding nominal prices or wages. This is the world of Tobin's grease effect.

There are a number of potential explanations for the presence of downward nominal rigidity. Chief among them is the view that social or bureaucratic norms discourage firms from either cutting the wages of good workers who face unfavourable market conditions or lowering the prices of goods with falling demand. This is the view originally expressed by Keynes, who thought that wage stickiness reflected social notions of fairness. Alternative explanations are based on the existence of long-term, nominal contracts (for example, for debt or wages) or money illusion (that is, workers resist cuts in their dollar earnings more than they resist equivalent rises in the prices of what they buy).[25] The common view is that nominal prices are less downwardly rigid than nominal wages because products themselves are not influenced by social norms, nominal contracts or money illusion. However, the producers and distributors that set prices may well be subject to the same influences that affect firms setting wages since product sales represent income to them, just as wages do to workers. As a result, downward nominal rigidity may extend beyond the labour market and, to at least some degree, be present everywhere.

Clearly, in an environment where cutting nominal prices or wages is difficult, inflation can play an important role. Following a real shock, firms may be faced with a need to reduce relative prices or wages. If they are unable to do so, firms will eventually respond by reducing production and employment. Inflation relaxes downward wage and price rigidity because, as other prices rise, firms can effectively lower real wages or prices without imposing nominal cuts. With this grease in place, wage and price signals travel more rapidly through the economy, reducing layoffs, providing more accurate incentives to workers choosing careers, and raising overall production while reducing its volatility. Thus, inflation reduces cyclical unemployment. An important corollary discussed in Tobin (1972) and further formalized by Akerlof, Dickens and Perry (1996) extends this reasoning to economies facing continual small 'background' disturbances. In that case, inflation reduces steady-state unemployment.

Returning to the question at hand, we find again that the conclusion is clear. In an economy with downward wage and price rigidity and real shocks, the output-maximizing (unemployment-minimizing) level of inflation will be somewhere above zero. It follows directly that the larger and more prevalent the shocks, the more beneficial is inflation, and the higher the inflation rate should be to maximize output. By the same token, however, inflation beyond that needed to accommodate these adjustments adds no further benefits.

Surely, however, the conclusions reached by looking exclusively at either the sand-induced costs or the grease-generated benefits of inflation are unrealistic. We expect that the two effects can and do coexist.[26] That is, economies can sustain both real and nominal shocks and have varying degrees of downward nominal rigidities. The optimal inflation goal depends on the balance between the nature of the shocks and rigidities in the economy. Thus, it is crucial that policy makers be aware of the empirical relevance of each effect to their current situation.

7.5.3 Empirical research on rigidities and inflation

How can we detect the relative size of the grease and sand effects in order to help fix an inflation goal? The task seems difficult because both raise the variance of relative price changes. But, as shown in Table 7.2, two key differences are potentially observable. Increased price-change variability from sand's disruptions should be symmetrical and should occur even among the prices of otherwise identical goods. Thus, sand can be measured in studies of inflation's impact on intra-market (same-good) price changes. By contrast, the grease effect of inflation allows an economy to adjust to shocks that alter the relative wages (prices) of different skill-groups (products). Hence, the grease effect is observed when inflation raises the dispersion of intermarket (that is, between skill-group or product) wage and price changes. In addition, its impact may be asymmetrical, as it facilitates downward movements more than upward ones.

Measures of sand effects

The sand phenomenon has been studied in both the goods and the labour market. Sand studies gauge inflation's costs by measuring its tendency to raise intra-market prices unevenly.

Recent research on price adjustment variability uses narrow product micro data. Some studies consider price changes in a single class of goods, generally in low-inflation countries;[27] others have explored price changes for a wide variety of goods in high-inflation environments.[28] Examining price changes in the United States during high inflation years (1980–82), Reinsdorf (1994) finds that the variation in prices within a single product category rose when inflation fell unexpectedly. The variation of price changes across product categories, however, was positively correlated with inflation, and so it fell. More support for the sand hypothesis comes from the observed tendency of inflation to raise forecast price-change dispersion.[29] On balance, these studies agree that price change and forecast variability rise with inflation, as predicted by the sand story.

Research using aggregate data on wages, however, seems to contradict the sand hypothesis. A number of studies find that the dispersion of wage changes fell as inflation rose in the late 1970s and early 1980s.[30] This seemingly contradictory result is attributed to the inflation-induced introduction of indexation, which makes wage changes more uniform across industries by tying them more closely to price inflation. In addition, since the datasets used in these studies leave investigators with a limited ability to control for business cycle variation in worker skill levels and workforce composition, the authors may be confusing intra-market sand effects with inter-market grease effects.

The work of Groshen and Schweitzer (1996, 1999) re-examines this question using transaction-level data over a long time period. Their data set includes detailed information on occupation, and so allows for the type of controls that effectively replicate the comparability across goods (intra-market variability) sought in the product-price literature. They find that, over the full observed range of 1 to 14 per cent, more inflation raises the variation of intramarket wage changes. Moreover, further increases in inflation appear to increase costs without bound.

Measures of grease effects

The original research investigating the existence of asymmetrical nominal rigidities examined aggregate time-series data. Testing whether aggregate real wages are pro-cyclical (as implied by downward wage rigidity), investigators have concluded that wages (in the United States) are probably rigid downward.[31] However, these results have been challenged by theorists who have provided models with identical predictions but fully flexible wages and prices.[32]

The response to this challenge has been to examine micro-level data and employ tests that are immune to the earlier criticisms. This research programme provides more direct evidence in support of the hypothesis that wages are rigid downward. Some studies examine this question using household survey data and find evidence of substantial nominal wage cuts, which they take to contradict the existence of downward rigidity. But the data are plagued by various measurement errors that may drive the conclusions.[33] More important, even if we take the evidence of these studies at face value, the existence of nominal wage cuts is neither necessary nor sufficient to demonstrate that wages are fully flexible, since we do not know how many wage cuts are needed to ensure efficient allocation of resources. Furthermore, the results obtained from looking at household survey data are contradicted by evidence obtained from interviewing employers and workers on the job. Employers report that their wage-setting policies have important downward rigidities built into them, and workers seem to agree. The studies all provide evidence that wages are downwardly rigid. Nominal wages are not cut unless there is explicit provision for flexible wages (such as through piece-rate or incentive systems) or the firm is under demonstrable financial distress.

More recent microeconometric studies, based on longitudinal datasets that allow investigators to control more fully for mismeasurement, detect evidence of downward rigidity in spikes at zero and the implied positive skewness of wage changes.[34] While spikes at zero or positive skewness of wage changes are neither necessary nor sufficient signs of downward rigidity, they add to the evidence in support of the grease hypothesis.[35]

Studies of firm-level micro-data take another approach to looking for downward nominal rigidities. Transaction-level data on wages paid by firms reflect employers' strategies to avoid downward wage rigidity and are not influenced by worker misreporting. Using such data, Groshen and Schweitzer (1996, 1999) find evidence consistent with downward wage rigidity and determine that the effect of inflation on wage changes is exhausted at inflation levels of about 7 to 9 per cent – consistent with the notion that grease benefits are bounded. Using employer data from the

Employment Cost Index, Lebow, Saks and Wilson (1999) find additional evidence of downward wage rigidity.

In sum, while each individual micro or macro test may not be fully convincing on its own, taken together the tests provide diverse and fairly consistent evidence that wages are rigid downward.

Net effects of inflation

Viewed from the policy maker's perspective, the question is whether inflation at low rates is in net terms beneficial or detrimental. How low should the monetary authority aim? At zero or something above that? Sand effects are clearly disruptive and rise with inflation, certainly wiping out the net benefits from the grease effects when inflation is high. But how do they compare at low rates? Beyond the impact on the price system's resource allocation mechanism, inflation can interact with the tax system, reducing the steady-state level of output. Furthermore, downward rigidity at the micro level may not translate into higher unemployment when inflation is low, implying that the grease effects themselves could be small. This would occur if the elasticity of demand for labour with respect to these distortions was low because employers honour implicit insurance-style contracts and absorb fluctuations of costs into profits. Finally, inflation may have different effects in different environments.

Thus far (the simulations in Akerlof, Dickens and Perry (1996) to the contrary), scant evidence of sizeable macro effects exists. Indeed, both Card and Hyslop (1996) and Lebow, Saks and Wilson (1999) find little net unemployment impact from downward wage rigidity under normal conditions. Groshen and Schweitzer (1999) estimate that at the point where benefits are maximized, for CPI inflation around 2.5 per cent, the net impact of inflation (grease minus sand) is positive but an order magnitude smaller than the gross benefits. They go on to estimate that raising inflation from zero to 4 per cent would lower unemployment by less than 0.1 of a percentage point. By contrast the net impact of raising inflation from 4 per cent to 8 per cent would add as much as 0.3 of a percentage point to the unemployment rate. Overall, these results suggest that there is little labour market justification for raising real inflation beyond about 1 per cent (using an unbiased measure of consumer prices) or raising CPI inflation beyond 2 per cent.

However, variation in general productivity growth rates will affect the choice of an optimal inflation target and the resulting monetary policy. The Groshen and Schweitzer results are based on the labour productivity growth experience during the sample period under study – that is, the 40-year period from 1957 to 1996. To understand why productivity growth matters for inflation targets, note that productivity growth has effects that are similar to those of inflation – it injects grease and sand into wage setting. Because general productivity growth is even harder to gauge than inflation, it adds confusion (sand) in wage-setting. Moreover, because productivity growth raises average nominal wages, it adds grease to the labour market in the same way as inflation does.[36] Thus, even though productivity growth appears as if it might be unrelated to monetary policy instruments or targets, it affects optimal inflation goals. In particular, as productivity growth strengthens, the amount of grease and sand in the labour market becomes greater, reducing the benefit of adding more inflation. Conversely, as productivity growth declines, the amount of grease and sand in the labour market also falls, increasing the net benefit of inflation.

As a final consideration, policy makers should bear in mind that studies of rigidities and shocks are necessarily specific to a particular economy and time. None of the papers cited provides comparative measures, even though, as we note above, differences in institutions and exposure to shocks may have important implications for policy. In particular, the studies implicitly treat shocks and rigidities as unchanged during the course of the study. While this assumption is entirely appropriate for the short run, it is certainly not true over the long run. Using short-run numbers to derive long-run estimates could bias results. Indeed, of particular policy interest are endogenous responses, such as the posited tendency for downward wage rigidity to relax in the face of persistent low inflation, lowering the grease benefits of raising inflation, and lowering the optimal rate of inflation. Similarly (but with contrasting implications), if low positive inflation rates were maintained with little uncertainty, some sand costs of inflation might dissipate as firms (no longer subject to stop-and-go shocks) were better able to plan for the future and distinguish between real and nominal shocks. Thus, if monetary policy has been the primary source of unpredictable nominal shocks, then to the extent that the policy itself can become more stable, a higher target level of inflation is justified.

A related caveat is that international differences have not yet been studied rigorously. All cited studies of the grease effect rely on US data. Hence, for other economies, the results must be considered suggestive, rather than definitive. By contrast, sand effects have been studied in a wide spectrum of countries, albeit individually rather than comparatively. Ultimately, given their importance for the conduct of sound monetary policy, comparative and longitudinal studies of shocks and rigidities will constitute an important area for further research.

7.6 Policy implications

What do we learn from our analysis? We began by noting that economies face both real and nominal shocks and that prices and wages are rigid in response. These rigidities may be asymmetrical (with decreases in prices and wages being more difficult to bring about than increases) or not. The implications for monetary policy are manifold.

First, we have described how theoretical models help guide us in developing measures of trend inflation. These models suggest that trimmed means are more efficient, timely measures of core inflation than the more commonly used indexes that systematically exclude certain components such as food and energy. Second, the research we have surveyed suggests that inflation is very difficult to control accurately, especially at short horizons. This explains why, in designing policy schemes, many central banks and governments have reconsidered the wisdom of adopting narrow inflation-targeting bands. Staying inside the bands may turn out to be an impossible task, damaging the credibility of the authorities that put the policy in place.

Finally, we address the question of how to select an optimal inflation target. We note that when prices adjust infrequently, inflation distorts price signals and leads to resource misallocations. But if wages and prices are rigid downward, some amount of inflation facilitates adjustment to real shocks. Recent research has produced measures of the relative size of these costs and benefits in an economy that suggest that inflation targets between 0 and 2 per cent (bias-adjusted) are optimal.

But there are two important caveats. First, to the extent that labour productivity is increasing on average, there is room to reduce the inflation target. Second, the optimal rate of inflation depends on the mixture of shocks and rigidities to which an economy is subject. Furthermore, a long-run steady rate of low inflation implies fewer nominal shocks and puts pressure on price and wage setters to reduce rigidities. Thus, the optimal rate of inflation may differ somewhat across countries and evolve over time.

Notes

1. Examples include Bolivia, Israel and Argentina.
2. The literature on the connection between inflation and growth is large and growing, with less than robust results. Andrés and Hernando (1999) is a recent example.
3. Mishkin (1999) provides a discussion of the recent international experience of various monetary regimes.
4. In their Table 1, Morandé and Schmidt-Hebbel (1999) also identify 34 countries that target primarily money and 36 that target exchange rates.
5. The political economy of monetary policy and the importance of credibility have been widely studied. The research in this area has focused on the importance of a structure in which the central bank is independent of the elected officials in the government. See, for example, Alesina and Summers (1993). With independence of operation comes the need for central banks to be accountable for their performance, usually relative to an inflation objective set by statute or agreement with other branches of government.

6. Throughout this section, we assume that the measurement of core inflation is a statistical problem associated with the estimation of long-run trend movements in prices. Other conceptions are surely possible, all of which would be based on structural economic models. For example, Quah and Vahey (1995), motivated by the concept of a long-run vertical Phillips curve, define core inflation to be the component of measured inflation that has no impact on real output in the long run. We shy away from such definitions, as they are highly parametric and therefore unlikely to provide timely evidence on structural breaks in the inflation process.

7. The literature on core inflation, now vast, began with Eckstein (1981). Wynne (1999) provides a recent survey.

8. A second difficulty is the presence of bias in price indexes. For recent work in this area, see the survey in Shapiro and Wilcox (1996).

9. See Bryan and Cecchetti (1994) and Bryan, Cecchetti and Wiggins (1997).

10. Cecchetti (1986) provides evidence of the rigidities in the price of one such good: magazines.

11. If there is significant downward rigidity, and a significant number of firms would wish to lower their prices, the problem is even more severe. The process of complete adjustment can be very slow, and in the meantime the aggregate price level can move significantly, making real shocks look like nominal ones.

12. Wynne (1999) discusses several other alternatives, including weighting individual prices by the inverse of their estimated variance: a procedure first suggested by Dow (1994).

13. Bryan, Cecchetti and Wiggins (1997) discuss a statistical rationale for computing trimmed means. They note that a trimmed mean can be a more efficient, reduced-variance estimator of the true mean when the underlying distribution of the data has fat tails. Inflation data generally exhibit very high kurtosis relative to the normal distribution, suggesting that trimmed means can provide improvements.

14. Cecchetti (1998a) discusses this problem in detail, noting that the objective is usually expressed in terms of a trade-off between output and inflation variability.

15. See Cecchetti (1995).

16. See Sims (1992) for a discussion of the problem that has come to be known as the *price puzzle*.

17. These estimates are derived from Cecchetti (1996).

18. The bulk of this work centres on the labour market, as this is presumed to be the source of some of the most important nominal rigidities in the economy. Researchers tend to focus on wages for a number of reasons. First, labour accounts for two-thirds of production costs. Second casual observation suggests that nominal wages are stickier than goods prices. Finally, wage data are more readily available than price data, making analysis easier.

19. Friedman has also argued that since the marginal cost of producing money is (nearly) zero, the social welfare maximizing level of real balances sets the nominal interest rate to zero. Optimal inflation is then minus the equilibrium real rate of interest. In our view, such a target would be extremely dangerous, since it dramatically increases the probability that policy errors force the real interest rate up unintentionally, since nominal interest rates will not be able to fall. For a further discussion on this point, see Cecchetti (1998b).

20. See Friedman (1977).

21. See Sheshinski and Weiss (1977).

22. Stigler and Kindahl (1970) and Reinsdorf (1994).
23. See Vining and Elwertowski (1976) and Huizinga (1993).
24. Some economists contend that the tax distortions created by inflation reduce the level of output permanently, and from this conclude that the optimal level of inflation is negative. The relationship between inflation and public finance is beyond the narrow scope of our essay.
25. See Haley (1990) for a review of the theories underlying downward wage rigidity.
26. Groshen and Schweitzer (1996) demonstrate this formally in a model of the labour market.
27. See Cecchetti (1986) for magazines' cover prices.
28. See Lach and Tsiddon (1992).
29. See Ball and Cecchetti (1990).
30. See the survey in Groshen and Schweitzer (1997) for discussion of these findings.
31. For a more detailed review of the results referred to in this section, see the survey in Groshen and Schweitzer (1997).
32. The earliest example we know of is Lucas and Rapping (1969).
33. Of particular concern is the fact that the data collection methods rely on individuals' memories and third-party reporting, creating large systematic errors in the measures of wage change.
34. See Akerlof, Dickens and Perry (1996) and Card and Hyslop (1996).
35. A spike is not sufficient because rounding in the data makes occurrences of zero-dollar wage changes common. It is not necessary since truncated workers may be laid off. As far as skewness is concerned, downward rigidities may also affect the upper tail of the distribution if employers limit other workers' salary increases to subsidize constrained workers.
36. From the firm's point of view, productivity growth lowers overall unit labour costs. This increases overall demand for workers, leading to generally higher wages. However, at any time some workers are facing reduced demand for their skills relative to others. The higher is productivity growth, the wider is the scope for employers of those workers to reduce unit labour costs without lowering their nominal wages.

References

Akerlof, G.A., Dickens, W.T. and Perry, G.L. (1996) 'The Macroeconomics of Low Inflation', *Brookings Papers on Economic Activity*, no. 1, pp. 1–74.

Alesina, A., and Summers, L.H. (1993) 'Central Bank Independence and Macroeconomic Performance', *Journal of Money, Credit, and Banking*, vol. 25, no. 2, pp. 151–62.

Álvarez, L.J., and de los Llanos Matea, M. (1999) 'Underlying Inflation in Spain', in *Measures of Underlying Inflation and their Role in the Conduct of Monetary Policy*, Proceedings of the Workshop of Central Bank Model Builders (Basle: Bank for International Settlements), June.

Andrés, J. and Hernando, I. (1999) 'Does Inflation Harm Economic Growth? Evidence from the OECD', in Feldstein, M.S. (ed.) *The Costs and Benefits of Price Stability* (Chicago: University of Chicago Press for NBER).

Ball, L. and Cecchetti, S.G. (1990) 'Inflation and Uncertainty at Short and Long Horizons', *Brookings Papers on Economic Activity*, no. 1, pp. 215–45.

Bryan, M.F. and Cecchetti, S.G. (1994) 'Measuring Core Inflation', in Mankiw, N.G. (ed.) *Monetary Policy* (Chicago: University of Chicago Press for NBER).

Bryan, M.F., Cecchetti, S.G. and Wiggins, R.L., II (1997) 'Efficient Inflation Estimation', NBER Working Paper no. 6183.

Card, D. and Hyslop, D. (1996) 'Does Inflation "Grease" the Wheels of the Labor Market?', NBER Working Paper no. 5538.

Cecchetti, S.G. (1986) 'The Frequency of Price Adjustment: A Study of the Newsstand Prices of Magazines', *Journal of Econometrics*, vol. 31, no. 3, pp. 255–74.

Cecchetti, S.G. (1995) 'Inflation Indicators and Inflation Policy', in Bernanke, B. and Rotemberg, J. (eds) *NBER Macroeconomics Annual* (Cambridge, MASS: MIT Press).

Cecchetti, S.G. (1996) 'Practical Issues in Monetary Policy Targeting', *Federal Reserve Bank of Cleveland Economic Review*, vol. 32, no. 1, pp. 2–15.

Cecchetti, S.G. (1998a) 'Policy Rules and Targets: Framing the Central Banker's Problem', *Federal Reserve Bank of New York Economic Policy Review*, vol. 4, no. 2, pp. 1–14.

Cecchetti, S.G. (1998b) 'Understanding the Great Depression: Lessons for Current Policy', in Wheeler, M. (ed.) *The Economics of the Great Depression* (Kalamazoo, MICH.: W.E. Upjohn Institute for Employment Research), pp. 171–94.

Dow, J.P., Jr (1994) 'Measuring Inflation Using Multiple Price Indexes', unpublished paper, Department of Economics, University of California at Riverside.

Eckstein, O. (1981) *Core Inflation* (Englewood Cliffs, NJ: Prentice-Hall).

Friedman, M. (1977) Nobel Lecture: 'Inflation and Unemployment', *Journal of Political Economy*, vol. 85, no. 3, pp. 451–72.

Groshen, E.L. and Schweitzer, M. (1996) 'The Effects of Inflation on Wage Adjustments in Firm-Level Data: Grease or Sand?', Federal Reserve Bank of New York Staff Report no. 9 (revised March 2000).

Groshen, E.L. and Schweitzer, M. (1997) 'Macro- and Microeconomic Consequences of Wage Rigidity', in Lewin, D., Mitchell, D and Zaidi, M. (eds) *Handbook of Human Resource Management* (Greenwich, CONN: JAI Press).

Groshen, E.L. and Schweitzer, M. (1999) 'Identifying Inflation's Grease and Sand Effects in the Labor Market', in Feldstein, M.S. (ed.) *The Costs and Benefits of Price Stability*, (Chicago: University of Chicago Press for NBER) pp. 273–308.

Groshen E.L. and Schweitzer, M. (1999) 'Firm's Wage Adjustments: A Break from the Past?' *Federal Reserve Bank of St Louis Review*, vol. 81 (3), pp. 93–111.

Haley, J. (1990) 'Theoretical Foundations for Sticky Wages', *Journal of Economic Surveys*, vol. 4, no. 2, pp. 115–55.

Huizinga, J. (1993) 'Inflation Uncertainty, Relative Price Uncertainty, and Investment in U.S. Manufacturing', *Journal of Money, Credit and Banking*, vol. 25, no. 3, part 2, pp. 521–49.

Lach, S. and Tsiddon, D. (1992) 'The Behavior of Prices and Inflation: An Empirical Analysis of Disaggregated Price Data', *Journal of Political Economy*, vol. 100, no. 2, pp. 349–89.

Lebow, D.E., Saks, R.E. and Wilson B.A. (1999) 'Downward Nominal Wage Rigidity: Evidence from the Employment Cost Index', Board of Governors of the Federal Reserve System, Finance and Economics Discussion Paper no. 99–32.

Lucas, R.E., Jr, and Rapping, L.A. (1969) 'Real Wages, Employment, and the Price Level', *Journal of Political Economy*, vol. 77, no. 5, pp. 721–54.

Mishkin, F.S. (1999) 'International Experience with Monetary Policy Rules', *Journal of Monetary Economics*, vol. 43, no. 3, pp. 579–606.

Morandé, F. and Schmidt-Hebbel, K. (1999) 'The Scope for Inflation Targeting in Emerging Market Economics', unpublished paper, Central Bank of Chile.

Quah, D. and Vahey, S.P. (1995) 'Measuring Core Inflation', *Economic Journal*, vol. 105, pp. 1130–44.

Reinsdorf, M. (1994) 'New Evidence on the Relation between Inflation and Price Dispersion', *American Economic Review*, vol. 84, no.3, pp. 720–31.

Shapiro, M.D., and Wilcox, D.W. (1996) 'Bias in the Consumer Price Index', in Bernanke, B. and Rotemberg, J. (eds) *NBER Macroeconomics Annual, 1996* (Cambridge, MASS: MIT Press).

Sheshinski, E. and Weiss, Y. (1977) 'Inflation and Costs of Price Adjustment', *Review of Economic Studies*, vol. 44, no. 2, pp. 287–303.

Sims, C.A. (1992) 'Interpreting the Macroeconomic Time Series Facts: The Effects of Monetary Policy', *European Economic Review*, vol. 36, no. 4, pp. 975–1000.

Stigler, G.J., and Kindahl, J.K. (1970) 'The Behavior of Industrial Prices', NBER General Series no. 90 (New York: Columbia University Press).

Tobin, J. (1972) 'Inflation and Unemployment', *American Economic Review*, vol. 62, no. 1, pp. 1–18.

Vining, D.R. and Elwertowski, T.C. (1976) 'The Relationship Between Relative Prices and the General Price Level', *American Economic Review*, vol. 66, no. 4, pp. 699–708.

Wynne, M.A. (1999) 'Core Inflation: A Review of Some Conceptual Issues', in *Measures of Underlying Inflation and Their Role in the Conduct of Monetary Policy*. Proceedings of the Workshop of Central Bank Model Builders (Basic: Bank for International Settlements).

Part III
Wages and Employment

8

Single-Peaked versus Diversified Capitalism: The Relation between Economic Institutions and Outcomes

Richard Freeman
Harvard University and National Bureau of Economic Research, USA,
and London School of Economics, UK

Capitalist countries have historically had quite different labour market institutions and social policies: high mobility and flexibility in the United States, lifetime employment and steep seniority profiles in Japan, corporatism in the Nordic countries and Austria, apprenticeships in Germany, the SMIC minimum wage and legislated work-time in France. Throughout the EU, 'social partners' negotiate arrangements, whereas in North America the term has no meaning. The labour market is potentially the most idiosyncratic market in advanced capitalism.

Do these different institutions and policies affect economic outcomes in important ways? Can institutional differences persist in a global economy or does competitiveness require that labour institutions converge to a single dominant form? Has the current lead candidate for peak economy, the US, found the right institutions for the twenty-first century?

To answer these questions, I develop criteria for determining whether there is a single optimum configuration of capitalist institutions; review evidence on how institutions affect outcomes; and assess the view that the US has found the dominant institutions for the new century. The evidence shows that:

1. The institutional organization of the labour market has identifiable large effects on distribution, but modest hard-to-uncover effects on efficiency.
2. Institutional diversity is increasing among advanced countries, as measured by the percentage of workers covered by collective bargaining.

These findings are more consonant with the view that capitalism is sufficiently robust for national differences in labour institutions to persist than with the view that all economies must converge to a single institutional structure. In the space of labour institutions, 'You can have it your way', albeit within some bounds.

The case that the US has found the institutions for peak economy status rests on its 1990s full employment experience, which arguably counterbalances its high level of economic inequality compared to other advanced capitalist countries. If the US maintains full employment *ad infinitum* while other advanced countries fail to reduce joblessness, even critics of US economic performance will have to accord it peak economy status. But if the post-Second World War experience is any guide to the future, the US will run into employment problems at some point in the 2000–10 period, which will give an economic model based on full employment grave problems, while other countries will modify their institutions in ways that will produce new candidates for lead economy.

8.1   The problem: single-peaked vs diverse capitalism

Every decade or so political or ideological groups, policy analysts, and, yes, even staid economists, herald the coming of a new Ideal Economic Model – a distinct set of institutions and organizations that has maximal fitness in the period's economic environment. In the Great Depression many thought centralized planning or government ownership of enterprises or government spending were needed for full employment. In the 1960s some saw French indicative planning as a viable compromise between centralization and decentralization. The 1970s oil shocks brought Nordic corporatist economic arrangements to the fore of discussion (Bruno and Sachs, 1985). In the 1980s the 900-pound gorilla on the economic scene was Japan – recall Ezra Vogel's *Japan as Number One*, or the best-selling business book, *A Book of Five Rings* by the fourteenth-century Samurai warrior Miyamoto Musashi. The early Clinton Administration looked jealously at parts of Germany's Rhineland Model and sought to expand the US welfare state through mandated health insurance. Major business-school thinkers and journalists bemoaned Anglo-Saxon short-termism in capital markets and saw virtue in the Japanese or German banking and ownership patterns (Porter (1990); Hutton (1996)). At the turn of the twenty-first century it is the turn of the United States to be the envy of the world, with many observers seeing US-style capitalist institutions as the lodestar for the next century.

Behind the claim that any particular set of institutions represents *the* ideal form of economic arrangements is the notion that institutions and outcomes are related by a 'landscape function' with a particular shape. Figure 8.1 depicts institutional arrangements along the X axis and a general measure of economic performance on the Y axis. Since there is a multiplicity of arrangements across economies – different modes of wage-setting, systems for training workers, patterns of ownership of enterprises, and so on – X should be viewed as a vector of arrangements, aggregated in some fashion. Similarly, since economic performance involves distribution, efficiency and growth, Y should also be viewed as a vector of outcomes, aggregated in some fashion. Landscape A represents the case of a dominant institutional structure. It has a single peak at N* (nirvana), with better efficiency and distribution than other institutional settings. Every move in the direction of N* raises well-being. Thus, it behoves all economies to adopt those institutions as quickly as they can: they are Pareto-efficient improvements over other arrangements. This landscape represents the economic world that adherents of any 'Ideal Capitalist Model' envisage. But A is not the only plausible institution-outcome landscape. Landscape B has multiple local peaks separated by valleys. To move from one peak to a higher one or to the global optimum requires that the economy descend from the local peak before it ascends the higher one. The fall in outcomes during the transition is an investment in change. If local optima are not much below nearby higher peaks or the global maximum it may not be worthwhile to make the investment, even though a country would choose the superior institutions *de novo*. *The expense of changing institutions permits variety in the institutional environment.*

Figure 8.1 Economic institutions – outcome landscapes

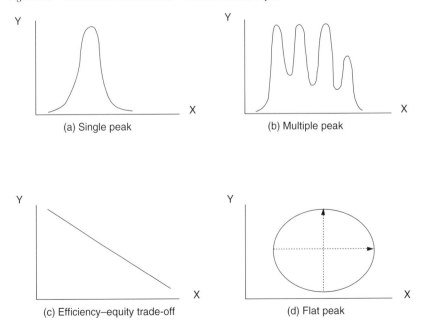

(a) Single peak

(b) Multiple peak

(c) Efficiency–equity trade-off

(d) Flat peak

Landscapes C and D decompose the Y outcome into two outcomes, efficiency and equity, and map them in a two-dimensional diagram. Both outcomes implicitly depend on institutional arrangements. In landscape C more equitable distributions and higher output are inversely related, possibly because the supply of effort or other resources needed for efficient production is highly responsive to the incentives that are the flip side of inequality. You either pay your local billionaire huge sums or see GDP fall. This is a world dominated by the efficiency–equity trade-off. If the trade-off is sufficiently steep, inequality may even raise the incomes of the poor so that more unequal distributions are desirable in terms of the income of all citizens.[1]

Landscape D shows a redistributionists' ideal: a flat efficiency-distribution outcome around the peak. Within the broad range of the circle in the figure, institutions can affect distribution and output independently of one another. The lack of an equity–efficiency trade-off opens the door to political battles, class warfare, and so on. Tax your local billionaire and give the money to the poor and GDP barely changes. Alternatively, give huge tax breaks to the billionaire or to special interest groups and again GDP barely changes. Even here, however, well-being falls sharply at some distance from the peak – outside the circle in Figure 8.1. The failure of the centrally planned economies, the retrogression of capitalist economies that fail to protect life and property (as in sub-Saharan Africa) and the problems of the former Soviet Union countries in moving to a successful market economy shows that the institution-landscape space is not a flat tabula rasa.

Which landscape best fits advanced economies as we move into the twenty-first century?

8.1.1 Criteria for deciding among landscapes

Belief in a single-peaked outcome function is deeply ingrained in economics. Models of optimizing behaviour assume convex functions so that first derivatives yield maximizing conditions and second derivatives have the appropriate sign. Globalization and information age technology have led more and more observers on both the right and left to adopt a single-peaked view of the world. The right argues for labour market flexibility or a smaller welfare state as the only way to attain efficiency in the modern world. The left worries about social dumping and the race to the bottom, out of fear that firms or countries with low labour standards will drive out those with high standards.

But there are arguments for diversified capitalism as well. Comparative advantage is a story of diversity; of gains that come from differing from one's neighbour, not from apeing him. If for historic reasons Germany can operate a tripartite social partnership and apprenticeship training model of capitalism better than the US while the US is more adept at a high mobility/market wage setting model, Germany will do better with its system and the US will do better with its system. Germany will outproduce the US in sectors that use skilled blue-collar labour and the US will outproduce Germany in low wage services and high-tech industries; and the two countries will trade the products in which they have an advantage. More broadly, game theory has shown that interactive decision-making creates many potential outcomes, with institutional rules or norms determining equilibrium (Kreps (1990)). Finally, there is the Coasian world where side payments guarantee an efficient outcome whatever the property rights.

What kind of evidence might help us to decide whether the modern institution-outcome landscape best fits a single-peak or a diversified capitalism?

Table 8.1 lists five factors that differentiate single peak landscapes from others.

The first criterion is that in a single-peak world we can identify a best-performing economy. Ideally, the peak economy should do better than other economies on all outcomes. More pragmatically, I will require that it does better on some weighted average of outcomes, recognizing that different folk may weigh outcomes differently.[2] If the US produces 20 per cent more than France, and has higher income for 95 per cent of the population but lower income for the bottom 5 per cent, I would accord the US the superior economic performance, though John Rawls presumably would not. Disagreement about the weights attached to multiple outcomes creates the possibility that two societies will see the 'same' institution-landscape space differently. *Differences in values across countries permits variety in institutions.* Greater preference by Europeans than by Americans for economic security and equality arguably produces different valuations of landscapes that allows each to prefer their own institutions.[3]

The second criterion is that the single-peak economy maintain its leading position over some extended period. In a world where landscapes change, the peak must be more than the flavour of the month in outcome space. Development economists usually make an even stronger demand. Since less-developed countries have low levels of income per capita, the outcome

Table 8.1 Evidence from single-peak landscape

Characteristics of N^*
1 N^* dominates on several outcomes; has higher well-being in much of distribution
2 N^* dominates over extended period
Landscape near N^*
3 Near neighbours are also high so that movements toward N raise well-being
Landscape away from N^*
4 Big jumps cost little so that radical reforms raise well-being
5 Institutions converge (or outcomes diverge)

---

that matters is the long-term growth of per capita income. But among advanced economies candidates for peak economy invariably have high levels of income per capita, which may give other economies a catch-up edge in growth, so I will again be more moderate. If the US produces 20 per cent more than Germany, and loses just a bit of that edge over time, I would still count the US as a candidate peak.

The third criterion relates to the convexity of the landscape space around the peak. Economies close to the peak economy should have outcomes close to those of the peak economy. Movements from the base of the mountain towards N* should raise well-being reasonably smoothly. This criterion will be important in assessing the candidacy of the US for peak since it requires that the US's closest neighbour in terms of economic institutions, Canada, perform about as well as the US.

The fourth criterion distinguishes single-peaked landscapes by how large or radical changes towards the peak from far-away values affect outcomes. In a single-peaked landscape, large-scale changes towards the peak economy raise output since other economies have no local peak from which to descend. In a multiple-peaked landscape, by contrast, changes in institutions may produce long periods of loss even in the direction of more efficient institutions.

The final criterion relates to the dynamics of institutional change. If the single peak hypothesis is correct, and if economies move towards better outcomes, there should be a long-term convergence in institutions towards the peak arrangements. The greater the advantage of the peak economy, the more rapidly will non-peak countries seek to mimic it. If, contrarily, institutions diverge in a single-peak landscape, countries moving away from the peak will be going in the wrong direction and should suffer accordingly.

My five criteria for the existence of a peak economy are, of course, nothing more than a verbal translation of the mathematical conditions for the existence of a global optimum, together with a dynamic process that makes the optimum an attractor in institution-outcome space, drawing more and more economies into its basin of attraction.

8.1.2   Measures of institutions

Thus far, I have been vague about what lies on the institution axis in Figure 8.1. The reason is that there is no generally accepted taxonomy for classifying economies into different institutional groupings, nor even a scale to measure the distance between particular institutional settings. Are Japanese institutions closer to those of the US or of Germany? Are UK institutions more American or European? We have no measures of institutions to answer these questions definitively. Lacking well-defined taxonomies or metrics of distance between institutions, researchers generally proceed in an *ad hoc* inductive manner, classifying institutions on the basis of observation and the differences relevant to policy discussion.

Most analyses of *institutions across country lines* treat the degree of centralization or coordination of wage-setting as the key determinant of outcomes. In part this is because the oil price shock of the 1970s produced different inflation and unemployment outcomes in corporatist and liberal countries, motivating much early work on the economic effects of labour institutions (Crouch (1985); Tarantelli (1986); Bruno and Sachs (1985)). Developments in the 1980s, however, suggested that corporatist and liberal economies did about as well in important outcomes, with the worst performances in countries that had institutions with industry-level bargaining (Calmfors and Driffill (1988); Freeman (1988)). Mancur Olson's arguments that an all-encompassing union would internalize the externalities of inflationary wage increases and favour non-inflationary wage agreements provide a theoretic base for this perspective. Studies in the late 1990s were largely concerned with the unemployment experience of countries in the 1990s and on the economic effects of labour market flexibility on unemployment. The OECD categorized countries by legislated restrictions on labour market behaviour, such as employment protection laws, modes of training, unemployment benefit systems, or active labour market policies (see OECD (1997a; 1997b; 1999)). The OECD *Jobs Study* came down strongly in favour of deregulation and active labour market policies, but succeeding analyses by the OECD have highlighted the weakness of that case. Countries with very different regulatory practices and policies have surprisingly similar outcomes.

It requires considerable expertise to determine accurately institutional arrangements for countries. You cannot visit Belgium on Tuesday and Denmark on Wednesday, or do a quick internet search for relevant statistics, code up the available indicators, and come up with a valid measure of how institutions operate in those countries, any more than you can understand how gorilla bands or ant colonies or dolphins behave by checking them out on your holiday. One problem is that readily available measures of institutions may not reflect actual practice. Spain and France have low levels of unionization, but collective bargaining determines wages throughout much of their economies. Published data show that Ukraine is the most highly unionized country in the world, with China not far behind (Visser (1998)), but unions surely do not affect those economies as they do the French or Spanish economies, much less the Nordic ones. Most EU countries mandate works councils at workplaces, but councils vary differently across countries (Rogers and Streeck (1995)). The EU has enacted more protective labour legislation than the US, but the US has pioneered affirmative action programmes and Americans regularly sue firms in court over alleged violations of labour rights. Does a works council and the EU Social Charter affect firms and market outcomes more than a court suit in the US? Many economists think the answer is yes, but there is no definitive study evaluating the costs/benefits of the two different forms of regulating market outcomes.

Turning to the developing world, many LDCs have extensive labour codes, often copied from advanced countries, and many subscribe to ILO conventions, but all too often the countries do not implement the codes or conventions. Does a country which adopts more ILO conventions or which has more interventionist laws intervene more in the labour market than other countries? It depends on whether the state enforces these regulations, which vary across countries and over time. Most LDCs have minimum wages, but during the 1980s debt crisis these wages proved to be sawdust rather than hardwood; and the existence of a sizeable informal sector may make them inapplicable to many employees in any case. In poorer countries, where public employees may be low paid, bribery offers a way around regulations to a greater extent than in a wealthier country.

Finally, there is the 'systems' problem that the same institution or policy may affect outcomes differently depending on other economic institutions. In the 1980s Germany and Spain enacted laws that encouraged temporary contracts. In Spain the proportion of workers covered by these contracts increased massively, until about one-third of employees worked under such contracts. In Germany there was virtually no growth of temporary contracts. German apprenticeships and works councils preserved permanent jobs. Prior to the Thatcher labour law reforms, British unions were the troglodytes of the advanced world, often dominated by small groups of leftists seeking industrial strife. In the 1990s British unions are arguably the most progressive in Europe, seeking partnerships with management and endorsing 'value added' unionism. The same institution, the trade union, adopted different policies in a different legal and economic environment. To treat UK unions as the same in the 1990s as in the 1970s would be a gross misreading of British labour institutions (Metcalf 1994)).

Analysts have struggled with the systems problem. Some add interactive terms in regressions of outcomes on particular institutions so that, say, employment protection legislation has a different effect on outcomes in countries with centralized wage-setting than on countries with decentralized wage-setting (OECD (1998)). Comparative social scientists have taken the interactive model to its natural limits by treating each configuration of institutions as a separate case in a Boolean 'qualitative comparative analysis' (Ragin (1987)). Other analysts have developed typologies that measure observed institutions along a uni-dimensional scale by summing different indicators. Another approach is to let measures of institutions 'speak for themselves' through cluster analysis or factor analysis or some related technique, which hopefully creates comprehensible groupings.

An alternative to categorizing institutions inductively is to take the competitive economic model as a point of departure and to measure the distance of actual economies from this polar case. The Heritage Foundation has developed an Economic Freedom index that rates economies by the degree to which the market is free to determine prices/wages and other outcomes. While one may object to the particulars of the Heritage rating scheme,[4] this 'thermometer' approach has the virtue of placing economies on a scale with a conceptual zero-point tied to economic theory. In a similar vein the World Economic Forum offers its 'competitiveness' ranking of economies. Both scales suffer from the problem that the teams that put together the scales cannot possibly know how things 'really' work in individual countries and may be overly sensitive to *au courant* views of what is the most successful set of institutional arrangements or policies.

8.1.3 Firm-level institutions

Studies of how the organization and policies of firms affect outcomes treat two issues: the allocation of decision-making powers within firms, and the effects of incentive pay on performance. Institutions that allocate decision-making range widely from employee involvement committees to works councils to diverse quality-of-work programmes. Incentive programmes range from group or individual bonuses to stock options to pension funds that invest in company shares, employee stock ownership plans, and stock options. In both cases, there is a serious problem in measuring the true policy or mode of operation. Top management may institute an open-door personnel policy, a formal affirmative action programme, quality-of-work and employee involvement committees, and so forth, but local managers may implement these policies in very different ways or they may ignore them almost completely. Anyone who has visited company headquarters and then gone to local branches or plants realizes that there is a huge gap between what the top of the company says and what actually happens on the ground floor. The result is that measures of the policies are subject to considerable error. Assessing the impact of incentive pay schemes is similar: many firms have multiple policies, whose net effect on workers' incomes is difficult to determine. The same firm may have an employee stock-ownership programme (ESOP), a bonus gain-share plan, a stock option plan, and a 401K retirement plan where the employee can put some funds into company stock. The fastest growing form of incentive pay in the US, all-employee stock option plans, poses a particularly stark problem for economic analysis. In the standard model of rational behaviour, options cannot motivate ordinary employees whose daily actions are too far removed and too modest to affect stock prices. Options may make lots of sense for the chief executive of Starbucks or Asda, but why should the firm also give them to clerks in local stores? One possibility is that the firm seeks to use this form of pay to help establish a particular type of corporate culture, rather than to create individual incentives.

The absence of a general mensuration for institutions at the national or firm level creates a problem for institutional economics. Measurement is, after all, the *sine qua non* of any scientific endeavour. The parallel problem in the biological sciences, defining species and varieties within a specie, has generated much attention and detailed work, with taxonomists battling over alternative ways to classify organisms: by function or evolutionary history (Ridley (1986)). But at the end of the day biologists can use differences in DNA to measure distances in familial heritage. We have no such instructional code to measure the relations among economic institutions.

From this litany of the weaknesses and problems in institutional analysis, one might expect that we have learned little from work in the area. To the contrary, empirical research has yielded important findings which seem robust to alternative measures of institutions and to varied empirical strategies for estimating the effect of institutions on outcomes.

8.2 Institutions, distribution and efficiency

Many studies have examined the links between institutions and the distribution of wages or incomes or the efficiency of production. There are cross-section contrasts of workers/firms covered by diverse institutional arrangements (unionized or non-unionized; employee-owned or not; profit-sharing or not); longitudinal contrasts of the same person/firm operating under different wage-setting systems; comparisons of countries with different institutions; and before/after analyses of changes in national policies. The vast bulk of studies support two empirical generalizations:

1. That *wage-setting institutions reduce inequality in economic rewards.*
2. That *most wage-setting and rule-making institutions have modest effects on efficiency outcomes.*

8.2.1 Distribution

Table 8.2 summarizes the results of studies that link the dispersion of wages to labour market institutions. The vast bulk of this literature takes the wages of individuals as the basic data and compares the distribution of wages among workers covered by the collective bargaining with the distribution of wages among nominally equivalent workers not covered by collective bargaining. Some studies use regression analyses to identify demographic equivalence; others contrast the pay of narrowly defined groups, such as production workers in union and non-union plants in a given industry. Regression analyses invariably find that years of schooling, age and other determinants of earnings have a smaller effect on union workers than on non-union workers in *ln* earnings equations, and that unions have a larger impact on the wages of low-paid and low-skilled workers than on the wages of high-paid and high-skilled workers. This explains part of the lower dispersion of wages among unionists. But most of the union/non-union difference shows up in the residuals from regressions: among workers of the same gender, age, years of schooling, occupation and industry, union employees have lower dispersion of pay than non-union employees. Consistent with this, studies that contrast pay structures within establishments show markedly smaller within-establishment dispersion of wages in organized establishments than in non-organized establishments. By its very nature, collective bargaining reduces the prevalence of merit pay and other forms of discretionary wage-setting within firms, lowering dispersion among similar workers, while it increases the pay of union members relative to management, professional workers and the like.

The sceptic may question the interpretation of these types of comparisons as reflecting the causal effects of unionism on outcomes. Perhaps the

Table 8.2   The effect of institutional wage-setting on distribution

---

Cross-sectional studies

Comparisons of individuals within countries: unions/collective bargaining (CB) reduces dispersion of wages; increases diffusion of pensions, health care coverage to lower paid
(Freeman (1982, 1992), Card (1992), Metcalf (1994), DiNardo, Fortin and Lemieux (1995)).

Comparisons of individuals within firms: Lower dispersion of pay; white collar/blue collar differences in pay in organized firms; no reduction in pay differentials ESOPs, but reduction in wealth inequality
(Freeman (1982), DiNardo, Hallock and Pischke (1997), Kardas, Scharf and Keogh (1998)).

Comparisons of countries: Countries with extensive collective bargaining; particularly centralized bargaining have lower dispersion; smaller industrial differentials in pay
(Freeman (1992), Blau and Kahn (1996), (OECD (1997b, ch. 3)).

Longitudinal

Comparisons of persons changing jobs: Unions/CB reduce dispersion of pay
(Freeman (1984), Card (1992)).

Comparisons of countries changing policies: Countries that shift from centralized to decentralized wage-setting have dispersion rise, and conversely for those that shift from decentralized to centralized bargaining
(Hibbs and Locking (1991), (Bell and Pitt (1995), Edin and Holmlund (1995), Erickson and Ichino (1995), Davis and Henrekson (1999), Manacorda (2001)).

Source: See References; some of these articles review additional studies and provide more references.

real reason for the difference in pay distributions is that workers in organized establishments differ from those in non-organized establishments in unobservable characteristics. Perhaps the market responds to union wage structures by reallocating workers so as to establish similar wage structures measured in efficiency units between organized and unorganized sectors. Assume, for instance, that collective bargaining initially compresses wages by raising pay for the least skilled and lowering pay for the most skilled. The narrower structure of wages in the organized sector will give firms an incentive to shun the least-skilled workers and search for the most skilled, but will give the most-skilled workers an incentive to look for jobs in the non-union sector. The interplay of demand and supply will produce an equilibrium in which both the most-skilled workers and the least-skilled workers will work non-union, while union firms will hire workers with middling skills. In this case, the fact that the dispersion of wages in the union sector is lower than in the non-union sector does not imply that unions reduce the distribution of pay in the entire economy. Instead, the compression of pay in the union sector would have reallocated workers by level of skill across sectors. Moreover, since virtually all studies of union/non-union pay differentials show higher pay for organized workers than for non-organized workers with comparable measured skills, the selectivity or reallocation interpretation of the difference between union and non-union pay structures implies that on average union workers should be more skilled than non-union workers.

One way to test this argument is to examine the wages of the same worker under union and non-union conditions. In its strongest form, the argument is that workers with the same characteristics earn the same pay in both sectors, so that differences in wages across sectors are due to the selectivity of workers into the sectors. Longitudinal studies show that the wages of workers who move from union to non-union jobs (and conversely) differ by less than do the wages of union and non-union workers in cross-section studies, implying some selectivity of workers into the sectors. But the estimated impact of unionism is still sizeable and much of the reduction appears due to the greater impact of measurement error in union status on the longitudinal estimates than on cross-sectional estimates on union wage effects. But, as argued above, to explain the smaller dispersion of pay among unionists requires a more subtle form of selectivity than union sectors attracting better workers: it requires that union firms have fewer workers at both the low end of the skill distribution but also at the high end of the distribution. A direct test of the potential effect of selectivity on the distribution of wages is to compare the pay of workers who leave union jobs with that of workers who move into union jobs. Such comparisons show that dispersion rises among those who leave union jobs (implying that their wages were truly compressed under unionism) while dispersion falls among those who enter union jobs (with the same implication).

There are other possible ways for firms to offset union negotiated wage increases so that the lower dispersion of pay among union workers could be spurious. Firms could reduce other costly benefits, such as private pensions or expenditures on health, and so on, for low-skilled union workers. This does not happen: the share of compensation going to supplementary benefits is higher under collective bargaining, and unions increase these benefits more for low-wage workers than for higher-paid workers. Rather than creating compensating differentials in benefits, collective bargaining diffuses fringe benefits such as private pension plans and privately provided medical insurance programmes to lower-paid and blue-collar workers, reducing the inequality in provision of these benefits. In countries with centralized wage-setting, wages drift – changes in wages in excess of collectively bargained settlements – at the plant or among individual workers could also undo the effect of centralized narrowing of the wage distribution. Wages drift does, indeed, operate in this way, but the effects of drift do not come close to undoing the narrowing of wages negotiated in central agreements (Hibbs and Locking (1991)).

The estimated effect of unionization on the dispersion of pay between unionized and non-unionized workers within a country does not, however, answer the question of what collective bargaining does to the distribution of pay economy-wide. This is because comparisons of the pay structure in the unionized and non-unionized sectors of the economy do not allow for the effects of pay-setting in one sector on the other. Consider, for example, what happens if non-union employers mimic union wage patterns to avoid unionization. In this case, the within-country difference in dispersion of pay between sectors will understate the effect of unionism on the overall wage distribution. Alternatively, non-union firms might increase their skill premium to keep their more skilled workers from organizing, so that the within-country difference in dispersion of pay across sectors might exaggerate the effect of unionism on the dispersion of pay.

The way to deal with this problem is to compare the dispersion of pay across countries with more or less extensive collective bargaining. Such comparisons show that centralized bargaining is associated with lower dispersion of pay in a country and with a much narrower structure of wages by industry than in countries with decentralized bargaining. Workers with nominally the same skills are more likely to be paid similar wages in different industries in Sweden or the Netherlands than in the US. One interpretation is that collective bargaining moves industrial wage structures closer to the competitive ideal than does market wage-setting. In decentralized markets, prosperous firms distribute economic rents to workers while firms that do poorly squeeze the pay of workers with high mobility costs. In markets with centralized wage-setting, all firms pay the same wage. Studies also show, however, that occupational differentials are smaller in countries with collective bargaining than in other countries, with potentially deleterious effects on investments in skill.

To illustrate the degree to which institutions affect the distribution of wages, Figure 8.2 shows the dispersion of wages of nominally comparable persons in highly-unionized Sweden and in the largely non-union USA. The figure records the ratio of pay in selected percentiles of the earnings distribution for persons of Swedish ancestry, defined as those with both parents of Swedish descent, in both countries.[5] When Anders Bjorkland and I first planned this tabulation, we expected that the Americans of Swedish parentage would have a more compressed earnings distribution than other Americans, probably somewhere between US and Swedish levels of inequality. After all, the Swedes in the US were persons with similar genetic and family background as the Swedes in Sweden, whereas all Americans included persons of more diverse backgrounds. Instead, we obtained the results in the exhibit: levels of inequality for Americans of Swedish descent nearly as large as those of all Americans, and nowhere near the levels of inequality in Sweden. By contrast, immigrants to Sweden, including non-Nordic immigrants who come from diverse places, have Swedish-level inequality. It is the wage-setting institutions, not ethnic background, that produces widely different distributions of incomes across countries.

Finally, if wage-setting institutions are critical determinants of the distribution of earnings in a country, changes in those institutions should be associated with changes in the distribution of pay. This is the case. The introduction of centralized bargaining in Sweden in the 1960s was accompanied by a substantial decline in the dispersion of wages and a reduction in the premium to education. The withdrawal of Swedish employers from centralized bargaining in 1983 was followed by a gradual rise in dispersion of pay across and within industries and a rise in the premium to education. Italian experience with the Scala Mobile tells the same story: a huge reduction in inequality during the period when the Scala Mobile determined wages, followed by an increase in inequality with the end of this centralized system of wage-setting (Manacorda (2001)). In the US the fall in union density from the 1970s through the 1990s explains about one-fifth of the rise in the dispersion of wages, while in the UK the fall in density also contributed to the rise in inequality in that country.

In sum, diverse forms of non-experimental evidence show that the primary wage-setting institution in modern capitalism, collective bargaining, reduces the dispersion of pay. Indeed, the inequality-reducing effect of institutional wage-setting is a more ubiquitous feature of unionism than is the widely studied effect of unions in raising the wages of members, as it is found even in countries where unions have little impact on members' pay

Figure 8.2 Evidence from single-peak landscape. Institutions determine districtions (earnings of males, 1989-91)

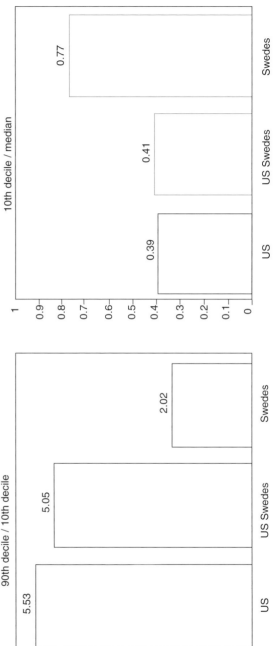

Source: Bjorklund and Freeman (1997).

relative to non-members because collective bargaining covers the vast bulk of the workforce.[6]

8.2.2 Efficiency

At the firm level

In contrast to the near-ubiquitous finding that institutional wage-setting significantly affects the distribution of pay, the evidence that labour market institutions have substantial effects on economic efficiency is frail (see Table 8.3). Analyses of firms that operate with different institutional forms shows that these forms have modest impacts on productivity. Studies of minimum wages (Card and Krueger (1995)), of employment protection legislation (OECD (1999)) and of diverse other social protection programmes (Abraham and Houseman (1994)) find little or no impact of these institutional interventions on economic efficiency. This does not mean that government interventions or union wage-setting or other policies cannot cause major economic problems (add a 0 after the US minimum wage and much of the economy would close tomorrow; give a trade union monopoly power over a critical part of the economy and it may very well act irresponsibly, as the Peronista unions did in Argentina for many years). Rather, the evidence indicates that the interventions that advanced capitalist economies implement rarely approach such levels, presumably because neither the government nor the citizenry can tolerate policies that reduce efficiency greatly.

Consider first the evidence on how different company institutions affect outcomes (Table 8.3). There are four main ways in which companies seek to motivate workers financially to be more productive: through direct incentive pay; through local group incentives, often called gain-sharing; through profit-sharing at the level of the firm; and through some form of ownership of shares. In addition, many US firms have instituted employee involvement programmes of various forms (team work, TQM, quality circles) that empower workers to make decisions without any immediate financial payoff to them, beyond the benefits that a more successful firm brings to employees in general.

Basic economic principles predict that companies which reward workers with incentive pay should reap higher productivity while at the same time increasing the dispersion of pay. This is found in studies that compare time rates of pay with piece-rate modes of pay. Linking incentives and productivity tightly at the individual level with piece rates increases individual output and the dispersion of pay, implying a steep equity–efficiency trade-off. The historic decline of piece-rate modes of payment is not because individual incentives do not work, but because companies have problems measuring output and controlling worker gaming in the setting of norms to which the rates apply in a rapidly changing technological environment. Gain-sharing and other forms of sharing of improvements in costs or

Table 8.3 The effect of institutions on efficiency (nature of evidence; findings; selected references)

Firm-based comparisons

Cross-section contrasts of firms: Profit-sharing raises productivity by 3–4%; employee ownership has more modest impacts, largely in small firms (Weitzman and Kruse (1990), Kruse (1993), Kruse and Blasi (1997)).

Unionized and non-unionized firms and industries: Unionized firms more productive but not by enough to be cost-effective to firm; unionized firms do less R&D/have slower productivity growth (Freeman and Medoff (1984), Addison and Hirsch (1989), Belman (1992)).

Firms with employee involvement/modern personnel practices: Modest effects from individual programmes; need complementary practices to succeed (Levine and Tyson (1990), Mitchell, Lewin and Lawler (1990), (Ichniowski, Shaw and Prennushi (1997), Kruse and Blasi (1998)).

Government interventions

Minimum wages have at most modest dis-employment effects (Card and Krueger (1995), Neumark and Wascher (1995), OECD (1998), Bernstein, Mishel and Schmidt (1999)).

Country-based comparisons

Cross-section contrasts of bargaining regimes: 1970s evidence that centralized wage-setting gave better outcomes; 1980s evidence that most and least centralized gave better outcomes; 1990s evidence that only major effect of bargaining systems is on wage dispersion (Bruno and Sachs (1985), Calmfors and Driffil (1988), Freeman (1988), Soskice (1990), OECD (1997b)).

Cross-section contrasts of employment protection laws: Laws have no effect on unemployment or employment but raise duration of joblessness and shift unemployment to the young (Jackman, Layard and Nickell (1996), Blanchard (1998), (OECD (1999)).

Changes in country policies: Weakening of employment protection laws has no effect on economic outcomes; widening of wage dispersion at end of centralized bargaining leads to expansion of employment in sectors with high wage inequality (Abraham and Houseman (1994), OECD (1999), Davis and Henrekson (1999)).

Source: See References; some of these articles review additional studies and provide more references.

profits at the local level, where the free-rider problem is modest, should also have positive effects on productivity and this too appears to be the case. Economic analysis predicts a more ambiguous effect for general profit-sharing, since the incentive to the individual will be largely offset by the diffusion of the gain from his or her effort to the group – the $1/n$ free-rider problem – and for employee ownership when large numbers of workers are involved. The danger that workers will free ride on the efforts of others, can, however, be offset by workers monitoring other workers, or by profit-sharing/ownership creating a team-oriented participative corporate culture.

Reviewing some 20 studies of profit-sharing, Weitzman and Kruse (1990) concluded that profit-sharing raises productivity by 4 per cent; while Kruse (1993) has found that profit-sharing firms also have less variability in employment fluctuations. Studies of employee-owned firms show weaker positive impacts of ownership on productivity, with more reliable results for smaller firms than for larger firms.

Finally, while some studies of employee involvement programmes find modest productivity results, others find negligible effects. Institutions that give workers a share in decision-making but not a share in the rewards of better decisions seem to be less effective in raising productivity than institutions that create financial incentives to be more productive. The most intriguing finding here, however, is that a firm that introduces a single advanced human resource practice – say job rotation – gains little or nothing from this policy unless it also implements an entire package of complementary policies, such as training, gain-sharing, grievance procedures, and so on (Ichniowski, Shaw and Prennushi (1997)).

Whether unionization is associated with higher or lower productivity has been extensively examined by estimating production functions with a union variable entered along with capital and labour as an input into production. Approximately two-thirds of extant studies find that unionized plants have higher productivity than do non-union plants, though the differential does not cover the extra costs that unions bring to the enterprise. The remaining one-third of studies find that unionism is associated with lower productivity. But there is also evidence that unionized sectors invest less in research and development, which is likely to have adverse effects on long-term productivity growth. Studies of the impact of firms on productivity growth in the US find such a relation, but studies for the UK tell a more complex story: an adverse union effect on productivity during the pre-Thatcher 'bad industrial relations' period but not afterwards, when unions modernized their policies.

The bottom line is that firms that give workers pecuniary incentives and institute participative labour relations practices have modestly higher productivity than other firms, with more extensive programmes having larger effects, but none of these variants has such a productivity edge as to dominate markets. Which is presumably why they coexist with firms that use more traditional wage and personnel practices, often in different market niches.

At the macroeconomic level

Consider next how unionism, collective bargaining and diverse government interventions in labour markets affect macroeconomic efficiency. Here, analyses have gone through several phases. In the late

1970s/early1980s, many analysts argued that centralized bargaining or corporatist arrangements were superior in efficiency since, as noted earlier,
these arrangements seemed to produce a better inflation–unemployment
trade-off. In the late 1980s, analysts held that either centralized or decentralized bargaining were superior to industry-level bargaining. But with the
success of the US economy in the 1990s, many have begun to argue that
decentralized institutions like those in the US were better suited for the
new information technology and global economy. But even here there is
some unease with the generalization. In 1997 the OECD, which had
endorsed deregulation of markets in its *Jobs Study*, reported 'a negative conclusion' that collective bargaining affected macroeconomic outcomes with
one exception: 'a fairly robust relation between cross-country differences in
earnings inequality and bargaining structure' (OECD (1997b, p. 64)).

What is one to make of these changing generalizations? One interpretation is that the generalizations correctly capture the link between institutions and outcomes in a specific time period, subject to a particular world
economic environment, but do not generalize to other periods or circumstances. But if this is correct, the generalizations are nothing more than
hindsight theories, explaining historical patterns, with little predictive
power for the future.

With respect to governmental interventions, the most widely publicized
intervention in the labour market is the minimum wage. Card and Krueger
(1995) found that late 1980s/early 1990s increases in minimum wages in
some US states and in the federal minimum had no effects (or even positive
effects) on employment. Using different research designs or data, some
economists have obtained similar results while others report losses of
employment with modest elasticities of demand (around –0.10). From the
perspective of economic efficiency, all of these estimates suggest that the
minimum wage at the level enacted in the US has no substantial economic
cost. A zero elasticity of demand implies that the only thing the minimum
wage does is redistribute earnings. An elasticity of –0.10 implies a minus-
cule efficiency loss using standard Harberger welfare triangles.

Many governments intervene on the employment side of the market
with employment protection legislation that gives some property rights to
jobs to workers rather than to management. Others such as the US or UK
have little such protection and rely largely on employment at will.
Economic theory in the form of the Coase theorem says that employment
protection legislation should not affect efficiency, as long as transactions
costs are small. In this case, employers and workers should reach the
efficient outcome through bargaining and side payments regardless of who
has the property right to the job. If my work is no longer valuable but I
own my job, the firm buys me out with some early retirement or severance
scheme. If the firm owns the job and my employment is no longer
efficient, it fires me. In both cases, I am gone, but in the former case, I gain

some of the rewards from the improved operation of the firm due to my departure, whereas in the latter, the firm obtains all of the gain. The implication is that employment protection legislation should have no effect on employment, but should affect the distribution of the benefits/costs of changes in employment.

Studies that contrast unemployment in countries with stronger/weaker employment protection laws generally support the predictions of theory. In its 1999 examination the OECD reported that 'simple cross country correlations suggest that EPL has little or no effect on overall unemployment' (OECD (1999, p. 50)) – and found that this negligible relation held up in multivariate regression modelling. In addition, countries that weakened their employment protection legislation in the hope of improving labour outcomes have not increased employment or reduced joblessness. Spain introduced fixed-term (temporary) contracts in the mid-1980s, but in the late 1990s Spain still had the highest rate of joblessness among advanced OECD countries. Employment protection legislation does appear, however, to affect the dynamics of joblessness: countries with strong employment protection laws have longer spells of employment and unemployment. In addition, some studies also find that it affects the composition of unemployment, lowering unemployment for adult men and raising it for other groups.[7] The bottom line is that employment protection legislation alters the distribution of work but not its volume.

8.2.3　Trends in institutional forms

The fifth criterion for a single-peaked landscape in Figure 8.1 is that economies with below-peak institutions should move towards those with peak institutions, or, if that does not occur, that countries moving away from the peak should fall further behind the peak economy. Given the lack of any accepted measure of the distance of institutions, it is difficult to test this criterion broadly. But the two most widely used measures of the extent of institutional wage-setting in a country – union density and the degree of collective bargaining coverage – have changed in a way that is inconsistent with the prediction that all forms of capitalism are converging on a single institutional pattern. Rather than converging, the extent of union-related pay-setting has *diverged* among advanced countries, without causing any parallel divergence in income per capita or productivity measures of economic efficiency.

Table 8.4 documents the divergence in the rate of union density and collective bargaining coverage across OECD countries between 1980 and 1994. It groups the country into several categories that reflect the pattern of change in the two measures of institutional influence on the labour market. Countries with high unionization/collective bargaining coverage maintained or even increased those levels over time, while countries with low levels of unionization/collective bargaining fell further behind the

Table 8.4 The increasing diversity of labour institutions, 1980–94.

	Density		Coverage	
	1980	1994	1980	1994
Declining density and coverage				
UK	50	34	70	47
US	22	16	26	18
Japan	31	24	28	21
New Zealand	56	30	67	31
Australia	48	35	88	80
Declining density and stable/rising coverage				
Austria	56	42	98	98
France	18	9	85	95
Germany	36	29	91	92
Italy	31	24	85	82
Netherlands	35	26	76	81
Portugal	61	32	70	71
Stable density/coverage				
Belgium	56	54	90	90
Canada	36	38	37	36
Denmark	76	76	69	69
Norway	57	58	75	74
Switzerland	31	27	53	50
Rising density and stable/rising coverage				
Finland	70	81	95	95
Spain	9	19	76	78
Sweden	80	91	86	89
Coef. of variation	42%	56%	29%	37%
#1/#19	8.9	10.1	3.5	5.4
# 5 relative to # 15	1.7	2.1	1.3	1.9

Source: OECD 1997, table 3.3.

OECD average. The summary measures of dispersion at the bottom of the table – coefficients of variation and ratios of high to low density or coverage – all increase.

What about the other side of this prediction – that if countries (foolishly) do not move to the peak institutional form, their economic performances will diverge? Figure 8.3 records the dispersion of GDP per capita in purchasing power parity (PPP) terms among advanced countries in selected years from 1970 to 1997. It gives the coefficient of variation in per capita incomes for all advanced OECD countries and for all of those countries less the three poorest: Ireland, Portugal and Greece.[8] Contrary to the peak economy prediction, the dispersion of GDP per capita fell over this period

Figure 8.3   The effect of institutional wage-setting on distribution. The disposal of GDP percapita in PPP terms, 1970–97

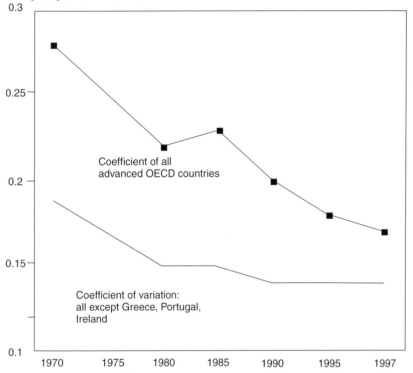

Source: Tabulated from *US Statistical Abstract 1999,* table 1363; *US Statistical Abstract 1993,* table 1392, for 1980.

for all countries and even fell, albeit modestly, for the higher-income advanced countries. The changes in GDP per capita among countries were, moreover, unrelated to institutional arrangements. Some economies with highly corporatist institutional arrangements like Sweden fell in the per capita GDP tables while others like Norway or Austria did not. Countries such as the UK or New Zealand which have adopted more US-style market arrangements did not improve their position relative to other advanced countries. All told, the convergence of GDP per capita provides little support for the notion that economic progress requires a single set of institutions.

8.3   The United States – peak economy?

Still, at the turn of the millennium, the performance of one economy holds centre stage as the potential single-peak capitalist economy: the United

States. Afficionados of American-style capitalism see a 'new economy' in the high employment, minimal inflation and rapid progress in technological frontier industries of the United States. Critics note that the US also has the highest level of inequality and child poverty among major economies, but the full employment boom of the late 1990s has lessened some of those concerns by narrowing inequalities and reducing poverty.

How well does the US fit the criterion for peak economy at the turn of the century? Columns 1–3 of Table 8.5 show that the US outperformed other advanced countries in employment and unemployment and has generated more hours worked per employed adult than other advanced countries. It is this record that makes the US the late 1990s candidate peak economy, supplanting the previous decades' candidate, Japan, which suffered rising unemployment and an extended recession. But the superior US performance in generating jobs did not carry over to some other important outcome variables, such as the level of productivity and growth or the economic well-being of lower-income citizens. In the 1990s output per hour worked in the US was roughly on a par with output per hour worked in

Table 8.5   US economic performance: peak landscape or pretender?

| | 1998 E-P | Panel A: 1990s economic performance | | | | |
| | | Quantities | | Growth rates, 1989–96 | | |
		Une	Hours	GDP/P	Comp.	Prod
US	73.5	4.5	1957	0.9%	0.1%	0.8%
UK	71.2	6.3	1737	0.1	0.5	1.8
Canada	69.0	8.3	1777	–0.1	0.5	1.0
Australia	67.2	8.0	1861	–	0.6	1.3
NZ	69.5	7.5	1825	–	–0.8	1.3
Eire	59.8	7.8	–	–	1.4	3.9
Japan	69.5	4.1	1879	1.9	0.7	2.2
Germany	64.1	9.4	1562	1.2	–0.1	1.1
France	59.4	11.7	1634	0.5	1.1	2.2
Italy	50.8	12.2	1682	1.2	0.7	2.1
Belgium	57.3	8.8	–	0.5	1.7	2.0
Neth	69.8	4.0	1365	2.1	0.4	1.6
Austria	67.2	4.7	–	1.0	1.3	2.3
Sweden	71.5	8.2	1551	0.0	0.8	2.0
Finland	64.8	11.4	1761	–	–	–
Norway	78.2	3.3	1401	2.1	1.4	2.4
Denmark	75.3	5.1	–	1.7	1.6	2.1

Source: OECD, 1999; table A for standardized unemployment rates; table B for employment-population rates; table F for hours worked, for total employment; Canada and France hours data are for 1997; Japan refers to dependent employment; Italy is 1994 dependent employment; Netherlands is 1997 dependent employment; Finland data are from labour force survey. Mishel, Bernstein and Schmitt, 1999, tables 8.4 and 8.5. Productivity and real compensation refer to the business sector, from OECD.

Table 8.5 continued

Panel B: per capita income relative to US per capita income, by position in the distribution of income 1996			
	Per capita	Lower decile	Upper decile
US	100	36	208
Switzerland	91	52	168
Norway	88	49	139
Japan	84	39	161
Denmark	81	44	126
Belgium	79	46	129
Canada	77	36	141
Austria	77	43	144
Germany	76	41	131
Netherlands	75	43	130
France	74	41	143
Australia	73	33	141
Italy	72	40	127
Sweden	69	39	110
Finland	68	39	107
UK	67	29	138
NZ	63	34	119

Source: Income per capita, *US Statistical Abstract, 1998*, table 1355. Income Distribution estimates based on percentile figures relative to median for household income Gottschalk and Smeeding (1997), usually 1991–2 figures.

Germany, France and some smaller EU countries (Freeman and Oostendorp (2001)). The US also did not outperform other economies in the rate of growth of GDP per capita or in the growth of productivity (columns 4 and 5 of Table 8.5 panel A), while the rate of growth of compensation was smaller than in most other countries (column 6). This would seem to suggest that productivity is not particularly sensitive to differences between US and EU institutions while wage settlements are responsive, consistent with the main theme of this essay. But there is an alternative interpretation. *The Economist* reads the comparable productivity experience of advanced OECD countries as evidence for the superiority of the American model, 'if Germany and Japan can grow as fast as America even when their incentives are blunted by an inflexible model, imagine what they might do were their economies to be set free'.[9] The not-so-subtle message, which Americans will have trouble digesting, is that Germans and Japanese would be better workers or managers than Americans if only they operated on a level playing-field with Americans.

With similar productivity per hour worked between the United States and many EU countries, the greater hours worked per adult employee and higher employment–population ratio in the US translates into a sizeable

American advantage in per capita income. Column 1 of Table 8.5 panel B shows that per capita income is on the order of 20–30 per cent higher in the United States than in other advanced countries. But this exaggerates the American edge in living standards. Greater hours worked in the market means fewer hours of leisure or of time worked at home. Since leisure is desirable, any social value function that combined leisure and goods per capita would bring EU countries closer to the United States in overall economic well-being. Moreover, given that hours worked per worker and per adult rose in the United States relative to other countries from the 1970s to the 1990s, the US advantage in living standards would seem to have eroded. But the real problem the United States has in passing the first criterion is its performance in distribution. Table 8.5 Panel B shows that the United States advantage in per capita incomes does not extend to the entire distribution of earnings. The US is no. 1 in per capita income, but no. 13 in per capita income for those in the lower decile of earnings. It is not until the 30th to 40th decile that the United States surpasses most other advanced countries in per capita income. So for the United States to meet the first criterion, we must weigh employment heavily and weigh distribution lightly in the social value function.

The second criterion for peak economic status relates to the time period in which the candidate peak economy has been in the forefront. At the time of writing (2000) the United States has had lower unemployment than the EU for roughly a decade, and lower unemployment than Japan for two years. From the 1950s to the 1980s, the rate of unemployment was higher than in countries with more institutional wage-setting, such as Germany, Sweden, Australia and Japan, among others. Measured by employment-to-population rates the US superior performance dates back to the mid-1970s. In 1973 the United States and OECD-Europe had the same employment–population rate. Since then the US rate has risen while the European rate has fallen to produce a 19-point differential in 1997! The $64,000 question is whether the United States can maintain its full employment edge. Many analysts believe that the 1990s combination of huge jobs growth with little inflation was largely a matter of luck – negative shocks to prices combined with temporary unease over job security. Others argue the opposite. While there are enough trouble-spots in the US economy to raise doubts about the sustainability of an unemployment rate of 4 to 5 per cent – the low savings rate; high consumer debt; the large trade deficit – the United States also has marked areas of strength. The US has a higher productive research and development sector, more venture capital than other countries, and a bankruptcy code that encourages risk-taking by entrepreneurs that may very well enable it to take a first mover's advantage on new technological developments and maintain its newly admirable employment record. In one sense, the United States has put all of its eggs in the full employment basket, and so far has reaped the rewards. With full employment, the United States does well enough to be a legitimate candidate for peak. Without full employment, believers in a single-peaked landscape will have to find another candidate – Ireland? (the Leprechaun model), the Netherlands? (the Polder model), or maybe even France? (the Asterix Model!).

Criterion 3 for the single-peak landscape requires that near neighbours to the proposed peak economy also do relatively well in outcome space. Even without a formal distance measure, most analysts will accept that Canada is the US's closest neighbour institutionally as well as geographically. For many years Canada and the US stood together at the top of the per capita GDP tables. In 1990 Canada stood third in the GDP per capita league tables, below Switzerland and the US, but sufficiently above EU countries to support the notion that North American institutions generated higher average living standards than those in other advanced countries. But the 1990s were a period of economic trouble for Canada. In 1997, following a decade of economic decline/stagnation Canada had fallen in the league tables to 7th position – the largest fall this side of the Swedish Third Way. The main reason for this fall was a drop in employment per capita – precisely the outcome on which the US did so well. One interpretation of the disparate performances of the US and Canada is that Canada has just not gone far enough towards the US model, but this explanation has trouble accounting for Canada's strong performance until the 1990s. An alternative interpretation is that the institutions-outcome landscape does not fit the single-peak paradigm. Rather the landscape is more jagged, subject to shocks having little to do with institutions, so that countries with similar institutions can do quite differently in any given time period.

The fourth criterion for a single-peak landscape is that economies making radical changes towards the peak economy should improve their outcomes. In the European Union, the UK is generally viewed as the economy most similar to the US, and the reforms enacted by the Thatcher, Major and Blair governments have brought the UK even closer to the American model. Has this improved the position of the UK in the league per capita income tables? No. In 1980 the UK was 16th in the league tables; in 1997 it was 18th.[10] Outside Europe, the economy which has undertaken the most radical reforms is New Zealand. New Zealand deregulated much of its labour market, freed its central bank from political control, and introduced a variety of free trade measures. It 'out-Thatchered Mrs T'. With what result? In 1996 New Zealand ranked last in per capita income with an income per capita some 20 per cent below that of its natural pair, Australia. In 1980 New Zealand was also last among the countries, with an income per capita 11 per cent below that of Australia.

It is possible that extenuating circumstances explain the failure of radical reform to produce the expected outcomes. Perhaps the UK would have fallen in the per capita output tables without the reforms. It was falling in per capita income compared to France and Germany from the 1950s through the 1970s. New Zealand may have had such serious problems prior to its reforms that without them it would have fallen more than 20 per cent below Australia. Perhaps, but once more a simpler explanation is that the single-peak landscape vision of capitalism is wrong.

In short, the safest reading of the past several decades is that there is no single-peak set of capitalist institutions, and that performances vary for many reasons rather than that the lead economy in any period has found the ideal institutional arrangements.

8.4 Conclusion

To return to the three questions that motivated this paper.

Do idiosyncratic labour market institutions or policies affect economic outcomes in important ways? My answer is yes, that the institutions associated with collective bargaining and other forms of institutional wage-setting substantially reduce the dispersion of earnings. They are not the mere crowing of Cantillon's cock, who imagines he raises the sun every morning with his cock-a-doodle-doo. But institutions have much weaker and uncertain effects on efficiency outcomes. At the company level, profit-sharing, employee ownership and other forms of devolving decision-making have modest effects on productivity. At the country level, many institutional interventions have barely discernible impacts on the allocation of resources. That economists can barely detect any impact of minimum wages on employment or of employment protection legislation on unemployment, or of collective bargaining on any outcome besides the distribution of earnings suggests that the null hypothesis should be that institutions have 'negligible effects' on national efficiency, at least within the experience of the advanced countries.

Why might institutions have a greater effect on distribution than on efficiency?

One possible explanation is that the relevant elasticities of response are small, at least within the time periods considered, with much of distributional differences among countries attributable to different allocations of economic rent. There is nothing in the logic of market economics that tells us that any particular response parameter is likely to be large or small, or that rents which do not motivate behaviour are common or uncommon. In a world of small elasticities/large rents, you can alter distributions without greatly affecting the supply of resources.

The Coase Theorem offers a somewhat different explanation. It is not that elasticities of response are intrinsically small, but that, given any distribution or redistribution of property rights/initial incomes, the parties will make side-payments or other bargains to attain the maximum outcome possible. Two societies with very different institutional arrangements will, barring large transactions cost, be able to reach the same efficient outcome. This line of thinking suggests further that only efficient institutional interventions or redistributions will survive in market economies. The unions and governments who intervene to reduce inequalities will take into account the potential loss of output from such interventions and choose those that cause the least harm to efficiency. If you set minimum wages, you set them relatively modestly so that they do not reduce employment noticeably. If you err and push for interventions that will harm efficiency, the potential losers from the intervention will oppose your initiative. The more inefficient the intervention, the greater the number of losers or the amount of potential loss, and thus the greater will be the opposition. The full Coase Theorem result may not apply, but the most prevalent institutional interventions are likely to be those that most efficiently redistribute incomes.

Can institutional differences persist in the modern global economy or does competitiveness require that labour institutions converge to a single dominant form? My answer is that institutional differences can persist. They can persist rather than converge to a single institutional form for three reasons: first, because changing institutions can be expensive, so that maintaining less than ideal arrangements may be better than investing in reform; second, because societies with differing values will value multi-dimensional outcomes differently and thus choose different arrangements; and third, because different institutions can attain similar outcomes through different Coase-type bargaining arrangements to reach efficiency.

Has the current leading candidate for peak economy, the United States, found the right institutions for the twenty-first century? My answer is no. It is safer to think of the United States as one of many well-performing economies in a multi-peaked landscape than as the only economy that really knows what it is about. On the basis of current information, the United States passes just one of the five criteria for being the peak economy, this being its admirable employment record. A few more years of full employment in the United States, accompanied by reductions in poverty, would lead me to happily revise this judgement. The problem with assessing institution–outcome landscapes is that even a correct reading of the current situation may fail to provide much guidance about the future. But here analysts of institutions are no more blind seers than any other economists.

Notes

1. Some may prefer to categorize a case like this as fitting landscape A with distribution measured in absolute rather than relative income terms. This would limit the trade-off to situations in which total output rises but some specified groups – presumably the poor – lose in absolute terms.
2. Empirical studies of macro-performance of economies often take a weighted average route: computing statistics such as misery indices (unemployment plus inflation), though usually without explicit counting of distributional outcomes.

3. These preference differences presumably result from past history through path-dependent changes in preferences or experiences about different outcomes and aversion to risk. I am not assuming any innate differences in preferences here.

4. There is no quantitative documentation for why it scales some countries higher or lower in particular areas, so that the scaling is a largely subjective one.

5. Note that the Swedes in the US are not immigrants, which rules out any differences in the dispersion of earnings due to the selectivity of immigrants, though some of the parents of the American-born Swedes might be immigrants.

6. Going beyond collective bargaining, some companies in the US have employee stock-ownership programmes (ESOP), which place company shares into retirement funds for workers, for which the firm receives certain tax advantages. These programmes reduce the dispersion of pension wealth among workers but do not change the dispersion of pay among workers, indicating that ESOPs (and by extension other specific programmes) have localized effects in the area on which they focus, rather than being an indicator of how the firm treats labour in general (Kardas *et al.* (1998)).

7. The effects of the legislation on the dynamics and composition of employment may have consequences for efficiency, creating a worse matching of employees with firms and concentrating joblessness on the young whose greater mobility may reduce the pain of unemployment. Whether these net out to be a positive or negative impact on efficiency is not clear.

8. I have excluded Luxembourg and Iceland from the calculations as well, as being too small.

9. 10 April, p. 20.

10. But perhaps the UK was not radical enough. Margaret Thatcher's reforms never touched the National Health Service, barely dented the ratio of tax revenues to GDP, and left macroeconomic monetary policy in the hands of the government rather than the Bank of England.

References

Abraham, K.G. and Houseman, S.N. (1994) 'Does Employment Protection Inhibit Labor Market Flexibility? Lessons from Germany, France and Belgium', in Blank, R.M. (ed.) *Social Protection Versus Economic Flexibility: Is There a Trade-Off?* (Chicago: University of Chicago Press for NBER).

Addison, J.T. and Hirsch, B.T. (1989) 'Union Effects on Productivity, Profits and Growth: Has the Long Run Arrived?' *Journal of Labor Economics*, vol. 7, no. 1, pp. 72–105.

Bell, B. and Pitt, M. (1995) 'Trade Union Decline and the Distribution of Wages in the UK: Evidence from Kernal Density Estimation', Nuffield College, Oxford, Discussion Paper no. 107, November.

Belman, D. (1992) 'Unions, the Quality of Labor Relations, and Firm Performance', in Mishel, L. and Voos, P. (eds) *Unions and Economic Competitiveness* (Washington, DC: Economic Policy Institute).

Bernstein, J., Mishel, L. and Schmitt, J. (1999) *The State of Working America: 1998–99* (Washington, DC: Economic Policy Institute).

Bjorklund, A. and Freeman, R. (1997) 'Generating Equality and Eliminating Poverty – The Swedish Way', in Freeman, R. Swedenborg, B. and Topel R. (eds) *The Welfare*

State in Transition: Reforming the Swedish Model (Chicago: SNS-NBER Conference volume, University of Chicago Press).

Blanchard, O. (1998) 'Thinking about Unemployment', mimeo, MIT.

Blau, F. and Kahn, L. (1996) 'International Differences in Male Wage Inequality: Institutions vs Market Forces', *Journal of Political Economy*, vol. 104, pp. 791–837.

Bruno, M. and Sachs, J. (1985) *The Economics of Worldwide Stagflation* (Cambridge, Mass.: Harvard University Press).

Calmfors, L. and Driffil, J. (1988) 'Bargaining Structure, Corporatism and Macroeconomic Performance', *Economic Policy*, vol. 6 (April).

Card, D. (1992) 'The Effect of Unions on the Distribution of Wages: Redistribution or Relabelling?' NBER Working Paper no. 4195, October.

Card, D. and Krueger, A. (1995) *Myth and Measurement: The New Economics of the Minimum Wage* (Princeton, NJ: Princeton University Press).

Crouch, C. (1985) 'Conditions for Trade Union Wage Restraint', in Lindberg, L.N. and Maier, C.S. (eds) *The Politics of Inflation and Economic Stagnation* (Washington, DC: Brookings Institution).

Davis, S.J. and Henrekson, M. (1999) 'Wage-Setting Institutions as Industrial Policy: Swedish Experience Seen from a U.S. Perspective', paper presented at the NBER Summer Institute Labor Studies Program Session, 28 July.

DiNardo, J., Fortin, N.M. and Lemieux, T. (1995) 'Labor Market Institutions and the Distribution of Wages, 1973–1992: A Semiparametric Approach', National Bureau of Economic Research Working Paper no. 5093 (April).

DiNardo, J., Hallock, K. and Pischke, J.-S. (1997) 'Unions and Managerial Pay', National Bureau of Economic Research Working Paper no. 6318 (December).

Edin, P.-A. and Holmlund, B. (1995) 'The Swedish Wage Structure: The Rise and Fall of Solidarity Wage Policy?' in Freeman, R.B. and Katz, L.F. (eds) *Differences and Changes in Wage Structures* (Chicago: University of Chicago Press for NBER).

Erikson, C.L. and Ichino, A.C. (1995) 'Wage Differentials in Italy: Market Forces, Institutions, and Inflation', in Freeman, R.B. and Katz, L.F. (eds) *Differences and Changes in Wage Structures* (Chicago: University of Chicago Press for NBER).

Freeman, R.B. (1982) 'Union Wage Practices and Wage Dispersion Within Establishments', *Industrial and Labor Relations Review*, vol. 36, no. 1, October, pp. 3–21.

Freeman, R.B. (1984) 'Longitudinal Analysis of the Effect of Trade Unions', *Journal of Labor Economics*, vol. 2, no. 1, pp. 1–26.

Freeman, R.B. (1988) 'Labour Market Institutions and Economic Performance', *Economic Policy*, vol. 6, pp. 64–80.

Freeman, R.B. (1992) 'How Much Has De-Unionisation Contributed to the Rise in Male Earnings Inequality?', ch. 4 in Danziger, S. and Gottschalk, P. (eds) *Uneven Tides* (New York: Sage), pp. 133–63.

Freeman, R.B. (1994) *Working Under Different Rules* (New York: Russell Sage Foundation and NBER).

Freeman, R.B. (1995) 'The Limits of Wage Flexibility to Curing Unemployment', *Oxford Review of Economics Policy*, vol. ii (i).

Freeman, R.B. and Medoff, J.L. (1984) *What Do Unions Do?* (New York: Basic).

Freeman, R.B. and Oostendorp, R. (2001) 'Wages Around the World: Pay Across Occupations and Countries', in Freeman, R.B. (ed.) *Inequality in the World Today*, vol. 2 of the Proceedings of the IEA Congress Held in Buenos Aires, Argentina (Basingstoke: Palgrave) forthcoming.

Gottschalk, P. and Smeeding, T. (1997) 'Cross-national Comparisons of Earnings and Income Inequality', *Journal of Economic Literature*, vol. 35, pp. 633–86.

Hibbs, D. and Locking, H. (1991) *Wage Compression, Wage Drift, and Wage Inflation* (Stockholm: FIEF).

Hutton, W. (1996) *The State We're In* (London: Vintage).

Ichniowski, C. Shaw, K. and Prennushi, G. (1997) 'The Effects of Human Resource Management Practices on Productivity: A Study of Steel Finishing Lines', *American Economic Review*, vol. 87, no. 3, pp. 291–313.

Jackman, R., Layard, R. and Nickell, S. (1996) 'Combating Unemployment: Is Flexibility Enough?' London School of Economics, Centre for Economic Performance, Discussion Paper no. 293.

Kardas, P., Scharf, A. and Keogh, H. (1998) 'Wealth and Income Consequences of Employee Ownership: A Comparative Study from Washington State', Washington State Department of Community, Trade and Economic Development.

Kreps, D. (1990) *Game Theory and Economic Modelling* (Oxford and New York: Oxford University Press).

Kruse, D. (1993) *Profit Sharing: Does It Make a Difference? The Productivity and Stability Effects of Employee Profit-Sharing Plans* (Kalamazoo, MI: W.E. Upjohn Institute).

Kruse, D. and Blasi, J. (1997) 'Employee Ownership, Employee Attitudes, and Firm Performance' in Mitchell, D., Lewin, D. and Zaidi, M. (eds) *Handbook of Human Resource Management* (Greenwich, CT: JAI Press).

Kruse, D. and Blasi, J. (1998) 'The New Employee/Employer Relationship', prepared for the Aspen Institute's Domestic Strategy Group, July.

Levine, D. and Tyson, L. (1990) 'Participation, Productivity, and the Firm's Environment' in Alan Blinder (ed.) *Paying for Productivity: A Look at the Evidence* (Washington, DC: Brookings Institution).

Manacorda, M. (2001) 'Changes in the Returns to Education and the Scala Mobile, Italy: 1978–1992', in Freeman, R.B. (ed.) *Inequality in the World Today*, vol. 2 of the *Proceedings of the IEA Congress Held in Buenos Aires, Argentina* (London: Macmillan) forthcoming.

Metcalf, D. (1994) 'The Transformation of British Industrial Relations? Institutions, Conduct and Outcomes 1980–1990' in Barrell, R. (ed.) *The UK Labour Market: Comparative Aspects and Institutional Developments* (Cambridge: Cambridge University Press), pp. 126–57.

Mishel, L., Bernstein, J. and Schmitt, J. (1999) *The State of Working America, 1998–99* (Ithaca and London: Cornell University Press for Economic Policy Institute).

Mitchell, D., Lewin, D. and Lawler, P. (1990) 'Alternative Pay Systems, Firm Performance, and Productivity', in Blinder, A. (ed.) *Paying for Productivity: A Look at the Evidence* (Washington, DC: Brookings Institution).

Miyamoto, M. (1974 edn) *A Book of Five Rings* (London: Allison and Busby).

Neumark, D. and Wascher, W. (1995) 'The Effect of New Jersey's Minimum Wage Increase on Fast-Food Employment: A Reevaluation Using Payroll Records, August, NBER Working Paper no. 5524.

OECD (1993) *Employment Outlook, July 1993* (Paris: OECD).

OECD (1994a) *Employment Outlook July 1994* (Paris: OECD).

OECD (1994b) *Jobs Study* (Paris: OECD).

OECD (1997a) *Employment Outlook, July 1997* (Paris: OECD).

OECD (1997b) *Jobs Study* (Paris: OECD).

OECD (1998) *Employment Outlook, July 1998* (Paris: OECD).

OECD (1999) *Employment Outlook, July 1999* (Paris: OECD).

Olson, M. (1989) *The Rise and Decline of Nations* (New York: Norton).

Porter, M. (1990) *The Competitive Advantage of Nations* (New York: Free Press).

Ragin, C. (1987) *The Comparative Method* (Berkeley, CA: University of California Press).

Ridley, M. (1986) *Evolution and Classification: The Reformation of Cladism* (London: Longman).

Rogers, J. and Streeck, W. (1995) *Works Councils: Consultation, Representation, and Cooperation in Industrial Relations* (Chicago: University of Chicago Press for NBER).

Soskice, D. (1990) 'Wage Determination: The Changing Role of Institutions in the Advanced Industrialized Countries', *Oxford Review of Economic Policy*, vol. 6, no. 4 (Winter), pp. 36–61; reprinted in Jenkinson, T. (ed.) *Readings in Macroeconomics* (Oxford: Oxford University Press, pp. 149–68).

Tarantelli, E. (1986) *Economia Politica del Lavoro* (Turin: UTET).

US Department of Commerce (1993) *Statistical Abstract of the United States 1993* (Washington, DC: US Government Printing Office).

US Department of Commerce (1999) *Statistical Abstract of the United States 1999* (Washington, DC: US Government Printing Office).

Visser, J. (1998) *Global Trends in Unionization: A Report for the ILO Task Force on Industrial Relations* (Amsterdam).

Vogel, E. (1985) *Japan As Number One: Lessons for America* (New York: Harper & Row).

Weitzman, M.L. and Kruse, D.L. (1990) 'Profit Sharing and Productivity', in Blinder, A. (ed.) *Paying for Productivity: A Look at the Evidence* (Washington, DC: Brookings Institution).

9
Institutions, Restructuring and Macroeconomic Performance

Ricardo Caballero
Massachusetts Institute of Technology and National Bureau of Economic Research, USA
and
Mohamad Hammour
DELTA, Paris, France, and Centre for Economic Policy Research, UK

'The American economy, clearly more than most, is in the grip of what … Joseph Schumpeter many years ago called "creative destruction," the continuous process by which emerging technologies push out the old. … It presupposes a continuous churning of an economy as the new displaces the old. … How is this remarkable economic machine to be maintained?. … [T]echnological advances alone will not buttress the democratic institutions, supported by a rule of law, which are so essential to our dynamic and vigorous American economy. … Institutions are needed that give free play to the inventive capacities of people and effectively promote the translation of conceptual innovations into increased output of goods and services that are the lifeblood of material progress.'

Alan Greenspan (1999)

9.1 Introduction: towards a 'structural macroeconomics'

9.1.1 Institutions and restructuring

The core mechanism that drives economic growth in modern market economies is the massive ongoing restructuring and factor reallocation by which new technologies replace the old. This process of Schumpeterian 'creative destruction' permeates major aspects of macroeconomic performance – not only long-run growth, but also economic fluctuations and the functioning of factor markets. At the microeconomic level, restructuring demands innumerable decisions to create or destroy production units. The efficiency of those decisions hinges on the existence of sound institutions that provide a proper transactional framework. Failure along this dimension can have dire macroeconomic consequences. By limiting the

171

economy's ability to tap new technological opportunities and adapt to a changing environment, institutional failure can result in dysfunctional factor markets, economic stagnation, and exposure to deep crises.

A growing body of new macroeconomic research, which is the subject of this chapter, has emphasized the macroeconomic consequences of *transactional* impediments in factor markets, and their role in the recurrent *restructuring* requirements of modern economies. This literature has added a body of analysis and evidence to the macroeconomist's toolkit that proved central in addressing many of the major macroeconomic developments of the last decade – which raised issues of little relation to the profession's continuing internal debates on nominal rigidities and the role of technology shocks. Many post-communist Eastern European economies have seen their great potential for restructuring and growth catch-up stifled by an underdeveloped legal and institutional environment. In Western Europe, the weight of labour-market regulation has caused persistently high unemployment, and deprived significant segments of the labour force from the fruits of economic growth. The recent emerging markets crisis exposed the fragility of economic systems that suffer from a lack of transparency and lax corporate governance standards. The prolonged US expansion of the 1990s reflects the powerful potential that technological progress and unshackled creative destruction can reach under an effective institutional environment.

For a prolonged period of time, postwar macroeconomics, driven by Keynesian ideas, had built a dichotomy between the analysis of long-run growth and short-run fluctuations. Long-run outcomes were essentially determined by a rather efficient supply side, and short-run outcomes by a highly problematic demand side. Supply-side notions of restructuring and creative destruction were considered essentially relevant to growth theory (as exemplified by the vintage models of Johansen (1959) and Solow (1960)), while institutions – mostly price-setting institutions – were relevant for business cycles.

This dichotomy placed severe limitations on the role restructuring and institutions could play in macroeconomic analysis. Those themes had been at the core of much pre-Keynesian thinking about aggregate economic phenomena, as exhibited in Schumpeter's work on creative destruction, and have retained their centrality in international and development economics. However, only recently did they regain strong theoretical and empirical footholds in mainstream macroeconomics. The literature on persistently high unemployment in Europe, for example, has made it clear that institutional obstacles are as relevant for long-run equilibrium as they are for the short run. To take another example, the literature that constructs and analyses high-frequency time series of gross job flows (Davis, Haltiwanger and Schuh (1996)) is essentially motivated by the importance of restructuring at high frequencies.

9.1.2 A common thread: specificity

There is a surprising degree of unity in the logic underlying analyses of institutions and restructuring. Essentially, our macroeconomic models need to be made more 'structural' in a precise sense. The first modelling instinct is to assume that decisions are fully flexible, but much of what happens in reality involves a degree of irreversibility. What we need to introduce is the notion of *specificity*. Specificity means that factors of production are not fungible. More precisely, we say that a factor is specific with respect to a production arrangement – its current production relationship with other factors using a given technology – when it would lose part of its value if used outside this arrangement. Specificity introduces *structure* into the collection of production arrangements in the economy.

Figure 9.1 depicts the context within which specificity of different types arises in factor markets. Starting with the upper box, consider an entrepreneur who needs to find external financing for a project. Given the entrepre-

Figure 9.1 Specificity relations

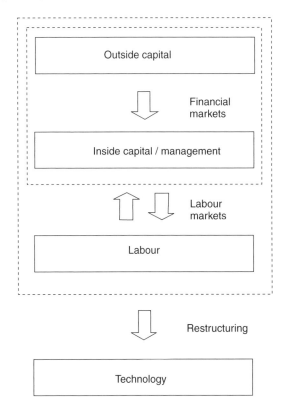

neur's informational advantage, special expertise, and effective control over the project, external capital becomes partly specific with respect to the entrepreneur once committed to the project. External financiers would lose some of their investment's value if they part with the entrepreneur. This gives rise to specificity in the *financing relationship*.

Moving down the figure, the entrepreneur next needs to hire labour. The resources he invests in searching for workers, training them, and building organizational capital are embodied in labour – both individually and as a group. Regulations may increase the specificity of capital with respect to labour. The right to strike or legal protection against dismissal, for example, effectively reduce the value of using capital outside its current labour relationships. This collection of factors gives rise to specificity in the *employment relationship*.

Finally, moving to the bottom of the figure, the entrepreneur dedicates the project's resources to producing a certain range of goods using a certain process, and therefore builds specificity with respect to a certain *technology* – understood in its broadest sense.

The project, therefore, gives rise to two types of specificity: 'relationship specificity' that characterizes financial or labour market relationships; and 'technological specificity' that characterizes production choices. Relationship specificity forms the underpinning of what *institutional arrangements* are about; technological specificity forms the underpinning of what *restructuring* is about. Most of the time, both are present simultaneously and interact in important ways.

It should be emphasized that the shift towards a more structural model has affected empirical as well as theoretical macroeconomics. We have already referred to what is perhaps the most notable empirical example of this shift: the extraordinary effort that has gone into reconstructing labour-market aggregates so as to distinguish between the gross job creation and destruction components of net employment change. This effort would be pointless if labour were fully fungible.

9.1.3 Outline

In this chapter, we attempt to describe the general principles at work in this structural type of macroeconomics, derive some of the lessons we have learned, and illustrate the usefulness of this approach with a number of applications. We do not attempt to provide a survey of the vast existing literature.

In section 9.2, we explore the function institutional arrangements play in facilitating transactions and give an overview of the macroeconomic consequences of poor institutions. As an application, we discuss the underpinnings of the European unemployment problem and the lessons that can be drawn from the phases of its evolution.

In section 9.3, we turn to the effect that the institutional environment can have on macroeconomic restructuring. In light of our framework, we revisit the question of the relationship between recessions and restructuring activity, and review the surprising evidence of reduced restructuring following recessions. We also discuss corroborating evidence from 'merger waves' in the restructuring of corporate assets.

Section 9.4 summarizes the main points of the chapter.

9.2 Institutions and macroeconomic performance

9.2.1 Why institutions?

Before we can explore the relationship between institutions and macroeconomic outcomes, we must take a step back to discuss the role institutions play in economic transactions.

Institutional arrangements are mechanisms that help address the problems that arise from the need to cooperate. Consider two factors of production that can either produce independently in an *autarkic* mode, or cooperate in a *joint-production* mode. This is illustrated in Figure 9.2. In the context of the financing relationship, our two factors are outside capital on the one hand, and inside capital or management on the other. In the context of the employment relationship, our two factors are labour and capital. Autarky for labour may correspond to producing in an informal sector where there is little need for capital, retiring from the labour force, or joining the unemployment pool. Autarky for capital may mean investment abroad, or consumption rather than saving.

Figure 9.2 Autarky and cooperation

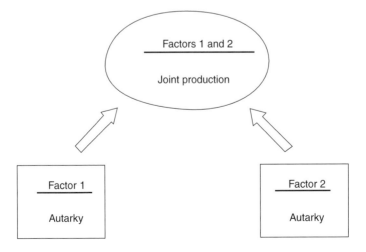

The main problem with cooperation is that it involves some irreversibility, some degree of specificity of one factor with respect to the other. This gives rise to *specific quasi-rents*. A generic account of the way such quasi-rents arise is the standard *'hold-up' problem* (Klein, Crawford and Alchian, 1978). While the terms of trade between the two factors may be competitive before they commit to joint production, they will find themselves in a bilateral monopoly situation *ex post*. The specific quasi-rents thus created become appropriable, and will have to be divided.[1]

Ideally, each factor should pre-commit to getting a share of the quasi-rents commensurate with its *ex ante* terms of trade. This arrangement would preserve the *ex ante* competitive terms of trade and guarantee transactional efficiency. But such pre-commitment is often problematic. The factor may have or acquire an informational advantage that would be tempting to exploit; its commitment may not be enforceable in court; or the contingencies that the contract in question would need to address may be hopelessly complex. The rules that govern the process by which specific rents are created and divided typically reflect, in their limitations, the problematic nature of pre-commitment, and result in less-than-efficient outcomes. We refer to those rules, be they the result of a private or a social contract, as 'institutional' arrangements.

Examples of the institutions that govern transactions in financial markets are corporate governance arrangements, financial accounting and auditing rules, debt covenants, or bankruptcy procedures. Examples of labour-market institutions are the tenure profile of wages, dismissal rules and procedures, or the regulations that govern collective action.

Institutions play two distinct functions: *efficiency* and *redistribution*. It is naïve to think that markets can generally function properly without an adequate institutional framework. In their efficiency role, the basic principle that determines institutions is that each factor ought to get out the social value of what they put in – i.e. without any externalities, their *ex ante* terms of trade. It is equally naïve to think that such institutions, being partly determined in the political arena, will not also be used as an instrument in the politics of redistribution. A poor institutional framework is the result of a combination of underdevelopment in the realm of contracting and regulations and of unduly powerful political interest groups who have tilted the institutional balance excessively in their favour.

9.2.2 Macroeconomic symptoms of poor institutions

A highly developed institutional framework that is relatively insulated from political tinkering can bring the economy close to its first-best efficient outcome. But what happens when institutions are poor? At this level of generality, it may seem that not much can be said. However, because the basic problem is common, one of unprotected specificity, a set of robust generic conclusions arises. When the hold-up problem is not resolved at the microeconomic level, it gives rise to a highly inefficient macro-economic 'solution' that is characterized by a number of symptoms (see Caballero and Hammour, 1998a).

At the level of individual interactions, a poor institutional environment *discourages cooperation* between factors of production. In equilibrium, this results in *under-employment, market-segmentation* and *technological exclusion* of the 'appropriating' factor. We explore those consequences in the context of the simple framework outlined in Figure 9.2, and illustrate them with the example of institutional failure in the labour market. More specifically, we assume that, starting from an efficient outcome, heavy regulation is introduced that gives an excessively strong advantage to labour in the employment relationship. In terms of Figure 9.2, we consider that autarky for labour corresponds to unemployment and autarky for capital corresponds to investment in the international financial marketplace.

The macroeconomic symptoms of poor institutions are multi-faceted:

(i) Reduced cooperation. The partial-equilibrium effect of poor institutions, by definition, is that one of the factors no longer gets its ex-ante terms of trade at the margin. We refer to this factor as the 'appropriated' factor, and to the other one as the 'appropriating' factor. The appropriated factor will be reluctant to enter into cooperative relationships. In our labour-market example, the introduction of heavy regulation shifts the *ex post* terms of trade from capital to labour. At the margin, capital no longer gets a return commensurate with what is obtainable in international capital markets, and becomes reluctant to invest in new job creation.

(ii) Under-employment. Naturally, in equilibrium, a factor will not agree to enter a new relationship knowing that its *ex post* terms of trade will fall short of its *ex ante* position. The free-entry condition of the appropriated factor will determine the new equilibrium, where fewer relationships are formed in the joint-production sector. The result is a misallocation of resources characterized by under-employment in joint production of the appropriating factor. In the labour market example, job creation will be insufficient and labour will be forced into an increasingly crowded unemployment pool. This weakens the outside option of labour in the employment relationship, and causes a terms-of-trade shift that helps restore equilibrium by raising the return on capital back to the level required by international markets. In this context, unemployment is an endogenous equilibrium response through which the economic system takes back from labour some of the advantage it had acquired through regulation.

(iii) The role of supply elasticities. The two factors' elasticities of supply into joint production are central determinants of the new equilibrium. This is easiest to see in a small-open-economy version of our labour market

example, where the supply elasticity of financial capital is infinite. In that case, the poor-institutions equilibrium exhibits the same return on investment as an efficient equilibrium – equal to the world interest rate. As far as new jobs are concerned, capital is not appropriable in equilibrium, and unemployment will have to be high enough to reduce labour compensation to a level compatible with this outcome. The regulatory burden backfires, and its inefficiency cost is entirely born by labour. In contrast, suppose that the appropriated factor in our example is not financial capital but land. The supply of land is fully inelastic. Land has nowhere else to run, and will have to accept the lower returns induced by regulation. In that case, the regulatory push will be much more successful, and will have much milder unemployment consequences. Generally speaking, the appropriated factor will be less appropriable in equilibrium the higher its supply elasticity is. This idea will play an important role in our discussion of the changing face of unemployment in Europe.

(iv) Market segmentation. We saw that, in partial equilibrium, poor institutions cause the appropriated factor to get less than its *ex ante* terms of trade. As a counterpart, the other factor – the 'appropriating' factor – can capture quasi-rents above its *ex ante* terms of trade. This creates a rush out of autarky, but the catch is that too few units of the appropriated factor are willing to join in production. Indeed, as we saw previously, it is the free-entry condition of the appropriated factor that determines the general-equilibrium level of joint-production activity. As a result, the limited number of joint-production opportunities for the appropriating factor will be *rationed*. The market for the appropriating factor will be segmented, with those who are successful in accessing joint-production opportunities earning rents above what they can get in autarky; and the market for the appropriated factor will clear. This rationing phenomenon is the direct result of the lack of contractual pre-commitment ability, which is the very root of institutional failure. In the labour market example, the implication is that unemployment is involuntary. Concretely, the persistence of market segmentation is due to labour's inability to pre-commit not to exploit its regulatory advantage – for example, its inability to waive its legal protection against dismissal, its right to collective action, or its right to receive a minimum wage.

(v) Technological exclusion. Institutions also affect the direction of technological development. Suppose there is a choice of joint-production technology, with different factor proportions. Which factor determines the technology to be used? It is effectively the appropriated factor that does so, because the other factor, being rationed, is in no position to impose its terms. The appropriated factor will choose a technology that reduces its

degree of specificity with respect to the other without being excessively inefficient. In the labour market example, this will typically imply a partial exclusion of labour from joint production and will translate into capital deepening. Technology choice is an escape route for capital that provides an alternative to investment abroad, and weakens the position of labour further through increased unemployment and reduced labour compensation. It also implies that under-employment in joint production is not necessarily accompanied by under-investment.

9.2.3 Application: European unemployment

As an application of the ideas presented above, we now turn to the European unemployment problem, which represents many of the macroeconomic symptoms of poor institutions. More particularly, we will concentrate on the representative case of France. The analysis in this sub-section is based on Caballero and Hammour (1998b).

Figure 9.3 summarizes three decades of French macroeconomic experience.[2] Panel (a) shows the well-known build-up of unemployment over the 1970s and 1980s. Although unemployment was rising for most of this period, its underlying nature had been changing. One can distinguish between two distinct phases. In the first phase, which lasted until the early eighties, the increase in unemployment was accompanied by brisk wage increases (panel b), a rise in the labour-share of value added (panel c), and a fall in the profit rate (panel d). Observers at the time saw a clear case of 'classical unemployment'. In the second phase, the rise in unemployment was, to the contrary, accompanied by a slowdown in wage growth and a fall in the labour share. As a consequence, the interpretation of unemployment became Keynesian. Observers started describing the situation as a 'European depression'. The problem is that the notion of a Keynesian depression did not fit well with the brisk recovery in the profit rate. Labour and capital had clearly parted company.

A highly parsimonious account of the French experience can be constructed based on the effect of an institutional push in favour of labour in face of a supply elasticity of capital that differs in the short and in the long run. The institutional push is well documented. There are indications that, until the late 1960s, labour had not shared evenly in the fruits of postwar prosperity. This caused tensions to build up, which exploded with the labour revolts of May 1968. The resulting Grenelle Accords started a process through which labour gained significantly in terms of union representation, wages, and the workweek. Similar events took place elsewhere in Europe, most notably in Italy during the Hot Autumn of 1969.

The political momentum of the late sixties' labour movement continued into the seventies. Following the oil shock of 1973, the agenda shifted to the regulatory protection of existing jobs. In France, the labour movement reached its apex following the 1981 presidential election of François

Figure 9.3   France, 1967–95

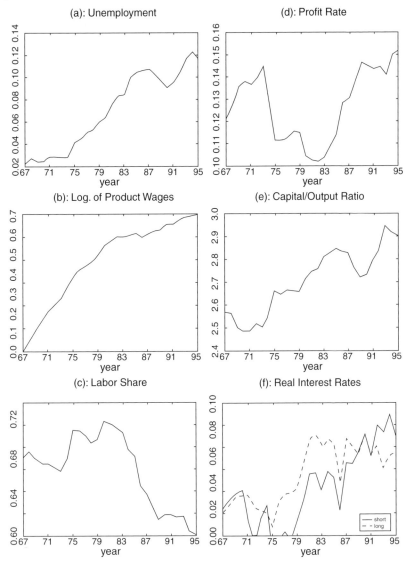

Mitterrand, when the *Programme Commun* coalition of socialists and communists came to power. Over the next two years, an array of regulations was put in place that covered wage increases, hours reduction, restrictions on temporary work, employee representation, and the creation of public-sector jobs.

The impact of this regulatory push during the first phase is best understood as characterizing a situation where capital had few short-run options. Investment was sunk and embodied a given labour intensity. Labour's gains during this period materialized in the form of brisk wage growth during the 1970s, despite the two oil shocks. Corporate profits plunged, and labour's share of value-added rose. While the rise in unemployment was to be expected as a result of the oil shocks, the brisk pace of wage growth in a recessionary period pointed to a more worrying prognosis.

Over time, as new investment was needed to replace outdated capital, the picture started to change. Uncommitted capital is very elastic. New investment must earn the rate of return available in the global economy. In the second phase, the reluctance to invest in jobs under heavy labour regulation led to a further build-up in unemployment, which induced wage moderation and permitted capital to earn the rates of return required by markets. The profitability of capital recovered progressively. At the same time, the technologies selected for new investments tended to economize on labour use, and the capital–output ratio climbed (see Figure 9.3, panel e). This led to further wage moderation and higher unemployment. As a result of both wage moderation and higher capital intensity, the labour share fell significantly below its initial level. Because of the high long-run elasticity of capital, labour's initial regulatory gains backfired and caused that factor ultimately to bear the bulk of the resulting inefficiency.

Figure 9.4   Capital-labour substitution and job protection

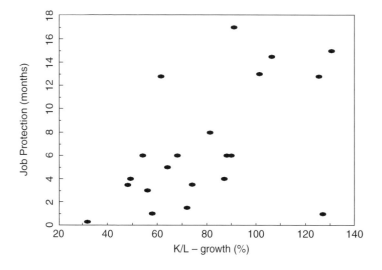

In fact, the relationship between job protection – as one dimension of labour market regulation – and capital–labour substitution can be found more generally in the data. This is shown in Figure 9.4 for the OECD countries over the period 1970–90.[3] The ability of the institutional shift to account parsimoniously for the rich joint dynamics of unemployment, wages, profits and capital intensity in Europe over the past three decades strongly supports the notion that institutions are the main culprit behind persistent unemployment in Europe.

9.3   Restructuring

9.3.1   Creative destruction, sclerosis and unbalanced restructuring

We now turn to restructuring, and the role of the institutional environment in that process. The need to restructure arises from the other dimension of specificity in production arrangements: specificity with respect to technology. Technology – taken in its broadest sense – is typically embodied in capital, in the experience of the workforce, and in the organization of production. This implies that a change in technology necessitates that factor components that are technology-specific be scrapped and replaced.

In a modern market economy, the productive structure is in a state of permanent adjustment. It must adapt to technological innovations, to the introduction of new products, to changes in modes of organization, and to the evolution of international competitiveness. Production units that incorporate the newest techniques and requirements must be continuously created, and outdated units must be destroyed. This process is what Schumpeter (1942) referred to as *creative destruction*. In this process of restructuring, production factors must be *reallocated* away from contracting activities and into newly expanding ones.

Recent empirical work allows us to quantify this process of ongoing restructuring. Traditionally, the construction of economic aggregates has often fallen short of the measures appropriate from a structural perspective. In terms of employment, flows were typically measured as net changes in stocks, without distinction between simultaneous positive and negative flows. Recent work has tried to remedy this state of affairs, and a rich literature developed that tries to measure gross job flows in the labour market (see Davis, Haltiwanger and Schuh (1996)). Measured gross job flows are surprisingly large, and reflect the extent of creative destruction. About 10 per cent of US manufacturing jobs disappear on average every year, and are replaced by new jobs.

The ongoing restructuring process requires innumerable transactions to create and destroy production units. The institutional environment is crucial for the efficiency of those transactions. Poor institutions are disruptive to the creative destruction process, giving rise to two additional macro-economic symptoms: *sclerosis* and *unbalanced restructuring* (see Caballero and Hammour (1998a)).

First, a poor institutional environment results in technological 'sclerosis' – it permits outdated, low-productivity units to survive longer than they would in an efficient equilibrium. This causes the creative destruction process to stagnate. Sclerosis is directly related to the under-employment and, therefore, under-valuation of productive resources. Under-employment causes the appropriating factor's autarky sector to be overcrowded, and its 'shadow' value of moving to autarky to be lower than in an efficient equilibrium. The result is weakened cost-pressures on outdated production units to be scrapped, and therefore technological sclerosis.

Second, poor institutions cause the restructuring process to be unbalanced. Although destruction is insufficient compared to an efficient equilibrium, it is, paradoxically, excessive given the economy's inefficiently sluggish creation rate. This is easiest to see in our labour market example in the special case where no social value – related to leisure or a matching function – is associated with unemployment. From a social perspective, as long as unemployment is positive, job destruction decisions should be based on a zero shadow wage. However, from a private worker's point of view, the shadow value of being unemployed is positive and determined by the opportunity of capturing quasi-rents in a new job. This puts excessively high private cost pressures on production units along the exit margin. Excessive destruction, given the depressed rate of creation, is not limited to the case where unemployment carries zero social value. It is a general consequence of the fact that capturing rents enters as a component of the appropriating factor's private but not social shadow values.

Crises are times when adjustment in factor prices is especially critical, and the unbalanced nature of restructuring is magnified. This mechanism is particularly relevant for an understanding of employment cirses during structural adjustment episodes, characterized by a surge in destruction that is not accompanied by a simultaneous rise in creation (Caballero and Hammour (1996a)). It is also relevant for the destruction-driven surge in unemployment observed during recessions, which we examine in the following section.

9.3.2 Recessions and restructuring: a reverse-liquidationist view

In addition to measuring the average pace of job reallocation, the new measures of gross job flows allow us to glimpse the way the creative destruction process is affected by the business cycle. Figure 9.5 presents the gross job creation and destruction time series constructed by Davis and Haltiwanger (1992) for the US manufacturing sector. Most notable in those series are the sharp peaks in destruction at the onset of each recession, while the fall in creation is much more muted. Although this asymmetry

Figure 9.5 Gross job creation and destruction rates in US manufacturing

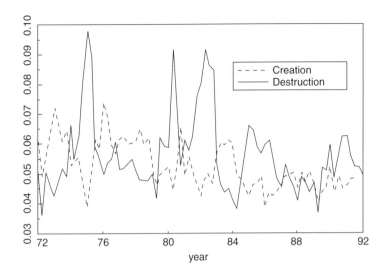

between creation and destruction may not be as strong in other sectors, or when the economy is subject to shocks of a different nature, this evidence confirmed the long-held view that liquidations are highly concentrated in recessions.

Concentrated liquidations were considered a central feature of recessions by pre-Keynesian economists. Unlike the Keynesian school that followed, those economists paid close attention to the supply side of the economy at high frequencies. Many of them – Hayek, Pigou, Robbins, Schumpeter – saw in liquidations the main reason for recessions (see De Long (1990). 'Liquidationists', as they came to be known, conceived of recessions as unavoidable times of intense restructuring. Lionel Robbins (1934) summarized this view as follows:

> In ... a boom many bad business commitments are undertaken. ... [Goods] are produced ... which it is impossible to sell at a profit. Loans are made which it is impossible to recover. ... [W]hen the boom breaks, these ... commitments are revealed. ... Nobody wishes ... bankruptcies. Nobody likes liquidation as such. ... [But] when the extent of malinvestment and over-indebtedness has passed a certain limit, measures which postpone liquidation only make matters worse.

Schumpeter (1934, p. 16) held a very similar view: '[D]epressions are not simply evils, which we might attempt to suppress, but ... forms of something which has to be done, namely, adjustment to ... change.'

Liquidationism was very influential in the Hoover administration's initial response to the Great Depression. President Hoover (1952) bitterly recollects:

> The 'leave-it-alone liquidationists' headed by Secretary of the Treasury Mellon ... felt that government must keep its hands off and let the slump liquidate itself. Mr Mellon had only one formula: 'Liquidate labour, liquidate stocks, liquidate the farmers, liquidate real estate'. ... He held that even panic was not altogether a bad thing. He said: 'It will purge the rottenness out of the system.'

Although few economists today would take the extreme position of early liquidationists, many see in increased factor reallocation a silver lining of recessions. Although recessions *per se* are undesirable events, they are seen as a time when the productivity of factors of production is low and, therefore, offers a chance to undertake much needed restructuring at a relatively low opportunity cost. Observed liquidations are seen as a prelude to increased restructuring.[4]

The evidence in Figure 9.5 supports the notion that recessions have a 'cleansing' effect on the production structure – in the sense that they are times of intense liquidations that affect mostly outdated, low-productivity jobs (see Caballero and Hammour (1994) Does cleansing constitute a silver lining of recessions? Under the presumption that poor institutions cause technological sclerosis, increased restructuring can be considered beneficial. However, there is an important difference between increased *restructuring* and increased *liquidations*. The fact is that lost jobs during recessions typically feed into unemployment, not job creation – which is not surprising, given the 'unbalanced' nature of restructuring in poor institutional environments. The question is whether, ultimately, increased liquidations lead to increased restructuring. In order to assess this question, one needs to examine the *cumulative* impact of a recessionary shock on creation and destruction. This is illustrated in Figure 9.6, which shows that an unemployment recession (bottom panel) that starts with a spike of liquidations may cumulatively result in increased, unchanged, or decreased restructuring.

We examined this question empirically in Caballero and Hammour (1999). Unfortunately, the available data are limited to the US manufacturing sector. The impulse-response function from our simplest regression is reported in Figure 9.7.[5] The bottom panel reports the cumulative impacts of a recessionary shock on creation and destruction. Surprisingly, recessions seem to *reduce* the amount of restructuring in the economy. This result of 'chill' following recessions is significant and robust in several dimensions, including the introduction of a second, reallocation shock. Given the limitations of the data, our conclusion can only be tentative. But, if there is any

Figure 9.6   Recessions and cumulative restructuring

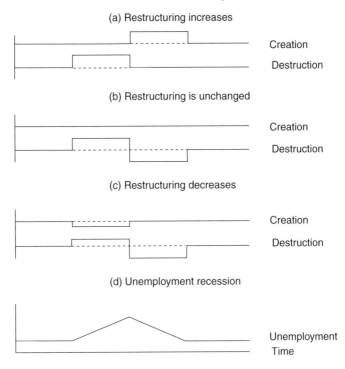

(a) Restructuring increases

Creation

Destruction

(b) Restructuring is unchanged

Creation

Destruction

(c) Restructuring decreases

Creation

Destruction

(d) Unemployment recession

Unemployment
Time

evidence, it does not support prevailing views that recessions are the occasion for increased restructuring.

Why would recessions freeze the restructuring process? Our interpretation is that the underlying factors are financial – again, a case of institutional failure. Recessions squeeze liquidity in financial markets and reduce firms' ability to undertake healthy restructuring.

9.3.3   Merger waves and the stock market

Fluctuations in the pace of restructuring can be approached from a very different angle, by moving from job reallocation to the *restructuring of corporate assets*. Looking at merger and acquisition (M&A) activity over time, and at its institutional underpinnings, we reach a conclusion that also amounts to a rejection of the liquidationist perspective (see Caballero and Hammour (2000)). Essentially, a liquidationist perspective in this context would consider fire sales during sharp liquidity contractions as the occasion for intense restructuring of corporate assets. The evidence points, on the contrary, to briskly expansionary periods characterized by high stock-market

Figure 9.7 A case of chill

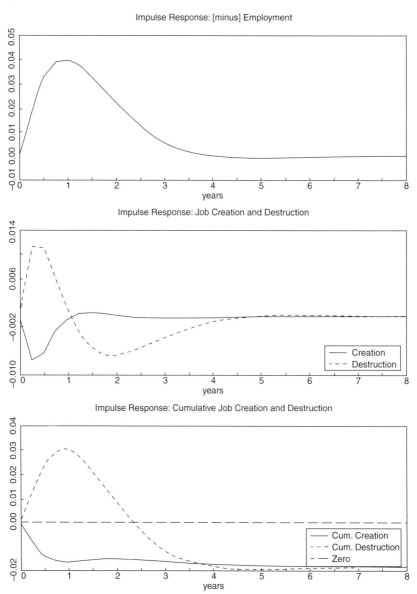

valuations and abundant liquidity as the occasion for intense M&A activity. Again, financial factors and their institutional underpinnings seem to be at the core of this restructuring phenomenon.

Figure 9.8   US merger waves, 1885–98

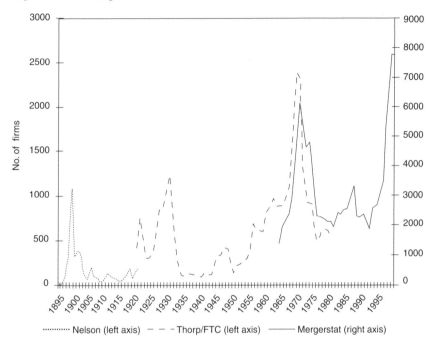

.... Nelson (left axis)   – – – Thorp/FTC (left axis)   ———— Mergerstat (right axis)

Figure 9.8 presents data on the number of mergers and acquisitions in the US over the past century. Without going into the data construction issues, it is important to note that the figure is based on three distinct data sets that are not directly comparable and contain a natural upward trend (see Golbe and White (1987)).[6] What the figure shows is the extreme concentration of US M&A activity over time, into essentially *four merger waves*.

The first merger wave took place at the turn of the century. It consisted, to a large extent, of the simultaneous horizontal consolidation of several enterprises that took advantage of scale economies and often created a near monopoly in their industry. The landmark transaction of this era was the Great American Steel Deal led by Andrew Carnegie, which combined ten companies into U.S. Steel. The second merger wave took place during the 'Roaring Twenties' and affected nearly one-fifth of manufacturing assets. Dozens of today's major US companies were formed at that time. The frenzy ended abruptly with the Great Crash of 1929. The third was the conglomerate merger wave of the late 1960s – the Go-Go Years of the stock market – and consisted mostly of corporate diversification across industries. Advances in management science were supposed to allow conglomerates to manage effectively a multitude of businesses that span a variety of industries. Retrospectively, much of the earnings-per-share growth demonstrated at the time

Figure 9.9   M&A volume and the stock market, 1963–98

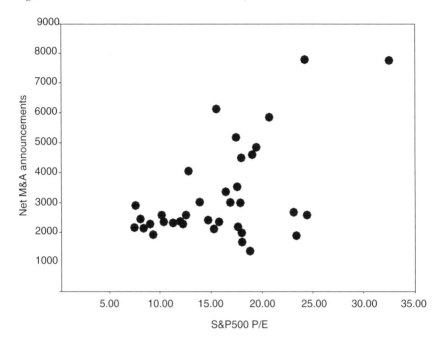

by leading conglomerates was financially driven. Finally, we are currently in the middle of another merger wave, which rivals in scale any of the previous ones. Enterprise restructuring is driven by trends towards globalization, corporate refocusing, and consolidation in the new IT industries. Overall, mergers have played a key role in the evolution of industrial structure in response to technological and organizational revolutions.

The one robust determinant for the aggregate volume of M&A activity – as documented in most studies on the subject – is the valuation of the stock market (Golbe and White (1987)). As an example, the positive correlation between US M&A volume and the rice/earnings (P/E) ratio of the Standard and Poor's (S&P) 500 index is illustrated in Figure 9.9 for the period 1963–98.

If we concentrate exclusively on the buyer's motives, the correlation between M&A activity and market valuations is difficult to explain. Why would the buyers of assets increase their demand when prices rise? It is true that – along the lines of Kiyotaki and Moore (1997) – a rising market will increase the collateral value of financially constrained buyers, thus increasing the volume of assets they are able to acquire. But, by the same token, a declining market also increases transactions volume, as shrinking collateral values force asset sales. This implies a correlation between M&A transactions and *changes* in market valuations – unless we introduce, as we discuss below, transaction costs on sellers.

Another piece of evidence that is difficult to interpret from the buyer's viewpoint concerns the method of payment in M&A, that is whether acquisitions are paid for with cash, with the buyer's stock, or a combination. Figure 9.10 plots the share of all-cash transactions in United States M&A against the market's P/E ratio over the period 1973–98. It is clear that the share of all-cash transactions is lower – and the share of stock transactions is higher – when the market's valuation rises. The question is, why should the volume of stock transactions, which raises no issue of collateral valuation for external financing, rise with the stock market? Why does it rise proportionally even more than the volume of cash transactions?

The evidence indicates that action is coming from the sellers' side. Our interpretation of merger waves centres on the 'liquidity' of the seller. When market valuations rise, sellers become more liquid and are more willing to sell control. Generally speaking, illiquidity arises when a *financially constrained* asset-owner faces a *transaction cost*. Transaction costs in the market for corporate control are mostly information-based. Financial constraints are central to the notion of illiquidity, because in the absence of such constraints the owner would be able to contractually transfer the asset's future cash flow without incurring the transaction cost. When a seller is illiquid, an increase

Figure 9.10   Method of payment in M&A, 1973–98

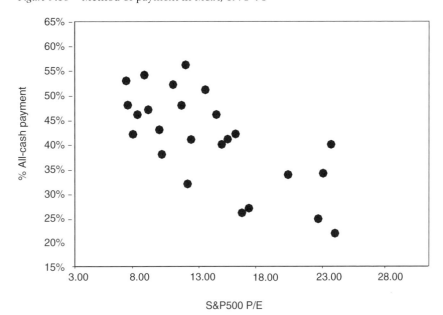

in the price of his asset does two things: *(i)* it increases his willingness to incur the transaction cost; and *(ii)* it relaxes his financial constraint. The latter effect enters as a pecuniary externality that helps explain the highly concentrated nature of merger waves. The fact that the share of stock transactions rises with market valuations confirms that the sellers' side is at work, because buyers who pay with their stock are, in fact, also a sort of seller.

The above interpretation of merger waves highlights another dimension of aggregate restructuring where institutions – here financial-market institutions – play a central role. The lesson that we draw from it reinforces the reverse-liquidationist view we developed based on labour market evidence. One could conjecture that times of crisis produce fire sales and increase the pace of corporate asset restructuring. That would correspond to the liquidationist perspective. But the evidence is otherwise. Great waves of asset restructuring have, on the contrary, come during good times, and have come about through waves of liquidity.

9.4 Summary

In this chapter, we outlined the basic ingredients that are needed to explore the macroeconomic effects of institutions and their impact on the restructuring process. We illustrated the usefulness of the approach in a few applications.

Our main propositions can be summarized as follows:

1. The study of the macroeconomic consequences of institutional arrangements and their impact on aggregate restructuring requires a 'structural' type of analysis, one which emphasizes the *technological* and *relationship specificity* that characterize the production structure.
2. Institutional arrangements determine the *rules* that govern the process by which specific quasi-rents are created and shared. In their *efficiency*-enhancing role, they help each party obtain the social value of what it put in; in their *political* role, they constitute an instrument of redistribution.
3. At the level of individual interactions, a poor institutional environment *discourages cooperation* between factors of production. In equilibrium, this results in *under-employment*, *market segmentation* and *technological exclusion* of the 'appropriating' factor.
4. *Application*: The European macroeconomic experience over the past three decades reflects the impact of shifts in labour relations when, in the *short run*, capital in place has few options, and, in the *longer run*, the supply of new investment is highly elastic and can choose from a range of technologies.
5. A poor institutional environment results in '*sclerosis*' – the inefficient survival of low-productivity jobs. Moreover, it causes the restructuring process to be *unbalanced*: given the level of creation, destruction is excessively high.

6. The concentration of liquidations during a recession is associated with productivity *cleansing*, but not necessarily with an overall increase in restructuring. On the contrary, the limited evidence we have from US manufacturing job flows contradicts the '*liquidationist*' view.

7. Similarly, the restructuring of corporate assets is not concentrated during times of liquidity crunch and fire sales. Merger waves are concentrated at times when stock-market *valuations* are *high* and *sellers* are highly '*liquid*'.

Notes

1. While it makes a world of difference for the contract theorist, for our purposes the specific rents that arise from the hold-up problem are similar to the informational rents that arise from asymmetric-information problems. In the latter case, one factor commits a production opportunity to another factor that has, or will have, an informational advantage. Specificity arises from the fact that the decision to commit the production opportunity cannot be reversed based on the outcome. For our purposes, we will treat specific rents as a single, generic type.

2. Data sources: OECD Business Sector Data Base and the IMF's *International Financial Statistics*.

3. The index of job protection is the sum of the maximum mandatory severance payments (in months of wages) and the advance notification period (in months). The source of both measures is OECD (1993), table 3-8, p. 97. The source of the K/L ratio is the OECD Business Sector Data Base. This figure was kindly provided to us by David Coe.

4. For a survey of this view of recessions as reorganizations, see Aghion and Saint-Paul (1993).

5. The regression underlying Figure 9.7 uses manufacturing employment (N_t), the flow of gross job creation (H_t), and the flow of gross destruction (D_t) in deviation from their mean. The data are quarterly for the period 1972:1–1993:4. We assume that employment fluctuations are driven by a single aggregate shock. Given the identity $\Delta N_t = H_t - D_t$, a linear time-series model for the response of job flows to aggregate shocks can generally be written either in terms of creation: $H_t = \theta^h(L)N_t + \varepsilon^h_t$; or in terms of destruction: $D_t = \theta^d(L)N_t + \varepsilon^d_t$, where $\theta^h(L)$ and $\theta^d(L)$ are polynomials in the lag operator L. Figure 9.7 portrays the estimated impulse-response functions for a 2-standard-deviation recessionary shock.

6. The 'Nelson' series can be found in Nelson (1959); the 'Thorp/FTC' series can be found in Thorp (1941) and in US Federal Trade Commission (1981); the 'Mergerstat' series can be found in Houlihan, Lockey, Howard and Zukin (1998).

References

Aghion, P. and Saint-Paul, G. (1993) 'Uncovering Some Causal Relationships between Productivity Growth and the Structure of Economic Fluctuations: A Tentative Survey', NBER Working Paper no. W4603.

Caballero, R.J. and Hammour, M.L. (1994) 'The Cleansing Effect of Recessions', *American Economic Review*, vol. 84, pp. 1350–68.

Caballero, R.J. and Hammour, M.L. (1996a) 'On the Ills of Adjustment', *Journal of Development Economics*, vol. 51, pp. 161–92.

Caballero, R.J. and Hammour, M.L. (1996b) 'On the Timing and Efficiency of Creative Destruction', *Quarterly Journal of Economics*, vol. 111, no. 3, pp. 805–52.

Caballero, R.J. and Hammour, M.L. (1998a) 'The Macroeconomics of Specificity', *Journal of Political Economy*, vol. 106, no. 4, pp. 724–67.

Caballero, R.J. and Hammour, M.L. (1998b) 'Jobless Growth: Appropriability, Factor Substitution and Unemployment', *Carnegie-Rochester Conference Series on Public Policy*, vol. 48, pp. 51–94.

Caballero, R.J. and Hammour, M.L. (1999) 'The Cost of Recessions Revisited: A Reverse-Liquidationist View', NBER Working Paper no. 7355.

Caballero, R.J. and Hammour, M.L. (2000) 'Technological Revolutions and Merger Waves', typescript.

Davis, S.J. and Haltiwanger, J. (1992) 'Gross Job Creation, Gross Job Destruction and Employment Reallocation', *Quarterly Journal of Economics*, vol. 107, pp. 819–64.

Davis, S.J., Haltiwanger, J. and Schuh, S. (1996) *Job Creation and Destruction* (Cambridge, MASS: MIT Press).

De Long, J.B. (1990) '"Liquidation" Cycles: Old-Fashioned Real Business Cycle Theory and the Great Depression', NBER Working Paper no. 3546.

Golbe, D. and White, L. (1987) 'A Time Series Analysis of Mergers and Acquisitions in the US Economy', in Auerbach, A. (ed.) *Corporate Takeovers* (Chicago: University of Chicago Press), pp. 265–305.

Greenspan, A. (1999) 'Maintaining Economic Vitality', Millennium Lecture Series sponsored by the Gerald R. Ford Foundation and Grand Valley State University, 8 September.

Hayek, F.A. von (1931) 'The "Paradox" of Saving', *Economica*, vol. 32, pp. 125–69.

Houlihan, Lockey, Howard and Zukin (1998) *Mergerstat Review 1998.*

Johansen, L. (1959) 'Substitution versus Fixed Production Coefficients in the Theory of Economic Growth: A Synthesis', *Econometrica*, vol. 27, pp. 157–76.

Kiyotaki, N. and Moore, J. (1997) 'Credit Cycles', *Journal of Political Economy*, vol. 105, no. 2, pp. 211–48.

Klein, B., Crawford, R.G. and Alchian, A.A. (1978) 'Vertical Integration, Appropriable Rents, and the Competitive Contracting Process', *Journal of Law and Economics*, vol. 21, pp. 297–326.

Nelson, R.N. (1959) *Merger Movements in American Industry: 1895–1956* (Princeton, NJ: Princeton University Press).

OECD (1993) *Employment Outlook* (Paris: OECD).

Robbins, L. (1934) *The Great Depression* (London: Macmillan).

Schumpeter, J.A. (1934) 'Depressions', in Brown, D. *et al.* (eds) *Economics of the Recovery Program* (New York: McGraw-Hill).

Schumpeter, J.A. (1942) *Capitalism, Socialism, and Democracy* (New York: Harper & Bros).

Solow, R.M. (1960) 'Investment and Technological Progress', in Arrow, K.J., Karlin, S. and Suppes, P. (eds) *Mathematical Methods in Social Sciences* (Stanford: Stanford University Press).

Thorp, W. (1941) 'The Merger Movement', in *The Structure of Industry*. Temporary National Economic Committee monograph no. 27, part III, pp. 231–34.

US Federal Trade Commission, Bureau of Economics (1981) *Statistical Report on Mergers and Acquisitions, 1979* (Washington, DC: FTC).

Williamson, O. (1985) *The Economic Institutions of Capitalism: Firms, Markets, Relational Contracting* (New York: Free Press).

10
Rigid Wages: What Have We Learnt from Microeconometric Studies?

Francis Kramarz
CREST, INSEE and CEPR, Paris, France

10.1 Introduction

In this survey, I intend to describe the latest efforts of labour economists to analyse wage rigidity both in its existence and in its consequences in various countries, in particular the United States and France. There has been recently a renewed interest in questions surrounding wage rigidity, a central concern of many macroeconomists. In addition, the existence of wage rigidities has been viewed by some analysts as the main reason for the high level of European unemployment, in contrast to the North American situation. The stakes are clear enough so that I do not need to spend much time in this introduction on justifying why we should, as economists, be interested in this topic.

The structure of this chapter is the following. I first describe in section 10.2 a simple theoretical framework that should help us understand where nominal and real wage rigidities enter macroeconomists' views on unemployment. Then in section 10.3 I describe in some detail several recent American studies – McLaughlin (1994); Card and Hyslop (1997), Groshen and Schweitzer (1997); Kahn (1997); Altonji and Devereux (1999) – all of which address this question of the existence of nominal rigidities and their consequences in terms of wage changes using survey data. I also present (section 10.4) some of the messages that emerge from Bewley's (1998) analysis of the same question based on interviews with managers, union leaders and others. Then in section 10.5 I present all the recent European studies of which I am aware – Goux (1997) for France; Dessy (1999) for Italy; Smith (1999) for the UK; Fehr and Goette (1999) for Switzerland – on the same topic. In section 10.6, I discuss the implications of the potential rigidities on employment, contrasting in particular the American and the French cases (using Card, Kramarz and Lemieux, 1999). In section 10.7 I try to go deeper in the understanding of the firm's behaviour when they face potential employment or wage rigidities, using once again the French situation as an example (based on

Abowd, Corbel and Kramarz, 1999; and Abowd, Kramarz and Roux, in progress). I briefly conclude in section 10.8.

10.2 Motivation: questions and theory

From my own reading of the various theoretical or empirical articles that have been written, I believe that we must ask the following questions: Are nominal wages downwardly rigid? Are real wages downwardly rigid? and, finally, why do wages not fall in recessions? Simple 'old-fashioned' theory can help us understand why these questions matter in the analysis of unemployment that, evidently, is central in our understanding of the functioning of modern economies. My presentation is based on models well described in Malinvaud (1977) or Grandmont (1989).

Consider an economy with three commodities (output, labour, money), a firm, a household, the government. The situation is described in Figure 10.1. If the couple (p,w) is right of L_2 and L_3 then the economy is in a Keynesian unemployment regime and policies that raise demand stimulate activity through multiplier effects. On the other hand, if the couple (p,w) is above L_1 and left of L_2 then the economy is in the so-called classical unemployment regime and policies that raise the profitability of firms are required. Now, assume that the output price p is flexible and adjusts to clear the goods market. Then, we can have involuntary unemployment and the short-run response to policy shocks depends on whether the *nominal* or the *real* wage is predetermined. In the former situation, a predetermined nominal wage, the economy has *Keynesian unemployment*. And going back to Figure 10.1, a positive demand shock shifts L_2 to the right: p increases, w/p decreases, output increases through multiplier effects.

Micro theories which tend to generate such nominal wage rigidity are menu costs theories, staggered contracts theories, as well as theories where there is imperfect information on wages. McLeod and Malcomson's (1993) hold-up problem when there are contracts and renegotiation, or Keynes's relative wage theory where workers compare their wage with those prevailing at other firms, are also theories that tend to generate nominal rigidities. Assuming as above price flexibility, but with the real wage being the predetermined variable, then the economy faces *Classical Unemployment* where output and employment are independent of aggregate demand. In particular, any increase in public expenditures would result in the crowding-out of private demand. Therefore, in such a situation, supply-side policies that restore profitability are needed. Micro theories which tend to generate real rigidities are numerous. Among them, we must cite implicit contracts, efficiency wage, bargaining or insider-outsider theories which all tend to generate real rigidities, at least in their simplest versions.

Hence, in the following sections, we will pay particular attention to the nature of the rigidity that is examined and, if so, demonstrated.

Figure 10.1 $L_2: Y(w/p) - C(R(Y(w/p))), p, w) = G$
$\ \ L_2: Y^* - C(R(Y^*), p, w) = G$

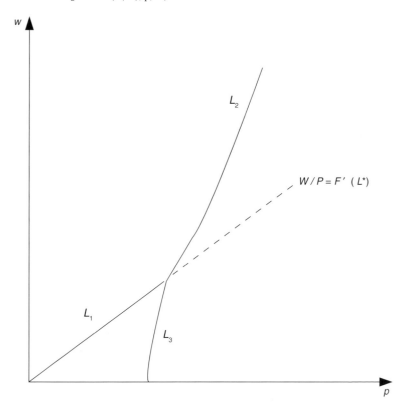

Source: Grandmont (1989).

10.3   Lessons from recent American microeconometric studies

For most of this section I adopt a chronological perspective that indeed fits with an increased complexity and care taken in the econometric analysis of the problem. Furthermore, I try each time to present

1. The data sources used in the analysis
2. The period of analysis
3. The observations used
4. The measure of wage used
5. The results
6. The econometric methodology and the underlying assumptions.

McLaughlin's paper in 1994 in the *Journal of Monetary Economics* revived the analysis of the existence of wage rigidity. The data source used in the analysis is the Panel Study of Income Dynamics (hereafter, PSID) for the period from 1976 to 1986, hence mostly a period of high or moderate inflation. As in most analyses of this problem, McLaughlin focuses on workers who did not change jobs in two consecutive years. This focus is crucial and we will discuss its validity in the final sections. The measure of compensation that he uses are two, earnings and hourly earnings. The results can be summarized as follows:

1. He observes that there is a lot of dispersion in wage changes.
2. More precisely, there are 43 per cent of real wage cuts and 17 per cent of nominal wage cuts, which are clearly very high percentages.
3. However, he finds that unions tend to induce wage compression when wages change.
4. In addition, he finds that very small wage cuts and raises are not rare (hence, he does not find support for the menu costs theory).
5. Very importantly, he claims that there is little evidence of important measurement errors. Since this issue is crucial, we will repeatedly discuss it and spend some time on the treatment of measurement errors in the various studies that we examine here.
6. Using time-series evidence, he shows that wage change is less than 1-to-1 with unanticipated inflation (all coefficients shown below are significantly different from 0 and the R-square of the regression is $R^2 = 0.84$):

$$\Delta \log w_t = 1.82 + 1.02 \pi_t^a + 0.42 \pi_t^u$$

The methodology which is adopted can be described as follows. First, McLaughlin looks for historical evidences and presents a number of them. In particular, his examination of wage cuts shows that they have historically not been rare. For instance, he finds repeated evidence of wage cuts in union contracts such as in the airline and steel industries in the 1980s. One must however remember that nominal wages in manufacturing were left unchanged by the large decline in nominal demand in the first two years of the Great Depression (O'Brien, 1989). Hence, there also exists historical evidence of strong nominal wage rigidity. Second, McLaughlin analyses the PSID. As mentioned above, his first task is to assess the quality of the wage data. Based on his own research as well as that of others, he concludes that hours are badly measured but that earnings information is correct. However, he takes into account, in a simple way, possible measurement errors and concludes that the above numbers are little changed: real wage cuts go from 43 to 39 per cent after accounting for errors, while the equivalent numbers for nominal wage cuts are from 17 to 12 per cent. Accounting for measurement error, the size of the average real cut goes from 9 to 6 per cent while the size of the average nominal wage cut goes from 12 to 8 per cent. In fact, much of his statistical analysis of measurement errors is based on skewness statistics and is therefore far from being non-parametric. In addition, he does not contrast years of low inflation with years of high inflation (see Figure 10.2, in which all years are pooled). In conclusion, it seems that McLaughlin believes in flexibility and finds strong evidence of it.

Shulamit Kahn (1997) uses the same dataset, the PSID, under a slightly longer period, 1970–88. In addition, she focuses, as usual in this literature, on the non-job changers. However, despite all these similarities, she uses different measures of pay than used in McLaughlin's study. More precisely, she considers wage and salary earners. And, as appears below, this has a strong effect on the view one has on rigidity. To obtain her results, she uses a methodology that we here briefly present. First, she calculates the proportion of pay changes

Figure 10.2 Nominal wage growth distribution, stayers, annual difference of log wages, PSID 1976–86

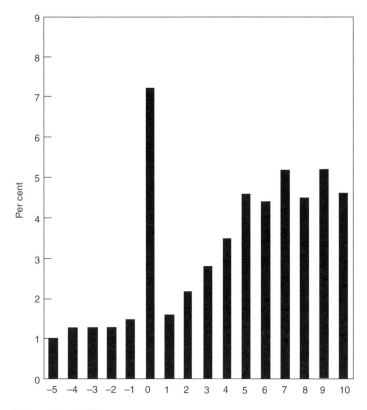

Source: McLaughlin (1994).

that fall into each bar of a histogram centred around the annual median pay change (for 12 bars and 19 years). Such histograms are presented in Figure 10.3. Then, Kahn regresses each bar for each year on bar dummies for zero, for negative nominal change, and for 1 per cent above and below nominal zero. Hence, she will be able to capture in some non-parametric form the importance of the various places in the distribution that are of interest (such as the spike at zero nominal change, the bars that surround the spike bar, the various bars strictly below zero nominal change).
Her results can be summarized as follows:

1. She finds strong evidence of nominal rigidity.
2. She also claims to find evidence of menu costs.
3. To assess the magnitude of rigidity and workers affected, she shows that there are fewer pay cuts for wage earners, 10.6 per cent, than for salary earners, 24.3 per cent.
4. There are also fewer pay cuts for low-skilled workers than for managers.
5. There is a large coefficient on zero nominal change that reflects the spike.
6. There are sizeable and negative coefficients on 1 per cent dummies above and below zero nominal wage change which are consistent with menu costs theories.
7. There is a large and negative coefficient on the negative dummy for wage earners (hourly pay) that reflects downward nominal stickiness.
8. However, there is a positive coefficient on the negative dummy for salary earners, reflecting that pay changes are more likely if they entail a pay cut. Interestingly, she claims that this result is not due to changing usual hours.

Hence, Kahn's paper brings the non-parametric dimension to the analysis. And she appears to have fewer biases in her interpretation than could be found in the previous analysis. Unfortunately, she does not incorporate in her study any assessment of the magnitude of measurement errors. Indeed, this methodology based on the analysis of histograms, albeit ingenious, may be difficult to extend because of its simplicity.

The issue of incorporating measurement errors in a non-parametric framework is addressed by David Card and Dean Hyslop's paper published in 1997. Card and Hyslop use, as before, the PSID, but they also use the matched year-to-year Current Population Survey (CPS, hereafter) for the period 1976 to 1993. Hence, they have more low-inflation years than in the two previous studies. Unfortunately, the CPS does not record information on tenure at the firm. Hence, when they use the CPS, to approximate non-job changers, they concentrate on all workers that had no change in occupation together with no change in sector. Note, however, that this choice

Figure 10.3 Distribution of annual differences in log real wages, hourly rated stayers, PSID

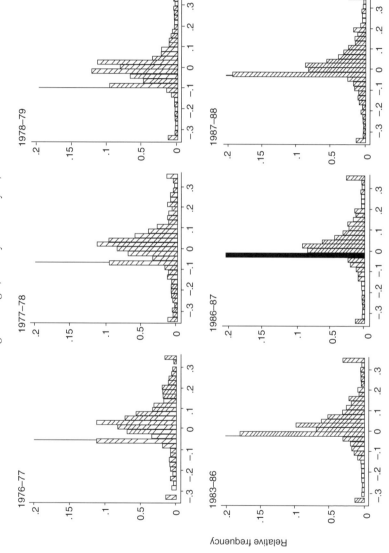

Source: Card and Hyslop (1997).

can bias the estimated amount of rigidity in both directions for various reasons. In their analysis, the measure they more often use is the hourly wage, concentrating mostly on workers paid by the hour, and very importantly, eliminating all minimum wage workers since, by construction, their wage must be downwardly rigid.

Their results can be summarized as follows:

1. In the data, many individuals appear to experience nominal wage reductions.
2. At the same time, there is evidence of a substantial spike at zero. In the high inflation era of the late 1970s, the spike amounts to 6 to 10 per cent of the workers; in the low inflation era (mid-1980s), it amounts to over 15 per cent. They also report estimation results that show that a 1 per cent decrease in inflation increases the proportion at the spike by 1.4 per cent.
3. Contrarily to some results presented above, they claim that there is the same amount of rigidity for workers with hourly rates than for workers with non-hourly rates.

Addressing some of the shortcomings of Kahn's analysis, their methodology takes care of potential measurement errors. In particular, they show that:

1. Even though there is evidence of rounding in reported hourly rates, this only accounts at most for 4 to 5 per cent of the apparent rigidity
2. All in all, correcting for rounding and measurement errors, they find that between a quarter and a half of non-job changers who might have experienced a nominal cut, instead had rigid nominal wages.
3. Finally, by aggregating the data at hand at a local level, they find that a market-level analysis displays no effect of inflation on the real wage response to local unemployment, contrarily to what one would expect given the previous evidence of wage rigidity.

The methodology that they adopt is of interest in its own right. It is a fully non-parametric analysis that examines the whole distribution of wage changes. However, as in any econometric analysis, there are some identifying assumptions that we list now:

H 1: in the absence of rigidities, the distribution would be symmetrical.
H 2: the upper-half of the distribution is unaffected by rigidities.
H 3: wage rigidities do not affect employment (an assumption that can be slightly relaxed).

Indeed, there is nothing here that tells us anything about the magnitude of measurement errors. Hence, they adopt the same information and approach that was used by Card (1996). They use the 1977 CPS that collected information both from the worker side and from the employer side on the same issues, such as wage, seniority, and so on. From the resulting counterfactual wage change distribution (see Figures 10.4a to 10.4c and compare with Figure 10.5), they are able to identify the effects of nominal wage rigidity. These effects are measured both in terms of number of persons affected by wage rigidity and in terms of wage changes (i.e. those which, in the absence of rigidity, would have been different). They find that:

1. The number of persons affected by such nominal wage rigidity amounts to 8 to 12 per cent in the mid-1980s.
2. The effects of such nominal wage rigidity on wage changes are such that wage changes have been 1 per cent higher every year than they would have been in absence of wage rigidity under the same time period of the mid-1980s.

Figure 10.4a   Theoretical illustration of the effect of downward nominal rigidity on the distribution of real wage changes

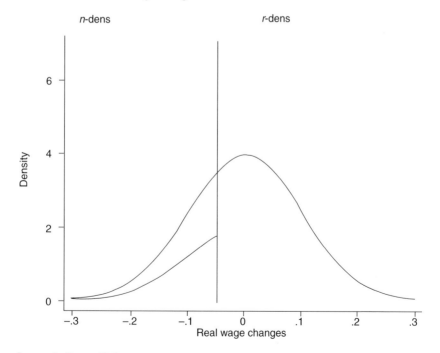

Source: As Figure 10.3.

Figure 10.4b Theoretical illustration of the effect of downward nominal rigidity and menu costs on the distribution of real wage changes

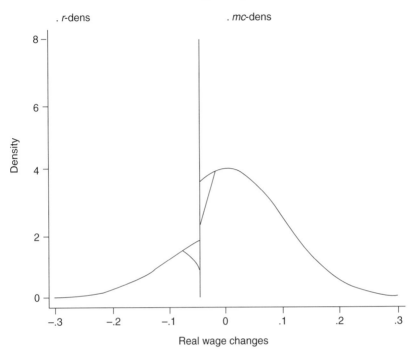

Source: As Figure 10.3.

To summarize, they present, as usual with David Card, a very well-written and well-executed paper with simple and clear results.

Joe Altonji and Paul Devereux, in a recent NBER Working Paper (Altonji and Devereux, 1999), take a completely different approach in that they adopt a fully parametric specification of the wage change process. In particular, they use a well-specified statistical model of nominal wage rigidity together with a measurement error model. We describe the estimated equations later. Using the same structure as for the other papers, we must note that their data source is the Panel Study of Income Dynamics (PSID) for the period starting in 1971 and ending in 1992. As other researchers, they concentrate on non-job changers paid by the hour. Hence, their measure of wage is the hourly wage.

To summarize the results that they obtain, we can say that:

1. Comparing the PSID with the personnel file of a large firm, they note that there are more nominal wage cuts in the PSID than in the large firm file.

Figure 10.4c   Theoretical illustration of the effect of measurement error in the presence of downward nominal rigidity and menu costs on the distribution of real wage changes

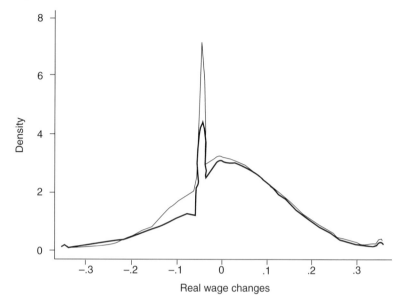

Source: As Figure 10.3.

2. But, controlling for measurement errors, they find evidence of substantial downward nominal wage rigidity.
3. They even conclude, based on the likelihood of their various estimated models, that perfect wage rigidity is a better approximation than perfect flexibility in terms of statistical fit.
4. However, explaining wage changes remains extremely difficult (indeed a statistical measure of a simple wage-change equation yields an R-square of approximately 0.05).
5. If they examine the impact of wage rigidity on employment stability, it appears that workers are slightly less likely to quit if they are protected by nominal wage floors.
6. Finally, and unfortunately, some conclusions depend highly on the exact estimated model. In particular, because of the estimated structure of the model, the identification power is very weak and relies mainly on the normality assumptions. Strong evidence of the lack of identification is given.

As already mentioned, their methodology is fully parametric and is based on a statistical micro-model of wage changes that is consistent with the theoretical

Figure 10.5 Kernal estimates of actual and counterfactual densities of real wage changes, stayers, CPS, 1979–80 to 1982–83

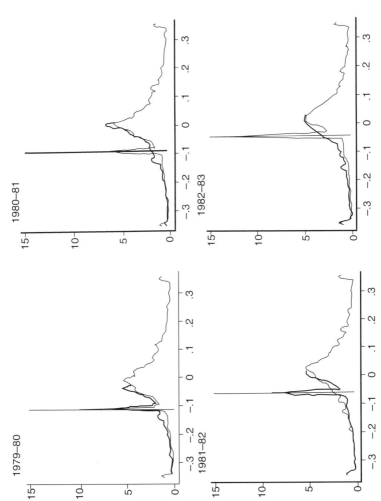

Source: As Figure 10.3.

micro-model of McLeod and Malcomson (1993). Their first equation gives the optimal wage that would prevail in the absence of rigidity:

$$w_{it}^* = x_{it}\beta + \varepsilon_{it}.$$

If there is wage rigidity, the equations become:

$$\Delta w_{it}^0 = x_{it}\beta - w_{it}^0 - 1 + \varepsilon_{it} \quad \text{if } 0 \le x_{it}\beta + \varepsilon_{it} - w_{it}^0 - 1$$
$$\Delta w_{it}^0 = 0 \quad \text{if } -\alpha \le x_{it}\beta + \varepsilon_{it} - w_{it}^0 - 1 \le 0$$
$$\Delta w_{it}^0 = \lambda + x_{it}\beta - w_{it}^0 - 1 + \varepsilon_{it} \text{ if } x_{it}\beta + \varepsilon_{it} - w_{it}^0 - 1 \le -\alpha$$

where α and λ represent rigidity parameters that should be both equal to zero in case of perfect flexibility, and where the shocks, ε_{it}, are normally i.i.d. error terms. In addition, Altonji and Devereux specify a model of measurement error which is a mixture of a model with no error and a normal measurement error. To conclude, it appears that the authors have a very promising statistical model that should be well suited to the analysis of this question of wage rigidity. But they obviously need better data, for instance data on workers and on their firms, to help them identify the effects of interest.

The final paper in this group of studies is unique in, at least, two aspects. First, Erica Groshen and Mark Schweitzer use an employer data source. More precisely, they analyse the Community Salary Survey that spans a very long period of time, from 1956 to 1996. This survey gives the wage distribution for each detailed occupation (mostly white-collar) for a group of employers of three American cities: Cleveland, Cincinnati, Pittsburgh. Hence, the data match employer information with job information. The measure they use is the median (or mean) wage in the occupation-employer cell. Second, their theoretical model consists of a two-stage process of the wage setting. This model helps them identify their estimated effects. More precisely, they assume that firms, based on their inflation expectations, first set the global change in the wage bill, and then allot the change across occupations (think for instance of a central management that would set the general wage-change rules giving the various profit centres the power to distribute the raises, freezes or decreases within their profit centres to the job holders). Therefore, mistakes being more likely when inflation is large, it is possible to examine the dispersion of employers' wage adjustments across firms at different moments. If this dispersion is growing when inflation rises (controlling for the firm-level changes in the occupation mix), the authors conclude that inflation has 'sand effects'. By contrast, inflation may have beneficial effects in the second stage of the wage-setting process, in a context where nominal wages are downwardly rigid. For instance, it helps decrease the real wage of employees in declining occupations. More generally, the authors conclude that inflation should help the firm in following market conditions for some occupations without firing workers. In fact, this 'grease effect' should be uncovered in the data by examining the dispersion of within-firm between occupations adjustments. This dispersion should be larger in years of higher inflation. Conversely, rigidity should imply a reduced variance.

Their empirical analysis relies on an analysis of variance in which wage changes are regressed on firm and occupation indicators. This analysis is performed for each year and for each locality. Then they take the coefficients on the firm and on the occupation indicators to measure dispersions between firms as well as between occupations in each year and locality. These measures are then regressed on inflation measures for the same years and localities. Their results are in agreement with the above model. Using wage changes for the various establishment-occupation cells in the Community Salary Survey, Groshen and Schweitzer find evidence in their data that, indeed:

1. Inflation-induced occupational adjustments represent beneficial grease (inflation expectations).
2. Inflation-induced wage changes across employers reflect distortionary sand (surprises in inflation expectations).

As already mentioned, their methodology is based on this two-stage wage determination process with errors in wage-setting due to inflation and downward rigid nominal wages in which the first stage yields the average nominal adjustment and in which the second stage yields the division of the raise among workers. In sum, I consider the authors to have taken two important steps in a very interesting direction but that their descriptive tools and estimation techniques might be further improved.

10.4 Lessons from a recent American interview study

Using a completely different approach, Truman Bewley (Bewley, 1998, as well as his forthcoming book) can help us understand the rigid wages problem from a different and complementary perspective. The data source, if it is possible to use this term, has been constructed by Bewley himself. He conducted interviews with 300 business people, labour leaders, consultants during the recession of the early 1990s. The basic question that was asked is reflected in the title of Bewley (1998) – *Why Not Cut Pay?*

As is done for all other studies, I will summarize the most important results of this line of research:

1. According to managers, pay cuts would have no impact on company employment.
2. Hiring new workers at reduced pay (or overqualified) would antagonize them.

3. Cutting the pay of existing workers is nearly unthinkable (attitudes).
4. Layoffs are better than pay cuts: 'they get the misery out of the door'.
5. Attitudes have an impact on performance.
6. Contrary to a widespread belief, the main resistance to wage cuts comes from employers (loss of morale) and not from union leaders.
7. After examining all theories of wage rigidity, it appears that there must be only one valid micro-theory. It is a theory that states that morale is incompatible with wage cuts (note that it is not a theory about levels like in Akerlof's norms theory but a theory about wage changes).

To conclude, I find Bewley's analysis quite interesting because he takes seriously both the collected interviews and theoretical work. Hence, his confrontation of collected data to various theories is of prime interest. In addition, he makes a lot of empirical suggestions at the end of the book at which any applied labour economist should look. However, if we are not disposed to accept the morale explanation of nominal wage rigidity but embrace his other conclusions, we must seek non-existing theories of nominal rigidity.

10.5   Lessons from recent European microeconometric studies

Recently, European scholars inspired by the earlier American analyses have started to examine the existence of wage rigidity using individual data. The first such study was based on French data and appeared in 1997, the year of publication of the Kahn and Card and Hyslop papers. Dominique Goux has examined the case of France using two complementary data sources. The first one is called the Déclarations Annuelles de Données Sociales (DADS, hereafter), an administrative data source based on companies' fiscal declarations. The second data source is the French Labour Force Survey (LFS, hereafter). The periods under study are respectively 1976 to 1992 for the former, and 1990 to 1996 for the latter. As in their American equivalent, the study focuses on non-job changers working full-time. However, due to the structure of the available data, Goux (1997) uses annual earnings as a measure of wages. Hence, hours are not controlled for.
The results are summarized as follows:

1. Even though the DADS, which are administrative data, have wages of excellent quality, the amount of wage cuts in the DADS is similar to the number of wage cuts observed in the LFS. Approximately 25 per cent of the workers (non-job changers employed full-time) experienced nominal wage cuts between 1991 and 1992.

2. As observed in the US, the frequency of wage cuts is negatively related to inflation.
3. Among full-time workers with pay cuts and without firm change:
   - 34 per cent have better working conditions (with respect, for example, to night work)
   - 22 per cent face a decrease in their annual bonus
   - 30 per cent change 4-digit occupation
   - More than 60 per cent are in one, at least, of these three situations.

Hence, what Goux (1997) shows is different from what was learnt from other studies: there are not as many measurement errors as usually thought in LFS-type data; better information on the job explains away many of the nominal wage cuts.

Three recent papers, all written in 1999, address the same questions for Italy, Switzerland and the UK. We review them in that order.

Dessy studies the situation of Italy using a data source coming from the Bank of Italy, the Bank of Italy panel data set for the period 1989 to 1995. Dessy studies both stayers and movers using as a wage measure the net income from employment.

The results are the following:

1. Confirming widespread prejudices on Italy, there is indeed more rigidity than in most other countries.
2. However, it appears that stayers and movers are similarly affected by nominal rigidity.

Fehr and Goette study the situation prevailing in Switzerland. Their data source is the Swiss LFS for the period from 1991 to 1996. They analyse earnings per working hour of non-job changers. Their methodology rests on the estimation of an econometric model in the spirit of Altonji-Devereux's.

The results are:

1. In periods of very low inflation, there are 12 per cent of rigid wages and 25 per cent of cuts
2. From the estimated model, one-third of what should be wage cuts turn into wage freezes for stayers and 15 per cent for movers, because of wage rigidity.
3. Full-time workers receive a pay freeze more often than part-timers.

The final study of the rigidity of nominal wages is by Smith for the UK. The data source that is used is the British Household Panel Study (BHPS) for the period 1991 to 1996. The earnings per week of non-job changers is the analysed measure of wage. An interesting feature of the BHPS is the following. When the reported earnings have been compared with the payslip, the

BHPS reports that this check has been performed. Hence, Smith can compare wage changes for workers with checked earnings with those of workers with unchecked earnings.

The results are summarized below:

1. There is a substantial amount of wage cuts and freezes: 22 per cent of pay cuts and 9 per cent of rigid wages.
2. After accounting for rounding, measurement error and long-term contracts, 1 per cent of the workers have rigid pay.
3. Contrarily to what is asserted by most analyses, measurement error *increases* apparent rigidity, since workers have an inflexible idea of their pay (this is shown using the BHPS reports when the pay has been checked with the payslip).

All these European studies point to very interesting results, often counter-intuitive given the American ones, that seem to show that either there is at least as much rigidity (or flexibility) in Europe as in the US (bar Italy), or American studies overestimate the importance of measurement errors.

10.6   Implications for employment

In a recent paper, David Card, Francis Kramarz and Thomas Lemieux analyse the implications of wage rigidity on employment in three countries: Canada, France and the United States (Krueger and Pischke (1997) examine a similar question by comparing Germany and the US). More precisely, they seek to answer the following simple question. Can we explain the dichotomy between the US, where real wages of unskilled workers fell and aggregate employment increased, and Continental Europe, where real wages of unskilled workers were constant and employment stagnant, by responses to common adverse demand shocks in an environment where wages are flexible versus an environment with high minimum wages and strong unions where wages are rigid? Is there evidence of this trade-off hypothesis? This hypothesis, formulated by Krugman (1993), therefore states that increasing inequality in the US and increasing unemployment in Europe are the two faces of the same coin. It is quite easy to summarize the results since they amount to a clear and negative answer to the above question. The trade-off hypothesis does not hold when confronted by the data. The same answer is also found in Krueger and Pischke for the US versus Germany. In all three countries, Card, Kramarz and Lemieux (1999) use similar data sources – LFS for all, under the same sample period, the 1980s. Since the result is important, it is crucial to detail the methodology. We specify the various steps that lead to the result:

1. The authors show that the three countries faced the same shocks (technological, such as computerization, or trade).
2. They construct sex-age-education cells at the beginning and at the end of the 1980s. The crucial variables are employment ratio and wage for each cell.
3. They construct for each cell a measure of the shocks (one is the wage at the beginning of the decade, the second is the percentage of computer users in the cell at the end of the decade).
4. They show that relative wages changed in the US in favour of the high-skilled.
5. They show that relative wages did not change in France over the period.
6. They show that Canada is in between.
7. They then look at the changes in the relative employment ratios across cells in the US.
8. They compare these with those observed for France and for Canada.
9. The trade-off hypothesis should imply that the shocks should have affected the relative employment ratios of the less-skilled in France much more than in the US since wage rigidity prevented the necessary adjustments.
10. The estimation results show that the changes in the relative employment ratios are similar across countries.

The conclusion should now be obvious: Krugman's trade-off hypothesis, in its simplest version at least, is rejected by the data.

10.7   Firms' behaviour

The previous result may seem surprising. How can we reconcile all the facts that we know on the United States, France and other countries? I tend to believe that the understanding of firms' behaviour is necessary at this point. A first attempt to show how French firms gain flexibility in a rigid world has been made by John Abowd, Patrick Corbel and Francis Kramarz. By using data on flows of workers (not stocks) with information on the type of contract, the skill, the age and the seniority of the exiting workers for a sample of French establishments followed over a period of four years (1987 to 1990), based on the Déclarations de Mouvement de Main d'Oeuvre (DMMO), Abowd, Corbel and Kramarz (1999) show the following result:

In France, when an establishment is changing employment, the adjustment is made primarily by reducing entry and not by changing the separation rates, except when establishments have to separate from a large fraction of their workforce, such as 15 or 20 per cent (see the left part of Figure 10.6). This result is robust to various controls and, in particular, to the introduction of establishment fixed-effects in all regressions.

From this result, we may conclude that, in a country that appears to have institutional rigidities, there are ways to circumvent wage rigidities and high firing costs. In particular, there is one institutional flexibility, the existence of short-term contracts, which helps firms to accommodate shocks, select workers, and so forth. Even without changing their employment, firms are in a position to make potential turnover savings, for instance by hiring less senior workers after a quit. Indeed, firms can control their total labour costs. This is what John Abowd, Francis Kramarz and Sébastien Roux have started to study. More precisely, they want to understand how firms make turnover savings and manage their wage bill. To accomplish this task, they rely on a newly available matched employee-employer administrative and exhaustive dataset on wages, hours, and so on, for the French private sector (there are more than 1 million observations when we study only one of the 22 French regions). Workers are followed from year to year (here 1996 to 1997). The available variables are total earnings, total hours, total days for each worker in each establishment of the region. Using these variables they are able to decompose the changes in the total wage bill into those due to changes of workers present in both years (stayers), changes due to entering workers (entrants), and changes due to workers leaving the establishment (exiters).

To summarize their preliminary results, we see that:

1. The total wage bill moves as that of entrants and exiters not as that of stayers.
2. Year to year changes in the wage bill are 8.3 per cent of the average wage bill.
3. Wage bill creation rate (defined similarly to what Davis and Haltiwanger, 1992, do for the job creation rate as $\frac{(e_{t+1} - e_t)}{\frac{e_t + e_{t+1}}{2}}$ where e denotes employ- 16.7 per cent (with 11.6 per cent for entrants and exiters, and 5.0 per cent for stayers).
4. Wage bill destruction rate (defined similarly to the use by Davis and Haltiwanger (1992) for the job destruction rate, when the above rate is negative) is 47.1 per cent (with 39.7 per cent for entrants and exiters, and 7.4 per cent for stayers).
5. Among stayers, wage-bill destruction hits the highly skilled.
6. Among entrants and exiters, wage-bill destruction also hits the highly skilled.
7. The last two statements are also true for wage-bill creation.

Hence, once more, in the face of strong wage rigidities, a firm may use various means to control its wage bill when hit by positive or negative

Figure 10.6 Entry and exit rates by establishment growth

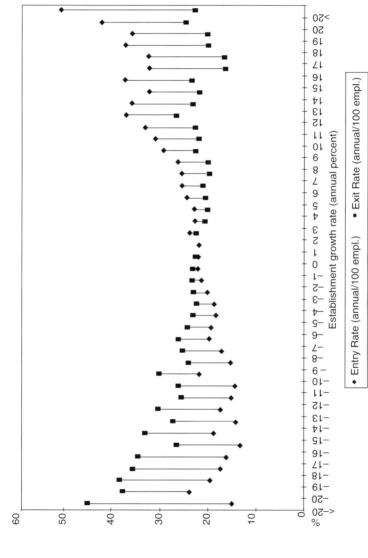

Source: Abowd, Corbel and Kramarz (1999)
Notes: Includes establishment and year effects.

economic shocks. Of course, this is only a start. But using this kind of data is obviously the way of the future for analyzing firms' simultaneous control of wages, hours, and employment.

10.8 Conclusion: understanding wage changes

I first summarize the main conclusions from this survey of the recent studies of wage rigidity:

1. The timing of the analysis is essential to identify most of the effects, since the level of inflation is obviously very important. In fact, it may be the most convincing piece of evidence showing the existence of nominal rigidities: wage change distributions in years of high inflation strongly differ from those observed in years of low inflation (see Kahn or Card and Hyslop for individual data and Groshen and Schweizer for establishment data). In addition, human-resource managers claim that they dislike cutting wages (Bewley).

2. Labour market institutions obviously matter. They explain the formidable amount of rigidity observed in Italy. In other parts of Europe, flexibility is achieved through other means than wage cuts (Goux, Abowd, Kramarz, Roux). This may also help explain the differences between Europe and the US where rigidity seems less pervasive. To uncover the precise mechanisms by which firms achieve their goals, it appears crucial to obtain data both on the job (such as schedules or a precise occupation) and on the employing firm.

3. Because of the above problems of time period or institutions, the evidence of wage rigidities may appear to be mixed: not all measures, not all datasets, not all types of employees indicate such rigidity, either nominal or real. In fact, even though the difference between real and nominal rigidity is important for theorists, it may matter much less in periods of low inflation for firm policies.

4. The evidence on measurement errors is also mixed: some authors claim that their data are clean whereas others do not. In addition, some authors view measurement error as leading to understating wage rigidity (it adds an error term to an otherwise inflexible wage: Card and Hyslop or Altonji and Devereux) whereas others claim that it may lead to overstating wage rigidity (because workers declare the same wage two years in a row, even when their wage has changed: Smith).

5. The data source seems to matter, in particular in the US, for instance when comparing results based on the PSID with those based on the CPS, since the sampling frame and the information available in the various sources make comparisons difficult. On the other hand, in France, the only European country for which such a comparison

is available, survey data and administrative data display the same amount of rigidity or flexibility. Recall also that data on individuals, from labour force surveys for instance, paint a different picture than that obtained using data from firms (the focus is different: no problem of measurement error, more information on the job or the occupation, less information on other environmental or social outcomes).

6. There are obvious differences between categories of workers. Rigidity widely differs for workers paid by the hour and for salaried workers in the US. The first face fewer pay cuts (Kahn). Also, rigidity widely differs for blue-collar workers and for white-collar workers in the US. The first also face fewer pay cuts (Kahn). However, the minimum wage may play a role (Card and Hyslop).

7. The insight that one obtains depends on the technique that is used. More precisely, non-parametric evidence is complementary to more structural approaches, estimated by maximum likelihood techniques. Unfortunately, there is very little that helps explain wage changes both theoretically and empirically. The explanatory power of classical variables is almost zero in any regression, even though we know how to explain wage levels (see for instance, Abowd, Kramarz and Margolis, 1999).

8. Indeed, new insights on the extent of rigidity and on its impact on employment will come from better data sources, more specifically matched employer-employee longitudinal data sets. In particular, such sources may help understand the within-firm composition effects that are described for the US by Groshen and Schweitzer and by Abowd, Corbel and Kramarz or Abowd, Kramarz and Roux for France. At this stage, I do believe that they are crucial fully to assess the magnitude of rigidity that, in reality, affects the firms. I tend to believe that in periods of low inflation, there are multiple ways of 'managing the wage bill' other than cutting pay.

After this little guided tour of recent empirical studies on nominal or real wage rigidity, could we draw conclusions that would be helpful to economic theory? I believe that evidence of wage rigidity exists, or to be more specific, firms appear to prefer to cut employment rather than cut wages in a downturn. This is really what economic theory has to explain. This is all the more crucial that, as already mentioned, microeconometricians are unable to explain individual wage changes. In fact, almost all studies that we have presented have adopted statistical models rather than more structural models inspired from theory. Indeed, theory seems to have little to say about the respective role of firm-specific policies versus person-specific explanations of wage changes that appears to be empirically relevant.

References

Abowd, J.M., Corbel, P. and Kramarz, F. (1999) 'The Entry and Exit of Workers and the Growth of Employment', *Review of Economics and Statistics*, vol. 81 (2), May, pp. 170–87.

Abowd, J.M., Kramarz, F. and Margolis, D.N. (1999) 'High-Wage Workers and High-Wage Firms', *Econometrica*, vol. 67 (2), March, pp. 251–333.

Abowd, J.M., Kramarz, F. and Roux, S. (in progress), 'The Wage Bill'.

Altonji, J.G. and Devereux, P.J. (1999) 'Extent and Consequences of Downward Nominal Wage Rigidity', NBER Working Paper no. 7236.

Bewley, T.F. (1998) 'Why Not Cut Pay?', *European Economic Review*, vol. 42, pp. 459–90.

Card, D (1996) 'The Effect of Unions on the Structure of Wages' *Econometrica*, 64 (4), pp. 957–79.

Card, D. and Hyslop, D. (1997) 'Does Inflation Grease the Wheels of the Labor Market?', in Romer, C.D. and Romer, D.H. (eds) *Reducing Inflation: Motivation and Strategy* (Chicago: University of Chicago Press, for NBER), pp. 71–114.

Card, D., Kramarz, F. and Lemieux, T. (1999) 'Changes in the Relative Structure of Wages and Employment: a Comparison of the United States, Canada, and France', *Canadian Journal of Economics*, vol. 32 (4), pp. 843–77.

Davis, S.J. and Haltiwanger, J. (1992) 'Gross Job Creation, Gross Job Destruction and Employment Reallocation', *Quarterly Journal of Economics*, vol. 107, pp. 819–63.

Dessy, O. (1999) 'Wage Rigidity in Italy', mimeo, University of Southampton.

Fehr, E. and Goette, L. (1999) 'Nominal Wage Rigidities in Periods of Low Inflation', mimeo, University of Zürich.

Goux, D. (1997) 'Les salaires nominaux sont-ils rigides à la baisse?', mimeo, INSEE.

Grandmont, J.M. (1989) 'Keynesian Issues and Economic Theory', *Scandinavian Journal of Economics*, vol. 91 (2), pp. 265–93.

Groshen, E.L. and Schweitzer, M.E. (1997) 'Identifying Inflation's Grease and Sand Effects in the Labor Market', Federal Reserve Board Report, no. 31.

Kahn, S. (1997) 'Evidence of Nominal Wage Stickiness from Microdata', *American Economic Review*, vol. 87 (5), pp. 993–1008.

Krueger, A.B. and Pischke, J.S. 'Observations and Conjectures on the U.S. Employment Miracle', NBER Research Working Paper no. 6146.

Krugman, P. (1993) 'Protection and Developing Countries,' in Dornbusch, R. (ed.) *Policymaking in the Open Economy* (Oxford: Oxford University Press), pp. 127–48.

Malinvaud, E. (1977) *The Theory of Unemployment Reconsidered* (Oxford: Blackwell).

McLaughlin, K.J. (1994) 'Rigid Wages?', *Journal of Monetary Economics*, vol. 34, pp. 383–414.

McLeod, W.B., and Malcomson, J.M. (1993) 'Investments, Holdup, and the Form of Market Contracts', *American Economic Review*, vol. 83 (4), pp. 811–37.

O'Brien, A.P. (1989) 'A Behavioral Explanation for Nominal Wage Rigidity During the Great Depression', *Quarterly Journal of Economics*, vol. 104 (4), pp. 719–35.

Smith J.C. (1999) 'Nominal Wage Rigidity in the UK, mimeo, University of Warwick.

Part IV
Econometrics

11
The Getting of Macroeconomic Wisdom*

Adrian Pagan
Research School of Social Sciences, Australian National University, Australia

'The beginning of Wisdom is this: get wisdom and whatever you get, get insight.'

(Proverbs, 4:7, RSV)

11.1 Introduction

As the proverb says, it is wisdom that we want and much of what we do is aimed at acquiring it. On reflection, the acquisition of wisdom is a two-stage process. In the first stage ideas are accumulated and explored; in the second those ideas that have withstood the 'experience test' are retained and recounted to others as insights. Macroeconometric modelling involves the same dichotomy and it was one that was fruitfully exploited by the Cowles Commission researchers, albeit informally. In the first stage, evidence needs to be assembled and *summarized* in a convenient and meaningful way, while, in the second, effort is devoted to *interpreting* the evidence through a set of principles or theories.[1] For the Cowles Commission the two stages were represented by the construction of a reduced form and a structure. Thus the distinction has a distinguished history in econometrics. However, all too often it has been ignored and the two stages are blurred together. Indeed, this blurring of the two categories goes back to the very beginnings of macroeconometrics and even features one of the most prominent members of the Cowles Commission, Tjalling Koopmans. The occasion was his famous critique of Burns and Mitchell's (1947) work on the business cycle. Although Koopmans (1947) seems to recognize that the latter are attempting to summarize the available data on the business cycle, he quickly complains that one needs theoretical models

---

* With apologies to Henry Handel Richardson. My thanks to Jacques Drèze for his comments on this chapter. An extended version is available at http://econrsss. anu.edu.au/staff/adrian/index.html.

to interpret the data, and so the steps of summarizing and interpreting the data are rolled together in his critique. I will place great emphasis on the distinction in this paper – and it actually provides headings for each of the sections that follow – as I believe that much more progress can be made by *hewing* to the division than trying to amalgamate the two stages into one. Moreover, important developments in econometrics in the past decade, namely the development of indirect estimation methods, as in Gourieroux *et al.* (1993), Smith (1993) and Gallant and Tauchen (1996), have this distinction at their core.

11.2 Summarizing the data

Consider first how one would want to summarize the data. On one level this is an easy question to answer. It is hard to avoid the impression that the exploration of issues in applied macroeconomics has always had a strong visual element to it. A very good example would be the Phillips curve, in which the rate of change of wages and unemployment were cross-plotted. Another would be the treatment of the relation between money growth and inflation in Lucas (1980). Indeed, some think that such evidence has been the most influential type in stimulating thought about the macroeconomy and in influencing policy actions – Summers (1991). Certainly, it does seem likely that the early history of applied macroeconomics largely involved an inspection of graphs. Such evidence can, however, be tricky to use. Accordingly, the development of statistical methods was greeted with great enthusiasm. These methods enabled many pieces of information to be reduced to a much smaller and manageable set, either in the form of a regression output or through parametric indices such as volatility, duration of a business cycle, and so on.

Early statistical methods focused upon the first two sample moments of a series but analysis of macroeconomic data clearly revealed that these moments failed to capture the temporal dependence that was a feature of such series. Eventually the deficiency was corrected by a computation of the auto-correlation function, and the resulting extended set of moments was used to describe the important characteristics of a time series. Thus the summarization stage is rightly viewed as one that largely involves the selection of the best statistical model for a series; economics really only enters into it through a naming of what variables it is that one seeks evidence on. Of course, the selection of the latter is not a trivial issue, and choosing a set of variables that is too narrow may well prejudice the answers obtained.

11.2.1 Summarizing the evidence on a single series

As mentioned above, the development of statistical science initiated a move from graphical displays to methods of summarizing the data which involved the estimation of a set of parameters – means, variances, and so on. Academics were naturally attracted to this, since the method promised both replicability and a variety of ways of estimating the quantity of interest, for example the aggregate inflation rate might be measured as either the mean or the median of the inflation rates of individual commodities. Moreover, the possibility was also raised that simple parametric models might be capable of summarizing a vast amount of information in a succinct way, for example while a first order auto-regression (AR(1)) of the form

$$y_t = \rho y_{t-1} + e_t \tag{1}$$

has an infinite number of auto-correlations, they depend upon the single parameter ρ, and so a complete auto-correlation function might be represented by a single parameter.

Linear models of the conditional mean

The simplification principle was central to the work of Box and Jenkins (1970). Those applying their techniques to macroeconomic data found that such series could be well represented with fairly simple forms, sometimes surprisingly so. A classical example was the finding that the log of GDP y_t could be well represented by making its growth rate, $z_t = \Delta y_t$, either an AR(1) or an AR(2)

$$z_t = \rho_1 z_{t-1} + \rho_2 z_{t-2} + e_t \tag{2}$$

that is, the time dependence was of a fairly simple form. What was perhaps more surprising, given that the second order process had been selected to capture the 'business cycle', was that the roots of the polynomial $(1 - \rho_1 L - \rho_2 L^2) = 0$ were *real and not complex* (see Pagan (1999) for evidence on this for 10 countries). This is a challenging finding for theory construction since, for a long time, textbooks had taught that one needed a complex root AR(2) process to produce the business cycle, and ingenious models had been constructed so as to achieve such an outcome.

Models of volatility

Although simple models such as (1) and (2) proved very effective at characterizing macroeconomic series, they could not capture all the characteristics that were observed. In particular, series of many asset prices showed 'clustering of volatility', in that a run of small or large values of $(\Delta y_t)^2$ or $|\Delta y_t|$ was clearly visible in the data. Extensions of models like (1) and (2) were deemed necessary and Engle's (1982) development of the Auto-regressive Conditional Heteroskedasticity (ARCH) class of models provided a good way of parameterizing this evidence. After that development it became the norm for describing this feature of the data. In the ARCH model $e_t = \sigma_t \, \varepsilon_t$, where ε_t was n.i.d. $(0,1)$ and σ_t, the conditional standard deviation, was related linearly to e^2_{t-1}. Many alternative mappings of σ_t into $\{e_{t-1}\}$ have been proposed – see the surveys in Bollerslev et al. (1994) and Pagan (1996). There can be little doubt about the existence of conditional volatility in asset prices and that it is a feature which must be accounted for in theorizing with any models that are capable of producing predictions about asset price behaviour.

Non-linear models for the conditional mean

Because financial prices generally had $\rho = 1$ one was effectively substituting $(\Delta y_t)^2$ or $|\Delta y_t|$ for y_t as the object to plot and for which auto-correlation functions and so on should be computed. But the processes describing the redefined variables could still be thought of as linear ones. The urge to complicate is a strong one, though, and gradually enquiries arose over whether some non-linearities might be introduced into the basic models. In the case of the modelling of volatility, such an extension proved to be useful at a very early stage in the development of ARCH models, mainly because of a feature that had been observed in the data, namely, what was termed 'leverage', wherein volatility seemed higher when the market was falling. The seminal work on extending the class of parametric models to capture this effect was that of the late Dan Nelson (1991) in his EGARCH (Exponential Generalised ARCH) model.

The situation is much murkier when it comes to assessing the progress in finding important non-linearities in the conditional means of y_t or Δy_t. Many non-linear models have been proposed. A simple example would be Potter's (1995) variant of a threshold auto-regression (the SETAR model):

$$\Delta y_t = a_0 + b_0 1(\Delta y_{t-1} < 0) + [a_1 + b_1 1(\Delta y_{t-1} < 0)] \, \Delta y_{t-1} + e_{1t} \qquad (3)$$

Others are the asymmetric persistence model of Beaudry and Koop (1993), the 'overheating' model of Pesaran and Potter (1997), and the Markov switching ('recurring states') model in Hamilton (1989).

All of the models described above are relatively simple to understand and, consequently, represent quite attractive extensions to the basic linear models that have been the norm in summarizing the data. The question that has to be asked, though, is whether they summarize important characteristics of the data. It is true that statistical tests tend to reject the linear model in favour of non-linear ones, but it is also well known that any regression can be very sensitive to a few influential points in the data, and there has not been enough work done to date in exploring the origins and benefits of a non-linear model.

11.2.2   Summarizing the evidence on multivariate series

Multivariate regressions

When faced with a number of series, data summary is often done through the estimated coefficients of multivariate regressions. Classic examples are the Phillips curve and growth regressions that relate cross-country growth rates to a large number of variables. Sometimes these relationships incorporate non-linear regression, either through simple functional forms or by using the recurring states way of inducing a non-linearity. There has also been some use of factor analysis to try to separate data into factors that might be later related to economic variables. For time series, examples of the latter would be Chauvet (1998) for output changes and Chauvet and Potter (1998) for the equity premium, while in cross-sections the decomposition is into factors that are local (idiosyncratic), and global.

VARs

The Cowles Commission chose to summarize multivariate sets of data through a reduced form in which endogenous variables were conditioned upon the exogenous and predetermined variables contained in a specified structure. There was nothing in this choice, however, that was specific to time series. As the subject of time series developed in statistics, though, the natural strategy was to extend the univariate approaches to multivariate series, and this meant a vector of AR processes (VARs). The idea seems to have first been proposed by Quenouille (1957) but it was Sims's (1980) paper which made them the dominant way of summarizing the multivariate dependence seen within macroeconomic data.

The p'th order VAR is

$$y_t = A_1 y_{t-1} \div A_2 y_{t-2} + \dots A_p y_t - p + e_t \qquad (4)$$

where y_t is an $n \times 1$ vector, $\text{cov}(e_t) = \Omega$, and one could summarize the data with $A_1, \dots, A_p$ and Ω. Alternatively, following Sims's advice, one could write out the vector moving average (VMA) representation

$$y_t = D_0 e_t + D_1 e_{t-1} + \dots \qquad (5)$$

and one might then use the *impulse responses* D_j and Ω rather than $A_1, \dots, A_p$ and Ω to summarize the data. Most of the available literature which deals with VARs as a way of summarizing the data has been concerned with choosing p and imposing some restrictions upon the A_j in order to help with forecasting.

Vector error correction models

If one feels that the y_t processes are integrated of order one, $I(1)$, and common stochastic trends are evident among them, then it is known that

$I - A_1 - \ldots - A_p$ is singular and the VAR is replaced by a vector error correction model (VECM) (assuming for convenience that $p = 1$)

$$\Delta y_t = \alpha\beta'y_{t-1} + e_t \tag{6}$$

Now the data is summarized by α (the loadings), β (the co-integrating vectors) and Ω, while the VMA representation is

$$\Delta y_t = C(L)e_t \tag{7}$$

In the VECM format some combinations of the e_t are permanent shocks and others are transitory. An extensive literature has evolved which suggests that there are often fewer stochastic trends than n in the data, that is, the number of permanent shocks is less than n.

Non-linearities in VARs

Just as VARs were the obvious extension of univariate models to the multivariate context, one might expect that non-linear VARs would have emerged to parallel the literature on univariate series. In fact, this development has been much slower, probably due to the need to develop some computationally tractable forms. To date no particular format seems to have gained favour. One relatively simple method that has had some application involves treating all of the series Δy_{jt} as being driven by a single common factor z_t and to then introduce the non-linearity through the evolutionary process for this factor. In most applications the common factor is not a common trend: that is, the y_{jt} are not co-integrated. Because z_t is a univariate process all of the non-linear structures mentioned earlier might be adopted for it, but the most popular approach has been to introduce the non-linearity through a Markov switching format, for example, Chauvet (1998).

Although the simple strategy outlined above has some appeal, other types of non-linearity might need to be accounted for. One example would be the possibility that impulse responses show asymmetric behaviour, depending on a particular outcome for some index ϕ_t, for example, ϕ_t might be either the sign of the change in a variable – Cover (1992) – or an index indicating whether the economy is in a contraction or expansion phase. Mostly these non-linearities are handled by interacting the index with some of the variables under discussion and it is these multiplicative variables that constitute the non-linearity. Other types of non-linearity can arise if variables change discretely, as with the Federal Funds target rate set by the Federal Open Market Committee (FOMC) – Hamilton and Jorda (1997) – and certain shifts in policy regimes – Sims (1999).

11.3 Interpreting the data

It is in the process of interpreting data, particularly in the context of considering policy options, that economic theory becomes important. Whilst a purely statistical summary of the data can be a useful source of 'stylized facts', drawing attention to what needs to be explained, and the statistical models underlying the summary can be useful for forecasting, ultimately one needs to have some way of explaining why the 'facts' are as they are. To do that we construct economic models of the series under investigation with the aim of providing a convincing story about the observed outcomes; as Dawes (1999, p. 29) says: 'People have a great deal of difficulty appreciating statistical contingency in the absence of a causal story that makes the contingency "reasonable".' How detailed this story is depends a great deal upon the nature of the storyteller and the audience he is addressing. Generally, the story we construct is about the behaviour of agents, and for this reason we will refer to these as behavioural models. Behaviour can be described by accounting for how choices are made. The methods to perform the latter task range from introspection through rules of thumb to optimizing frameworks.

It is imperative that the interpretation step be clearly demarcated from that producing the statistical summary. Identifying a good statistical model for summarizing the data should not be confused with the model we wish to use for storytelling.[2] Often this principle has been ignored. Many of those who implemented the Cowles Commission's ideas wrote down a series of structural equations as a statement of the way they saw the economic system as operating and then deduced a reduced form from that, which they subsequently utilized to summarize the data. There was some flexibility in what they did, in that many behavioural structures could be compatible with a given reduced form, but it is nevertheless the case that the choice of model as the vehicle to summarize the data came from the stories they were trying to tell and not, as I would argue, from the principle of selecting the statistical model that best fits the data.

11.3.1 Interpreting univariate series

There is little doubt that the nature of univariate series such as output behaviour, price inflation and asset prices are often used as quick checks on whether the interpretation of the data being offered is a reasonable one. For example, the fact that US GDP growth has positive serial correlation has often been used to argue that many RBC models are incapable of generating the correct process for the path of aggregate economic activity – see Cogley and Nason (1995) and Ramey and Watson (1997) – while the magnitude of the equity premium has also cast doubt upon many models based on simple capital asset pricing principles. Another example would be E. Nelson's (1998) use of the fact that inflation is a very persistent process to query models of inflation and fluctuations such as that of King and Wolman (1996), since the latter imply relatively weak persistence in inflation. Almost all quantitative economic models do contain predictions about univariate series and so it seems a good strategy to elicit these in a first round assessment. Zellner and Palm (1974) recommended such a strategy quite a while ago.

We have learned a lot from studying such simple comparisons and discovering how models would need to be adjusted to be able to interpret those features of the data. For example, as we noted earlier, volatility clustering in asset prices demands some explanation. Some optimizing behavioural models have emerged in which volatility clustering comes from behavioural choices rather than from the nature of the exogenous processes that drive the system, for example, den Haan and Spear (1998), but the most successful methods seem to be those in which agents are assumed to have rather simple trading strategies, for example Lux and Marchesi (1999). Perhaps this is not surprising. The volume of literature on algorithms to detect turning points in asset prices ('technical analysis') points to the need to develop heterogeneous agent models in which some traders do not optimize in any clearly defined way but follow rules that are data dependent.

11.3.2 Interpreting multivariate data

SVARs

In the past two decades macroeconomics has wholeheartedly adopted the idea of shocks as the driving forces of the economic system, and discussion of their role is either carried out by reference to particular names such as money and supply or to some of their characteristics such as permanent or transitory. Given such a development, it is inevitable that any data will often be interpreted in terms of a set of shocks. In their simplest incarnation most economic models can be written either as a structural VAR (SVAR)

$$B_0 y_t = B_1 y_{t-1} + \varepsilon_t \tag{8}$$

or a 'structural VMA'

$$y_t = C_0 \varepsilon_t + C_1 \varepsilon_{t-1} + \dots \tag{9}$$

where y_t is a vector of n variables and there are k ($\leq n$) shocks ε_t that drive the system. These shocks are assumed to have a covariance matrix Σ that is diagonal. The unknown parameters in B_0, B_1 and Σ are then chosen to replicate the data as summarized in A_1 and Ω.

Some restrictions must be placed upon B_0, B_1 and Σ in order to differentiate the shocks. Most often this is done by specifying the nature of the C_j for the different types of shocks and by making the shocks uncorrelated. In his original work Sims made B_0 triangular so that C_0 also inherited that property.[3] Such a restriction requires that one be able to identify which shocks have a non-zero contemporaneous influence on which variables, for example, money shocks might be assumed to affect output and prices only with a lag but interest rates and the exchange rate contemporaneously, and this leads to some zeros in C_0. In almost all instances in which SVARs are adopted the system is treated as being *exactly identified*, in that the number of parameters in B_0, B_1 and Σ is identical to that in A_1 and Ω. Thus the transition from summarization to interpretation simply involves a rotation, and the story being told cannot be invalidated using the data. There is a downside to this robustness since there are many economic models which are exactly identified and so there are many stories that would be consistent with any given data summary. Consequently, the choice between them must be made on other grounds than the ability to fit the data. In practice discrimination has generally involved judgements about the plausibility of the C_j associated with different models.

Although one cannot deny the popularity of just identified SVAR's among academic researchers, some of this popularity arises from inappropriate uses of the information they supply. One often sees results being cited that have been established with a particular interpretation of the data, that is, an assumption about the nature of B_0, as if these were summaries of the data. For example, it is often said that money shocks from a given SVAR system show a certain pattern for the C_j and that this justifies a behavioural model favoured by the author, even when the said model would never imply the type of B_0 that was used to find the money shocks. There is no reason at all why the C_j found under one interpretation will hold under another: that is, the effects of a shock are not facts from the data but are specific to a particular interpretation of the data. All one learns from the data is the likely magnitude of the C_j for a given interpretation. One caveat to this complaint needs to be entered. If the series y_t are $I(1)$, a transient change in ε_t may now effect a permanent change in y_t, and a division of shocks into those that are permanent and those that are temporary can be done using the parameters of (6), that is, from the data summary alone. Therefore, if one knows that certain shocks in a model are permanent (say those to technology), while others are only transitory, then it is possible to regard the C_j associated with the permanent shocks as facts, in that they do not depend upon the provision of a story (except in so far as one needs to believe the names given to the permanent shocks).

Just identified SVARs have not been very popular among those involved in policy formulation. Forecasts are often at the heart of the policy process but, since predictions made from an exactly identified (8) are identical to those from (4) ($p = 1$), there would be no reason to go through the steps to find B_0 and ϵ_t if all one wanted to do was to produce predictions. It is only restrictions upon (4) that are of use in forecasting. They are also not a good vehicle for performing policy experiments. This occurs for a number of reasons, each connected with problems involving the objects they focus on, ε_t. Rudebusch (1998), for example, observes that the time series of estimates of ε_t are hard to reconcile with known policy changes. Whilst unanticipated policy shocks can occur, the ε_t really measure the extent of the failure to predict y_t from the past history of those variables included in the VAR, and thus the errors are composed of a myriad of influences other than policy actions. Consequently, treating the ϵ_t literally as policy variables is not particularly appealing. It is also the case that policy generally relates directly to variables in y_t rather than to ε_t and it becomes torturous to try to convert policy actions into a history for ε_t.

SEMs

SVARs tend to be rather small systems with large numbers of parameters due to the fact that there are no excluded dynamics from each structural equation, that is, no zeros are imposed upon B_1, ..., B_p. Macroeconomic models popular in the 1960s and 1970s generally involved large numbers of variables. These models were often referred to as simultaneous equation models (SEMs) and imposed restrictions upon the dynamics as well as upon B_0. To some extent their size is misleading as many variables were determined through identities, with the number of stochastic structural equations being relatively small, and it is this latter number which should be used in any comparison with SVARs. Whether one prefers to impose restrictions upon dynamics (SEMs) rather than to make an assumption that shocks are uncorrelated (SVARs) seems to be more a matter of taste than truth. SEMs are still quite widely used in the policy process, although the models are somewhat different to those of the 1960s and 1970s in that rational expectations generally play a key role in them, for example, some of the models in Bank of England (1999). SEMs almost always involve over-identified systems and the policy variables in them are directly manipulated, so it is probably these elements that account for their popularity in institutions concerned with policy formation.

Academic calibrated models

Although the SVAR and SEM approaches represent ways of moving from a purely statistical model (the VAR) towards a parametric economic model that captures many characteristics of the data, they do so by using economic theory in a loose way, and relying a good deal upon a modeller's prior views of the nature of short-term adjustment mechanisms. A different tradition, rather loosely termed 'calibration' here, has taken the opposite tack of utilizing economic theory in a very *precise* way, at the same time dispensing with the objective of holistically capturing the data generating process (DGP). Instead, the intention is to replicate only a few features of the data, for example, some moments. There are many models that fall into this class – RBC models are well-known members of the set but do not exhaust it – for example, King and Wolman (1996) construct models of this type featuring money and monopolistic competition. It cannot be emphasized too strongly that the specification of these models is predominantly influenced by the need to have a story about events that is based on optimizing agents. Thus, whilst these models provide a story about the macroeconomy, it is not necessarily one about the macroeconomy under observation. The models provide an interpretation of the data, but it is unclear how valid the interpretation is, and it is this latter caveat that has caused the most heartburn, particularly if they are to be used to shed light on policy options.

Certainly for learning about the validity of a theory and for convincing policy makers that it tells a story that is worth listening to, one needs some information upon how well the model fits the data and in what way it doesn't. A large number of procedures have emerged to do this and they can be usefully classified into three groups:

1. Methods that examine the Euler equations which are at the core of these models.
2. Methods that focus on the historical tracking record of the model.
3. Methods that aim to make inferences robust to the fact that the calibrated model is almost certainly mis-specified.

Tests of the Euler equations have either used the standard J-test for the validity of the implied moment conditions or have adopted transformations of it that may have more appeal from an economic perspective, for example, Durlauf and Hall (1990) and Durlauf and Maccini (1995) derive a 'noise ratio' index that is equivalent to studying an R^2 rather than an F statistic (as the J-test is). Whilst it is important to compute these indices, there can be little doubt that a useful supplement would be a visual impression of how well the model fits a series of data points, that is, how well can (say) an RBC model reproduce the actual movements in GDP rather than just (say) the mean and variance of output growth? Tracking performance of a model was always regarded as an important piece of information in the SEM tradition, and extensive graphical information was generally presented on its ability to do this. Such information was regarded as being particularly valuable when the models were dynamic.

To explore this further, let y_t^* be the calibrated model output, y_t the data, and $u_t = y_t - y_t^*$ the 'model error'. Historical tracking means comparing u_t to zero. However, because calibrated models are generally driven by *unobserved* processes such as technology shocks, it is possible to describe the moments of y_t^* but rarely y_t^* itself. One attempt to circumvent this difficulty has been the use of 'Solow residuals' in order to measure the technology shocks that enter into RBC models. Whilst it is true that technology shocks are linear combinations of output, capital and labour in these models, the latter trio should be measured using their *predictions* from the model and not their *actual* realizations. Only if this is done will the technology shocks be consistent with the model itself and allow a proper evaluation of its tracking performance. But then one no longer has an observed measure of the shocks.

In the above analyses the central idea was that the calibrated model was the DGP. However, most builders of these models would maintain that this is unlikely to be true: that is, the calibrated model is mis-specified. This fact raises some difficult issues of inference. If all one was interested in doing was to test if the calibrated model was the DGP, the standard testing procedures as discussed above would be adequate. However, if one is making some inferences about a quantity $g(\theta)$ that depends on the calibrated model parameters θ, then the fact that the calibrated model does not describe the DGP must be taken into account. Mostly this problem has been ignored in the literature: for example, Eichenbaum (1991) and Christiano and Eichenbaum (1992) assume that the calibrated model is the DGP and perform inferences about $g(\theta)$ using Generalised Method of Moments estimators of θ. However, when the model is not the DGP the estimators of θ will not have standard properties and this will impact upon the distribution of the estimator of $g(\theta)$. Consequently, it seems important that estimators and test statistics be made robust to this mis-specification in some way.

Statistical methods to do this are given in Pagan (1994) and Diebold *et al.* (1998). The basic idea is very simple – find a good approximation to the DGP and use it to make inferences. To appreciate how this would work, consider a true regression relation which contains a dependent variable y_t and two independent variables ξ_{1t} and ξ_{2t}. An investigator adopts a model (y_t^*) that only incorporates the first of these variables. Consequently, y_t^* involves ξ_{1t} while u_t is a function of ξ_{2t}. Because we know what the true DGP is in this instance we can always figure out the consequences of the mis-specification upon any estimators of the impact of ξ_{1t} upon y_t. In this simple case the effects of mis-specification can be found analytically, but in more general cases they need to be measured by simulating from the DGP. This latter fact suggests that we apply the same idea to calibrated models. In Pagan (1994, p. S8), I proposed such a strategy for calibrated models. The approach is simple to implement and merely requires one to select a statistical model as the DGP from which pseudo-observations can be simulated. Based on the arguments of the current paper, such a model would naturally be whatever has been selected as the way of summarizing the data. I did not give any empirical examples of how the method would work, but Diebold *et al.* (1998) do.

Calibrated policy models

There is another type of calibrated model used in macroeconomics which is on a much larger scale than those used by academics and which has become increasingly popular in institutions concerned with providing advice to policy makers: see for example McKibbin and Sachs (1991), Black *et al.* (1994), McKibbin and Wilcoxen (1995), Black *et al.* (1997) and Laxton *et al.* (1998). Such models have many similarities to their academic cousins but also display significant differences. Apart from size, they place less emphasis on stochastic variation in shocks, and are concerned to make allowances for liquidity-constrained consumers, and so on, in an attempt to capture actual short-run dynamic responses. One of the similarities to academic models is that many of the parameters are either chosen from a literature search or are selected to produce 'realistic' impulse responses to particular shocks. Another is that minimal attention is paid to a precise fitting of the data, with many of the models being designed to inform policy makers through the production of a story about the economic mechanisms rather than the provision of a forecast. However, the latter requirements cannot be entirely ignored. Policy is almost always about actions based on forecasts: as has often been said, inflation targeting should really be described as 'inflation forecast targeting', and so one sees models such as the Canadian and New Zealand ones mentioned above being integrated into the forecasting process.

A good example of the role of these models in leading to wisdom is their use in studying the adjustment of the world economy to the Asian crisis; for example, see McKibbin and Martin (1998) for an analysis of this event with McKibbin and Wilcoxen's (1995) calibrated G-cubed model of the world economy. Many policy-setting institutions utilize such models for understanding some of the longer-term issues of macro policy; the exact values of variables such as output and asset prices from the simulations are rarely regarded as being as important as the insight one obtains into how the factors are likely to play out in response to a specified shock.

There are many interesting issues about how to use these models to generate wisdom and it is an area that is still under-researched. To some extent we do want to know how well they explain features of the data, and certainly we would wish to know what their failures on this score might be. Somehow then one needs to find relatively small models that effectively capture enough of the dimensions of the larger ones as to effect a comparison with the data. Under certain circumstances, it is possible to utilize the output from simulations of the larger models to perform this task. Once performed, such simulations indicate what the implied impulse responses of the artificial economies embedded in the large models are to permanent and transitory shocks, that is, values of $C_M(L)$ in (7) and (9) can be found, where M stands for model. With this information we can always determine a VAR (or VECM) in a given set of variables that would be capable of replicating the $C_M(L)$ up to some specified degree of L (clearly one can never exactly represent an infinite number of C_j with a finite order VAR). The approximating VAR found in this way might then be used as prior information when a VAR is estimated from the data, as in Ingram and Whiteman (1994).

11.4 Conclusion

In line with the fundamental division of this paper we can ask what has been learned about the execution of the two steps of summarization and interpretation. I think a great deal of knowledge has been accumulated through the first of these, and a consensus has emerged on useful ways of parameterizing the features that we see. To some extent the consensus is stronger for univariate data, although even there one encounters questions relating to the need for non-linear structure. In the multivariate case we may not all agree on the best ways of summarizing the data, but important lessons have emerged along the way: for example, in the case of the US, one should incorporate commodity prices into any VAR involving consumer prices. I also suspect that substantial agreement could be reached about the list of variables that would need to be adopted to capture the essential macroeconomic data of small open economies.

The interpretation stage is much more challenging and open. It has never been hard to find stories about the data, but it has been much harder to have them formulated in such a way that they can be assessed via the data summary. In many respects the developments in macroeconomics of the past twenty years has been helpful in this regard, as there has been a strong emphasis in this literature upon producing quantitative models that are in 'real-time'. Moreover, we have seen certain theories, such as monetarism, 'monetary mis-perceptions', pure RBC theories, and so on, lose a lot of their appeal after many failures to adequately characterize the data. There is never a single dramatic experiment which causes this. Rather credibility is lost via repeated failures. Perhaps the biggest problem we still face in this endeavour is exactly how to perform a confrontation with the data, and it is for this reason that I have spent some time sketching what I see as some promising developments to assist us in this task.

Notes

1. Levtchenkova *et al.* (1998) emphasize the distinction.
2. It is not clear that they can be completely divorced. Although the selection of variables to be modelled should arise naturally from what phenomenon is being studied, it is likely that the set of variables selected will stem from the theories that the investigator knows about.
3. There have been other proposals involving a different pattern of zeros in B_0 and also some suggestions about using linear restrictions involving B_0 and $B_1, \ldots, B_p$.

References

Bank of England (1999) *Economic Models at the Bank of England* (London: Bank of England).

Beaudry, P. and Koop, G. (1993) 'Do Recessions Permanently Change Output?', *Journal of Monetary Economics*, vol. 31, pp. 149–64.

Black, R., Cassino, V., Drew, A., Hansen, E., Hunt, B., Rose, D. and Scott, A. (1997) 'The Forecasting and Policy System: The Core Model', Reserve Bank of New Zealand Research Paper no. 43.

Black, R., Laxton, D., Rose, D. and Tetlow, R. (1994) 'The Steady-State Model: SSQM – The Bank of Canada's new Quarterly Projection Model, Part 1', Bank of Canada Technical Report no. 72.

Bollerslev, T., Engle, R.F. and Nelson, D.B. (1994) 'ARCH models', in Engle, R.F. and McFadden, D. (eds) *The Handbook of Econometrics*, vol. IV (Amsterdam: North-Holland).

Box, G.E.P and Jenkins, G.M. (1970) *Time Series Analysis: Forecasting and Control* (San Francisco: Holden-Day).

Burns, A.F. and Mitchell, W.C. (1947) *Measuring Business Cycles* (New York: NBER).

Chauvet, M. (1998) 'An Econometric Characterization of Business Cycle Dynamics with Factor Structure and Regime Switches', *International Economic Review*, vol. 39, pp. 969–96.

Chauvet, M. and Potter, S. (1998) 'Economic Turning Points and Stock Market Expectations – An Empirical Approach to the Equity Premium Puzzle', Staff Paper, Federal Reserve Bank of New York.

Christiano, L. and Eichenbaum, M. (1992) 'Current Real Business Cycle Theories and Aggregate Labor Market Fluctuations', *American Economic Review*, vol. 82, pp. 430–50.

Cogley, T. and Nason, J. (1995) 'Output Dynamics in Real-Business-Cycle-Models', *American Economic Review*, vol. 85, pp. 492–511.

Cover, J.P. (1992) 'Asymmetric Effects of Positive and Negative Money Supply Shocks', *Quarterly Journal of Economics*, vol. 107, no. 4 (November), pp. 1261–82.

Dawes, R. (1999) 'A Message from Pyschologists to Economists: Mere Predictability Doesn't Matter Like It Should (without a good story appended to it)', *Journal of Economic Behavior and Organization*, vol. 39, pp. 29–40.

den Haan, W.J. and Spear, S. (1998) 'Volatility Clustering in Real Interest Rates: Theory and Evidence', *Journal of Monetary Economics*, vol. 41, pp. 432–54.

Diebold, F.X., Ohanian, L.E. and Berkowitz, J. (1998) 'Dynamic Equilibrium Economies: A Framework for Comparing Models and Data', *Review of Economic Studies*, vol. 65, pp. 433–51.

Durlauf, S.N. and Hall, R.E. (1990) 'Bounds on the Variances of Specification Errors in Models with Expectations', mimeo, Stanford University.

Durlauf, S.N. and Maccini, L.J. (1995) 'Measuring Noise in Inventory Models', *Journal of Monetary Economics*, vol. 36, pp. 65–89.

Eichenbaum, M. (1991) 'Real Business Cycle Theory: Wisdom or Whimsy', *Journal of Economic Dynamics and Control*, vol. 15, pp. 607–21.

Engle, R.F. (1982) 'Autoregressive Conditional Heteroskedasticity with Estimates of the Variance of U.K. Inflation,' *Econometrica*, vol. 50, pp. 987–1008.

Gallant, A.R. and Tauchen, G. (1996) 'Which Moments to Match?', *Econometric Theory*, vol. 12, pp. 657–81.

Gourieroux, C., Monfort, A. and Renault, E. (1993) 'Indirect Inference', *Journal of Applied Econometrics*, vol. 8, pp. S85–S118.

Hamilton, J.D. (1989) 'A New Approach to the Economic Analysis of Nonstationary Time Series and the Business Cycle', *Econometrica*, vol. 57, pp. 357–84.

Hamilton, J.D. and Jorda, O. (1998) 'A Model of the Federal Funds Rate Target', mimeo, University of California at Davis.

Ingram, B.F. and C.H. Whiteman (1994), 'Towards a New Minnesota Prior: Forecasting Macroeconomic Series Using Real Business Cycle Priors', *Journal of Monetary Economics*, vol. 47, pp. 497–510.

King, R.G. and Wolman, A.L. (1996) 'Inflation Targeting in a St Louis Model of the 21st Century', *Federal Reserve Bank of St Louis Review*, vol. 78, pp. 83–107.

Koopmans, T. (1947) 'Measurement without Theory', *Review of Economics and Statistics*, vol. 29, pp. 161–72.

Laxton, D., Isard, P., Faruqee, H., Prasad, E. and Turtelboom, B. (1998) 'MULTIMOD Mark III: The Core Dynamic and Steady-State Models', *International Monetary Fund Occasional Paper*, no. 164.

Levtchenkova, S., Pagan, A.R. and Robertson, J. (1998) 'Shocking Stories', *Journal of Economic Surveys*, vol. 12, pp. 507–32.

Lucas, R.E. (1980) 'Two Illustrations of the Quantity Theory of Money', *American Economic Review*, vol. 70, pp. 1005–14.

Lux, T. and Marchesi, M. (1999) 'A Micro-Simulation of Interacting Agents', mimeo, University of Bonn.

McKibbin, W. and Martin, W. (1998) 'The East Asian Crisis: Investigating Causes and Policy Responses', mimeo, Australian National University.

McKibbin W.J. and Sachs, J. (1991) *Global Linkages: Macroeconomic Interdependence and Co-operation in the World Economy* (Washington: Brookings Institution).

McKibbin, W. and Wilcoxen, P. (1995) 'The Theoretical and Empirical Structure of the G-Cubed Model', *Brookings Institution Discussion Paper in International Economics*, no. 119.

McKibbin, W., Pagan A.R. and Robertson, J. (1998) 'Some Experiments in Constructing a Hybrid Model for Macroeconomic Analysis', *Carnegie-Rochester Conference Series on Public Policy*, vol. 49, pp. 113–42.

Nelson, D.B. (1991) 'Conditional Heteroskedasticity in Asset Returns: a New Approach', *Econometrica*, vol. 59, pp. 347–70.

Nelson, E. (1998) 'Sluggish Inflation and Optimizing Models of the Business Cycle', *Journal of Monetary Economics*, vol. 42, pp. 303–22.

Pagan, A.R. (1994) 'Calibration and Econometric Research', in Adrian Pagan (ed.) Calibration Techniques and Econometrics, *Journal of Applied Econometrics*, vol. 9S (1994), pp. S1–S10.

Pagan, A.R. (1996) 'The Econometrics of Financial Markets', *Journal of Empirical Finance*, vol. 3, pp. 15–102.

Pagan, A.R. (1999) 'Some Uses of Simulation in Econometrics', *Mathematics and Computers in Simulation*, vol. 48, pp. 341–49.

Pesaran, M.H. and Potter, S. (1997) 'A Floor and Ceiling Model of US Output', *Journal of Economic Dynamics and Control*, vol. 21, pp. 661–96.

Potter, S. (1995) 'A Nonlinear Approach to US GNP', *Journal of Applied Econometrics*, vol. 10, pp. 109–25.

Quenouille, M.H. (1957) *The Analysis of Multiple Time Series* (London: Griffin).

Ramey, G. and Watson, J. (1997) 'Contractual Fragility, Job Destruction and Business Cycles' *Quarterly Journal of Economics*, vol. 112, pp. 873–911.

Rudebusch, G. (1998) 'Do Measures of Monetary Policy in a VAR Make Sense?' *International Economic Review*, vol. 39, pp. 907–31.

Sims, C. (1980) 'Macroeconomics and Reality', *Econometrica*, vol. 48, pp. 1–49.

Sims, C. (1999) 'Drifts and Breaks in Monetary Policy' (E.J. Hannan Lecture given to the Australasian Econometric Society Meetings, Sydney).

Smith, A.A. (1993) 'Estimating Non-Linear Time Series Models Using Simulated Vector Autoregressions', *Journal of Applied Econometrics*, vol. 8, pp. S63–S84.

Summers, L.H. (1991) 'The Scientific Illusion in Empirical Macroeconomics', *Scandanavian Journal of Economics*, vol. 93(2), pp. 129–48, reprinted in Hylleberg, S. and Paldam, M. (eds) *New Approaches to Empirical Macroeconomics* (Oxford: Blackwell, 1991), pp. 1–20.

Zellner, A. and Palm, F. (1974) 'Time Series Analysis and Simultaneous Equation Econometric Models', *Journal of Econometrics*, vol. 2, pp. 17–54.

Part V
Dynamics

12
Learning Dynamics: Complete and Incomplete Learning*

Seppo Honkapohja
University of Helsinki, Finland

12.1 Introduction

Rational expectations (RE) is currently the standard approach to modelling expectations in macroeconomics. However, refinements to modelling expectations formation have recently been developed and the literature on learning dynamics has grown rapidly. The basic idea in models of learning is that agents have limited information about the structure of the economy and they have to act inductively like scientists when they forecast the relevant aspects of its future course. Some forecasting is necessary since, as is common in economics, the decisions of individual agents depend on the future and these agents are forward looking in their decision-making. The RE hypothesis is weakened to the assumption that expectations follow a real-time learning rule which often will make expectations converge to RE over time.

An example of a learning rule is one in which agents use a linear regression model to forecast the variables of interest. They estimate the required parameters by least squares and update the parameter estimates each period to incorporate new data. This approach may be termed econometric learning, and the greatest concentration in research has been here. A different but related approach is to use formulations from computational intelligence, such as genetic algorithms or classifier systems. The different approaches to modelling learning behaviour are discussed in the survey paper (Evans and Honkapohja 1999) which provides detailed references to the development of the subject.[1] The book (Evans and Honkapohja (2001)) provides an extensive treatment of learning in macroeconomics.

* This chapter is based on extensive collaboration with George W. Evans over many years. Certain other commitments save him from co-authorship. I thank Jacques Drèze for helpful comments. Financial support from the Academy of Finland and Yrjö Jahnsson Foundation is gratefully acknowledged.

It should be noted that modelling expectations in this fashion puts the agents in the economy in a symmetric position with the economic analyst since, when studying real economies, we economists use econometrics and statistical inference. In contrast, under RE the agents in the model economy have much more information than the outside observer, so in fact the standard formulation of RE turned the quest of Muth (1961) on its head.

The learning approach to macroeconomics has several possible motivations and goals. First, learning has been used to address the issue of the plausibility of the RE assumption in particular models: could boundedly rational agents arrive at RE through a learning rule? This issue is of interest as it provides a justification for the RE hypothesis.

Second, some widely used models have multiple rational expectations equilibria (REE). If some REE are locally stable under a learning rule while others are locally unstable, then learning acts as a selection device for choosing the REE which we can expect to observe in practice. Extensive work has been devoted to obtaining stability conditions for convergence of learning to particular REE, and at present a systematic stability theory for REE under econometric learning is available.

Third, it may be of interest to take seriously the learning dynamics itself, for example, during the transition to RE. Dynamics with learning can be qualitatively different from, say, fully rational adjustment after a structural change. This has been the focus of some policy-oriented papers. It has also been the focus of some recent work on asset pricing. Brian Arthur (see for example papers reprinted in Arthur (1994)) has emphasized path dependence of adaptive learning dynamics in the presence of multiple equilibria.

If the model is mis-specified by the agents, then this can effectively lead to persistent learning dynamics as in Evans and Honkapohja (1993a), Timmermann (1996), Marcet and Nicolini (1998), Honkapohja and Mitra (1999), Sargent (1999), Cho, Williams and Sargent (2000) and Evans and Honkapohja (2001). I call this kind of situation *incomplete learning*, since the learning economy fails to converge even asymptotically to an RE. When there is convergence to some REE, we have the case of *complete learning*.[2] The research on incomplete learning is very recent and this area is undergoing further development. We note also that even if the model is not mis-specified, particular learning dynamics may not fully converge to an REE and the learning dynamics may be of intrinsic interest. This arises, for example, in Evans and Ramey (1995) and Brock and Hommes (1997).

The implications of these results have led also to one further set of issues: the effects of policy and appropriate policy design in models with multiple REE. For example, if there are multiple REE which are stable under learning, then policy may play a role in the selection of equilibrium, and policy changes may also exhibit hysteresis and threshold effects. The appropriate choice of policy parameters can eliminate or render unstable inefficient steady states, cycles or sunspot equilibria. For examples, see Evans and Honkapohja (1993b) and Evans and Honkapohja (1995).[3]

A further application of learning algorithms is that they can also be used as a computational tool to solve a model for its REE. This point has been discussed by Sargent (1993). An advantage of such algorithms is that they find only 'learnable' REE.

The purpose of this paper is to illustrate different aspects of the dynamics of learning. I do this by means of a model of increasing social returns and coordination failures. It should be stressed that this model is adopted for illustrative purposes just to show how learning adds to and interacts with standard macroeconomic theory. As already noted, for complete learning there exists a systematic theory of stability and dynamics applicable to a wide variety of models in which expectations are pertinent. In incomplete learning the research is very recent, and the state of knowledge far less systematic but the initial results on the possible dynamics are intriguing and worth illustrating.

I will consider both complete and incomplete learning with the aid of the same model. I start with complete learning and consider the set of steady-state REE which are stable under learning. I also show how policy can be used to steer the economy to a steady state with high welfare.

As a second step I introduce unobservable random shocks which lead to occasional structural shifts in the economy. In response to structural shifts agents utilize a 'constant gain' learning rule, which is a common way in statistics and engineering to account for such possibilities. This kind of learning is incomplete in that it does not converge to an REE, even if it is often unbiased (i.e. its mean is correct asymptotically). Dynamics of incomplete learning can provide further patterns of dynamics, as will be illustrated by the analysis.

12.2 A model of increasing social returns

12.2.1 The model

I consider the basic Samuelson overlapping generations model with money, but I make an important modification to the production structure.[4] The consumption side of the model is standard. The economy consists of overlapping generations of identical agents who live each for two periods. Agents work when they are young and consume when old. The utility function of an agent in generation t takes the form

$$U(c_{t+1}) - V(n_t)$$

where c_{t+1} is consumption at old age and n_t is labour supply. $U(\cdot)$ is concave and $V(\cdot)$ is convex and both $U(\cdot)$ and $V(\cdot)$ are twice continuously differentiable. Assume that the money supply is constant. For simplicity I will assume isoelastic utility functions, so that

$$U(c) = c^{1-\sigma}/(1-\sigma) \text{ and } V(n) = n^{1+\varepsilon}/(1+\varepsilon)$$

On the production side I assume that the production activity of every young consumer takes place in accordance with a production function

$$Q_t = f(n_t, N_t)$$

where N_t denotes aggregate labour effort and represents a positive production externality. We assume $f_1 > 0$, $f_2 > 0$ and $f_{11} < 0$. Here $N_t = \ell n_t$ where ℓ is the total number of agents in the economy. ℓ is assumed large enough so that each agent has negligible effect on N_t. For concreteness, I assume the multiplicative form

$$Q_t = n_t^\alpha \, \psi\,(N_t)$$

The consumer's budget constraints take the form

$$p_t Q_t = m_t$$

$$P_{t+1} c_{t+1} = m_t$$

Here m_t denotes the nominal saving by the representative agent, and p_t the prevailing price of output in period t. Money is the only means of saving.

In the maximization each agent then treats the externality N_t as given, so that the first order condition becomes

$$V'(n_t) = E_t^\star \frac{p_t}{p_{t+1}} f_1(n_t, \ell n_t) U'\,(c_{t+1})$$

Here $E_t^\star(\cdot)$ denotes the (in general subjective) expectations about the next period, given current information. I formulate the model entirely in terms of n_t. Using $p_t/p_{t+1} = Q_{t+1}/Q_t$ and $c_{t+1} = Q_{t+1}$ we have

$$V'(n_t)f(n_t, \ell n_t)/f_1(n_t, \ell n_t) = E_t^\star f(n_{t+1}, \ell n_{t+1})U'(f(n_{t+1}, \ell n_{t+1})) \qquad (1)$$

It is convenient here to choose average employment n_t as the variable to be forecast. (Since n_t is in 1-1 correspondence with the price level, this is an innocuous assumption.) I will thus analyse the model in terms of employment.

Letting $W(n_t)$ denote the left-hand-side function in (1), it can be verified that $W(n_t)$ is a strictly increasing function of n_t. Solving for n_t yields that the (interior) perfect foresight equilibria satisfy

$$n_t = F(n_{t+1}) \qquad (2)$$

for a suitable F. Steady state REE n^* satisfy $n^* = F(n^*)$.

For appropriate specifications of the utility function and the production function (such as those specified above) it is possible to obtain reduced form functions F which yield three interior steady states, as shown Figure 12.1. Examples are given in Evans and Honkapohja (1995). Employments levels $n_L < n_U < n_H$ correspond to low, medium and high output levels. The steady states n_L and n_U can be interpreted as coordination failures since the steady states can be Pareto-ranked and steady-state welfare is higher in n_H than in either n_L or n_U.[5] (Also welfare in n_U is higher than in n_L.)

Figure 12.1

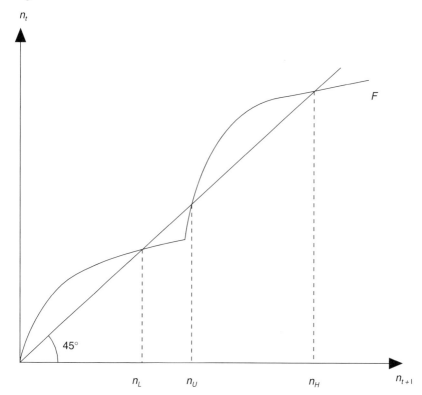

12.2.2 Formulation of learning

Suppose that there is no uncertainty, so that the representative consumer of generation t needs to forecast average employment for next period n_{t+1}^e. Substituting given expectations n_{t+1}^e in place of n_{t+1} in (2) gives the temporary equilibrium for this economy.

I assume that people form expectations from past data in the following way:

$$n_{t+1}^e = n_t^e + \gamma_t(n_{t-1} - n_t^e) \tag{3}$$

Here $0 < \gamma_t < 1$ is usually referred to as the 'gain sequence'. Two main cases of interest are $\gamma_t = t^{-1}$ and $\gamma_t = \gamma$, a constant. It should be noted that in the overlapping generations model learning is done by successive generations with an implicit transfer of knowledge across generations.

The first case corresponds to agents taking the average of n_i, $i = 0, \ldots, t - 1$, i.e.

$$n_{t+1}^e = t^{-1}\sum_{i=0}^{t-1} n_i$$

This corresponds to estimation of an unknown constant through the sample mean. From this point of view the forecast method leads to a learning rule in which agents update their estimate of an unknown mean which they treat as a constant. Note that in this kind of learning rule each new data point has a smaller weight with $\lim_{t\to\infty} \gamma_t = 0$. Such gain sequences are known as 'decreasing gain'. The second case $\gamma_t = \gamma$ can be seen as a version of the traditional adaptive expectations assumption, but it can also be interpreted as a constant gain learning rule. I come back to such rules in a later section.

Substituting (2) into (3) yields the difference equation

$$n_{t+1}^e = n_t^e + \gamma_t(F(n_t^e) - n_t^e)$$

and n_0^e is treated as an arbitrary initial expectation. It can be shown that a steady state $n^* = F(n^*)$ is locally stable under learning if $F'(n^*) < 1$. It follows that n_L and n_H are locally stable, while n_U is unstable. In this model it is, therefore, possible for the economy to become stuck in a low-activity, low-welfare steady state. Globally, this learning economy exhibits path-dependence, since the eventual outcome depends on its history (starting point) and any possible random shocks.

12.2.3 Learning and policy

Suppose that we modify the preceding model, so that (because of the positive externality) the government provides a production subsidy which, for simplicity, is assumed to be financed by a lump-sum tax. If the subsidy to output is constant with rate ρ, the basic equation (1) describing the temporary equilibrium is modified to

$$(1 - \rho)V'(n_t)f(n_t, \ell n_t)/f_1(n_t, \ell n_t) = E_t^* f(n_{t+1}, \ell n_{t+1})U'(f(n_{t+1}, \ell n_{t+1}))$$

Geometrically, this corresponds to a leftward rotation of the map $n_t = F(n_{t+1})$ and this can alter the number of steady-state REE in the economy. Since the mapping $F(n_{t+1})$ continues to have a finite asymptote as $n_{t+1} \to \infty$ the low and middle steady states n_L and n_U in Figure 12.1 can sometimes disappear in this rotation while the high steady state n_H will continue to exist.

Suppose now that the economy has had a coordination failure and has stayed in n_L. If an unanticipated production subsidy is introduced and it makes n_L and n_U disappear, then learning dynamics will start (as n_L is no longer an REE) and it will take the economy to n_H. This is a favorable bifurcation of the economy.[6]

It should be noted that an unfavourable bifurcation as a result of bad policy is also possible for this economy. Suppose that in the basic model (without the subsidy) the government starts to purchase a share ξ of output and finances this by printing money. It is easy to show that the basic equation of the model (1) is then changed to

$$n_t = [\alpha X_{t+1}^e]^{1/(1+\varepsilon)}, \text{ where } X_{t+1} = (1 - \xi) f(n_{t+1}, \ell n_{t+1})$$

Geometrically, under perfect foresight this corresponds to a rightward rotation of the map $n_t = F(n_{t+1})$ and it can be the case that the economy has only a low-employment steady state left after the government policy change. Figure 12.2 illustrates various possibilities. Then the economy can possibly move from a high-employment, high-welfare steady state to the (unique) low-welfare one through a learning process.

12.3 Incomplete learning

Nonconvergence of learning dynamics has also been discussed in the literature. One case is that the economy has no stable REE for particular values of the model parameters. (This is discussed, for example, by Bullard (1994) and Grandmont (1998).) Another one is that *learning dynamics is incomplete* in the sense that it has no chance of converging to an REE for any parameter configuration, see e.g. Section 5 of Evans and Honkapohja (1999) or Honkapohja and Mitra (1999) for discussions and references. Several studies in recent literature have considered situations of incomplete learning. (The case of instability of REE will not be treated as a case of incomplete learning.)

Figure 12.2

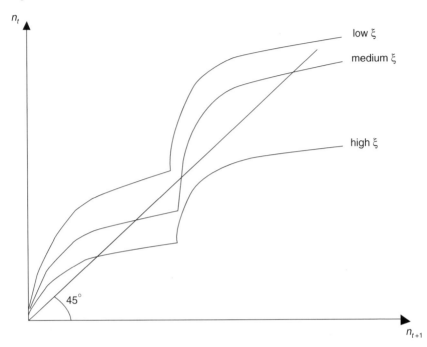

The incompleteness of learning may arise for different reasons. First, the perceptions of the agents (and thus their forecasts about the motion of the economy) may be incorrectly specified, so that they do not nest any REE.[7] Second, the procedure for estimating the perceived law of motion of the economy may not yield exact convergence. This latter case arises, for example, when the economy is subject to structural shifts or regime changes, and the agents try to account for possibility of shifts by using a suitable incomplete procedure.

As already noted, constant gain algorithms in stochastic frameworks are one case leading to incomplete learning, so that under them learning dynamics are persistent, that is, never cease.[8] Such procedures are employed in statistics and engineering when the possibility of structural changes exists, see for example the discussion in part I, chapters 1 and 4 of Benveniste, Metivier and Priouret (1990). Another case leading to incomplete learning is the use of bounded memory rules in frameworks with random shocks, see Honkapohja and Mitra (1999). When learning is incomplete, dynamics may nevertheless give a good approximation to actual economic data as discussed in the concluding section. The resulting dynamics can take interesting new forms and this part of my paper is devoted to an exposition of some of the possibilities using the model of coordination failures outlined above.[9]

12.3.1 Constant gain learning

I introduce random shocks into the preceding model of increasing social returns and coordination failures. Assume that there is a proportional productivity shock to the production function which now takes the form

$$Q_t = f(n_t, N_t)v_t$$

Here v_t is an i.i.d. positive random shock with mean equal to one. I continue to postulate that government purchases a fraction ξ of output and finances it by seignorage. The model can be written in the form

$$n_t = H(G(n_{t+1}, v_{t+1})^e)$$

where

$$X_t = G(n_t, v_t) = [(1 - \xi)f(n_t, ln_t)v_t]$$

represents after-tax output, and

$$H(X) = (\alpha X)^{1/(1+\varepsilon)}$$

is an appropriate function, depending on preference and production parameters, which arises from the first order condition.

Under adaptive learning we write

$$\theta_{t-1} = G(n_{t+1}, v_{t+1})^e$$

for the expectations of the agents, and I assume that expectations are updated according to the rule

$$\theta_t = \theta_{t-1} + \gamma_t(X_t - \theta_{t-1})$$

The analysis of the previous section is now modified by replacing the decreasing gain assumption by the assumption of constant gain

$$\gamma_t = \gamma \text{ for some } 0 < \gamma < 1$$

For the time being, the gain parameter γ is held fixed at some value $0 < \gamma < 1$. The choice of γ is considered later.

The key difference from the case of a decreasing gain is that under constant gain algorithms there exists the possibility of endogenous fluctuations. This is because the economy occasionally escapes from the basin of attraction of one stochastic steady state to the basin of attraction of another stochastic steady state. This possibility of endogenous fluctuations arises even if agents do not condition their estimates on an extraneous exogenous variable, but try to estimate a steady state using a constant gain algorithm. Endogenous fluctuations can arise in which the economy shifts between high and low activity levels in a random way.[10]

Recall from above that there will generically be one or three steady states. When there are three steady states I label them as $n_L < n_U < n_H$ as before. Recall also that increases in the tax rate ξ rotate F downward, lowering both n_L and n_H. Sufficiently large increases in γ can bifurcate the system, eliminating n_H. Similarly, sufficiently low values of ξ may also bifurcate the system, eliminating n_L.

The following properties of the function

$$n = F(n) \equiv [\alpha(1 - \xi)f(n, \ell n)]^{1/(f + \varepsilon)} = H(G(n, 1))$$

will be used below: (i) $F(n)$ is continuous and strictly increasing with $F(0) = 0$. (ii) If there is a single interior steady state $\bar{n}$ then $F(n) - n > 0$ for $0 < n < \bar{n}$ and $F(n) - n < 0$ for $n > \bar{n}$. If there are 3 distinct steady states $n_L < n_U < n_H$ then $F(n) - n > 0$ for $0 < n < n_L$ or $n_U < n < n_H$, and $F(n) - n < 0$ for $n_L < n < n_U$ or $n > n_H$. Furthermore, $F(n) - n \to -\infty$ as $n \to \infty$. (iii) $F(n)$ is differentiable almost everywhere and $F'(0) = +\infty$, $0 < F'(n_L)$, $F'(n_H) < 1 < F'(n_U)$.

The 'size' of the productivity shock v_t plays a key role under constant gain learning. I restrict attention to distributions with compact support, that is, the support of v_t is the interval $I_v = [\bar{v}_1, \bar{v}_2]$, where $\bar{v}_1 < 1 < \bar{v}_2$, and v_t has continuous positive density over $[\bar{v}_1, \bar{v}_2]$.

The first result is that if the support of v_t is sufficiently small, then n_t will become trapped in a small region around either n_L or n_H. We focus on the case in which three steady states exist. Let $\theta_L = G(n_L, 1)$, $\theta_U = G(n_U, 1)$ and $\theta_H = G(n_H, 1)$ be the after-tax levels of output corresponding to n_L, n_U and n_H, respectively. The following results are proved in chapter 14 of Evans and Honkapohja (2001):

Proposition 1. Suppose there are three steady states. There exist $\bar{v}_1 < 1 < \hat{v}_2$ so that for all $\bar{v}_1$, $\bar{v}_2$, satisfying $\hat{v}_1 < \bar{v}_1 < 1 < \bar{v}_2 < \hat{v}_2$, there are neighbourhoods $N(\theta_L) = (a_1, a_2)$ and $N(\theta_H) = (b_1, b_2)$, with $0 < a_1 < \theta_L < a_2 < \theta_U < b_1 < \theta_H < b_2$, such that $\theta_{t-1} \in N(\theta_L)$ implies $\theta_t \in N(\theta_L)$ and $\theta_{t-1} \in N(\theta_H)$ implies $\theta_t \in N(\theta_H)$.

Thus, for a sufficiently small support for the productivity shock v_t, expectations will remain trapped in a neighbourhood of θ_L or θ_H if they start in or enter that neighbourhood. Since $n_t = H(\theta_t)$, this also implies that n_t will be confined to a neighbourhoods of n_L or n_H.

Next consider what happens if the support of v_t is increased:

Proposition 2. Suppose there are three steady states. Suppose $\bar{v}_1 < \hat{v}_1$ and $\bar{v}_2 < \hat{v}_2$. Then for every interval $J = (\bar{\theta}_1, \bar{\theta}_2)$, $0 < \bar{\theta}_1 < \bar{\theta}_2$, and for all neighbourhoods $N(\theta_H)$ of θ_H and $N(\theta_L)$ of θ_L there is a positive integer T such that if $\theta_t \in J$ then, for all $s > t + T$, $\theta_s \in N(\theta_H)$ with positive probability and $\theta_s \in N(\theta_L)$ with positive probability.

This proposition shows that, for a given constant gain γ, there is a critical size of the support of the exogenous shock v_t which prevents θ_t (and hence n_t) from remaining trapped for ever in a neighbourhood of the low-level state or in a neighbourhood of the high-level steady state. Occasional sequences of large shocks can lead to paths which 'escape' the basin of attraction of θ_L to a neighbourhood of θ_H for a period of time. Similarly, an occasional sequence of shocks leads can lead θ_t to escape the basin of attraction of θ_H and return toward θ_L.

Simulations illustrating this phenomenon were first presented in Evans and Honkapohja (1993a) and are further discussed in chapter 14 of Evans and Honkapohja (2001). These 'endogenous fluctuations' are induced by the learning rule in conjunction with the random shocks and they depend on the constant gain assumption.

The following figure, taken from chapter 14 of Evans and Honkapohja (2001), illustrates the phenomenon. I use the production function developed in Evans and Honkapohja (1995):

$$f(n, N) = An^\alpha \{\max(I^*, \lambda N(1 + \alpha\lambda N)^{-1})\}^\beta$$

with parameters $A = 0.0805$, $\alpha = 0.025$, $\lambda = 0.5$, $I = 40$, $\beta = 1.007$ and $I^* = 19.5$. The other model parameters are set at $\varepsilon = 0.25$, $\sigma = 0.1$, and $\xi = 0.04$. The random productivity shock is distributed as a i.i.d. lognormal random variable, that is, $\ell n \, v_t$ is normal with mean one and standard deviation 0.0577. We choose the gain parameter $\gamma = 0.15$.

Figure 12.3 exhibits the time path of employment n_t over a simulation of 2500 periods by plot of a line graph of n_t plotted against n_{t-1}. Most of the time the dynamics stay near one of the two steady states, as is illustrated by the very dark areas. However, occasionally the path from a neighbourhood of one steady state escapes to a neighbourhood of the other steady state. This requires a specific series of productivity shocks, so that the estimates can move from one region to another. The important features of the *escape routes* is that, while the probability of their occurrence is low but positive, these routes do not go to any arbitrary direction but tend to move in specific ways.[11]

This escape route phenomenon was also discovered by Sargent (1999) in the context of a standard natural rate Phillips curve inflation model,

Figure 12.3

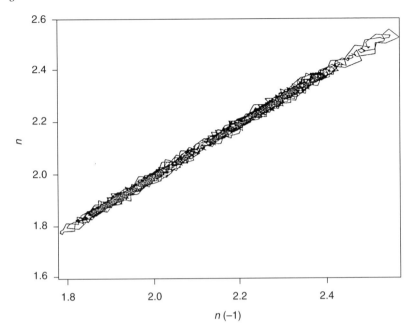

but with the central bank trying to learn a mis-specified 'naïve' Phillips curve. A further analysis of the inflation model is in Cho, Williams and Sargent (2000).

Without going to details I also want to point out that learning dynamics with constant gain learning can sometimes produce a hysteresis. This happens when there is a time-varying structure to the model leading to bifurcations in the set of steady states and agents use a constant gain learning algorithm in order to take account for the possibility of structural shifts.

12.3.2 Equilibria in learning rules

What determines the choice of the gain parameter γ? So far I have just examined the effects on economic dynamics of a particular choice of γ by the agents. This poses a natural question: is there an optimal gain parameter γ from the point of view of an individual agent?

It should be noted that this issue is not so important when the dynamics converge to rational expectations. If the economy converges to rational expectations, the agents are asymptotically using a fully optimal way of forming expectations. With constant gain learning there is typically convergence to a stationary stochastic process and agents are not forming expectations optimally even in the limit. This kind of reasoning suggests the concept of an equilibrium in learning rules, following Evans and Honkapohja (1993a).

I take up this issue using the above model of increasing returns and coordination failures. Dynamics with fixed gain γ_0 learning defines a Markov process in $n_t^{(\gamma_0)}$, and $\theta_t^{(\gamma_0)}$, where the superscript (γ_0) denotes the stochastic process induced by a particular value γ_0. Consider now the optimal choice of γ. Let $\theta_t^{(\gamma_0)}(\gamma)$ be defined by

$$\theta_t^{(\gamma_0)}(\gamma) = \theta_{t-1}^{(\gamma_0)}(\gamma) + \gamma(G(n_t^{(\gamma_0)}, v_t) - \theta_{t-1})$$

That is, $\theta_{t-1}^{(\gamma_0)}(\gamma)$ is the sequence of forecasts $G(n_{t+1}, v_{t+1})^e$ that would be obtained from using the fixed gain parameter γ when all the other agents in the (large) economy are actually using gain γ_0. Let also

$$MSE^{(\gamma_0)}(\gamma) = \lim_{t \to \infty} E(G(n_{t+1}, v_{t+1}) - \theta_{t-1}^{(\gamma_0)}(\gamma))^2$$

provided this limit exists, be the asymptotic mean-squared error from using the fixed gain rule γ when agents are in fact using γ_0. If

$$\gamma_0 = \arg \min_{\gamma} MSE^{(\gamma_0)}(\gamma)$$

then we say that we have an *equilibrium in learning rules*.

In this kind of equilibrium no agent has an incentive to change to an alternative value of γ if there is a large number of agents and each agent treats its actions as having negligible effects.

The possibility for this equilibrium was investigated numerically in Evans and Honkapohja (1993a) and in Evans and Honkapohja (2001). Table 12.1 gives $MSE^{(\gamma_0)}(\gamma)$, the estimated values of $MSE^{(\gamma_0)}(\gamma)$ obtained as[12]

$$MSE^{(\gamma_0)}(\gamma) = T^{-1} \sum_{t=1}^{T} (G(n_{t+1}, V_{t+1}) - \theta_{t-1}^{(\gamma_0)}(\gamma))^2$$

using a stochastic simulation with $T = 100{,}000$.

From the table it is seen that $\gamma = 0.15$ is an approximate equilibrium in learning rules. The simulation in Figure 12.3 was based on the value $\gamma = 0.15$, so that it represents an equilibrium in learning rules. These parameter values give rise to endogenous fluctuations in the sense shown above: the path of n_t periodically shifts between regions near the high and low level steady states. It is important to stress that the notion just discussed yields a self-fulfilling prophecy at the metalevel of learning rules, though not in terms of expectations.

Table 12.1

γ	$MSE^{(\gamma_0 = 0.15)} (\gamma)$
0.05	0.0276
0.10	0.0256
0.15	0.0253
0.20	0.0255
0.25	0.0259
0.30	0.0265
0.40	0.0278
0.50	0.0295
0.60	0.0314
0.70	0.0336
0.90	0.0395

12.4   Concluding remarks

The model I used to illustrate some of the characteristics of learning dynamics is obviously too simple for estimation or calibration and thus for empirical application. Hopefully, my discussion has shown how learning dynamics can lead to a rich set of possibilities and that they can provide possibilities for empirical work in the future.

So far, empirical work based on learning has been scarce. Before considering applications, I note that experimental work has been recently done to provide broad support for the types of dynamics that can emerge from complete learning (see Section 5 of Evans and Honkapohja (1999) for discussion and references). Let me conclude by mentioning three interesting areas of empirical work.

Since learning offers an alternative to RE dynamics, it is in principle desirable to develop applications where learning does better than RE dynamics. Marcet and Nicolini (1998) argue that the recurrent episodes of inflation and disinflation in several Latin American countries since the Second World War are difficult to account for by an RE approach. They suggest that a model of learning based in part on constant gain algorithms can account for this period in an otherwise standard inflation model.

Recently Sargent (1999) has suggested that the disinflationary process in the US since the 1980s is difficult to explain by means of the model based on the natural rate hypothesis and a time-consistent monetary policy maker. He suggests that an alternative explanation might be that the central bank has continued to believe in the simple (non-natural rate) Phillips curve and has estimated the slopes continuously using a constant gain learning rule. In Sargent's model the disinflationary period is an escape route of the type illustrated above (though his model has only one REE).

A third application of learning has been to financial markets. The papers by Timmermann (1993, 1996) suggest that two major anomalies of the stock market, the excess volatility of stock prices and the predictability of stock returns, can be accounted for by certain models of learning dynamics. This list is short even if there are some other studies, see Evans and Honkapohja (1999) for references. The 1990s have seen major structural changes in a number of countries which suggests rich possibilities for empirical work based on the learning approach. This viewpoint is a progressing research programme, and further work, both applied and theoretical, is highly valuable.

Notes

1. See also Marimon (1997).
2. This distinction is made in Honkapohja and Mitra (1999).
3. Here policy is modelled as a rule which atomistic private agents take as part of the economic structure. Modelling policy maker's learning is a different approach, see e.g. Sargent (1999).
4. The model was first developed in Evans and Honkapohja (1995), where further details can be found. All the results and illustrations shown here are developed more extensively in the forthcoming book Evans and Honkapohja (2000).
5. Evans, Honkapohja and Romer (1998) show the possibility of multiple steady state REE in growth rates in a model of innovations and endogenous growth.
6. The possibility of favourable and unfavourable bifurcations for a model of growth and trade is investigated in Honkapohja and Turunen-Red (1999). They show that opening autarkic economies for trade can lead to large positive increases in growth and welfare.
7. Note that in complete learning leading to convergence to an REE the agents mis-specify the dynamics during the adjustment, but this mis-specification will disappear asymptotically.
8. Evans and Honkapohja (1993a) pioneered the use of constant gain learning.
9. The treatment here summarizes the analysis in Evans and Honkapohja (1993a) and in ch. 14 of Evans and Honkapohja (2000).
10. These fluctuations are different from sunspot equilibria which in fact also exist for this model, see Evans and Honkapohja (1993b). Sunspot solutions are a particular type of REE. I will not consider them in this paper.
11. The term 'escape routes' is due to Sargent (1999).
12. For this table the model parameters are those as above and with the lognormal shock and $\xi = 0.04$. The simulation is taken from Evans and Honkapohja (2000).

References

Arthur, W.B. (1994) *Increasing Returns and Path Dependence in the Economy* (Ann Arbor: University of Michigan Press).

Benveniste, A., Metivier, M. and Priouret, P. (1990) *Adaptive Algorithms and Stochastic Approximations* (Berlin: Springer-Verlag).

Brock, W.A. and Hommes, C.H. (1997) 'A Rational Route to Randomness', *Econometrica*, vol. 65, pp. 1059–95.

Bullard, J. (1994) 'Learning Equilibria', *Journal of Economic Theory*, vol. 64, pp. 468–85.

Cho, I.-K, Williams, N. and Sargent, T.J. (2000) 'Escaping Nash Inflation', Working Paper, Stanford University.

Dixon, H. and Rankin, N. (eds) (1995) *The New Macroeconomics: Imperfect Markets and Policy Effectiveness* (Cambridge: Cambridge University Press).

Evans, G.W. and Honkapohja, S. (1993a) 'Adaptive Forecasts, Hysteresis and Endogenous Fluctuations', *Federal Reserve Bank of San Francisco Economic Review*, no. 1, pp. 3–13.

Evans, G.W. and Honkapohja, S. (1993b) 'Learning and Economic Fluctuations: Using Fiscal Policy to Steer Expectations', *European Economic Review*, vol. 37, pp. 595–602.

Evans, G.W. and Honkapohja, S. (1995) 'Increasing Social Returns, Learning and Bifurcation Phenomena', in Kirkman, A. and Salmon, M. (eds) *Learning and Rationality in Economics* (Oxford: Basil Blackwell), ch. 7, pp. 216–35.

Evans, G.W. and Honkapohja, S. (1999): 'Learning Dynamics', in Taylor, J. and Woodford, M. (eds) *Handbook of Macroeconomics*, vol. 1 (Amsterdam: Elsevier Science), ch. 7, pp. 449–542.

Evans, G.W. and Honkapohja, S. (2001) *Learning and Expectations in Macroeconomics* (Princeton, NJ: Princeton University Press).

Evans, G.W. and Ramey, G. (1995) 'Expectation Calculation, Hyperinflation and Currency Collapse', in Dixon, H. and Rankin, N. (eds) *The New Macroeconomics* (Cambridge: Cambridge University Press), ch. 15, pp. 307–36.

Evans, G.W. Honkapohja, S. and Romer, P. (1998) 'Growth Cycles', *American Economic Review*, vol. 88, pp. 495–515.

Grandmont, J.-M. (1998) 'Expectations Formation and Stability of Large Socioeconomic Systems', *Econometrica*, vol. 66, pp. 741–81.

Honkapohja, S. and Mitra, K. (1999) 'Learning with Bounded Memory in Stochastic Models', Working Paper, University of Helsinki.

Honkapohja, S. and Turunen-Red, A. (1999) 'Complementarity, Growth and Trade', Working Paper, University of Helsinki.

Marcet, A. and Nicolini, J.P. (1998) 'Recurrent Hyperinflations and Learning', CEPR Working Paper no. 1875.

Marimon, R. (1997) 'Learning from Learning in Economics', in Kreps, D. and Wallis, K. (eds) *Advances in Economics and Econometrics*, vol. 1 (Cambridge: Cambridge University Press), chap. 9, pp. 278–315.

Muth, J.F. (1961) 'Rational Expectations and the Theory of Price Movements', *Econometrica*, vol. 29, pp. 315–35.

Sargent, T.J. (1993) *Bounded Rationality in Macroeconomics*. (Oxford: Oxford University Press).

Sargent, T.J. (1999) *The Conquest of American Inflation*. (Princeton, NJ: Princeton University Press).

Timmermann, A.G. (1993) 'How Learning in Financial Markets Generates Excess Volatility and Predictability in Stock Prices', *Quarterly Journal of Economics*, vol. 108, pp. 1135–45.

Timmermann, A.G. (1996) 'Excessive Volatility and Predictability of Stock Prices in Autoregressive Dividend Models with Learning', *Review of Economic Studies*, vol. 63, pp. 523–57.

13

Standard-of-Living Aspirations and Economic Cycles*

David de la Croix
National Fund for Scientific Research and IRES, Université Catholique de Louvain, Belgium

13.1 Introduction

One of the main tasks of macroeconomists is to explain why there are fluctuations in output and employment and why growth is not a steady process.

Three different ways to explain the existence of fluctuations can be found in the literature. The first one, which is the mainstream approach, considers stochastic disturbances affecting the fundamentals of the economy. These shocks can take the form of productivity shocks, fiscal shocks, tastes shocks … . Shocks and propagation mechanisms are studied by the use of calibrated theoretical models or by econometric techniques. The second approach looks at mechanisms that can be responsible for fluctuations in the absence of exogenous shocks. In this case, it is the non-linear, complex, nature of the economy that generates endogenous fluctuations. In the third approach, the fundamentals are not sufficient to determine the actual growth path of the economy. The way expectations are coordinated plays then a crucial role in selecting the type of equilibrium that will emerge. Shocks to expectations, like pessimistic waves, can then be responsible for fluctuations.

For these three approaches, the elaboration of models which can propagate cycles through empirically realistic mechanisms is a central challenge: One of the findings of Hodrick and Prescott (1980) is that the deviations of output from trend display a moderately high degree of persistence. Accordingly, one the major tasks of the dominant paradigm is to build models that account for this persistence, without needing to assume that the exogenous shocks themselves are highly persistent. This proves to be a difficult task and it is often objected to real business cycle models that the

---

* I am thankful to Jacques Drèze for his suggestions on an earlier draft. The financial support of the PAI program P4/01 is gratefully acknowledged.

persistence displayed by output is simply the mirror of the persistence of the shocks. In other words, the model does not bring any insight as far as persistence is concerned.

A main objective for studying models which are able to generate endogenous cycles is to set up a theory of fluctuations that can compete with the dominant paradigm. A variety of mechanisms may be responsible for self-driven oscillatory phenomena. As stressed by Boldrin and Woodford (1990) in their survey, the construction of examples that allow endogenous cycles in the case of empirically realistic mechanisms and parameters is one of the main challenges of this line of research. Using a scalar overlapping generations model Grandmont (1985) shows that complicated cycles may occur if savings are sufficiently decreasing in the interest rate. An extension of this model to account for elastic labour supply shows that cycles are possible even though savings are not a decreasing function of the interest rate. In this case, the production factors should be highly complementary (Reichlin (1986)).[1] Finding a propagation mechanism that neither requires a negative effect of the interest rate on savings nor low values of the elasticity of substitution in production is on the research agenda.

One of the relevant propagation mechanisms can be the adaptation of preferences – or tastes – to the environment. Accordingly, we intend to show in this paper the contribution of such set-ups to the explanation of fluctuations. We shall in particular focus our attention on three specific forms of endogenous adaptation of preferences. These are respectively the formation of consumers' habits, the inheritance of standard-of-living aspirations and the formation of the fair wage.

Before studying these cases we present some selected stylized facts on growth and cycles.

13.2 Selected facts on growth and cycles

13.2.1 Long-run growth

One problem to the study of long-run growth is the lack of data over a very long period of time. There is some partial evidence, however, that economic growth was very slow before 1700. Real wages and per capita GDP were roughly the same in 1700 as they were 2000 years before (see Jones (1999) and the references therein). For the recent past, Maddison (1995) has performed a huge task of building GDP and population series for many countries over more than one century. Figure 13.1 presents the GDP per capita of selected years for the whole set of countries for which the data are available (i.e. starting in 1820). Each point broadly reflects the standard of living of one generation in one country. The first fact that emerges clearly from this picture is that growth is a monotonic process at this frequency and that the standard of living of successive generations is rising over time.

Figure 13.1 World GDP per capita

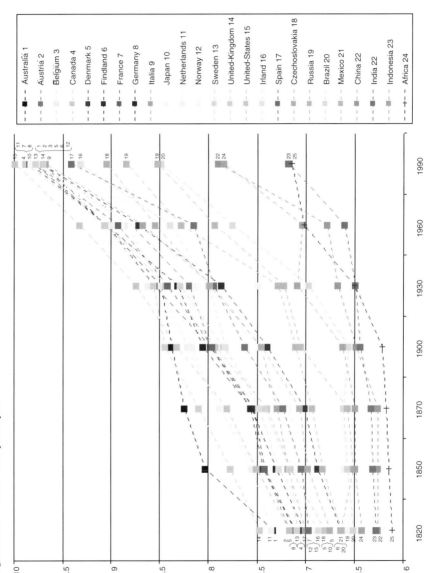

13.2.2 Long cycles

The fact that there is positive growth in the long run does not imply that long-run growth rates are constant. To illustrate this, we take GDP per capita series and extract their long-run component using a very smooth moving average of the Hodrick and Prescott (1980) filter type.[2] Figure 13.2 displays the long-term component for two countries. Clearly, the trend does not grow at a constant rate. There are very long periods of time during which growth is low, followed by lasting booms. This also stresses that predicting growth over long periods of time is a hazardous game.

If one goes further and computes the growth rate of the long-term component, one finds that the growth rate attains a peak approximately every 30 years. However, it is not possible to prove that these fluctuations at low frequencies come from the functioning of the economic system itself rather than from the filtering procedure. Note, however, that the presence of long-term cycles is broadly consistent with what we know on growth over a long period of time (see for instance the spectral estimates of the Kondratieff cycle by van Ewijk (1982) and Reijnders (1990) and the study by Solomou (1986)).

13.2.3 Short cycles

The short-term cycles have been widely documented in the real business cycle literature (see for instance Prescott (1998)) as well as in the applied econometric literature. The standard theory is able to document a wide series of stylized facts. There are, however, many puzzles left and we would like to mention some of them here.

The equity-premium puzzle. Returns on the stock market exceed the return on Treasury bills by an average of 6 percentage points, in the US. This strong risk-premium is puzzling in the context of an economy populated by agents endowed with standard preferences (Mehra and Prescott (1985)).

The excess smoothness puzzle. Consumption is slow to adjust to innovations in income and the changes in consumption are related to averages of previous innovations (J. Campbell and Deaton, 1989).

The international risk-sharing puzzle. Output is more highly correlated across countries than consumption. This weak correlation of consumption levels is in contradiction with international risk-sharing (Backus, Kehoe and Kydland (1992)).

13.2.4 Satisfaction

A fourth set of facts is less conventional. It relates to the results of surveys dealing with the overall satisfaction of people.

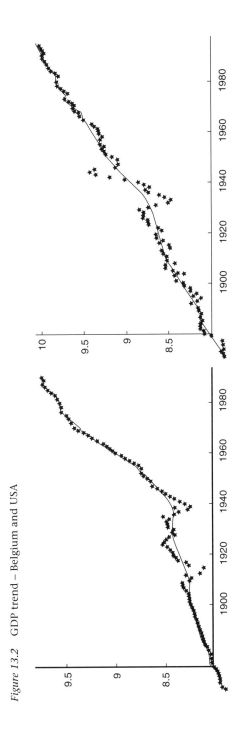

Figure 13.2 GDP trend – Belgium and USA

Neoclassical growth theory suggests that utility increases with consumption and, as a consequence, with wealth. Accepting that satisfaction and instantaneous utility are equivalent, this implies that the rich should feel more satisfied than the poor, that reported satisfaction levels should be higher in more developed countries and that satisfaction should grow in line with wealth. As a matter of fact, only the first of these three consequences of standard models seems to be weakly verified.

According to various studies, international differences in satisfaction are very small and almost unrelated to economic prosperity.[3] Surveys undertaken by Gallup simply consisted of asking a question on people's satisfaction in different parts of the world. These are some puzzles about these results. Why are the impoverished Latin Americans so satisfied? Are Europeans really less happy than Americans and Australians? (Argyle (1987, p. 103)).[4]

The Gallup-type studies give useful information on the non-existence of the simple link consumption → utility only if satisfaction levels are comparable across countries, that is, if the preference orderings are monotonically related. If this is not the case, one has to use a method that is robust to cultural discrepancies and, possibly also, to other sources of bias such as translation problems. Such a study has been carried out by Cantril (1965) and further analysed by Easterlin (1974). People were asked to imagine the best possible life and the worst possible life they could lead. They then had to say where their present life fell on a scale from 0 to 10:

> The inference about a positive association (between wealth and satisfaction) relies heavily on the observations for India and the USA. ... the values for Cuba and the Dominican Republic reflect unusual political circumstances. ... there is not much evidence, for these 10 countries[5] of a systematic association between income and happiness. ... a similar lack of association would be found between happiness and other economic magnitudes such as income inequality. (Easterlin (1974, pp. 105–6)).

Even if the methods and concepts of happiness studies are subject to criticism, one conclusion is that there is no evidence at the aggregate level in favour of the idea that wealth buys satisfaction.

Despite continually rising prosperity in the developed countries, there were considerable fluctuations in the percentage of those who said they were very satisfied. In Figure 13.3 we compare the US data gathered by Veenhoven (1993) with EC data from the Euro-barometer (some data points for Japan and Sweden are also displayed). The observed fluctuations for the USA and the astonishing constancy for EC 10 data are two puzzles which standard models are confronted with. Note finally that, behind the aggregate variable for EC 10, the various European countries display very contrasting experiences (de la Croix and Deneulin (1996)).

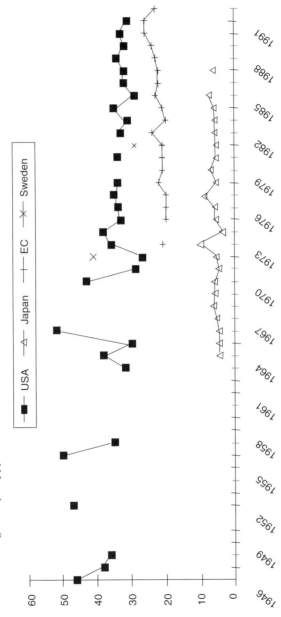

Figure 13.3   Percentages 'very happy' over time

13.2.5 Labour market

One major challenge of macroeconomics is to propose rigorous and convincing explanations of why real wages may be rigid and why employment fluctuates largely in response to shocks. Indeed, the inspection of the US business cycle characteristics of the labour market aggregates shows that the volatility of labour input is high and greater than the volatility of wages. Moreover, the correlation between wages and output is moderate (see Cooley and Prescott (1995)). The standard Real Business Cycle model, see for example King, Plosser and Rebelo (1988), fails to fit these facts. Solving this business cycle puzzle has become one of the most challenging task for the RBC research programme.[6]

Moreover, the contrast between the US pattern of the labour market and its European counterpart has attracted wide attention (see e.g. Card, Kramarz and Lemieux (1996)). Indeed, in the last two decades, the US labour market was characterized by constant or even declining real wages and rising employment, while the European labour market experienced steadily rising real wages and falling employment, and a substantial and persistent high level of unemployment.

13.3 The principle of extended preferences

The standard approach to economics is to assume that agents maximize an objective function with preferences that depend at any point in time on the control variables chosen at that time (consumption, leisure ...). In the simplest growth model one has:

$$u(c_{it})$$

where u is the instantaneous utility function and c_{it} is the consumption at time t of individual i. The preferences under which the utility function is derived are, by definition, independent of past choices and others' choices. This simplification is quite useful to address many economic issues, but it is fair to recognize that most economic models have adopted a very naive approach to the determination of utility and that a large number of choices depend very much on past actions and inter-individual relationships. As stressed by Frank (1989), there is a lack of context: 'The neoclassical economic model of choice abstracts from context, saying that utility depends only on the level of consumption. ... one must not only know the relevant levels of consumption, but also have an appropriate frame of reference within which to evaluate them.'

Accordingly, the standard microeconomic approach to preferences has been extended by Becker (1996) and others to incorporate past experiences and social forces into tastes in order to analyse issues such as addiction, peer pressure and catching up. We can thus use these 'extended preferences' to model the making of standard-of-living aspirations and their effect on macro-economic variables. An extended utility function can be written

$$u(c_{it}, s_{it})$$

where s_{it} is a stock variable that represents the level of aspirations, habits ..., of individual i. We shall now analyse to what extent these mechanisms provide plausible frameworks to understand how fluctuations in output and employment are propagated. The question is now to specify how the stock variable s_t is formed.

13.4 Personal capital

A first class of models consider that s_{it} is built from the past actions of the agents:

$$s_{it} = s(s_{it-1}, c_{it-1}) \tag{1}$$

In this case s_{it} is called a 'personal capital'. The easiest example is habit formation. The past consumption of the agent modifies its desire to consume today. Tastes thus evolve as a function of the agent's decision.

13.4.1 Principle

The idea dates back to Duesenberry (1949), has been used in many empirical studies and has been applied in general equilibrium set-ups by Wan (1970) and Ryder and Heal (1973). It amounts to assuming that tastes are changing and that these changes depend on past decisions (i.e. past consumption levels or expenditure levels). Things are judged by the extent to which they depart from a baseline of past experiences. Experiences that are salient or extreme and relevant to other experiences imply important changes in instantaneous satisfaction. However, another important aspect of habit formation is that, 'gradually, the most positive events will cease to have impact as they themselves are absorbed into the new baseline against which further events are judged' (Brickman, Coates and Janoff-Belman (1978)). This is a consequence of adaptation, a theory developed by biologists and psychologists, 'which is a mechanism for acquainting us with changes in the environment. If the same stimulation continues, adaptation gradually counteracts its effects to the point where it may no longer be sensed or its quality becomes neutral' (Helson, 1964). The power of adaptation has been explored by Brickman, Coates and Janoff-Belman (1978). They study whether quadriplegic patients are just as satisfied some time after their accident as other people. The impact of their accident is completely eroded by an habituation process. Some authors then claim that happiness is totally relative and that the initial gain or loss in satisfaction after a big shock is completely eroded by habituation to the new consumption standard. Economists would then have in mind a utility function of the form:

$$u = \left(\frac{c_{it}}{s_{it}} \right)$$

where the function (1) is homogeneous of degree one. This is of course an extreme case of habit formation.

A related problem in the context of habit formation is to capture the degree of forward looking behaviour of the agents (see Pashardes (1986) and Muellbauer (1988)). The agent is called myopic if in each period he takes into account his consumption history but does not recognize the impact of his present consumption on his future tastes and decisions. In contrast, a 'rational' agent refers to one who takes into account the effect of his current decision on his future tastes. This was a important debate in the seventies but now all rational expectations models assume no particular myopia on behalf of the consumers. Let us now explore in more detail the macroeconomic consequences of habit formation.

13.4.2 Macroeconomic implications

Several papers in the literature show that habit formation is helpful to explain the fact that the return on the stock market exceeds so much the return on risk-free deposits. The first attempt to do so (Constantinides (1990)) was criticized because it implied counterfactual high risk aversion. Subsequent research has shown (Boldrin, Christiano and Fisher (1995)) that this equity premium puzzle can be accounted for without assuming counterfactual risk aversion if one assumes both habit formation and a multi-sector technology with limited mobility of factors.[7] The main force at work is a general equilibrium feature: as agents with habits have an additional motive to smooth their consumption, they will extensively sell and buy assets in the face of unexpected shocks. When the stock of capital is fixed, the price of assets is more volatile, and, other things being equal, the equity premium is increased.

The second implication of models with habit formation is obviously to smooth consumption. This is a nice property as standard models tend to overestimate the sensitivity of consumption to income shocks. With habit formation, the response of consumption to income shocks is smaller, and the response to a distributed lag of past permanent incomes is positive (see Winder and Palm (1996) and Seckin (1999)).

To smooth consumption in the face of income shocks agents obviously need to adjust their saving rate. This implies that investment is more volatile with habit formation. As a consequence, a negative shock will have deeper consequences in the future, as investment is more depressed than in standard models because agents try to adjust slowly their consumption level.

With respect to the international risk-sharing puzzle, Fuhrer and Klein (1998) first show that habits are important in the G7 countries' aggregate consumption, and second that the introduction of habit formation makes the puzzle even worse than we think. Indeed, in the face of common shocks to interest rates, habits can generate positive international correlations, even in the absence of risk-sharing.

On the econometric side, the habit formation model has been used in empirical studies of consumer behaviour (see Ferber (1973) for a survey). If we only consider relatively recent contributions, Muellbauer (1988), Eichenbaum, Hansen and Singleton (1988), Ferson and Constantinides (1991) and Ogaki and Park (1998) find that habit formation helps to account for consumption dynamics. Winder and Palm (1996) show in an explicit model that 'ignoring habits or other forms of nonseparability may explain the frequent rejection of the life cycle hypothesis'. Finally, de la Croix and Urbain (1998) show that habit formation can be useful to obtain stable preference parameters in household's Euler equations.

13.4.3 Comparison with the best previous experience

Modigliani (1949) introduces the highest past income in the consumption function. Following Michalos (1980), the best previous experience is one of the two main determinants of aspirations and of the goal-achievement gap, which itself explains quite well the reported levels of satisfaction. His study is carried out over 12 specific domains (e.g. health, family life, etc.) and his conclusion seems rather robust. When comparisons are made with the best previous experience, the function (1) is of the form:

$$s_{it+1} = \max[s_{it}, c_{it}]$$

This introduces a unit root in the model and the economy displays path dependency. In this framework, reported satisfaction depends on the whole history, including the initial level of habits. This case provides interesting elements for explaining international differences in reported satisfaction.

13.5 Social capital

In the personal capital case the stock of habits is built from the personal past experience of the agent. An alternative is to suppose that aspirations are built from the past consumption of a reference group of agents, either peers or the whole society. This is the social capital case also called in the literature the 'catching-up with the Joneses' approach. The main references are Abel (1990) and J. Campbell and Cochrane (1995). The stock s is now given by:

$$s_{it} = s(s_{it-1}, C_{t-1})$$

where c_{t-1} is aggregate consumption.

13.5.1 Principle

The norm–achievement gap model often presented in the psychological literature can be seen as embedding both personal and social capital. According to Michalos (1980), 'the hypothesis regarding satisfaction as a function of the gap between aspiration and achievement has been almost uniformly successful.' In this model satisfaction is a function of the perceived gap between goal and achievements, and the goal is a function of previous personal experience and other achievements. This norm– achievement gap model is demonstrated by the scheme shown in Figure 13.4.

Norms are fed by (real and/or imaginary) comparisons with one's own and with other persons' past. The studies of Michalos (1980) conclude, on the basis of questionnaire data, that comparisons with the most-liked previous experience and with a reference group of other people are the main factors of the norm–achievement gap and, hence, of satisfaction. Using the terminology of Scitovsky (1976), the 'enjoyment of novelty' may come from comparisons with the past, and 'satisfaction of status' from comparisons with other people.

13.5.2 Macroeconomic implications

The key difference between social and personal capital models is that social capital postulates a consumption externality. Indeed, the future norms of the society are formed from the current and past consumption choices of its members. Each individual member does not internalize the effect of his current choice on social norms and thus on his future tastes. Agents who increase their consumption do not take into account their effect on the aggregate desire of all other agents to catch up. This externality allows room for beneficial government intervention. Optimal – first-best – policies can take different forms depending on the structure of the model:

- If there are different types of goods, it is obvious that the optimal policy consists in taxing the positional goods. The possibility is explored in a growth model by Cooper and Garcia-Peñalosa (1999). This taxation allows a reduction in the aggregate desire to catch up.
- In the face of exogenous shocks on income, Ljungqvist and Uhlig (1999) show that it can be optimal to adopt a Keynesian policy. Indeed, in a model without capital, pro-cyclical taxes allow to cool down the

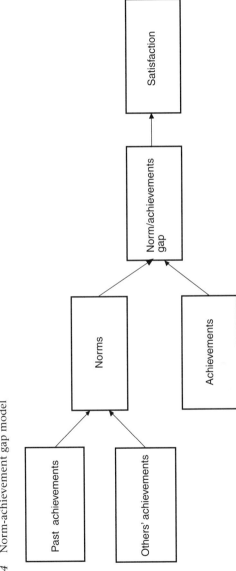

Figure 13.4 Norm-achievement gap model

economy when it is overheating following a positive shock. As households cannot smooth consumption as much as they wish, it is optimal to avoid over-consumption during expansion periods.

- On the contrary, when capital is introduced, the catching-up-with-the-Joneses model leads to too smooth consumption. It is then optimal to amplify the effect of the shocks by means of taxes (see de la Croix (1998) and Lettau and Uhlig (2000)). This illustrates that reducing the variance of consumption is not always an optimal policy.

Government spending policies can also help in reducing the externalities. In models with a direct effect of government spending on utility, including possibly some habituation mechanism, there are potential cross-effects with the norms derived from private consumption. An example of the positive role of government spending on externalities is provided by Ng (1987) in a static framework: the external cost of the resources used to produce private goods which are imposed on others through relative-income effects no longer exists in the case of public expenditure on pure public goods. The production of public goods is thus a means to reduce the inter-individual externalities. An extension of this to a dynamic setting is left for future research.

Finally, Layard (1980) suggests altering utility functions in order to reduce the importance of externalities. Education policies could play a role so as to make people more altruistic and less concerned about their status. The effect of education on the norm–achievement gap is not straightforward, however, as some empirical studies show that the positive effect of education on satisfaction can be offset by the fact that education may lead to higher aspirations and, hence, frustrations (see e.g. Woittiez and Theeuwes (1995)). In order to analyse such policies, it is necessary explicitly to introduce human capital to the model (or, at least, leisure) and to assume that the function describing how norms are built depends either on the level of human capital or on the time spent on leisure.

13.6 Family capital

Let us now turn our attention to another form of endogenous tastes, more adapted to the study of long-run issues. It is a framework in which agents evaluate their own consumption with respect to a baseline that depends on the consumption of their parents when they were still living with them. Indeed parents' influence on children is not limited to resource transfers or human capital transfers. Becker (1992) notices that

> The habits acquired as a child or young adult generally continue to influence behavior even when the environment changes radically. For instance, Indian adults who migrate to the United States often eat the same

type of cuisine they had in India, and continue to wear the same type of clothing. ... Childhood-acquired habits then continue, even though these would not have developed if the environment when growing up had been the same as the environment faced as an adult.

A comprehensive survey of evidence of vertical transmission (i.e. from parents to children), including the fear of insects but also career aspirations, is provided in Boyd and Richerson (1985). These vertical transmission mechanisms are modelled in different strands of literature. All of them lead to the conclusion that intergenerational taste externalities are particularly important for thinking about long-term evolution processes like economic growth.

13.6.1 Principle

The intergenerational spillover can take the form of what social scientists call social capital (to be distinguished from the concept of social capital used above). Following Coleman (1990), physical capital is wholly tangible, being embodied in equipment; human capital is embodied in the individuals through skills and knowledge; social capital is embodied in the relations among persons. The family relationships are important vectors of social capital allowing for intergenerational spillovers. Chapter 22 of Coleman (1990) analyses how different family structures generate social capital and how the decline in the role of the family in recent decades can be important for the social capital of the next generations. In Coleman (1990), social capital can be seen as a vector of growth; he does not investigate situations in which some sort of social capital can hamper the growth process.

The most comprehensive analysis of intergenerational spillovers can be found in the work of Cavalli-Sforza and Feldman (1981) and Boyd and Richerson (1985). They study cultural transmission across generations, and in particular the link between the transmission of culture and the transmission of genes.

After having assessed the huge importance of social learning within the family, Boyd and Richerson (1985) build different models in which the distribution of beliefs, attitudes and values in a population is transmitted and modified. The most important source of ambiguity is the empirical difficulty of disentangling cultural inheritance from genetic inheritance. However, linking the models of cultural transmission to models of genetic evolution helps to determine the circumstances under which natural selection might favour the modes of cultural transmission observed among human beings. Given detailed assumptions about the structure of cultural transmission and the nature of the environment, they predict the kinds of culturally transmitted behaviours that should characterize a particular population.

In Cavalli-Sforza and Feldman (1981), the vertical transmission of culture is measured using the Stanford survey of beliefs and values. Vertical transmission appears clearly important concerning dietary habits, religious habits, sports participation and political interest. The authors next study the interaction between the inheritance of culture, the inheritance of genes and the environment. One interesting aspect is that cultural selection is distinguished from natural selection. Cultural selection is determined by the acceptance or refusal by the individual after his exposure to the trait. Cultural selection is important to determine the type of dynamics that can emerge. For instance, negative reactions to examples set by parents may generate cyclical dynamics. Once cultural selection has occurred, the Darwinian fitness of the trait is tested. Indeed, the inheritance of a trait can alter the viability of the next generation, depending on how this trait 'fits' with the process of natural selection. This can lead to unstable dynamics, and to the extinction of some traits. Their socio-biological approach is not that far from the economic approach, in which the role of the natural selection is played by market forces.

13.6.2 Modelling intergenerational taste externalities

In a simple general equilibrium model, intergenerational taste externalities can be modelled in the following way. Using the same notation as above, the instantaneous utility depends on a stock variable s_t which is here interpreted as family capital. We thus have $u(c_t, s_t)$ and we may distinguish two cases depending on the sign of the intergenerational spillover.

When $u'_s > 0$, the consumption of the parents has a positive influence on the utility of their children. This is the case, for instance, when the children learn an 'art-of-living' with their parents; this stock of cultural knowledge presents some durability and still exerts a positive influence when the children become adults. The effect of s on the consumption behaviour of the new adult depends on u''_{cs}. If $u''_{cs} < 0$, the desire to consume is reduced by the stock of cultural knowledge, when for instance the agents have learned how to withdraw a maximum satisfaction from what they consume, and we say that they are repleted. If $u''_{cs} > 0$ the desire for consumption is increasing with the parents' consumption and we say that there is addiction.

When $u'_s < 0$, which is the case studied in this paper, parents' consumption has a negative influence on children's utility. As in the psychological models of the 'goal-achievement gap', the instantaneous satisfaction depends on the gap between the actual consumption and the aspirations, that is, the consumption of the previous generation. If $u''_{cs} < 0$, the aspiration effect generates distaste. If $u''_{cs} > 0$, which is the interesting case, the aspirations serve as a benchmark consumption level determining a goal to reach for the new generation. They induce a desire of catching up, pushing the new generation to consume more than their parents did. The utility function used in de la Croix (1996, 2000) and de la Croix and Michel (1998, 1999) displays this catching-up effect. They use the following utility of a representative individual:

$$\log(c_t - s_t) + \beta \log(d_{t+1})$$

where c_t is the consumption when adult, d_{t+1} is the consumption when old and β is the psychological discount factor. Aspirations s_t are linked to the consumption of the parents when adults:

$$s_t = \gamma c_{t-1}$$

As $u''_{cs} > 0$, the aspiration effect induces a desire of catching up, pushing the new generation to consume more than their parents did. We also assume that the depreciation rate of aspirations (i.e. forgetting) is high so that they no longer affect the evaluation of consumption when old. This simplifying assumption proxies the idea that aspirations are less important for older persons.[8]

13.6.3 Macroeconomic implications

As stressed by Easterlin (1971), income growth from one generation to another is a two-edged sword. His argument is that 'in a steadily growing economy, successive generations are raised in increasingly affluent households and hence develop successively higher living aspirations.' This 'inter-generational taste effect' is a *negative* externality making the future generations more and more demanding along the growth process. This is dramatically illustrated by the results of a survey of the experience in a rapidly growing economy – Taiwan – analysed by Freedman (reported by Easterlin (1974)): 'Only 20 per cent of the respondents said their financial position had improved during the last five years, although real per capita income increased about 40 per cent during that period.'

How the negative externality linked to inherited standard-of-living aspirations interacts with positive inherited human capital is studied in de la Croix (2000) who wonders whether the interaction of inherited higher skills and higher aspirations could explain why development and economic growth are not as successful and widespread as the standard theory predicts. For instance, if aspirations rise faster than productivity, households can be tempted into lowering savings and/or education spending in order to maintain the growth of their consumption. This mechanism can be responsible for oscillations around the balanced growth path. The economic rationale for oscillations in this case is the following. The spillover from one generation to the next has two components: (*a*) savings of the old generation finance the capital stock required to produce and to pay the wages of the young generation; this process that transforms income/savings of the old into income for the young displays decreasing returns; (*b*) past consumption levels of the parents generate standard-of-living aspirations for the young generation, leading them to spend more on consumption; this process displays constant returns. At one point, due to the decreasing returns in the production process, the bequest in terms of higher wages is not sufficient to cover the bequest in terms of higher aspirations. This leads to a drop in savings to maintain the standard of living and induces a recession. When the consecutive impoverishment is strong enough, aspirations revert to lower levels, allowing a rise in savings and the start of an expansion period. Depending on the relative strength of the two effects and on the current state of the economy compared to its stationary state, this process can either converge, or explode.

A second implication of the model is the existence of a poverty trap: for some initial conditions, the economy is led to a no-growth stationary state. This model can thus explain differences in income levels and growth rates across countries in terms of (slight) differences in fundamentals and initial conditions. The difference with the existing literature on the subject, surveyed by Benhabib and Gali (1995), Galor (1996) and Azariadis (1996), is that the initial conditions include, in addition to the standard levels of human and/or capital stock variables, an initial level for the stock of norms/aspirations. This model implies that the economies will be divided into two classes as a function of their initial combination of aspirations – human capital: one class experiencing a positive growth rate (that may furthermore oscillate over time) and one class characterized by low or no growth. This dualization may take place even if the initial distribution of initial conditions is concentrated. This is in accordance with the description of covergence proposed by Quah (1996) in which two convergence clubs emerge with their own basin of attraction. The presence in one of our examples of a repelling limit cycle reinforces the idea of small basins of convergence around endogenous growth stationary states. Notice that the picture proposed by Quah (1996) does not exclude the transition of a poor country to the club of the rich; in our model this would be explained by a favourable initial mix of aspirations and human capital in this poor country.

A third consequence is the occurrence of a decline scenario. In the existing literature, education below a critical level may lead to a poverty trap, and economies starting with too low a stock of human capital may be unable to reach the higher stationary state. This remains true in our framework, yet countries starting with too *high* education spending may also end in a poverty trap. In that case, the high revenues generated by the high human capital stock may rapidly induce a boom and high standard-of-living aspirations. If aspirations rise too rapidly compared to the potentialities of the economy, savings are depressed and investment in education and physical capital drops.

An empirical question implied by the above theoretical research consists in analysing whether excessively high aspirations can effectively slow growth. A documented example concerns the 'golden' sixties in the US and the following recession. In the model, recession periods are preceded by a time of high aspirations, and hence, low satisfaction. Easterlin (1974) and Easterlin (1995) use the happiness survey carried out by the American Institute of Public Opinion (Gallup) in the years 1946–70 and by the National Opinion Research Centre (University of Michigan) since 1957. The conclusion that can be drawn from the two independent surveys is that there was a decline in happiness between the late 1950s and the mid-1960s. The drop in happiness came in a boom before the drop in growth that started in the mid-sixties. This view is also corroborated by the comprehensive study of A. Campbell (1981) based on 45 happiness surveys. He concludes first that there was a swing in American happiness with a peak in the late fifties, and second that movements in happiness sometimes occur in direct opposition to what one would have expected on the basis of economic trends. Further research on the idea that aspirations above a critical level can be a cause of economic stagnation for certain developing countries could be pursued using cross-sectional data.

13.7 The fair wage

Habit formation and social norms mechanisms can be helpful in understanding labour market characteristics. For countries where unions play an important role, the utility of the union may depend on the history of wages, making an income cut undesirable to the union. Stated differently, the unions' utility function may depend on the growth of wages, that is, the level of past wages is progressively included in the reservation wage. Union's habit formation relates to 'built-in' taste changes depending on past decisions. The assumption that '[a] once and for all increase tends after a period to be forgotten and assumed part of the accepted wage structure' was applied to unions by Kotowitz and Portes (1974) and de la Croix, Palm and Pfann (1996). Frank and Hutchens (1993) relate this idea to the empirical evidence that people prefer jobs with rising wage profiles.

Another promising line of research relies on an extension of the efficiency wage model.

13.7.1 Principle

Assuming that productivity and workers' effort are affected by the wage paid by the firm, efficiency wage theories have been judged to be very promising given the goal of understanding labour market characteristics (see e.g. Blanchard and Fischer (1989, p. 463)). Danthine and Donaldson (1995) list four kinds of efficiency wages: (*a*) those that discourage shirking by raising the opportunity cost of being fired (shirking model), (*b*) those that reduce quits (turnover cost model), (c) those that improve the applicant pool (screening model), and (d) those that improve efforts by improving morale with a fair wage (gift exchange model). These theories have first been developed in static models, explaining the existence of involuntary unemployment in terms of the optimal response of firms to workers' behaviour. For instance, in the gift exchange model of Akerlof (1982), the effort of an individual worker depends on a comparison between the current wage and a norm which includes the salaries perceived by other workers, the level of unemployment and unemployment benefits, and the actual wage of the individual in previous periods. Notice that this last element has been omitted in the various subsequent analyses because the majority of them are performed in static frameworks.

The optimal response of the firm to this behaviour is to offer a wage above the market-clearing level in return for which workers would provide a higher level of effort. This view of labour relationships is supported by a large number of studies both in applied economics and experimental psychology. A representative study in this category which precedes the theoretical formulation of the efficiency wage models is the one of Adams and Rosenbaum (1962). The agents in this experiment were male college students who were hired on a part-time basis to conduct interviews at a given salary per hour. After completing an extensive questionnaire, agents in the control group were informed that they were suitably qualified for the job. In the experimental group, agents were told that their questionnaires revealed them to be underqualified, but that they would be hired and paid the pre-established rate nevertheless. This manipulation led agents in the experimental group to feel they were overpaid compared to the agents in the control group. The results revealed that the agents in the experimental group conducted more interviews per hour than those in the control group, thereby lending support to the theory.

Several papers pursuing the efficiency wage route embed shirking or gift exchange motives in the framework of stochastic dynamic general equilibrium models.[9] The hopes generated by the efficiency wage theories were then strongly dashed by these studies.

In a gift exchange set-up, Danthine and Donaldson (1990) conclude that

> The most striking implication to emerge from these data is the inability of our gift exchange example to account for the business cycle puzzle. This result is important because it demonstrates that in efficiency wage models involuntary unemployment ... is not synonymous with wage sluggishness. ... most of the adjustment to productivity shocks is in terms of wages. There is almost no adjustment in terms of quantities.

A similar disappointment with regard to efficiency wage theories can be found in models of the shirking category as in Uhlig and Xu (1995) and

Gomme (1999). Uhlig and Xu (1995) find that, in order to reproduce an adequate level of employment variability, they need to assume implausibly large movements in the technological shock. The reason is that effort moves counter-cyclically, because the wage norm depends negatively on unemployment. Gomme (1999) also finds that wages are too volatile and too pro-cyclical compared to the data.

Taking inspiration from what has been developed on consumers' habits and social norms, it is possible to extend the gift exchange model of Danthine and Donaldson (1990), allowing for the reference wage to include past wages of the individual himself or of others. Indeed, the conclusion that efficiency wage considerations based on the gift exchange paradigm are not sufficient to resolve the business cycle puzzle (Danthine and Donaldson (1995)) seems too hasty because the aforementioned studies have never used the original idea of Akerlof (1982) that the wage norm depends also on past wages. It is fair to recognize that this time-non-separability in the disutility of effort could not have been analysed in the initial static studies of gift exchange models, but it seems feasible and desirable to use it in the more sophisticated dynamic models of the RBC type. This position is reinforced by the bunch of empirical studies which stress the importance of inter-temporal wage comparisons for effort and job satisfaction.

For instance, examining the benchmarks used in the evaluation of payments, Goodman (1974) found that an important proportion of respondents to his survey used their own payment in the past as a comparison standard. Another interesting study has been carried out by Lord and Hohenfeld (1979). They compared the performance of baseball players who were paid less one season than they were the season before. Using their own salaries during the previous year as a basis for comparison, they were expected to have felt underpaid. As the theory predicts, these players lowered their performance. A more recent microeconometric study of Wadhwani and Wall (1991) uses a panel on UK manufacturing enterprises to estimate their production function (including the effort function). They allow the wage norm to depend on past wages and show that there is some evidence in favour of this dependence. Additional inference on the role of past wages on effort can be done by analysing job satisfaction studies. Using a panel data on British employees, Clark (1996) provides evidence that job satisfaction is strongly positively correlated with the change in the worker's payment between the two waves of the panel.

Very recently the survey undertaken by Bewley (1998) brings interesting insights to model wage behaviour. He interviewed business people, labour leaders and counsellors of unemployed people in the US to understand why wages were almost never declining. The key result is that firms dislike pay cuts because they hurt morale. Good morale promotes high productivity, less turnover, and a good company reputation that helps recruiting. Pay cuts hurt morale because of discomfort from reduced living standards and because of an insult effect – workers associate pay increases with approbation and reward. A key point of the survey is that morale depends on the level of wages, but most importantly, on wage changes.

Applying the terminology of Becker (1996) to our problem, the inclusion of past wages in the norm can be achieved in two distinct ways: (*a*) the personal norm includes the relevant past wages perceived by the individual; (*b*) the social norm incorporates the influence of past actions by peers and others. This distinction is crucial for the type of dynamics which will emerge from the model. In the personal norm case, the firm recognizes the impact of the current wage on the future effort levels of its workers. In the social norm case, the firm has no control on the 'social capital' of its workers since it is mainly determined by the situations of peers and relevant others. In the majority of the mentioned empirical studies, the authors have implicitly in mind the social norm case. However, in a fully specified dynamic model with rational expectations, the alternative of the personal norm case could also be of interest.

13.7.2 Macroeconomic implications

Collard and de la Croix (2000) evaluate whether incorporating past wage comparisons in gift exchange models can help to solve the business cycle puzzle related to the labour market and hence promote a new direction for research. The evaluation of the performance of the model is carried out using standard real business cycle techniques, including the comparisons between the properties of the data generated by a stylized calibrated model and those from the real world. The moments on which the comparison will bear are essentially the volatility and the correlation of hours and wages with respect to output. They also examine the ability of the model to mimic the dynamic pattern of wages and hours.

In both social and personal norm models, the high variability of employment and the low variability of wages are reproduced without requiring additional features such as nominal rigidities, tastes shocks or indivisible labour. The social norm model also makes it possible to mimic closely the slightly positive actual correlation between real wages and employment. In the personal norm case, fair wage considerations induce a propagation mechanism that magnifies the effect of productivity shocks on activity and implies a pro-cyclical effort.

de la Croix, Palm and Urbain (2000) propose a dynamic model in which a representative firm chooses employment and a wage level designed to motivate its employees. The effort of these employees depends both on the level and on the growth rates of wages compared to those of the alternative wages (i.e. in the rest of their sector). With the aim of understanding wage and employment dynamics, the implications of this model are confronted with data for manufacturing sectors in the US, Germany, Great Britain and France. Their conclusion is twofold. First, the implications of the model seem in accordance with the non-stationarity present in the data and the restrictions imposed on the dynamics are not rejected. Parameter constancy is not rejected in three countries among four.[10] Second, effort is less sensitive to wage growth comparisons in the US than in the three European countries. European workers seem more attached to previous wage conditions and put more weight on wage increases. According to these results, the optimal wage growth set by the firm is more sensitive to the level of unemployment in the US than in Europe.

13.8 Summary and conclusion

One of the major challenges of research in macroeconomics is to explain why there are economy-wide movements in output and employment. Different approaches have been pursued to model fluctuations, including shocks to fundamentals, endogenous cycles and self-fulfilling expectations. For all approaches, the elaboration of frameworks that can propagate cycles in the case of empirically realistic mechanisms is one important challenge. Our aim was to study the contribution of habit formation set-ups and standard-of-living aspirations to the explanation of fluctuations.

The standard approach to economics is to assume that agents maximize an objective function with preferences that depend at any point in time on the control variables chosen at that time (consumption, leisure). These preferences are, by definition, independent of past choices and others' choices. This simplification is quite useful for addressing many economic issues, but it is fair to recognize that a large number of choices depend very much on past actions and inter-individual relationships. Accordingly, the standard microeconomic approach to preferences has been extended to incorporate past experiences and social forces into tastes in order to analyse issues like addiction, peer pressure, catching-up. Our aim was to use these 'extended preferences' to model the making of standard-of-living aspirations and their effect on macroeconomic variables; we then analysed to what extent these mechanisms provide plausible explanations of why growth is not a steady process and how fluctuations in output and employment are propagated.

In section 13.3 we concentrated on consumption behaviour when there is habit formation. We showed that such behaviour can be in accordance with several empirical facts and has important policy implications. Long-term issues were analysed in section 13.6 in which we assumed that children become habituated to a certain standard of living whilst still with their parents. We showed that this assumption introduces a powerful mechanism that can be responsible for long-term oscillations. As the labour market is a key element of the macroeconomic dynamics, we investigated in section 13.7 whether habit formation set-ups applied to wage formation can explain the relative volatility of wages and employment and the persistence of unemployment at high levels.

We conclude that the microeconomic approach to extended preferences can be fruitful for analysing macroeconomic issues like cycles and growth. Including past consumption expenditure in the utility function is helpful to model the desire to maintain or enhance inherited standard of living. The notion of fair wage as depending on the history of wages, either personal or social, is also important to an understanding of labour market facts. Many further extensions are possible. In pursuing this line of research, one should, however, keep in mind that when one puts things like status into the utility function one should be careful not to lose the discipline standard economic modelling provides (Postlewaite (1999)). A careful analysis of both the theoretical and empirical foundations of the modelling choices is thus required to build parsimonious macroeconomic models with endogenous tastes.

Notes

1. Another overlapping generations model is proposed by Farmer (1986) in which cycles arise only if the government pursues a particular policy, namely a policy of fixing the value of the deficit. As in Reichlin (1986), low values of the elasticity of substitution in production are required for cycles to occur.
2. Note that there exists an infinity of arbitrary ways to decompose a given series into a long-term trend and a cycle.
3. This conclusion of various aggregate studies is to some extent contradicted by panel data analysis, such as in Veenhoven (1994).
4. A second study of the Gallup type *comforts* the idea that there is no positive association between wealth and satisfaction. 'The results are ambiguous. The four lowest income countries are neither at the top nor at the bottom of the table' (Easterlin (1974, p. 108)). Another useful source for making international comparisons of satisfaction is the survey carried out twice a year in the EC (Eurobarometer). The inference about a positive association between wealth and satisfaction relies heavily on the observations for two countries, Denmark and Greece. The other eight countries do not display any clear association.
5. Nigeria, Egypt, Philippines, Panama, Brazil, Yugoslavia, Japan, Poland, Israel, West Germany.
6. See for instance the contributions of Christiano and Eichenbaum (1992) and Fève and Langot (1994).
7. The resolution of the equity premium puzzle by means of habit-forming preferences is, however, still at stake (Otrok, Ravikumar and Whiteman (1998)).
8. This is supported by the empirical observation that reported satisfaction increases from the age of 30 onwards. On the basis of their empirical study on job satisfaction, Clark, Oswald and Warr (1996) conclude that 'the rise in job satisfaction at these ages could come from *reduced aspirations*, due to a recognition that there are few alternative jobs available once a worker's career is established ... . Alternatively, aspirations themselves could remain the same but older workers might put less weight on such comparisons.'

9. To our knowledge, the two other types of efficiency wage models have not been analysed within stochastic dynamic general equilibrium models.
10. From a practical point of view, parameter constancy appears as a necessary but not sufficient condition for robustness to the Lucas critique.

References

Abel, A. (1990) 'Asset Prices under Habit Formation and Catching up with the Joneses', *American Economic Review Papers and Proceedings*, vol. 80, pp. 38–42.
Adams, J. and Rosenbaum, W. (1962) 'The Relationship of Worker Productivity to Cognitive Dissonance about Wage Inequalities', *Journal of Applied Psychology*, vol. 46, pp. 161–64.
Akerlof, G. (1982) 'Labor Contracts as Partial Gift Exchange', *Quarterly Journal of Economics*, vol. 97, pp. 543–69.
Argyle, M. (1987) *The Psychology of Happiness* (London: Methuen).
Azariadis, C. (1996) 'The Economics of Poverty Traps – Part One: Complete Markets', *Journal of Economic Growth*, vol. 1, pp. 449–86.
Backus, D., Kehoe, P. and Kydland, F. (1992) 'International Real Business Cycles', *Journal of Political Economy*, vol. 100, pp. 745–75.
Becker, G. (1992) 'Habits, Addictions and Traditions', *Kyklos*, vol. 45, pp. 327–45.
Becker, G. (1996) *Accounting for Tastes* (Cambridge, Mass. Harvard University Press).
Benhabib, J. and Gali, J. (1995) 'On Growth and Indeterminacy: Some Theory and Evidence', *Carnegie-Rochester Conference Series on Public Policy*, vol. 43, pp. 163–211.
Bewley, T. (1998) 'Why Not Cut Pay?', *European Economic Review*, vol. 42, pp. 459–90.
Blanchard, O. and Fischer, S. (1989) *Lectures on Macroeconomics* (Cambridge, Mass. MIT Press).
Boldrin, M. and Woodford, M. (1990) 'Equilibrium Models Displaying Endogenous Fluctuations and Chaos', *Journal of Monetary Economics*, vol. 25, pp. 189–222.
Boldrin, M., Christiano, L. and Fisher, J. (1995) 'Asset Pricing Lessons for Modeling Business Cycles', NBER Working Paper no. 5262
Boyd, R. and Richerson, P. (1985) *Culture and the Evolutionary Process* (Chicago: University of Chicago Press).
Brickman, P., Coates, D. and Janoff-Belman, R. (1978) 'Lottery Winners and Accident Victims: Is Happiness Relative?', *Journal of Personality and Social Psychology*, vol. 36, pp. 917–27.
Campbell, A. (1981) *The Sense of Well-Being in America* (New York: McGraw-Hill).
Campbell, J. and Cochrane, J. (1995) 'By Force of Habits: A Consumption-Based Explanation of Aggregate Stock Market Behavior', *Journal of Political Economy*, vol. 107 (2), pp. 205–51.
Campbell, J. and Deaton, A. (1989) 'Why is Consumption so Smooth?', *Review of Economic Studies*, vol. 56, pp. 357–74.
Cantril, H. (1965) *The Pattern of Human Concerns* (New Brunswick, NJ: Rutgers University Press).
Card, D., Kramarz, F. and Lemieux, T. (1996) 'Changes in the Relative Structure of Wages and Employment: Comparison of the United States, Canada and France', NBER Working Paper, *Canadian Journal of Economics*, vol. 32 (4), pp. 843–77.
Cavalli-Sforza, L. and Feldman, M. (1981) *Cultural Transmission and Evolution: A Quantitative Approach* (Princeton, NJ: Princeton University Press).
Christiano, L. and Eichenbaum, M. (1992) 'Current Real Business Cycle Theories and Aggregate Labor-Market Fluctuations', *American Economic Review*, vol. 82, pp. 430–50.

Clark, A. (1996) 'Are Wages Habit Forming?' Evidence from Micro-Data', OECD Working Paper.

Clark, A., Oswald, A. and Warr, P. (1996) 'Is Job Satisfaction U-Shaped in Age?', *Journal of Occupational and Organizational Psychology*, vol. 69, pp. 57–81.

Coleman, J. (1990) *Foundations of Social Theory* (Cambridge, MASS: Belknap-Harvard).

Collard, F. and de la Croix, D. (2000) 'Gift Exchange and the Business Cycle: The Fair Wage Strikes Back', *Review of Economic Dynamics*, vol. 3, pp. 166–93.

Constantinides, G. (1990) 'Habit Formation: A Resolution of the Equity Premium Puzzle', *Journal of Political Economy*, vol. 98, pp. 519–43.

Cooley, T. and Prescott, E. (1995) 'Economic Growth and Business Cycles', in Cooley, T. (ed.) *Frontiers of Business Cycle Research* (Princeton, NJ: Princeton University Press).

Cooper, B. and Garcia-Peñalosa, C. (1999) 'Status Effects and Negative Utility Growth', University of Oxford Department of Economics.

Danthine, J.-P. and Donaldson, J. (1990) 'Efficiency Wages and the Business Cycle Puzzle', *European Economic Review*, vol. 34, pp. 1275–301.

Danthine, J.-P. and Donaldson, J. (1995) 'Non-Walrasian Economies', in T. Cooley (ed.) *Frontiers of Business Cycle Research* (Princeton, NJ: Princeton University Press).

de la Croix, D. (1996) 'The Dynamics of Bequeathed Tastes', *Economics Letters*, vol. 51, pp. 89–96.

de la Croix, D. (1998) 'Growth and the Relativity of Satisfaction', *Mathematical Social Sciences*, vol. 36, pp. 105–25.

de la Croix, D. (2000) 'Growth Dynamics and Education Spending: The Role of Inherited Tastes and Abilities', *European Economic Review*, forthcoming.

de la Croix, D. and Deneulin, S. (1996) 'Relativité de la satisfaction et croissance économique', *Actes du 12ème congrès des économistes belges de langue française*, vol. 1, pp. 153–69.

de la Croix, D. and Michel, P. (1998) 'Altruism and Self-Refrain', *Annales d'Economie et de Statistique*, forthcoming.

de la Croix, D. and Michel, P. (1999) 'Optimal Growth When Tastes are Inherited', *Journal of Economic Dynamics and Control*, vol. 23, pp. 519–37.

de la Croix, D. and Urbain J.-P. (1998) 'Intertemporal Substitution in Import Demand and Habit Formation', *Journal of Applied Econometrics*, vol. 13, pp. 589–612.

de la Croix, D., Palm, F. and Pfann, G. (1996) 'A Dynamic Contracting Model for Wages and Employment in Three European Economies', *European Economics Review*, vol. 40, pp. 429–48.

de la Croix, D., Palm, F. and Urbain, J.-P. (2000) 'Labor Market Dynamics When Effort Depends on Wage Growth Comparisons', *Empirical Economics*, vol. 25, pp. 393–420.

Duesenberry, J. (1949) *Income, Saving, and the Theory of Consumer Behavior* (Cambridge, MASS: Harvard University Press).

Easterlin, R. (1971) 'Does Human Fertility Adjust to the Environment?', *American Economics Review Papers and Proceedings*, vol. 61, pp. 399–407.

Easterlin, R. (1974) 'Does Economic Growth Improve the Human Lot? Some Empirical Evidence', in David, P. and Reder, M. (eds) *Nations and Households in Economic Growth* (New York: Academic Press).

Easterlin, R. (1995) 'Will Raising the Incomes of All Increase the Happiness of All?', *Journal of Economic Behaviour and Organization*, vol. 27, pp. 35–46.

Eichenbaum, M., Hansen, L. and Singleton, K. (1988) 'A Time Series Analysis of Representative Agent Models of Consumption and Leisure Choice under Uncertainty', *Quarterly Journal of Economics*, vol. 103, pp. 51–78.

Farmer, R. (1986) 'Deficits and Cycles', *Journal of Economic Theory*, vol. 40, pp. 77–88.

Ferber, R. (1973) 'Consumer Economics, a Survey', *Journal of Economic Literature*, vol. 11, pp. 1303–42.

Ferson, W. and Constantinides, G. (1991) 'Habit Persistence and Durability in Aggregate Consumption', *Journal of Financial Economics*, vol. 29, pp. 199–240.

Fève, P. and Langot, F. (1994) 'The RBC Model Through Statistical Inference: An Application with French Data', *Journal of Applied Econometrics*, vol. 9, pp. S11–S35.

Frank, R. (1989) 'Frames of References and the Quality of Life', *American Economic Review, Papers and Proceedings*, vol. 79, pp. 80–5.

Frank, R. and Hutchens, R. (1993) 'Wages, Seniority, and the Demand for Rising Consumption Profiles', *Journal of Economic Behavior and Organization*, vol. 21, pp. 251–76.

Fuhrer, J. and Klein, M. (1998) 'Risky Habits: On Risk Sharing, Habit Formation, and the Interpretation of International Consumption Correlations', NBER, Working Paper no. 6735.

Galor, O. (1996) 'Convergence? Inferences from Theoretical Models', *Economic Journal*, vol. 106, pp. 1056–69.

Gomme, P. (1999) 'Unemployment and Aggregate Fluctuations', *International Economic Review*, vol. 40, pp. 3–21.

Goodman, P. (1974) 'An Examination of Referents Used in the Evaluation of Pay', *Organizational Behavior and Human Performance*, vol. 12, pp. 170–95.

Grandmont, J.-M. (1985) 'On Endogenous Competitive Business Cycles', *Econometrica*, vol. 22, pp. 995–1037.

Helson, H. (1964) *Adaptation-Level Theory: An Experimental and Systemic Approach to Behavior*, (New York: Harper and Row).

Hodrick, R. and Prescott, E. (1980) 'Post-War U.S. Business Cycles: An Empirical Investigation', mimeo Carnegie-Mellon University.

Jones, C. (1999) 'Was an Industrial Revolution Inevitable? Economic Growth over the Very Long Run', mimeo, Stanford University.

King, R., Plosser, N. and Rebelo, S. (1988) 'Production, Growth and Business Cycles: IBC', *Journal of Monetary Economics*, vol. 21, pp. 196–232.

Kotowitz, Y. and Portes, R. (1974) 'The Tax on Wage Increases', *Journal of Public Economics*, vol. 3, pp. 112–32.

Layard, R. (1980) 'Human Satisfactions and Public Policy', *Economic Journal*, vol. 90, pp. 737–50.

Lettau, M. and Uhlig, H. (2000) 'Can Habit Formation be Reconciled with Business Cycle Facts?' *Review of Economic Dynamics*, vol. 3, pp. 79–99.

Ljungqvist, L. and Uhlig, H. (1999) 'Tax Policy and Aggregate Demand Management under Catching up with the Joneses', *American Economic Review*, vol. 90 (3), pp. 356–66.

Lord, R. and Hohenfeld J. (1979) 'Longitudinal Field Assessment of Equity Effects on the Performance of Major League Baseball Players', *Journal of Applied Psychology*, vol. 64, pp. 19–26.

Maddison, A. (1995) *Monitoring the World Economy, 1820–1992*, (Paris: OECD).

Mehra, R. and Prescott, E. (1985) 'The Equity Premium: A Puzzle', *Journal of Monetary Economics*, vol. 15, pp. 145–61.

Michalos, A. (1980) 'Satisfaction and Happiness', *Social Indicators Research*, vol. 8, pp. 385–422.

Modigliani, F. (1949) 'Fluctuations in the Saving–Income Ratio: A Problem in Economic Forecasting', *Studies in Income and Wealth*, vol. 11, pp. 371–443.

Muellbauer, J. (1988) 'Habits, Rationality and Myopia in the Life Cycle Consumption Function', *Annales d'Economie et de Statistique*, vol. 9, pp. 47–70.

Ng, Y.-K. (1987) 'Relative-Income Effects and the Appropriate Level of Public Expenditures', *Oxford Economic Papers*, vol. 39, pp. 293–300.

Ogaki, M. and Park, J. (1998) 'A Cointegration Approach to Estimating Preference Parameters', *Journal of Econometrics*, vol. 82 (1), pp. 107–34.

Otrok, C., Ravikumar, B. and Whiteman, C. (1998) 'Habit Formation: A Resolution of the Equity Premium Puzzle?' Working Paper, University of Iowa.

Pashardes, P. (1986) 'Myopic and Forward Looking Behaviour in a Dynamic Demand System', *International Economic Review*, vol. 27, pp. 387–97.

Postlewaite, A. (1999) 'Social Arrangements and Economic Behaviour', Working Paper, presented at the International Conference on Social Interactions and Economic behaviour, University of Paris I-Panthéon Sorbonne.

Prescott, E. (1998) 'Business Cycles Research: Methods and Problems', Working Paper 590, Federal Reserve Bank of Minneapolis.

Quah, D. (1996) 'Empirics for Economic Growth and Convergence', *European Economic Review*, vol. 40, pp. 1353–75.

Reichlin, P. (1986) 'Equilibrium Cycles in an Overlapping Generations Economy with Production', *Journal of Economic Theory*, vol. 40, pp. 89–102.

Reijnders, J. (1990) *Long Waves in Economic Development* (Cheltenham: Edward Elgar).

Ryder, H. and Heal G. (1973) 'Optimal Growth with Inter-Temporally Dependent Preferences', *Review of Economic Studies*, vol. 40, pp. 1–31.

Scitovsky, T. (1976) *The Joyless Economy* (Oxford: Oxford University Press).

Seckin, A. (1999) 'Consumption with Habit Formation', mimeo University of Montreal.

Solomou, S. (1986) 'Non-balanced Growth and Kondratieff Waves in the World Economy, 1850–1913', *Journal of Economic History*, vol. 46, pp. 165–9.

Uhlig, H. and Xu, Y. (1995) 'Effort and the Cycle: Cyclical Implications of Efficiency Wages' Working Paper, Centre (Tilburg).

van Ewijk, C. (1982) 'A Spectral Analysis of the Kondratieff-Cycle', *Kyklos*, vol. 35, pp. 468–99.

Veenhoven, R. (1993) *Happiness in Nations: Subjective Appreciation of Life in 56 Nations 1946–1992*. (Rotterdam: Erasmus University).

Veenhoven, R. (1994) 'Is Happiness a Trait? Tests of the Theory that a Better Society Does not Make People any Happier', *Social Indicators Research*, vol. 32, pp. 101–60.

Wadhwani, S. and Wall, M. (1991) 'A Direct Test of the Efficiency Wage Model using UK Micro-data', *Oxford Economic Papers*, vol. 43, pp. 529–48.

Wan, H. (1970) 'Optimal Saving Programs under Intertemporally Dependent Preferences', *International Economic Review*, vol. 11, pp. 521–47.

Winder, C. and Palm, F. (1996) 'Stochastic Implications of the Life Cycle Consumption Model under Rational Habit Formation', *Recherches Economiques de Louvain*, vol. 62, pp. 403–12.

Woittiez, I. and Theeuwes, J. (1995) 'Well-Being and Labour Market Status' Working Paper, Tinbergen Institute Rotterdam.

Part VI
Development

14

Development Policies Beyond Export-led Growth*

Vittorio Corbo
Pontificia Universidad Católica de Chile

14.1 Introduction

In recent years, developing countries in different regions of the world have been struggling to create an economic and social environment conducive to sustainable growth with a reduction of poverty. In the process, countries have introduced policy and institutional reforms aimed at restoring macroeconomic stability, improving overall economic efficiency and promoting opportunities for the poor. Progress has differed among countries, depending on the government objectives, the strategies followed, and the capacity of the governments to gather support and to carry through their policies. However, most countries have made substantial progress in the narrow area of stabilizing their economies and in opening their economies to foreign trade. A more stable macroeconomic situation and the resultant dismantling of protection reduced the anti-export bias of the trade regime, facilitating an expansion of export activities. In turn, for a given size of the trade balance deficit, export expansion led to a higher level of imports. The higher level and better quality of imports, in turn, have had positive effects on consumers' welfare and on total factor productivity.

To restore growth with equity requires much more than stability and opening to trade, as economic growth depends ultimately on the rate of growth of factor accumulation, the efficiency with which factors are employed, and the overall rate of growth of total factor productivity, the famous 'Solow residual'. Achieving higher growth and improving the access of the poor to social services have proved to be the most efficient strategy to enhance the capacity of the poor to generate income and to escape from poverty. Much is known from theory and empirical work about policies that promote growth. However, much less is known on how to improve social services. Difficulties here arise from both lack of knowledge on what

---

* I thank Andrés Elberg and José A.Tessada for their comments and suggestions.

works and what does not work and from entrenched political economy problems that act as an impediment to attempts at reforms.

But in spite of innumerable unresolved problems, changes in the way of thinking about development policies have been so radical that the overall model of development has been turned upside-down. In the process, the old import-substitution-cum-government intervention model of the 1950s and 1960s, with a weak concern for macroeconomic stability, has been replaced by a model where restoring and maintaining macroeconomic stability is a central element and where the role of markets and the government have been radically changed. In the old model, the central premise was that in developing countries most markets were incomplete and did not work properly, and therefore they could not be counted on to play a central role in resource allocation. In contrast, development policies in the 1990s have been guided by the central principle that markets could play an important role in facilitating an efficient allocation of resources. In the new model the government is as important as in the previous one, but its areas of specialization are radically different. In the new model the role of government is to ensure macroeconomic stability, to provide a regulatory and institutional infrastructure for the development of a competitive market economy, and to improve the supply of public goods, especially social services for the poorest groups in the population.[1] Now, the economic principles required to study the problems of developing countries are not so different from the ones required to study advanced countries; however, one still needs to take into account the specific institutional and market characteristics of the developing countries.[2]

These changes have been major if one considers that up to the mid-1980s, most developing economies, especially in Latin America, did not have much urgency to restore macroeconomic stability, had very restrictive trade regimes, and had very intrusive and large government sectors.[3] Macroeconomic imbalances took the form of high and sometimes accelerating inflation and large current account deficits. As fiscal deficits were endemic and financed at the central bank, inflation and balance-of-payments problems were more the rule than the exception. Governments were also much involved in altering price incentives and in allocating resources. The arsenal of instruments included: price controls; high levels and highly dispersed import tariffs; a wide variety of non-tariff barriers; multiple exchange rates; a distorted process of credit allocation; very restrictive labour practices; and social expenditures targeted towards the powerful middle class groups in urban areas.

The old development model not only led to a highly distorted and inefficient economy but also failed to achieve the ultimate objectives of a higher and sustainable rate of output growth, improved income distribution, and a significant reduction of poverty. Failures on this front were due both to the poor results in terms of output growth and to the failure to make advances in improving the social services geared to the poor. Indeed, government expenditures favoured mainly the powerful urban middle-class groups. A clear example of the latter was the complete lack of targeting among education and health expenditures. In particular, a substantial part of the education budget was typically spent on tertiary education, while the quality and coverage of primary and secondary education remained very poor.

Many factors contributed to the radical change in policies. In some countries it was the debt crisis of the early 1980s that set the stage for the introduction of widespread reforms, while in others it was the prospect of reduced access to foreign aid or the conditionality attached to aid flows. In many parts of the world the reform process was facilitated (and even accelerated) thanks to the existence of a critical mass of well-trained economists that took an interest in assessing the welfare effects of existing policies and in proposing alternative policies.[4] In other countries the intensity of the crisis diminished the political power of the rent-seeking groups (that had benefited from the earlier policies and had previously resisted this type of reform) and increased the capacity of the governments to carry out reforms.

In the case of Latin America the new winds of reform led the UN Economic Commission for Latin America and the Caribbean (ECLAC), the once major advocate of the import substitution-cum-government intervention model, to endorse the new development strategy. Thus ECLAC (1992) proposed a new development model, based on restoring and maintaining macroeconomic balances, increasing outward orientation, broadening the role of market forces, and introducing social programmes targeted towards the poorest groups of the population.

Typically, a country suffering an external crisis or facing the prospects of reduced access to foreign aid also had a large and unsustainable fiscal deficit, and, in many cases, was also experiencing very rapid inflation. Thus, macroeconomic problems were at the roots of the crisis and macroeconomic adjustment programmes were at the forefront of the adjustment efforts.

The adjustment programmes had to find quick ways to reduce current account deficits, while reducing inflation and simultaneously creating the basis for future growth. In the short run, to restore macroeconomic stability, it was necessary to focus policy measures more on expenditure reduction than on boosting output, as the latter type of policy produces results much more slowly. Thus, adjustment programmes were dominated by stabilization components, often with the support of the IMF and other international financial institutions.

Thus, macroeconomic adjustment was accompanied early on by a reduction in the anti-export bias of trade policies, creating, in the process, the conditions for export-led growth. But opportunities to improve the prospects for growth went far beyond stability and opening to trade, as there were a host of other inefficiencies with negative effects on growth. Thus, once the worst of the crisis was over, countries initiated more profound policy and institutional reforms to complement stabilization and trade reforms. These changes in policy and institutions have emphasized actions to maintain macroeconomic stability, to make markets operate more efficiently, and to reduce government interference; while putting in place the appropriate institutions to guarantee that the changes become more permanent and credible.

In the process, during the last decade, policies and institutions have been radically altered in the areas of inflation stabilization, fiscal reform, trade and financial liberalization, privatization, regulation of newly privatized enterprises, and a major overhaul in the social security system.

The rest of this chapter is divided in four sections. Section 14.2 discusses the initial reforms in the macroeconomic and trade regime, section 14.3 discusses the role of 'deeper' reforms beyond export-led growth, and section 14.4 discusses some new issues that have arisen recently in the area of macroeconomic management. Finally, section 14.5 presents the conclusions.

14.2 The initial priorities: macroeconomic stability and trade opening

In the first phase of policy reform, given the initial conditions of severe macroeconomic imbalances and the quite distortionary trade policies, macro stability and trade reform were prominent. Furthermore, as countries decided to use the market to allocate resources, the small size of their economies required competition from foreign trade to avoid the monopolization of a large number of industrial branches and to achieve the level of efficiency that usually comes with economies of scale.

The adjustment programmes included drastic reductions in public sector deficits, a reorientation of monetary and exchange rate policies towards achieving a reduction of inflation, and the privatization of public enterprises. The first spell of privatization included mostly enterprises that were producing private goods and operating at a loss. The reduction in public sector deficits relied also on improving tax collection and the efficiency of the tax system.

On the resource allocation side, policies were adjusted to reduce large price distortions, in particular, for tradable goods. The only way to rationalize the existing trade regimes was a combination of a lack of understanding of the economic costs of it, and (even more important) the existence of strong political economy factors that generated a strong opposition to the change in the status quo. Once the economic costs of the restrictive trade regime were well understood and widely documented – following the work of Johnson and Corden on effective protection theory, the main problem left was to deal with the political economy problems created by the groups that were benefiting from the restrictive trade regime and were defending the status quo.

Indeed, the protection system, once in place, created important rents to the producers of import-competing goods, to the importers that benefited from the allocation of (non-auctioned) import quotas, to the organized labour that was sharing part of the monopoly profits resulting from the protection, and to the bureaucracy that was administering the restrictive trade policies. The political economy difficulties with initiating a drastic reduction of protection in a very restrictive trade regime are by now well understood. As Paul Krugman (1993, p. 147) has put it:

> long-standing protectionist regimes end up being defended by 'iron triangles' of interested groups – firms that depend on the barriers, organized labour that extracts wages above the level in unprotected sectors, and government officials who gain influence and perhaps profits from their role in controlling trade. The strength of these triangles is such that major trade reforms usually occur only following severe political or economic crisis.

Most developing countries in the 1980s fitted Krugman's description quite well, both on the strength of the 'iron triangles' and on the role of the crisis in increasing the demand for reforms and decreasing the powers of the actors involved in the triangles. The debt crisis of the 1980s and the severely restricted access to foreign aid created a drastic change in the power of the different groups in the society, making possible the introduction of radical trade reforms.

In general, the initial objective of trade reforms was to achieve compression in the structure of effective rate of protections by a larger reduction in the highest tariff levels to be followed by the compression of the nominal tariff rates. Non-tariff barriers were converted into tariff equivalent, leaving tariffs as the main instrument of protection. One can say that the first stage of reforms created a first wave of productivity growth. The latter has been based on: achieving a first round of correction in tradable goods prices, improving the information content of relative prices – through the reduction of inflation – and reducing the frequency and the intensity of balance-of-payments crises. In small countries, the efficiency gains that arose out of the reduction in the discrimination against export-oriented activities unleashed a period of export-led growth.

14.3 From export-led to economy-wide growth

Once enough progress had been made on stabilization and trade reforms, the attention shifted towards setting in place the conditions for economy-wide growth with a reduction of poverty.

14.3.1 Policies that promote economy-wide growth

The belief that economic policies – through their effects on total factor productivity – and the investment rate are major determinants of economic growth has long been expressed in the writings of economists. However it has been only recently that the links between policy, investment and long-term growth have been captured in simple analytic models. These models are of the endogenous growth variety (Romer (1986, 1990), Lucas (1988), Easterly (1993).

This literature highlights a number of channels through which public policies can affect growth. The promotion of human capital accumulation, through education and even through improvements in nutrition, can foster growth. So can investment in R&D. These models also point to the possibility of economies becoming stuck in a poverty trap: a situation in which low income and low human capital levels create incentives for high population growth and low human capital investment, thus perpetuating the state of poverty. Policies that stimulate investment in human capital can help the economy break out of the trap.

The ideas underlying these models – economies of scale, externalities and public goods – and the argument that the removal of distortions promotes investment and growth, have been familiar in the development literature for a long time. At a minimum, the new models provide a framework that may improve understanding of the operation of growth-promoting policies that have been proposed in the past; perhaps they will also improve the quality of growth-promoting policies in the future.

One can summarize this literature concluding that it is expected that stabilization and the introduction of efficiency-enhancing reforms would result in an increase in the demand for physical and human capital investment and in a jump in total factor productivity. Then, through these two channels, a country could achieve a higher and more sustainable growth rate. Indeed, it has been shown that the investment rate is much affected by the stability of the macroeconomic framework and by the existing (or lack of) clear and predictable tax rules and property rights (Rodrik (1989), Servén and Solimano (1992)). However, as in the early stages of an adjustment programme it is inevitable that there will be doubts about the final success of it, the supply response of investment will be slow.[5] This slow response is a common characteristic of most adjustment programmes (Dornbusch (1990), Servén and Solimano (1992)).

For countries that are more successful in getting an investment response, a problem could be how to finance the investment. In principle, the increase in investment could be financed by borrowing in the international capital markets, though it is rare that as much as 5 per cent of GNP can be borrowed on a sustainable basis (Krugman (1993)). Further, heavy reliance on capital inflows in the early stages of an adjustment programme could lead to a premature real exchange rate appreciation. One way or another an effort has to be made to increase national saving.

The weight of the empirical evidence suggests that private saving rates are not very sensitive to policy variables, and in particular to interest rates (Giovannini (1985); Corbo and Schmidt-Hebbel (1991); Edwards (1995); and Schmidt-Hebbel and Servén (1999)). However, negative real interest rates probably discourage saving – certainly they reduce the amount and the efficiency of financial intermediation and encourage capital flight. Increased public saving will contribute to increasing national saving provided it is not offset by a decrease in private saving. Empirical evidence presented by Corbo and Schmidt-Hebbel (1991) shows that changes in public savings generally are not greatly offset by the response of private saving. This evidence on saving highlights the central importance of improving fiscal balances as an effective way to increase national savings rates.

A separate channel to promote a higher rate of growth is through policies that improve total factor productivity. Here one would include measures that affect directly the efficiency in the allocation of resources: improving the efficiency in the provision and distribution of non-tradable goods and services (especially electricity and telecommunications; ports and airports and a host of other services); resolving supply bottlenecks in infrastructure; reducing transaction costs, and so on.

Indeed, severe bottlenecks in infrastructure are a common problem in many developing countries. As the fiscal adjustment programmes of the 1980s reduced the spending capacity of the public sectors, investment in infrastructure and human capital was substantially reduced. Thus, for the public sector to be able to invest in the upgrading of its infrastructure and human capital base with a public good character – such as rural roads and social services for the poor – it has to get out from investing in infrastructure where ways can be found to have a private provision of the services. For this purpose, an institutional framework has to be developed in advance, to regulate private sector investment in infrastructure that belongs more properly to the category of private goods (i.e. high density roads, ports, airports and others). Here, progress has been made recently in the development of a regulatory framework to promote efficient solutions for the participation of the private sector in infrastructure, including roads and port facilities (Engel, Fischer and Galetovic (1997)). It is also the knowledge derived from modern industrial organization that has made it possible to develop regulation aimed at obtaining efficient solutions for the private provision of services which have a natural monopoly characteristic – energy generation and distribution, telecommunications, ports and water services. It has been thanks to these advancements that many countries have taken the decision to privatize the provision of this type of services. However, much still needs to be done to improve the efficiency of the newly privatized firms. As a result, there is a wide consensus now that the regulatory capacity of the state must be improved to promote competition in the production and distribution of these services. Although modern regulatory theory provides the analytical underpinnings for efficient regulation, much remains to be done with regard to improving the training and qualifications of the regulators and ensuring that regulators are more independent of the political process.

14.3.2 Pension system reform

A policy area that is closely related to fiscal stance is the reform of the pension systems. The experience of countries with pay-as-you-go (PAYG) defined benefit systems has revealed the unsustainable nature of this kind of scheme. As life expectancy of people increases and fertility rates fall, the aggregate contributions made by the active portion of the population tend to shrink, while the promised benefits of the system keep growing. Thus, the system is fatally flawed.

The first steps towards a fully-funded defined contribution private pension system were taken in Chile in 1981. Although the above-mentioned demographic trends did not represent an imminent threat for the Chilean pension system in the early 1980s, there were other problems – shared by most developing countries – that pointed to the need to reform the system. One of the most evident of these problems was a political economy one. As the state institutions that managed the PAYG scheme offered differentiated benefits to different groups of workers, the system was highly vulnerable to political manipulation. In fact, populist governments used it as a tool to satisfy the demands of pressure groups, giving higher benefits to lobbies and unions with a greater political weight. In this way, the system's inherent unfairness – given the fact that the benefits received by initial pensioners are paid by subsequent cohorts – was greatly magnified. Citing Schmidt-Hebbel (1999): 'The major beneficiaries of generous net pension benefits were urban, middle income and formal sector employees of the government or large state or private sector enterprises'. Another associated problem with the PAYG system was the use of the contributions and benefits structure for fiscal purposes, which increased the instability of the taxes paid by the active population and the transfers made to the pensioners. In addition, the pension funds managed by the social state institutions were usually misallocated, being destined to finance low-return investments and lend at subsidized terms to privileged beneficiaries.

The reforms implemented in Chile were soon followed by several other countries (the list in Latin America includes Argentina, Peru, Bolivia, Uruguay, Colombia, El Salvador and Mexico, among others), involved a shift from the PAYG system to a fully funded defined contribution scheme. Under this scheme, workers contribute a fraction of their wage to individual accounts in pension funds that are invested in financial markets and managed by privately owned pension-fund management companies (PFMC). In this way, the new system creates a direct link between a person's contribution and the benefits that he/she obtains as a pensioner, avoiding, by this means, the need to deal with a growing pension debt burden. At the same time, the significant amount of funds collected by the PFMCs helps to develop the domestic financial markets, as these institutions demand long-term assets to hedge their pension debt. As in most cases, the shift to the fully funded scheme was not complete; the new system coexisted with the old one, and the people were given the option to choose between the two.

The implementation of this kind of reform has been, however, very complex. In the first place, there is a public finance issue that must be considered before embarking on the reform. It is clear that, as workers switch from the old PAYG system to the new one, the flow of contributions received by the government will shrink suddenly, while the government will have to continue paying benefits to pensioners. Thus, as an immediate result of the reform, the government will have to deal with a higher (but transitory) fiscal deficit. Experience shows that countries have managed this problem mainly in four ways: by generating fiscal surpluses in the period previous to the reform, as in the case of Chile; by using funds proceeding from the privatization of public enterprises to finance the revenue losses, as in the cases of Peru and Bolivia; by setting up a separate fund, as in the case of El Salvador; or, by the funds provided by earmarked taxes, as in Argentina.

Another difficulty that complicates the implementation of the pension system reform is the opposition faced from pressure groups. Typically, the opposition has come from three groups: the privileged beneficiaries of the PAYG system; the functionaries involved in the administration of the state social security institutions; and the generations that have to bear the costs of the transition from the old PAYG to the new fully funded system. To a great extent, the depth of this type of reform hinges on the capacity of the government to negotiate with these groups and reduce their opposition.

With regard to the effects of the reform, the evidence provided by empirical studies and simulations shows that it has a substantial impact on factor markets, savings and growth. The reform of the pension system affects positively total labour supply, labour-force participation of aged people, reallocation of labour from informal to formal sectors, and structural employment levels (Schmidt-Hebbel (1998)). Also, as mentioned above, the pension reform contributes to the deepening of capital markets, encouraging the development of longer-term instruments and a wider variety of financial services. Thus, the pension reform, through higher factor productivity and higher saving and investment rates, has a positive impact on long-term growth.

14.3.3 Social service reforms

Efficiency and equity-enhancing improvement are also required in the provision of social services (i.e. education, health, judicial system, etc.). The upgrading of the human capital base, that has a public-good character, requires a profound restructuring of the public sector. Here what is usually required is to dispose of activities that are more efficiently undertaken in the private sector and to make space in the public sector budget for this type of expenditure (i.e. health and educational services geared towards the poor). One can go a step further and develop a framework in which the private sector can provide these activities with the public sector subsidizing its demand.[6]

In the area of education, much progress has been made in the last twenty years in expanding enrolment at all levels. However, there are still major deficiencies in the average level of academic achievement and in the opportunities offered to the different groups in society. Improving education is not only a problem of resources as there is extensive evidence that expenditures in this area are allocated in highly inefficient ways and that, in spite of major expenditure increases, standard measurements of school performance and parental satisfaction have not improved much (IADB (1997); World Bank (1999)). Moreover, school attendance is low and the time spent in school is short. The most pressing problems are the quality of education, as education in many countries is still of poor or mediocre quality. There is also much inequity in the quality of the education to which poor people have access, while pre-primary school coverage for girls and for the poorest groups in the population is very low, especially so in rural areas.

Some simple reforms would increase inputs going into the school system: school buildings, books and standard supplies. More input would permit increasing the coverage of pre-primary and secondary education, especially in rural areas, and lengthen the school day throughout the educational system. However, much must still be learned about the most efficient ways to improve education. This is not surprising, as information problems are endemic in this area. There are information problems in assessing the quality of the services provided and in enhancing the information set of parents, who make most decisions on primary and secondary school choices. Policy reforms in the area of education (and health) services have to deal with: (i) ways to give more authority to those with more information – users and local providers – by the way of decentralizing; (ii) improving the information on school quality and making this information more accessible; (iii) using the knowledge on curricula and new technologies to improve quality (World Bank (1999)).

Here, some countries are moving in directions different to the ones that are suggested by the findings of research. Thus, Hanushek (1995), Kremer (1995) and Kremer (1998) have found that, contrary to standard practice, reducing the size of classes is not an important and significant determinant of school performance. The same studies have found that the experience and the education of teachers have a positive – but not too important – effect on performance. In contrast, the quality of the school facilities *is* an important determinant of performance. This literature has also found evidence in favour of developing institutional arrangements that decentralize the optimization of school inputs to an accountable group far removed from central authorities (Kremer (1995); Filmer and Pritchett (1999). Recent work by Kremer, using experimental rather than econometric techniques, shows that the quality of education depends on teaching techniques (audio-visual systems, radio, TV, etc.), the quality of the schools and the incentive system facing the agents involved in the production of education (Kremer (1998)).

It is surprising that contrary to what has been done in other areas, in the area of education not much progress has been made in introducing competition in the provision of this service, although there are some well-known techniques to promote private provision. Thus, it has been found that the use of vouchers, by increasing competition in the provision of school services, improves the quality of education.[7]

Chile has made some progress in getting the private sector involved in the production of education by providing incentives through the tax system for corporations to finance and get directly involved in the production of education. This involvement includes primary and secondary education and vocational training. Innovations include also matching grants from the public sector for contributions made by the parents (Larrañaga (1995)).

One can say also that reforms in this area have become very difficult due to political economy problems (Graham and Naim (1998)). Teachers' trade unions and groups of intellectuals have opposed the introduction of freedom of choice and of private initiative in the provision of school services. Typical arguments that have been used to oppose these types of reform include: that they discriminate against poor children, that they do not promote national values, that parental choice is not well informed, and so on. Although some of these problems could be real, the alternative is a public monopoly that has all the problems listed above and many more.

Although here we are far from having a unified view of what is the best way of producing 'good' education, problems are so acute that it is necessary to start making progress with methods that could make an obvious contribution now, although they could be improved later on. Among the methods that have proved to be effective are (i) the extension of the student day from half a day to a full day; (ii) the extension of the coverage of pre-primary school to include girls and the poorest groups in the population (this strategy is specially recommended for rural areas); (iii) improvements in the basic school infrastructure; (iv) investment in teacher training; and (v) the decentralization of provision through appropriate incentives and regulations. One problem with the introduction of reforms in this area has been the lack of incentives to pursue alternative paths. In particular, the central government bureaucracy in charge of public education does not want to give power away by encouraging private provision and it is not interested in trying unknown (for them) alternative methods and procedures.

In the case of health services, although progress in medicine has made it possible to reduce infant mortality and increase life expectancy, the current provision of services is very inefficient and the degree of user satisfaction remains very low, in spite of substantial increases in the amount of resources spent. Furthermore, there are serious problems of inequity in the access to and quality of health services. Here problems are not of resources. For example, Latin America spends $234 per patient while Asia spends only $21. However, the access to health services is very limited for the poor and the rural population (IADB (1996)). Furthermore, it has been found that given the low quality of the services provided, the poor spend in health services more than twice what is spent by comparable groups in other parts of the world (Londoño and Frank (1996)).

The practice today is that most ministries of health and social security systems finance and provide health care through their own network of hospitals and clinics. There are a host of problems with this system: the service providers are not accountable; they have rigid staffing; few degrees of freedom on how to use their budget; and they are often highly inefficient. In the allocation of the health budget, it has been found that a large share goes to treatment and a much smaller portion to prevention. Here, it is more than a problem of changing incentives: what is required is a major change in the microeconomic organization of the provision of services, separating the funding from the provision of services and strengthening the responsibilities of the funding agencies (Oxley and MacFarland (1994)). Also the responsibility for the provision should be given to local units and efforts should be made to get the private sector involved in the provision of services (Gertler and Hammer (1997)).

In the health sector, political economy factors are as important as in the education sector (Graham and Naim (1998)). The strongest opposition to reform in this sector comes from the trade unions, the medical associations, and from intellectuals who claim that health should be a universal service. It is the collapse and profound inequities of the current system that are forcing reform.

The judicial system plays a key role in a market through many channels: the definition and the enforcement of property rights; the cost of transactions; the limitation of the discretion of the public sector; and the reduction of corruption in society at large. It is widely acknowledged that the current system is highly unpredictable; is very slow; provides very poor access to the poorest groups in the population; is very costly; and is subject to widespread political intervention. Reforms here must address the independence of the judicial system, the training of judges and a major overhaul of the judicial process.

In the area of the design of reforms in health and education services some experiences are beginning to emerge in the use of demand subsidies instead of direct public provision. In Latin America, Chile and Colombia have gone far in this direction by introducing demand subsidies in education and health services and, in this way, promoting the participation of the private sector in the production of these services. In particular, for the access of the poorest group of the population, a system such as that used in Colombia of targeting expenditures through the use of vouchers is an interesting innovation.

14.3.4 Civil service reform

In the area of the public sector efforts have also been made to improve the efficiency of public administration. Progress here includes the introduction of performance criteria in government programmes and a better definition of responsibilities and tasks within the public sector. However, the change of government model also requires a complete overhaul of the public sector, upgrading its regulatory capacity and downsizing its interventionist capacity. Here there are complex issues of workers' redundancy, severance payments and introducing a wage scale consistent with the need to improve the quality of civil servants. Here, in Latin America, important progress has been made in Argentina, Mexico and Nicaragua, but much still has to be done (Burki and Perry (1997)).

14.3.5 Infrastructure reforms

The participation of the private sector in investment in infrastructure, including roads, airports and port facilities, can be promoted through the development of an appropriate regulatory framework to ensure that such concessions are operated efficiently while the government concentrates its activities on the provision of pure public goods.[8]

A major challenge is to carry out this second generation of reforms, while preserving the newly gained macroeconomic prudence which is necessary to increase the pay-off of the first and second generation of reforms.

14.4 New macroeconomic management issues

Of the many which have arisen in the area of macroeconomic management we single out three main issues – the choice of exchange-rate regime; the choice of monetary policy regime; and the potential role of current-account objectives.

14.4.1 The choice of an exchange-rate regime[9]

In choosing an exchange-rate regime, recent experience provides evidence that, for countries which are well integrated into world capital markets, there are only two feasible options: a fully credible fixed exchange-rate system and different varieties of a flexible exchange-rate system. Argentina's currency board system comes close to the first type. But even this system still leaves open the possibility of an eventual adjustment of the peg. Thus, as has been shown by the peso discount in the forward market, the market is not fully convinced that the exchange rate will remain fixed. As a result, Argentina is paying the costs of having higher interest rates to compensate peso asset holders for the probability of a sudden devaluation of its currency. The premium was especially high on three recent occasions: after the Mexican crisis, after the Brazilian crisis, and during the last presidential election. The lack of credibility of the currency board has persisted even after its central bank made, following the Mexican crisis, considerable efforts to strengthen the financial system. These efforts included the establishment of a large credit line with foreign banks to be used when the financial system faces a sudden withdrawal of funds.

In spite of these measures, many questions still remain open with regard to the monetary arrangement which would be appropriate for Argentina and for other countries in the region. In particular, in the case of Argentina, given the high proportion of its trade with Brazil, and that its country-specific shocks are very different from those which affect the United States, it is unclear that a monetary union with the United States would be part of an 'optimal currency area' *á la* Mundell. What is clear now is that the idea of having a common currency with Brazil, which has been discussed as a means of improving the integration within Mercosur, will need to wait until the Mercosur countries make sufficient progress in macroeconomic policy coordination.

Some economists have gone further and suggested that Brazil should also introduce a currency board.[10] However, one must remember that currency boards are not a panacea. To start with, a country has to have sufficient foreign reserves to finance the short-term monetary liabilities of the monetary system; otherwise, the system will not be credible. Furthermore, the financial system must be strong enough to be able to survive without a lender of last resort. If this is not possible, arrangements must be made for access to emergency lending from foreign commercial banks – as in Argentina – or from an external institution, most likely the Fed or the European Central Bank (ECB). Moreover, wage flexibility and labour mobility must be high enough to facilitate changes in the relative prices between tradable and non-tradable goods when a change in the macroeconomic fundamentals evokes such a change. However, ultimately, the discipline of a currency board requires that a government must be ready and have the political support to live with the high interest rates and high unemployment which are an integral part of the adjustment dynamics of a country that operates with a currency board. In the case of Argentina, a country with a history of abusing its monetary and exchange-rate policies, a currency board has served well, since there was essentially no alternative.

For open economies with a large tradable sector in which exports are not very diversified, fixed rates are not a viable option. For this type of country, a real depreciation – when a change in fundamentals requires one – could become too costly, given that it depends on the downward flexibility of prices of non-tradables. In this case, a more flexible exchange-rate regime would be preferable. Indeed, the combination of prudent monetary policy and exchange-rate flexibility has facilitated adjustment in most countries in the region. With capital mobility, exchange-rate flexibility also leaves the door open for the use of monetary policy for stabilization purposes to response to unexpected domestic and external shocks affecting the demand for local output.

Given that few countries are willing to go down the avenue of dollarization, most are moving towards the use of more flexible systems. However, more flexible systems must be accompanied by the development of forward and future exchange-rate markets, to enable market participants to be able to buy protection against exchange-rate volatility. Otherwise, the real costs of real exchange-rate variability could be high.

As countries move to the use of more flexible exchange-rate regimes, they will need to make the selection of the monetary anchor more explicit.

14.4.2 Choosing a monetary policy regime[11]

Three basic strategies can be envisaged for the choice of a monetary policy regime to anchor inflation. The first would be fully orthodox: a monetary targeting, relying on a pre-committed path for the money supply to anchor inflation. The second, exchange-rate targeting, would use the nominal anchor of the exchange rate. The third is the increasingly popular use of inflation targeting, where the anchor for inflation is the inflation target itself.

In all these cases, in the initial stages, the stabilization attempt would probably induce slower growth, more so in the first and third cases. The exchange-rate anchor is usually first accompanied by an expansion, followed by a recession (Calvo and Végh (1999)). In choosing between these three approaches, it is important to take into account the degree of openness of the economy and the stability of the relationship between the chosen monetary aggregate and inflation. The latter depends mostly on the stability of the demand for money. In particular, in a small open economy, the exchange rate provides an anchor for the price level through its effect on the price of tradable goods. The stability of the relationship between a monetary aggregate and inflation presents a problem in cases where there is considerable financial innovation or when there is a sudden change in the rate of inflation.

In an economy which has experienced a period of high and variable inflation, the demand for money generally becomes very unstable as economic agents develop ways to economize in the use of money balances. And, therefore, when the rate of inflation is reduced, hysteresis effects emerge, generating a breakdown in the old demand for money relationship. In cases such as these, predicting the quantity of money demanded becomes very difficult and the use of a monetary target could result in too high a cost for lower inflation. Therefore, in these cases, it could be more appropriate to use an exchange-rate anchor in the initial stages of the stabilization programme, to be followed later on by a more flexible exchange-rate system accompanied by a monetary or inflation target. Another advantage of an exchange-rate target is that the public much more easily understands it than a monetary rule, given that the information content of the exchange rate is much more direct than the one provided by a monetary aggregate.

However, the use of an exchange-rate anchor also has some important disadvantages. The first is that a country which pegs its currency to the currency of another country loses the ability to use monetary policy to respond to domestic shocks (Obstfeld and Rogoff (1995)). Furthermore, with perfect capital mobility, the use of an exchange rate anchor exposes the country to speculative attacks. Defence against these attacks involves the use of high interest rates for a protected period of time. High interest rates are costly in terms of the high unemployment and the deterioration of bank portfolios. There are also costs when a peg is abandoned in favour of a large devaluation (Obtsfeld and Rogoff (1995)).

But this is not all. The fixing of the exchange rate also requires that other indexation mechanisms in the economy be discarded and that the appropriate institutional structures be developed to prevent the financial system from becoming too vulnerable to an eventual exchange-rate correction. Potential problems along these lines are best illustrated by the experience of Chile in the late 1970s (Corbo and Fischer (1994)), Mexico in 1994

(Dornbusch and Werner (1994)), and the Asian countries in 1997 (IMF (1997)), when the exchange rate was used as a nominal anchor.

Another potential side-effect of exchange-rate fixing, with an open capital account, is undue risk-taking and, as a consequence, an unsustainable expansion of credit which could result in a financial bubble, increasing financial fragility in the process (Corbo and Fischer (1995); Edwards and Végh (1997); and Mishkin (1997a and b)). This problem is illustrated by the experience of Chile in the early 1980s, of Mexico in the first half of the 1990s, and in the recent experience of Asia (Thailand, Korea, Malaysia and Indonesia). In all these cases, following the fixing of the exchange rate, the initial spread between the domestic and the foreign interest rate – adjusted for the expected rate of devaluation – rose sharply, providing substantial encouragement for capital inflows and credit expansion. The final result was a combination of large capital inflows, an expenditure boom, and sharp real appreciation. In these cases, a sudden reversal of capital flows is all that it took to set the stage for a major crisis.

The exchange-rate anchor usually takes the form of a predetermined nominal path for the rate of currency devaluation, but it could also be a fixed rate against the currency of another country. Fixed rates come in three varieties: (i) just fixed; (ii) fixed within a stronger institutional framework, as in Argentina's currency board system; and (iii) the abandonment of the local currency in favour of a common currency, as in the Euro, or the currency of another country, as in Panama and Liberia. In the latter case, the probability of an adjustment in the peg (a devaluation of the local currency) is negligible.

Given the problems which could emerge from the use of both a monetary and an exchange-rate anchor, in recent years some countries have moved to use a third type of anchor, inflation targeting. In inflation targeting, the target rate of inflation serves the purpose of a monetary anchor and monetary and fiscal policies are geared towards achieving the inflation target.[12] The advantage of this system is that its effectiveness does not rely on a stable relationship between a monetary aggregate and inflation and, at the same time, it avoids the problems associated with the fixing of the exchange rate. An additional advantage is that the trajectory of the market exchange rate provides important information on the market evaluation of present and future monetary policy (Bernanke *et al.* (1999)).

As mentioned above, in this system the established inflation target is the ultimate objective of policy, and an inflation forecast, sometimes not made public, is the intermediate objective. The interest rate is the main instrument used to pursue the target. Thus, when the conditional inflation forecast, made with existing policies and the expected path of the exogenous variables, is above the inflation target, the level of the intervention interest rate is raised. One advantage of inflation targeting is that inflation itself is made the target, committing monetary policy to achieve the set target and thus helping to shape inflation expectations. However, herein also resides its main disadvantage.

As inflation is an endogenous variable, that is, the authorities do not directly control it, it becomes difficult to evaluate the monetary stance on the basis of the observed path of inflation. Furthermore, as monetary policy works with a substantial lag, to pre-commit an unconditional inflation target – independently of changes in external factors which do affect the inflation rate – and to change monetary policy to bring the inflation rate back to the set target could be costly. In particular, to try to reach the inflation target, when a shock results in an (temporary) increase in the inflation rate, could be costly in terms of a severe slowdown or increased output volatility (Corbo (1999), Cecchetti (1998)).

To address some of these problems, several options have been proposed: (*i*) to set the inflation target in terms of a range rather than a point estimate; (*ii*) to set a target for core inflation rather than observed inflation; (*iii*) as in New Zealand, to exclude from the price index the effects of changes in indirect taxes and in terms of trade; (*iv*) to set the target as the fourth-quarter-to-fourth-quarter rate of change rather than the December-to-December rate of change. In this last case, it is assumed that the use of quarterly averages for the price level smoothes out the effect of unexpected shocks.

Another problem with inflation targeting has been the effects of this policy on the exchange rate. This problem could be especially acute for countries that are in the middle of a stabilization effort and that have an open capital account. Thus, countries that use inflation targeting face, at times, the dilemma that the monetary policy enacted to achieve the target could result in excessive nominal and real appreciation and large capital inflows. If real appreciation is pronounced, it could jeopardize export growth and, eventually, even the sustainability of the external account. The problem here is that with two objectives, an inflation rate target and an implicit real exchange-rate target (or a current-account deficit target), one needs two instruments, and monetary policy provides only one.

The selection of nominal anchors in Latin America is quite wide. Bolivia uses monetary targets as the main nominal anchor and does not have an explicit target for inflation. However, in its programmes, supported by the IMF, there is an inflation forecast that at times appears to take the form of a target. Peru uses a monetary target that takes the form of a ceiling on the expansion of net domestic assets, but it also announces an inflation target and has been moving lately from the explicit use of a monetary target to an inflation target. Mexico, until the 1994 crisis, and Brazil, in its 'Real' plan, used the nominal exchange rate as the monetary anchor, but both countries have now shifted to the use of an explicit inflation target. Chile and Colombia use inflation targeting. Indeed, Chile is one of the first countries that started to use an inflation target. Figure 14.1 summarizes the type of monetary anchors used in the stabilization strategy of a group of Latin American countries.

14.4.3 Setting a target for the size of the current-account deficit?

Traditionally, when private capital flows were rare, balance-of-payments problems were the result of excessively expansionary monetary and fiscal policies.[13] In such cases adjustment programmes, usually formulated within the context of an IMF programme, included fiscal and monetary reforms aimed at reducing the current-account deficit to a level consistent with the amount of official capital inflows available. In the 1990s, private capital inflows became a major force, and the expenditure effects of capital inflows now mostly drive current-account deficits.

However, the size of the current-account deficit is still important for two reasons. First, a larger current-account deficit requires real appreciation, and this real appreciation works, in many cases, at cross-purposes with the

Figure 14.1 Latin American monetary policy regimes in the 1990s

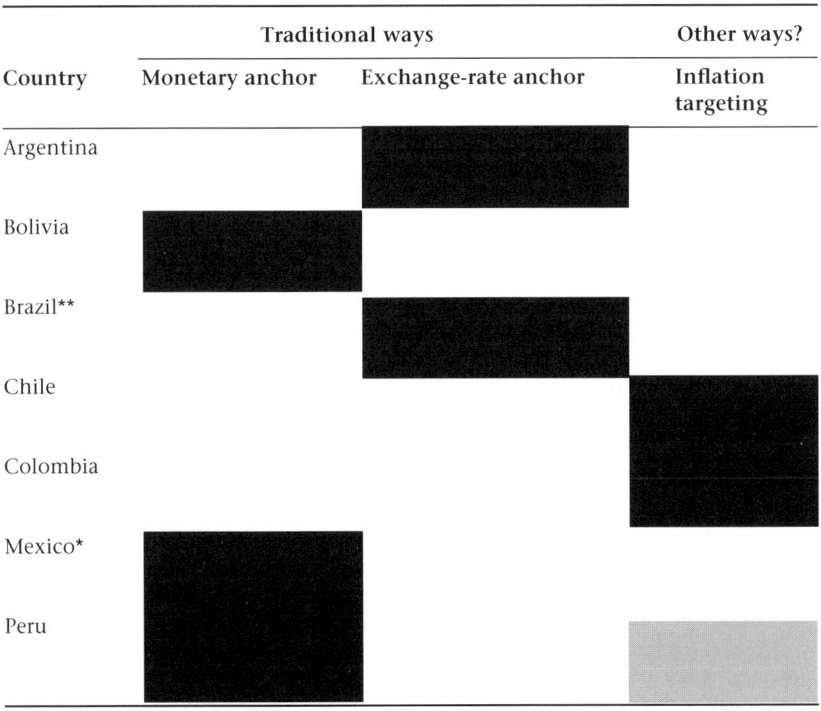

Country	Traditional ways		Other ways?
	Monetary anchor	Exchange-rate anchor	Inflation targeting
Argentina		■	
Bolivia	■		
Brazil**		■	
Chile			■
Colombia			■
Mexico*	■		
Peru	■		▤

* Starting in early 1998, it shifted to an explicit inflation target.
** Starting in March 1999 it shifted towards an explicit inflation target.
The grey shading indicates that there was also an implicit use of this regime.

export-led growth model chosen by Latin American countries in the 1990s (Dornbusch (1980, ch. 6)). Second, as the recent experience of Mexico and Thailand illustrates, it makes a country vulnerable to a sudden reversal of capital flows. As a result of a sudden reversal, and of the policy adjustments required to adjust to this type of shock, large real adjustment costs could emerge. In particular, in the period during which the current-account deficit is rising, the financial system is expanding. But, as the liabilities of the banks have a shorter maturity than their assets, a sudden capital reversal could result in severe financial problems.

Disregard for the size of the current-account deficit already played a role in the Chilean crisis of the early 1980s, in the Mexican crisis of 1994, and in the recent crisis of Thailand and Malaysia.

Constraints on the size of current-account deficits can also be justified by the externalities created by a sudden crisis and the information problems associated with external borrowing by a weak financial system. As a result, it appears that a self-imposed limit on the size of the current account deficit should be a basic rule of prudence. Increasingly, some Latin American countries are adopting this practice. In practice, this limit operates in such a way that when the current account deficit reaches a pre-established threshold, aggregate demand policies are tightened to reduce the deficit.

The most explicit use of a current account target is made in Chile. Since the 1990s, the now independent central bank has been working with two targets: a gradual reduction of inflation towards international levels and a target for the current account deficit. The current account deficit target, established in terms of normal values for the terms of trade (long-term trend), has been set by the Central Bank at less than 4 per cent of GDP. In practice this target has been expressed as a loose commitment to a competitive real exchange rate, given a trajectory for domestic absorption and GDP.

However, whenever the two objectives – the inflation and the current account – come into conflict, the central bank implicitly trades off between them.[14] In fact, when the inflation target has been in jeopardy, the real exchange rate has been allowed to appreciate, as capital flowed in at the set level of the real interest rate.[15]

Peru also decided to introduce restrictive monetary and fiscal policies in late 1995, when, as a result of a domestically originated expansion, the current-account deficit went above 7 per cent of GDP. This is an area where much work still must be done to determine appropriate deficit levels.[16]

14.5 Conclusions

Development policies have been drastically changed during the last 15 years. The reforms have included drastic reductions of public sector deficits, the opening of the economies to foreign trade, the promotion of competition through openness to trade, the elimination of discrimination against direct foreign investment, the deregulation or privatization of public utilities, and a radical redefinition of the role of the state.

As a result of the reforms, the state has reduced its role as a producer and distributor of private goods and has increased its role in macroeconomic management, the provision of public goods, and the improvement of access by the poorest groups in the population to social services.

In the case of the second generation of reforms there is much that has to be learned about how to improve the quality of services in the most efficient way. In the case of education this includes teaching methods, input relations and the industrial organization of the sector. Similar problems emerge in the case of health care.

On the macroeconomic front, countries have been moving away from a rigid exchange-rate system towards more flexible ones. But the abandonment of rigid exchange-rate systems has also required the introduction of alternative monetary regimes. Here the main innovation has been the increasing use of inflation targeting.

Notes

1. Although problems of incomplete markets are not dismissed, they are considered to affect a narrower set of activities.
2. For an assessment of the consensus on policy reforms, see ECLAC (1992) and Corbo and Fischer (1995).
3. Macroeconomic imbalances were more extreme in Latin America than in other regions of the world.
4. In many countries, this new breed of professional economists working in universities and think tanks had prepared specific proposals of alternative policies which were later used as a blueprint by reformist governments.
5. Typically investors will wait to have a clearer assessment of the most likely evolution of the economy, both the level of activity and relative prices, before committing themselves to investment.
6. Chile has gone far in this direction by promoting the participation of the private sector in the production of education and health services.
7. West (1997) presents evidence in this direction based on the experience with this system in Milwaukee, but see Carnoy (1997) for a critique. It has been found that the voucher system also increases the motivation and commitment of the parents with the schooling of their children (Witte *et al.* (1995) present this type of evidence for Milwaukee).
8. In Latin America, Argentina, Chile and Mexico have made important progress in getting private sector participation in the production and operation of the infrastructure, but they have been less successful in involving the private sector in the provision of health and education services (World Bank (1999)).
9. Following the Mexican and the Asian crises, the debate on the most appropriate exchange-rate system has taken a new twist. Now the discussion is framed more in terms of feasibility than of optimality (see in particular, Obtsfeld and Rogoff (1995) and Eichengreen (1999)).
10. Dornbusch (1999), Cavallo (1999).

11. On monetary anchors, see Bernanke, and Mishkin (1997), Bernanke *et al.* (1999) and Calvo and Végh (1999). On the choice of monetary anchors in Latin America, see Corbo, 1999.
12. In Latin America, Chile, Colombia and now Mexico use inflation targeting. For an analysis of the Chilean experience with inflation targeting see Corbo (1998).
13. Indeed, this was the main motivation for Krugman's classic paper on currency crisis (Krugman, 1979).
14. A way out of this conflict would be to control aggregate demand through fiscal policy instead of monetary policy. The latter could be done either by increasing taxes or reducing government expenditures. In the case of Chile, the use of fiscal policy has been very limited due to political economy factors. Difficulties have arisen, first, because the government lost some credibility when it negotiated a temporary increase in taxes which then became permanent. Second, it is politically difficult to implement a fiscal adjustment for a government that has been running a non-financial public sector surplus every year since 1986.
15. There was much less possibility of conflict between the two objectives in the 1980s when Chile's access to international capital markets was severely curtailed. Then, the link between domestic and international interest rates was broken and the Central Bank could set real interest rates without affecting the level of capital inflows.
16. For some interesting work along these lines, see Milesi-Ferreti and Razin (1998).

References

Baker, D., Epstein, G. and Pollin, R. (eds) (1998) *Globalization and Progressive Economic Policy: What Are the Real Constraints and Options?* (Cambridge: Cambridge University Press).

Banco Central de Bolivia (1997) *Memoria Anual.*

Banco Central de Reserva del Perú (1998) *Nota Semanal*, various issues.

Bernanke, B.S. and Mishkin, F.S. (1997) 'Inflation Targeting: A New Framework for Monetary Policy', *Journal of Economic Perspectives*, vol. 11 (2), pp. 97–116.

Bernanke, B.S., Laubach, T., Mishkin, F.S. and Posen, A.S. (1999) *Inflation Targeting* (Princeton, NJ: Princeton University Press).

Burki, S. and Perry, G. (1997) *The Long March: A Reform Agenda for Latin America and the Caribbean in the Next Decade* (Washington, DC: World Bank).

Calvo, G. and Végh, C. (1999) 'Inflation Stabilization and BOP Crisis in Developing Countries', NBER Working Paper no. 6925.

Carnoy, M. (1997) 'Is Privatization through Educational Vouchers Really the Answer? A Comment on West', *World Bank Research Observer*, vol. 12 (1), pp. 105–16.

Cavallo, D. (1999) *Financial Times*, 3 February.

Cecchetti, S.G. (1998) 'Policy Rules and Targets: Framing the Central Banker's Problem', *Economic Policy Review*, Federal Reserve Bank of New York, June, pp. 1–14.

Corbo, V. (1988) 'Problems, Development Theory and Strategies of Latin America', in Ranis, G. and Schultz, T.P. (eds) *The State of Development Economics: Progress and Perspectives* (Oxford: Blackwell).

Corbo, V. (1998) 'Economic Policy Reform in Latin America', paper presented at the Conference on 'Economic Policy Reform: What We Know and What We Need To Know', Center for Research on Economic Development and Policy Reform of Stanford University, September 16–19; also in Krueger, A. (ed.) *Economic Policy*

Reform: What We Know and What We Need to Know (Chicago: University of Chicago Press, 2000).

Corbo, V. (1999) 'Monetary Policy in Latin America in the 1990s', paper presented at the Third Annual Conference of the Central Bank of Chile 'Monetary Policy: Rules and Transmission Mechanisms', 20–21 September, Santiago.

Corbo, V. and Fischer, S. (1994) 'Lessons from the Chilean Stabilization and Recovery', in Bosworth, B., Dornbusch, R. and Laban, R. (eds) *The Chilean Economy: Policy Lessons and Challenges* (Washington, DC: Brookings Institution).

Corbo, V. and Fischer, S. (1995) 'Structural Adjustment, Stabilization and Policy Reform: Domestic and International Finance', in Behrman, J. and Srinivasan, T.N. (eds) *Handbook of Development Economics*, vol. III (Amsterdam and New York: Elsevier).

Corbo, V. and Schmidt-Hebbel, K. (1991) 'Public Policies and Saving in Developing Countries', *Journal of Development Economics*, vol. 36, pp. 89–115.

de Gregorio, J., Edwards, S. and Valdés, R. (1998) 'Capital Controls in Chile: An Assessment', paper presented at the International Seminar on Economics, Rio de Janeiro, Brazil.

Díaz-Alejandro, C. (1983) 'Stories of the 1930s for the 1980s', in Aspe-Armella, P., Dornbusch, R. and Obstfeld, M. (eds), *Financial Policies and the World Capital Market: The Problem of Latin American Countries* (Chicago: University of Chicago press), pp. 5–35.

Dornbusch, R. (1980) *Open Economy Macroeconomics* (London: Basic Books).

Dornbusch, R. (1990) 'Policies to Move from Stabilization to Growth', *World Bank Conference on Development Economics* (Washington DC: The World Bank), pp. 19–48.

Dornbusch, R. (1997) 'Brazil's Incomplete Stabilization and Reform', *Brookings Papers on Economic Activity*, no. 1.

Dornbusch, R. (1999) 'Brazil beyond Tropical Illusions', mimeo, MIT Economics Department (February).

Dornbusch, R. and Werner, A. (1994) 'Mexico: Stabilization, Reform and No Growth', *Brookings Papers on Economic Activity*, no. 1.

Easterly, W. (1993) 'How Much Distortions Affect Growth', *Journal of Monetary Economics*, vol. 32, pp. 187–212.

ECLAC (1992) *Equidad y Transformación Productiva: Un Enfoque Integrado* (Santiago: ECLAC).

Edwards, S. (1995) *Crisis and Reform in Latin America. From Despair to Hope* (Oxford: Oxford University Press).

Edwards, S. and Végh, C. (1997) 'Banks and Macroeconomics Disturbances under Predetermined Exchange Rates', *Journal of Monetary Economics*, vol. 40 (2), pp. 239–78.

Eichengreen, B. (1999) 'Kicking the Habit: Moving from Pegged Rates to Greater Exchange Rate Flexibility', *Economic Journal*, vol. 109, pp. C1–C14.

Engel, E., Fischer, R. and Galetovic, A. (1997) 'Highway Franchising: Pitfalls and Opportunities', *American Economic Review*, vol. 87 (2), pp. 68–72.

Filmer, D. and Pritchett, L. (1999) 'What Education Production Functions Really Show: A Positive Theory of Education Expenditures', *Economics of Education Review*, vol. 18, pp. 223–39.

Gertler, P. and Hammer, P. (1997) 'Strategies for Pricing Publicly Provided Health Services', *Policy Research Working Paper* no. 1762, World Bank.

Giovannini, A. (1985) 'Saving and the Real Interest Rate in LDCs', *Journal of Development Economics*, vol. 18, pp. 197–217.

Graham, C. and Naim, S. (1998) 'The Political Economy of Institutional Reform in Latin America', in Birdsall, N., Graham, C. and Sabot, R. (eds) *Beyond Tradeoffs: Market Reform and Equitable Growth in Latin America* (Washington, DC: Inter-American Development Bank and Brookings Institution Press).

Hanushek, E. (1995) 'Interpreting Recent Research on Schooling in Developing Countries, *World Bank Research Observer*, vol. 10, no. 2, pp. 227–46.

Hernández, L. and Schmidt-Hebbel, K. (1999) 'Capital Controls in Chile: Effective? Efficient? Endurable?', paper presented to a World Bank Conference, April.

IADB (Inter-American Development Bank) (1996) *Progreso Económico y Social en América Latina: 1996* (Washington, DC: IADB).

IADB (Inter-American Development Bank) (1997) *Progreso Económico y Social en América Latina: 1997* (Washington, DC: IADB).

IMF (International Monetary Fund) (1997) *World Economic Outlook*, December (Washington, DC: IMF).

IMF (International Monetary Fund) (1998) *World Economic Outlook*, May (Washington, DC: IMF).

Kremer, M. (1995) 'Research on Schooling: What We Know and What We Don't. A Comment on Hanushek', *World Bank Research Observer*, vol. 10 (2), pp. 247–54.

Kremer, M. (1998) 'Education Reform', paper presented at the Conference 'Economic Policy Reform: What We Know and What We Need to Know', Stanford University, September 1998; also in Krueger, A. (ed.) *Economic Policy Reform: What We Know and What We Need to Know* (Chicago: University of Chicago Press, 2000).

Krugman, P. (1979) 'A Model of Balance-of-Payments Crisis', *Journal of Money, Credit and Banking*, vol. 11, pp. 311–21.

Krugman, P. (1993) 'Protection and Developing Countries', in Dornbusch, R. (ed.) *Policymaking in the Open Economy* (Oxford: Oxford University Press), pp. 127–48.

Larrañaga, O. (1995) 'Descentralización de la Educación en Chile: Un Análisis Económico', *Estudios Públicos*, vol. 60, pp. 243–88.

Londoño, J. and Frank, J. (1996) 'Structured Pluralism: A New Model for Health Reform in Latin America and the Caribbean, Latin American Technical Department Working Paper, World Bank.

Lucas, R. (1988) 'On the Mechanics of Economic Development', *Journal of Monetary Economics*, vol. 22, pp. 151–83.

Milesi-Ferreti, G.M. and Razin, A. (1998) 'Current Account Reversals and Currency Crises: Empirical Regularities', NBER Working Paper no. 6620.

Mishkin, F.S. (1997a) 'The Causes and Propagation of Financial Instability: Lessons for Policy Makers', in *Maintaining Financial Stability in a Global Economy* (Kansas City: Federal Reserve Bank of Kansas City), pp. 55–96.

Mishkin, F.S. (1997b) 'Understanding Financial Crises: A Developing Country Perspective', in Bruno, M. and Pleskovic, B. (eds) *Annual World Bank Conference on Development Economics* (Washington DC: World Bank).

Mishkin, F.S. (1998) 'Financial Market Reform', paper presented at the Conference 'Economic Policy Reform: What We Know and What We Need to Know', Stanford University, September; also in Krueger, A. (ed.) *Economic Policy Reform: What We Know and What We Need to Know* (Chicago: University of Chicago Press, 2000).

Obtsfeldt, M. (1998) 'The Global Capital Market: Benefactor or Menace?', NBER Working Paper no. 6559, May.

Obtsfeldt, M. and Rogoff, K. (1995) 'The Mirage of Fixed Exchange Rates', *Journal of Economic Perspectives*, vol. 9, pp. 73–96.

Oxley, H. and Macfarland, M. (1994) 'Health Care Reform: Controlling Spending and Increasing Efficiency', OECD Working Paper no. 149.

Rodrik, D. (1989) 'Promises, Promises: Credible Policy Reforms via Signalling', *Economic Journal*, vol. 99, pp. 756–72.

Romer, P. (1986) 'Increasing Returns and Long-Run Growth', *Journal of Political Economy*, vol. 94 (5), pp. 1002–37.

Romer, P. (1990) 'Endogenous Technological Change', *Journal of Political Economy*, vol. 98 (5), part II, pp. S71–S102.

Schmidt-Hebbel, K. (1998) 'Does Pension Reform Really Spur Productivity, Saving and Growth?', Banco Central de Chile Working Paper no. 33.

Schmidt-Hebbel, K. (1999) 'Latin America's Pension Revolution: A Review of Approaches and Experiences', in Bruno, M. and Pleskovic, B. (eds) *World Bank Annual Conference on Development Economics 1998* (Washington: World Bank).

Schmidt-Hebbel, K. and Servén, L. (1999) (eds) *The Economics of Saving and Growth* (Cambridge: Cambridge University Press).

Servén, L. and Solimano, A. (1992) 'Private Investment and Macroeconomic Adjustment: A Survey', *World Bank Research Observer*, vol. 7 (1), pp. 95–114.

Stiglitz, J. (1994) 'The Role of State in Financial Markets, in Bruno, M. and Pleskovic, B. (eds) *Annual World Bank Conference on Development Economics 1994* (Washington: World Bank).

West, E. (1997) 'Education Vouchers in Principle and Practice: A Survey', *World Bank Research Observer*, vol. 12 (5), pp. 83–103.

Williamson, J. (1989) *Latin American Adjustment* (Oxford: Oxford University Press).

Witte, J, Thorn, C. and Prichard, K. (1995) *Fourth Year Report: Milwaukee Parental Choice Program* (Madison WI: State Department of Public Instruction).

World Bank (1999) *Global Economic Prospects* (Washington, DC: World Bank).

15
Macroeconomic Policies: Can We Transfer Lessons Across LDCs?

Carlos Rodriguez
Universidad del CEMA, Buenos Aires, Argentina

'Many of you are too young to remember, but it was not long ago that the policies pursued by many governments in Latin America, and the courses taught in most universities across the region, reflected more bad economics than good.'

Harberger (1998)

15.1 Introduction

Less-developed countries (LDCs) have provided the economics profession with a wide range of macroeconomic experiences. Many are experiences of failure, a few of success. It is my belief that useful lessons can be obtained from all those experiences. Contrary to the widely held belief that it is not possible to transfer to LDCs theories and policies designed for developed countries, I hold the position that there is only one body of economic theory and that the best policies apply to all patients and are, for most cases, the simplest: market rules, free trade and orthodox monetary and fiscal policy.

The numerous failed stabilization experiences of LDCs teach us what should not be done. They also tell us what to expect from markets subject to macroeconomic mismanagement. High country-risk premiums and currency substitution (dollarization) are two of the most common responses. They also tell us about the fundamental role of credibility for the viability of a set of macroeconomic policies. Credibility is built on fundamentals and experience. Governments that have repeatedly fooled their populations in the past find they must pay much higher adjustment costs when they decide to follow the right policies.

LDCs by definition lack enough savings and need foreign capital to develop. They also need to follow the right policies. In previous decades, while institutional capital was flowing in, some could afford to use it to finance the wrong policies. Nowadays the big difference is that while LDCs continue to need investment, they are already in debt and private creditors are reluctant to continue financing without a much stricter scrutiny of the policies being followed.

Highly indebted countries following the wrong policies are punished twice: once by the wrong policies and again by investors taking away their money. The 'flight to quality' experienced during the last crisis hit the LDCs drastically by raising to unprecedented levels the interest rates at which they should roll over their debts. Nowadays, more than ever, it is imperative for LDCs to instrument the correct macroeconomic policies.

This chapter focuses on several topics related to macroeconomic policies in LDCs. The selection is biased towards those cases I have dealt with during my last 20 years of professional experience, home based in Argentina. Inflation, dollarization and stabilization policies are old friends of Latin Americans. Currency boards, lender of last resort and country risk are newer concepts that have gained special relevance in the 1990s, the decade of globalization.

15.2 Economic development and country risk

Less-developed countries are not a homogeneous group. They differ as much between each other as from the developed countries. They differ in cultural level, income level, degree of functioning of markets and of institutions. Some LDCs have a culture and institutions similar to those of developed countries but they are poorer. Some LDCs were born poor and others impoverished themselves: the per capita income of Argentina was 85 per cent of that of the United States at the beginning of this century; today it is only 34 per cent.

Since the 1970s, many LDCs have frequently tapped the world's financial markets. Perhaps due to an optimistic view of the development process, less-developed countries saw their name changed first to developing countries and later to emerging countries, a denomination more akin to the bullish spirit of financial markets. There is no unique listing of emerging countries. According to the Bloomberg page on emerging markets, the set includes any country with nascent stock and bond markets, as well as small economies. However, Bloomberg also mentions the World Bank definition of an emerging market as a country with a per capita income smaller than US$8950!

In general, a common characteristic shared by the members of the emerging markets (EM) club, one which is useful to our macroeconomic analysis, is that they all possess an elevated degree of 'macroeconomic weakness' that manifests itself into a high level of the denominated *'country risk'*. This is the additional return requested by an investor in order to put money in the EM instead of placing it into a risk-free country (such as the United States or Germany). We measure the country-risk premium as the difference in return of a bond issued in hard currency by the EM and a similar bond issued in the same currency by the risk-free country. One of the major traders in sovereign debt, J.P. Morgan, lists prices for sovereign bonds of 12 emerging countries (Table 15.1). The risk premiums differ grossly across countries depending on the creditors' expectations of recovering their money. On the given day Russia, Ecuador, Venezuela and Brazil were the least preferred EMs (for widely known reasons). In a couple of cases the risk premium exceeded 30 per cent annual rate (in dollars), which was about five times the risk-free dollar rate for the 10-year Treasury Note.

Ignoring the high variance of the individual risk premiums in the Table 15.1, we can illustrate the cost of high risk by assuming an average risk premium that is of 10 per cent (1000 basis points) over the equivalent American Treasury bond. Assuming a representative average debt/GDP ratio of 50 per cent, the average risk premium mentioned would imply that an amount equivalent to about 5 per cent of GDP is being transferred to creditors annually just to compensate them for investing in risky countries. Economic activity is directly affected by country risk through its impact on investment flows and financial behaviour. Some effects are of a short-run nature – through the impact on aggregate demand – and others are long lasting, due to modification of the capital accumulation path. Figure 15.1 shows concisely the negative effect of country risk on short-run economic activity using Argentine quarterly data for the period 1991–99.

Clearly, being risky is an expensive business. We should therefore observe considerable efforts on the part of risky emerging countries to improve their appearance in the eyes of the investors. This implies improving on their institutions, and optimizing their macroeconomic policies. In the

Table 15.1   Average spread over US Treasury bonds of selected emerging market issues

Issuer	Basis points
Argentina (FRB)	722
Brazil (BRA C)	1081
Bulgaria (Discount)	1042
Ecuador (Discount)	3167
Morocco (loan)	677
Mexico (Discount)	787
Panama (PDI)	409
Philippines (FLRB)	485
Peru (FLIRB)	555
Poland (Discount)	303
Russia (INT)	6026
Venezuela (DCB)	1473

* Spreads correspond to representative Brady Bonds on 18 March 1999.
Source: J.P. Morgan.

Figure 15.1 Relation between output and country risk: Argentina, 1991–98

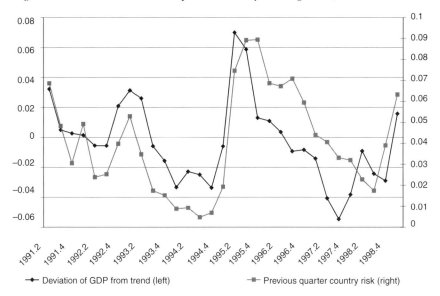

globalized economy open to international capital flows, the principal jurors about the macroeconomic situation are investors. Investors in international markets lack ideology, sentiments or nationalisms. International capital flows respond faster than any other economic variable. They can stop suddenly or reverse sign on the expectation of a policy change. The effect of these sudden changes on the real and financial structure of the economy may be drastic. Since LDCs need foreign capital, this behaviour reinforces the case for reasonable and predictable macroeconomic policies.[1]

In the 1960s and 1970s, many LDCs went through a process of unsustainable growth based in good part on multilateral help, government borrowing and the inflation tax. The debt crisis of the early 1980s marked the beginning of the decade of adjustment. In the 1990s, with globalization already in place, LDCs started the implementation of much more sensible macroeconomic policies from the viewpoint of their effectiveness and sustainability – notably fiscal prudence, monetary control and market-oriented allocation of scarce resources.

15.2.1   Some determinants of country risk: macroeconomic performance, flight to quality and contagion effect

We accept that lack of development comes hand-in-hand with high risk for investors which in turn implies a high cost for the capital needed. Breaking the vicious circle requires implementing policies and adopting institutions that allow for a decrease in the country risk premium as perceived by investors. We believe that such set of policies and institutions are those of a market economy with conservative monetary and fiscal management.

This belief seems to be shared by the largest of the international rating agencies assessing country risk for investors. A recent paper by Cantor and Packer (1996) studies the determining factors for the sovereign credit ratings given by Standard and Poor's (S&P) and Moody's. Using econometric analysis they find that eight factors explain more than 90 per cent of the cross-sectional variation in the ratings. These variables are GDP per capita, growth record, debt burden, inflation, default history, level of development, fiscal deficit and current-account deficit. Beyond the circularity involved in the fact that several of the variables are endogenous (development, GDP growth, inflation) we rescue the fact that evaluators do pay attention to indebtedness, credit record and macroeconomic equilibrium as represented by inflation, current account and fiscal variables.

In spite of the importance attributed to conventional variables in the determination of country risk, past performance and performance by peers seem to be also excessively important. Markets tend to hold to memories of past performances and, in the absence of or inability to process new information, they tend to rate a country by the performance of what they consider to be similar countries. From this last perspective, being a member of the club of emerging markets may imply receiving a high-risk premium that may be quite irresponsive to policy improvements in the short run. This phenomenon has been called the *contagion effect* and implies that the risk premium of any single EM is partly determined by that of the average. On the other hand, the risk premium for the 'average' EM is set so as to equilibrate the market's risk perception for EMs as a whole versus the non-risky assets. As EMs become more risky, investors seek better assets and increase the demand for those perceived as 'safe'. This process has been called the *'flight to quality'* and was responsible during the last crisis for unprecedented increases in prices of US bonds and stock markets while the EM's real and financial markets crashed. Figure 15.2 shows the opposite impact of the Russian crisis on interest rates in EMs and the United States, a result explained by the 'flight to quality'. For a well-managed but indebted EM the contagion effect undeservedly raises the interest rate at which it may borrow new funds. On the other hand, the service of the existing stock of debt is likely to be indexed to the risk-free interest rate (such as the US Treasury Bill) which is bound to fall due to the 'flight to safety' effect. *We see therefore that in a crisis the 'flight to safety' reduces the service cost of existing debt and the 'contagion effect' raises the cost for increases in debt.*

The contagion effect may imply that in the middle of a crisis originated elsewhere, the risk premium of an EM may rise and not respond to any additional efforts at improving macroeconomic policies which the country may simultaneously undertake. This does not mean that the country should abandon the practice of good policies because the only chance of altering the perception of being a member of the EM club is to persist in the good policies.

In sum, good policies may have a cumulative effect. If they are followed for a sufficiently long period, investors may perceive the country as a different member of the EM club, as in the case of Chile, which consistently receives a better risk evaluation than the other Latin American countries: the reason is that it is the pioneer of structural change in the region and that it has always regularly serviced its foreign debt.

Chile, Uruguay and Colombia are the only large countries in the region that regularly continued foreign debt service during the crisis of the 1980s, and are also the only three which are ranked as 'investment grade' by both Moody and S&P. It is clear that regular servicing of foreign debt is one of the most important factors in determining country risk. Figure 15.3 illustrates the significance of the contagion effect by comparing the stripped yield demanded by markets on a basket of sovereign bonds constructed by J.P. Morgan (the EMBI) and the stripped yield on the Argentine Bonex. It is quite evident that the two series respond to similar shocks most of the time, as predicted by the hypothesis of the contagion effect.

In some cases the common shocks are readily identifiable: (1) marks the turn around in Fed interest rate policy (towards higher rates) that most affected the highly indebted group of LDCs and acted as the trigger for the Mexican crisis labelled as (2). After the peak of the rates at the beginning of 1995 comes a period of tranquillity in world markets, and rates fall sharply both for the EMs as a group and for Argentina as well. Point (3) marks 'Black October' and the beginning of the Asian crisis, followed by the sharp peak due to the Russian crisis (4) and a hitherto smaller one due to the Brazilian crisis (5). It is clear that in all six years Argentina has not been able to differentiate itself from the overall group of EMs represented by the EMBI index.

15.3 Policies for differentiation: are fiscal surpluses contractive or expansive?

In the short run, emerging countries are at the mercy of the mistakes made by other members of the group due to the contagion effect: differentiation is the name of the game. However, there are fundamental reasons determining why a country is classified by investors as emerging and its position within the group. Even worse, it is very easy for a country's position

316

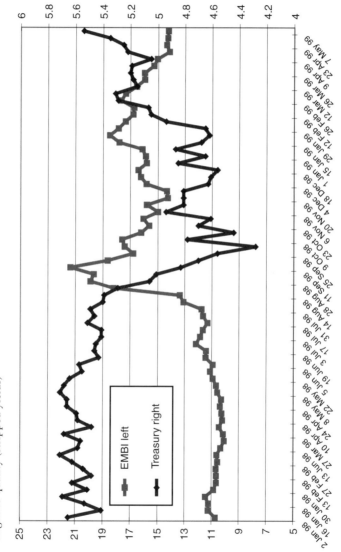

Figure 15.2 Flight to quality (stripped yields)

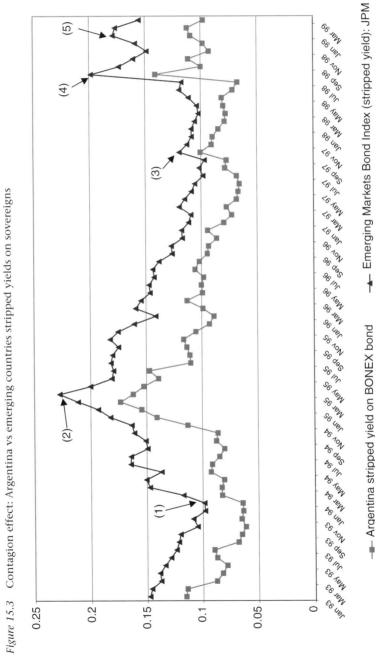

Figure 15.3 Contagion effect: Argentina vs emerging countries stripped yields on sovereigns

■ Argentina stripped yield on BONEX bond

▲ Emerging Markets Bond Index (stripped yield): JPM

quickly to deteriorate if the wrong policies are followed, but it is very hard to improve fast by announcing the implementation of the right policies: *markets are fast to downgrade but very slow to upgrade.*

Differentiation is a slow process. Surviving the exogenous shock while doing better than those directly affected is one way to move in the right direction. Persisting in doing the right policies will eventually attract the attention of investors and help to generate the required credibility on the intention permanently to follow such policies. A fiscal surplus for a single half-year may do little to impress investors, but a consistent surplus, however small, may attract their attention and induce differentiation of a permanent nature.

Policy makers in EM face a dilemma when their economies are exposed to exogenous shocks which sharply raise the country-risk premium. The rise in interest rates and the reduction in capital inflows slows economic activity and also reduces tax revenue, thereby widening the fiscal deficit. Standard textbook analysis indicates that the optimal policy response should be to allow for a larger fiscal deficit and to finance it through more debt. However, if investors determine country risk by looking at fiscal performance and debt levels, it may pay not to allow the deficit to increase by raising taxes or lowering expenditures. Under these circumstances, fiscal surpluses may not be contractive as in the standard Keynesian analysis, but expansive because they contribute towards moderating country risk and promoting capital inflows.

Figure 15.4 illustrates the policy dilemma created by the endogeneity of country risk. The equilibrium in the fixed exchange-rate economy is determined at point (1) on the intersection of the IS curve with the supply of international capital at the fixed rate $r^* + crisk(0)$, where r^* is the risk free rate and $crisk(0)$ is the initial level of country risk. Aggregate demand is at the level $Y(0)$. A larger fiscal surplus will shift the IS curve down to $IS(1)$ and, if the supply of foreign funds remains unchanged the result is the lower level of demand at $Y(1)$ as shown by point (2). However, if the fiscal surplus has the effect of reducing the country-risk premium to $crisk(1)$, the reduction of the cost of funds will provide an expansive stimulus on the economy and aggregate demand may in fact rise, as shown by the level $Y(2)$ in Figure 15.4 where the equilibrium lies at point (3).

It may be argued that the expansive effects of a fiscal stimulus (deficit) are immediate, whereas the effect of the deficit on the stock of debt and the risk premium will only take place later in time as the deficits accumulate. This may be true in a Keynesian world with static expectations[2] but need not be the case with more rational expectations. The increase in the deficit may be interpreted by analysts as a signal that debt will rise, and therefore they will project greater difficulties for its service and in consequence they will raise country risk at once.

Figure 15.4 Endogeneity of country risk

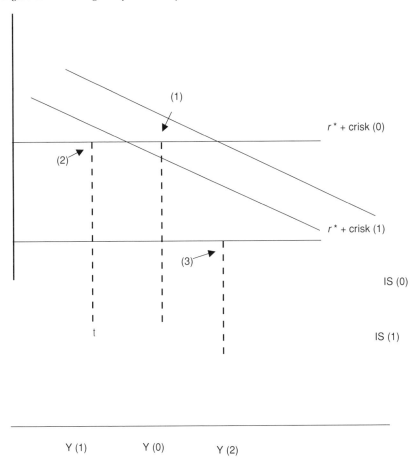

15.4 Dollarization is irreversible: Uruguay, Peru, Argentina

One of the legacies of the macroeconomic instability in the region during the preceding decades has been the preference of residents of many countries for the use of dollars instead of the local currency. The dollarization phenomenon is at the core of many financial crises affecting LDCs. While in some cases central banks lose reserves to distrustful foreign creditors, in others it is the country's residents demanding the dollars in order to carry out the transactions that they previously carried in the local currency. As more and more lines of activity start being transacted in dollars (including savings) the economy dollarizes. In a dollarized economy the central bank loses the role of lender of last resort for the simple reason that in a crisis the public wants dollars and not local currency and the central bank cannot print dollars (which is of course the prerogative of the US Fed).

The thesis of our paper (Guidotti and Rodriguez (1992)) on dollarization in Latin America was that the phenomenon appears as a hedge against high inflation and that transitory increases in inflation may result in permanent changes in the degree of dollarization. Peru, Argentina and Uruguay are some examples of countries that started dollarization in response to the high inflation rates experienced in the 1970s and 1980s. In the 1990s all three countries implemented significant adjustments and drastically reduced the inflation rates for several years. However, as predicted in our paper, dollarization did not show any sign of reversing. In the case of Peru, annual inflation fell from 56 per cent in 1992 to only 6 per cent in 1998; the ratio of dollar to sol deposits increased from 2.64 in January 1992 to 3.78 in December 1998. Uruguay also saw the dollarization ratio practically unchanged between January 1992 and December 1998, despite a decline in inflation from 110 per cent to only 10 per cent. It is noteworthy that both Peru and Uruguay have managed exchange rates.

In Argentina the central bank operates as a currency board, exchanging pesos for dollars at a 1:1 rate and holding 100 per cent dollar reserves

Figure 15.5   Dollarization in Uruguay, Jan. 1992–Sep. 1998

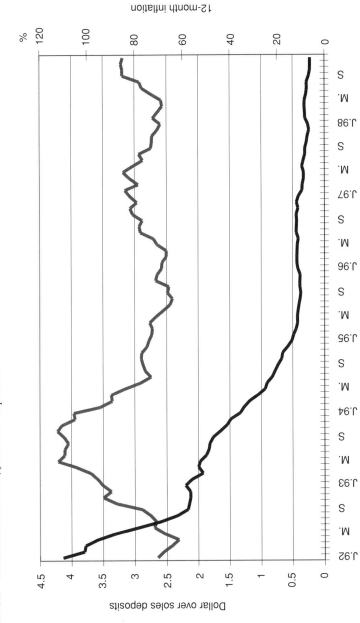

Figure 15.6 Dollarization in Peru, Jan. 1992–Sep. 1997

Figure 15.7 Dollarization in Argentina, Jan. 1992–Sep. 1997

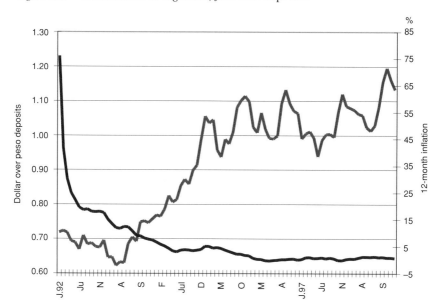

against all pesos issued. Inflation has fallen from 18 per cent in 1992 to just 1 per cent in 1998. In addition, the peso deposits pay a premium of about 2 per cent annually over the dollar deposits. Despite the interest rate premium and an inflation rate even lower than in the United States, the ratio of dollar to peso deposits has increased from 0.72 in January 1992 to 1.13 in December 1998. The recent financial crises in Asia, Russia and some Latin countries may result in new processes of dollarization; Brazil, of course, is a likely candidate.

For those countries starting or deepening dollarization the best message is: as dollarization is practically irreversible, do not fight it. Rather, accommodate institutions to permit the public to obtain what it wants without generating unnecessary disturbances in payment mechanisms or financial markets. Fighting dollarization may result in black markets, disappearance of credit and unbearably high interest rates in local currency.

15.4.1 Lender of last resort and dollarization

In many LDCs the role of lender of last resort is often confused with the need to have some government institution which lends to those to whom nobody else wants to lend! In Argentina the National Development Bank, before being shut down, lent billions of dollars to enterprises that went bankrupt but whose owners remained rich. Of course, this has nothing to do with the concept of lender of last resort discussed in the context of monetary policy institutions. An example may clarify this role of the lender of last resort. It is often suggested that part of the blame for the Depression of the 1930s was the failure of the Federal Reserve Board in performing its duty as lender of last resort. The reasoning goes as follows: with the collapse of the stock market the public became worried about the financial situation of banks and tried to draw out their deposits. The outcome was a fall in the demand for bank deposits and an equal increase in the demand for banknotes. Since the Fed could print dollar bills at its discretion, it should have provided those banknotes until the public recovered confidence in the banking system. That is the role of the lender of last resort: to lend the currency to those who want to hold it, not to those who want to spend it!

Most LDCs have local currencies printed by their own central banks. However, whenever there is a crisis in an LDC one can be almost 100 per cent sure that what the public wants is to convert the deposits into hard currency, not local currency. What the public wants is dollars, not pesos. Therefore if the central bank feeds the banks with pesos it will be feeding a currency run. When the public loses confidence in their national currency the local central bank cannot perform the role of lender of last resort for the simple reason the public wants to get rid of the local currency in exchange for hard currency. The outcome of a weak local currency is typically indexation (with the loss of monetary policy) or dollarization. Argentina is an example of the last outcome: dollarization has been validated through a charter that makes the central bank behave like a currency board. However, the Central Bank of Argentina cannot print dollars and therefore cannot perform the role of lender of last resort. This real-life impediment has been circumvented in the following ways:

1. By law all currency has a one-to-one counterpart in liquid dollar reserves.
2. Liquidity requirements are 20 per cent of banks' deposits and they are deposited in dollars in authorized foreign banks. Contrary to non-remunerated reserve requirements, the banks keep the interest earned on these liquidity requirements.
3. The Central Bank has arranged with several foreign banks for open credit lines to be used exclusively at times of serious crisis. Government bonds are used as collateral in case the credit lines are used. The amount of these lines is equivalent to 12 per cent of deposits.

Point (3) is the real innovation of the Argentine system in that it effectively creates the lender of last resort by use of the capital market. So far the credit lines have been arranged with commercial banks, but nothing precludes in the future further deals being made with international institutions, or even the US Treasury or the Federal Reserve Board itself.

15.5 Currency boards or currency areas?

The recent sequence of currency crises has revived the discussion over alternative monetary arrangements, particularly in relation to the convenience of staying with monetary arrangements that guarantee monetary independence. There have been several actions in recent years that imply a revival of the concept of 'optimum currency areas' originally developed by Robert Mundell (1961), specifically the revival of 'currency boards' and the implementation of the new European currency. There is also talk about creating a common currency in Mercosur. Mundell's analysis dealt with finding circumstances under which it would be appropriate for a country to forgo monetary policy and join another country in a common currency. Mundell's analysis was carried on in non-inflationary Keynesian world in which the only role for the exchange rate was to change the relative costs of labour between the countries. Under those circumstances the analysis shows that labour mobility can substitute for relative price changes and therefore the countries can peg their exchange rates, forming a 'currency area'. The world of the 1980s and 1990s did not experience nominal wage rigidity. Rather, it has been an inflationary world (until the last two years) and the main purpose for countries pursuing monetary independence has to be sought in reasons other than the ability to devalue for changing competitivity. The main reason for monetary independence, at least among most LDCs, has been to be able to apply the inflation tax. However, in the globalized economy, capital is averse to surprise taxes through devaluations and flows away from countries with a propensity to apply this tax. This creates currency crisis and generates incentives for providing for exchange rate stability in order to attract international capital.

Many countries have resorted to permanently fixed exchange rate arrangements of the currency board type in order to guarantee credibility to their monetary arrangements. On the other hand, the European Union significantly advanced its integration by forming a multicountry currency board under the European Monetary System aiming at a single currency for the area.

Argentina has adopted a currency board which pegs the peso to the US dollar, integrating unilaterally and freely to the Federal Reserve System. I say freely because even though Argentina uses dollars, it does not share in other rights available to Fed members, such as representation in the Board and, most importantly, access to the function of lender of last resort or share in the distribution of the seignorage. The suggestion has been made that Argentina and the United States form some sort of a monetary area under a pact for monetary cooperation which should incorporate some collaboration in the issues of representation, lender of last resort and seignorage. This possibility would imply a profound institutional change in the functioning of the Fed because it was not created as a multicountry central bank. However, the European Central Bank is a multicountry organization, endowed with the institutional requirements for accepting new members. The quality of the Argentine currency would be significantly improved if it were accepted formally to be part of either of the two dominant currency areas: the dollar (Fed) or the Euro (ECB). The fall in the country-risk premium would be drastic.

Such logic and tradition implies that Argentina should seek membership of the Federal Reserve System, with all relevant obligations and advantages, even some form of representation on the Board. Argentina is a case of 'taxation without representation' because it pays the seignorage for using dollars but has no say in the dollar's monetary policy. The latest estimate accepted by the IMF shows that Argentines have non-interest-earning dollar bills amounting to $21 billion and the central bank has dollar reserves of $25 billion (albeit interest-bearing). In recent testimony to a Joint Subcommittee of the US Congress, Guillermo Calvo (1999) estimated that under a bilateral seignorage-sharing treaty the United States would gain $150 million a year and Argentina could set up a $10 billion stabilization fund. Under the envisioned cooperation arrangement both countries would gain.

The Argentine government has recently expressed its desire to gain a monetary cooperation treaty with the United States, which would allow dollarization to go beyond the present currency board. Despite expressed reservations by some US authorities, the discussion continues at both the official and the academic level. It has also been mentioned that other countries (possibly Mexico and Canada) may be interested in joining such a monetary agreement. The US has indeed shown interest in hemispheric commercial integration. If we follow the European experience of first the Common Market and then the Euro, the proposal of a common currency for the Americas does not sound any more far-fetched than the proposal for the Free Trade Area for the Americas.

15.6 Devaluations: can they help?

Few policy measures are more powerful than devaluation in affecting daily life and in passionate discussion between academics, policy makers and interest groups. Latin Americans have significantly contributed to the history of this much used and abused instrument. It is not clear, however, that all participants in the discussion have arrived at agreement about what a devaluation can do. One way to illustrate the present state of confusion about the topic is to describe three recent devaluation experiences in our region that systematically ended up creating a crisis of far bigger magnitude than the situation they were meant to correct.

First it was Argentina in February 1981: faced by the unanimous conclusion of the 'experts' that the peso was overvalued between 10 and 20 per cent, the outgoing Economy Minister (at the suggestion of the incoming minister) abandoned the fixed exchange rate that had been in place since December 1978. The devaluation was 10 per cent. The change in the rules of the game backfired: an unstoppable loss of reserves began immediately. Contrary to commonly held beliefs, the devaluation generated a run against the currency: the year ended with four more devaluations, each equal or larger than 30 per cent (all implemented by the new Economy Minister, who lost his job at the end of the year). GDP fell by 5.4 per cent in that year while inflation was 131 per cent. The year 1981 had the privilege of starting the sequence of three-digit annual inflation that persisted until the implementation of the Convertibility Plan in 1991.[3] Some refer to those years as 'the lost decade'.

Then it was Mexico on a fateful 20 December 1994 when, also counselled by 'experts' talk of a 20 per cent overvaluation, the central bank devalued by 13 per cent. The next day $13 billion of reserves were lost *en route* for the Tequila crisis. After three months, the accumulated devaluation reached 114 per cent and GDP that year fell by 6.2 per cent.

Finally, it was Brazil's turn. This time the 'experts' also diagnosed serious competitiveness problems due to overvaluation. On 13 January 1999 the Central Bank devalued by 9 per cent from 1.21 to 1.32. Financial panic developed and the resulting reserve losses forced the authorities to float the real. Two weeks later the rate reached 2 reales per dollar and interest rates skyrocketed, aggravating the problem of servicing the public debt. In just one month Brazil had three presidents of the Central Bank. Later in 1999 an agreement was reached with the IMF, and significant fiscal adjustment was implemented. One year after the initial devaluation, the real stands at 1.77, implying a nominal devaluation of 46 per cent. During the same period the wholesale price index rose by 29 per cent, implying that the real devaluation (assuming constant international dollar prices) was only 13 per cent.

Official predictions of an unprecedented trade surplus of $11 billion in 1999 were soon revised downwards after first-quarter results showed a deficit of half a billion dollars and a fall in the nominal value of exports. In fact, the year 1999 ended with a trade deficit of $1.2 billion. Contrary to initial expectations of a large fall in output, real GDP increased by slightly under 1 per cent during 1999.

The three crises described above have one element in common: all three countries experienced large fiscal deficits which were financed by issuing short-term debt at interest rates that rose by the day. Those high interest rates attracted short-term capital which helped finance the fiscal deficit and the counterpart of the current account deficit. The 'experts' saw the current account deficit as the problem and recommended devaluation in order to improve the real exchange rate and competitiveness. The devaluationist diagnosis was quite wrong: in all three cases the source of the problem was fiscal disequilibrium which had taken governments close to bankruptcy. The correct solution was fiscal adjustment and debt restructuring to a level and maturity compatible with the best possible fiscal effort. Devaluations were totally unnecessary and they simply triggered currency runs. In the Mexican case the resulting crisis helped to create the political environment for a deep fiscal adjustment. However, in the case of Argentina in 1981, the devaluations simply opened the way for a decade of three-digit annual inflation. It is still too early to assess what the effect of the currency crisis will be on Brazil's much-needed fiscal adjustment.

As is often the case in economics, there was confusion between nominal and real variables. *Nominal devaluations may not improve competitiveness, particularly if they are the result of financial crisis and market panic.* The distinction between nominal and real variables is fundamental to economic policy analysis. From theory we may say that devaluations *per se* do not change relative prices unless they do something else. *Two usual outcomes of devaluation are to increase the price level and to scare investors.* By raising prices, devaluation melts down the real value of cash balances and induces people to save in order to restore them to their desired level. The forced savings effect of the price-level increase is bound to reduce aggregate demand and this may temporarily improve the relative price of traded goods in terms of non-traded.

The effect of devaluations on investor sentiment is less clear. If the devaluation is expected to be the last one for some time, investors are most likely to sell foreign exchange to get local money and take advantage of the usually much higher local interest rates. The game here is to stay in 'pesos', earning the high local rates as long as possible before the new devaluation comes and melts down the 'peso' earnings. However, the amount of hard currency that the central bank obtained is at most growing at the dollar interest rate so that the peso liabilities grow faster than the dollar assets.

Speculators know they are playing musical chairs with everybody trying to outguess the rest. To survive it is fundamental to have privileged information about the authorities' intentions. This is a very unstable equilibrium and is likely to be permanently disturbed by any new piece of information, however irrelevant it may be. In many instances the authorities try to correct the growing exposure differential by a small devaluation – a signal that produces the stampede. More often than not, devaluations are the last resort of a financially strangled government that chooses to debase the currency in order to erode the real value of its internal debt. In other cases the fiscal imbalance is monetized and devaluation is the necessary validation of the inflation tax. In these cases in which devaluation operates as a tax instrument it is only natural that investors are scared away from the country, generating a capital outflow.

When a country experiences a capital outflow, foreign exchange becomes scarce and expensive: the real exchange rate is high when capital flows out. The real depreciation is not the result of the nominal devaluation but of the panic of local asset-holders. If confidence is restored, investors will come back and real appreciation will take place, as many successful stabilization plans can attest. The Argentine experience is ideal to illustrate the real effects of nominal devaluations. Table 15.2 shows the values in three selected years of four nominal variables: price level, wages, exchange rate (corrected by the US CPI) and money supply. The lower part of the table shows the three corresponding real variables: real wages, real exchange rate and real cash balances. In the 25-year period nominal prices increased by 3 trillion per cent and money by 10 trillion! However, the real wage increased only 4 per cent in the period and the real exchange rate fell only 2 per cent. Real cash balances rose by 218 per cent over the 25 years. The distinction between the universe of the nominal and the real variables is too clear to need any additional explanation.

However, one should note that in 1980 the real exchange rate was about half its level in 1972 or 1998. The explanation is that in 1980 the country was experiencing a much higher rate of capital inflow (which culminated in the debt crisis of 1982) than in the other two periods. One also observes real cash balances increasing by 55 per cent in 1980 and to more than triple in 1998. These variations can be explained by changes in the conventional variables determining money demand: inflationary expectations and

Table 15.2   Devaluation: nominal and real effects in Argentina

	Nominal wage	Nominal exchange rate*	Money supply	Wholesale prices
1972	1	1	1	1
1980	852	452	1305	841
1998	34 831 460 674	33 087 800 382	107 047 439 490	33 635 336 699

	Real wage	Real exchange rate	Real cash balances	
1972	1.00	1.00	1.00	
1980	1.01	0.54	1.55	
1998	1.04	0.98	3.18	

* Nominal rate multiplied by the US WPI.

GDP. On account of lower expected inflation and higher GDP, real cash balances tripled between 1972 and 1998 despite the fact that the nominal exchange rate showed a trillionaire jump.

15.7 Are currency boards the panacea for macroeconomic instability?

It was a surprise to many that the Hong Kong currency board was able to survive the sequence of currency attacks that tumbled most of its South Asian neighbours. It is also a surprise that the Argentine currency board has lived through the Asian, the Russian and the regional crises without receiving even a single speculative attack. It is often stated that in the light of such successful experiences, countries under speculative attack should seek to implement a currency board, notably Brazil and Ecuador. The reasoning behind this suggestion seems to be that upon the announcement of the new policy the risk premium would fall and the normal flows of refinancing would be restored; but this assigns money and exchange-rate policies more power than they effectively have. Currency boards are not the proper tool to cope with a crisis due to structural macroeconomic disequilibrium, usually of fiscal origin.

If a country is under speculative attack because it cannot service its debts, the only feasible set of instruments lies in a combination of fiscal adjustment and debt restructuring. In this situation the monetary system cannot effect a miracle: debts should be paid and convertibility alone cannot pay debts! Of course, a firm commitment of the central bank to spend any reserves still left in defence of an exchange rate will discourage speculators for some time, but it cannot solve the fundamental fiscal disequilibrium. The same temporary result can be obtained by getting fresh money from the IMF and announcing that it will be used to defend the currency, as Brazil did in March 1999: the markets will rest only while the fresh money lasts and then all participants will go back to paying attention to the fundamentals.

Hong Kong and Argentina survived the crises because they had their houses in order and large stocks of reserves relative to short-term debt, with the consequence that speculators did not think they could succeed. A country facing a run because it cannot service its short-term debt would gain very little in credibility and possibly lose whatever reserves it had left by trying to implement a currency board as a substitute to fiscal adjustment.

In sum, currency boards are no substitute for macroeconomic adjustment: countries facing fiscal problems would do better by solving them straightforwardly. There is, however, a situation in which a currency board may be warranted in the absence of any other way of obtaining some credibility. This is a situation of a country under hyperinflation and experiencing serious fiscal collection problems because of price instability. In this vicious circle inflation forces the government to monetize the fiscal deficit as tax revenue declines. To break the vicious circle some transitory price stability is needed in order to design and implement a new tax system and to restructure government spending.

Under normal circumstances, the announcement of a fiscal reform plan, if consistent, would be enough to raise demand for money and reduce price inflation. It may nevertheless be the case that the government has already used all its credibility capital in previous failed stabilization attempts. In such circumstances credibility cannot be bought with words but only with hard currency. The initial devaluation needed to implement a currency board (with 100 per cent backing) reduces financial claims on the central bank, leaving whatever money supply is left backed by convertible currency. In this situation the announcement of the currency board may prove to be credible and allow for a period of price stability during which the authorities may produce and implement the fiscal proposal now required. A currency board should be viewed as one input in the process of fiscal adjustment and not as the alternative to it. The German stabilization after the second hyperinflation as described by Tom Sargent (1983) may prove to be a case in which the creation of a strong currency was an essential input for the implementation of the required fiscal adjustment. In this case the initial mega-devaluation of the currency board was replaced by the direct repudiation of the existing stock of currency.

One such case, where a currency board was warranted, was Argentina in early 1989 when the government had lost all credibility to implement any fiscal adjustment because of the persistent practice of monetary financing that had led to the ongoing hyperinflation. Under those circumstances the only alternative was for the government to renounce permanently its ability to issue money: a currency board rendered that promise credible.

Notes

1. On the economics of sudden stops see Calvo (1998).
2. This case was analysed in Rodriguez (1979).
3. The exception was 1986 with 82 per cent; this was due however, to the price freeze decreed under the Austral Plan.

References

Calvo, G. (1998) 'Capital Flows and Capital Markets Crises: The Simple Economics of Sudden Stops', *Journal of Applied Economics*, vol. 1 (1), pp. 35–54.

Calvo, G. (1999) 'Testimony on Full Dollarization', presented before the Joint Hearing of the Subcommittees on Economic Policy and International Trade and Finance, Congress of the United States (Washington, DC: Government Printing Office), 22 April.

Cantor, R. and Packer, F. (1996) 'Determinants and Impact of Sovereign Credit Ratings', *Federal Reserve Bank of New York Economic Policy Review*, vol. 2 (2), pp. 37–53.

Guidotti, P. and Rodriguez, C. (1992) 'Dollarization in Latin America: Gresham's Law in Reverse', *IMF Staff Papers*, vol. 39 (3), pp. 518–44.

Harberger, A. (1998) 'Letter to a Younger Generation', *Journal of Applied Economics*, vol. 1 (1), pp. 1–33.

Mundell, R. (1961) 'A Theory of Optimum Currency Areas', *American Economic Review*, vol. 51, pp. 657–65.

Rodriguez, C. (1979) 'Short and Long Run Effects of Monetary and Fiscal Policies under Flexible Exchange Rates and Perfect Capital Mobility', *American Economic Review*, vol. 69 (1), pp. 176–82.

Sargent, T. (1983) 'The Ends of Four Big Inflations', in Hall, R. (ed.) *Inflation: Causes and Effects* (Chicago: University of Chicago Press), pp. 41–97.

16
Cross-Country Growth Comparison: Theory to Empirics*

Danny Quah
London School of Economics and Political Science, UK

16.1 Introduction

In this chapter I describe some empirical regularities in cross-country patterns of aggregate economic growth, and discuss how theoretical reasoning has guided their analysis.

I will use three themes in addressing the topic. The first builds on an observation in the literature that appears, at first, obvious and perhaps trivial. This observation is that *cross-country comparisons matter*, both empirically and theoretically. By this, I do not mean the near-afterthought where a researcher looks at what happens across countries only as a way to provide variation in a cross-country regression equation describing a representative economy. Instead, I refer to empirical and theoretical analysis that looks at why differences across, relations among, and interactions between countries matter for economic growth.

The well-known Kaldor stylized facts on growth mention the variation in economic performance across countries. But until recently, this point had not been picked up on as much as Kaldor's other enumerations – on constancies of ratios and income shares, and on the relations between aggregate variables, all within a single growing economy. Credit for this reorienting towards cross-country analyses must go to the different projects to construct, for many different countries, comparable cross-country data on macro-aggregates. This then is my second theme.

* I thank the British Academy, the Economic and Social Research Council (ESRC), and the Andrew Mellon Foundation for financial support. This paper draws on a range of ideas jointly developed in earlier collaboration with Steven Durlauf and with Louise Keely. Tony Atkinson, Gavin Cameron, Stephen Redding, and seminar participants at the Reserve Bank of Australia provided helpful comments. I alone, however, am responsible for (mis)interpretations and errors in the paper. I used *tSrF* to perform all the calculations.

Summers and Heston (1988, 1991) provide the key and best-known data compilation here. As with the developers of theorems on estimators in econometrics, those authors cannot be held responsible for how their data are used or misused. But that their 1988 and 1991 papers have to date seen 900 citations in scholarly economics publications is surely testament to how they have shifted the debate since Kaldor.[1]

There is a final third theme in this chapter – actually more subtext and spin than a theme proper. That is *technology*. By this, I mean not just a factor that shifts production functions. Instead, I refer more to knowledge in the form of ideas, blueprints and design.

Certainly knowledge perturbs production technologies. Accumulating knowledge shifts out the production possibilities frontier. It has done so since at least the Industrial Revolution of the late eighteenth century. But of at least equal concern, I believe, when we discuss growth relations across countries is the 'non-rivalry' of knowledge (or what Thomas Jefferson called its 'infinite expansibility'), and the healthy disrespect that knowledge shows for physical geography, the political boundaries of nation states, and other artificial barriers constructed by economic agents.[2] Some of these – in the work of Aghion and Howitt (1992), Grossman and Helpman (1991), Romer (1990), and others – provide key insight into so-called 'endogenous growth'. But other implications for economic performance follow as well.

Many have remarked how knowledge cannot be exchanged as a standard Arrow-Debreu commodity. But we have other ways of modelling its production and dissemination. By happy coincidence, the same economics that helps us analyse these is useful also for thinking about other, in my view, exclusively modern (and therefore post-Kaldor) features of economic performance. Those features acquire ever greater prominence when progressively more of aggregate economic value is generated in commodities like computer software, communications technology, biotechnology and genetic databases, and internet-mediated activity. What is significant now and different from earlier times is that the economic concerns surrounding technology do not centre exclusively on technical developments in the shipbuilding dock or aircraft hanger, on the shopfloor or manufacturing assembly line, or in the R&D cleanroom or engineering laboratory. Instead the interest in information, knowledge and technology centres on their direct impact on and immediacy to consumers. It is irrelevant whether one regards software such as Windows 95 or cryptography algorithms, or for that matter, a video game to be scientific knowledge. These commodities happen to have *all* the essential properties of scientific knowledge – infinite expansibility, disrespect for geography, and so on. In this view, knowledge is no longer only something produced in R&D labs through Schumpeterian competition. Instead, commodities that behave like knowledge have now been taken out of the domain of scientists and engineers, and brought upfront to the final consumer. How does this influence patterns of economic growth from here on?

These last changes I have just described do not yet have enough of a data presence for me to discuss their cross-country growth empirics. However, acknowledging them helps explain why my subsequent discussion is structured the way it is.

16.2   Growth and development across countries

In a key paper re-igniting professional interest in economic growth, Robert Lucas (1988, p. 3) described the question to address as follows:

> By the problem of economic development I mean simply the problem of accounting for the observed pattern, across countries and across time, in levels and rates of growth of per capita income. This may seem too narrow a definition, and perhaps it is, but thinking about income patterns will necessarily involve us in thinking about many other aspects of societies too, so I would suggest that we withold judgment on the scope of this definition until we have a clearer idea of where it leads us.

Lucas quickly concedes that for some, his definition has too much a hard-nosed, mainstream economics focus on only per capita income.[3] However, Debraj Ray's excellent textbook on development economics, among others, notes that while a broader, multi-faceted view is, in principle, the appropriate perspective, per capita income is a pretty good proxy for many of the important dimensions to development (Ray, 1998, p. 29).

This 1988 statement of Lucas's usefully contrasts with a comparable one from 1969: Stiglitz and Uzawa (1969, p. 3) introduced the then-modern theory of economic growth as follows:

> The primary objective of the modern theory of economic growth is to explain, on the one hand, the movements in the output, employment, and capital stock of a growing economy and the inter-relations among these variables, and on the other hand, to explain the movements in the distribution of income among the factors of production.

The difference between the two positions can be simply stated. Stiglitz and Uzawa were concerned with explaining conditions *within* a single economy through time. Lucas's evocative statement, on the other hand, removed the limits confining that analysis to within national boundaries and asked, 'Can we understand what is happening over time to the entire cross section of countries?'

Earlier growth theorists and empiricists might simply have confined themselves to within-country studies because they thought different countries were, well, different. Researchers have long known about the biases and omissions in developing-country national income accounts. Comparison of those data with the data of developed countries can be unreliable even when within-country analysis over time for a given economy is perfectly sensible. That Switzerland's per capita income is 400 times Tanzania's at official exchange rates probably does not mean the same thing as Bill Gates's being 400 times wealthier than the 95th-percentile household in the US. But this excuse for excess caution in cross-country comparison has lost some of its punch with World Bank, UN, and Summers-Heston efforts at purchasing power parity corrections in aggregate income data across countries. Such adjustments cannot remove all problems in cross-country comparisons, but the obvious analytical difficulties are now minimized.

Between 1960 and 1990, average per capita income in the world grew by 2.25 per cent per annum. Individual country performance fluctuated around this worldwide average growth path. Table 16.1 shows the evolution of country per capita incomes over this period. The figures take countries as the basic unit of observation and are relative to world average per capita income. Thus, the first entry in the table shows that over the five-year period 1960–64 the 10th percentile country had per capita income only 22 per cent of the world average. The ratio of the 90th percentile per capita income to the 10th percentile averaged over 1960–64 was 12. By the beginning of the 1990s, this ratio had increased to 21, a 67 per cent increase over 25 years. That rise in disparities came from both a relative decline at the bottom of the cross-country income distribution *and* a relative increase at the top end.

Table 16.1 also shows the fraction of the world's population contained in the top and bottom deciles of countries. We see a remarkable decline in population share of the bottom decile from 26 per cent to 3 per cent. This, however, is due to a single economy, China, exiting the group of very

Table 16.1 Evolution of country per capita incomes

Per capita income in national economies	Times world per capita income	
	1960–64	1985–89
10th %-ile	0.22 × (26.0% world popn.)	0.15 × (3.3% world popn.)
90th %-ile	2.70 × (12.5% world popn.)	3.08 × (9.3% world popn.)
(25th–15th) %-iles	0.13 ×	0.06 ×
(95th–85th) %-iles	0.98 ×	0.59 ×

poorest countries. Taking out China, the modified Table 16.1 (not presented here) says two things. First, the richest countries are usually larger, and the poorer countries smaller. Second, over time, the share of the world's population living in the very richest countries has declined, while that in the very poorest has increased.

What I have just described suggests to me that if one is interested in the worldwide distribution of incomes across people – not just that across countries – additional insights are available by looking directly at the distribution of incomes across people within these countries, and then merging that information with the data underlying Table 16.1. It will take us too much out of the way to go into that discussion here, but some quick comments are in order. China's transition out of the bottom decile of countries has been associated with an increase in its personal income inequality. Thus, it might seem misleading to suggest that only 3.3 per cent of the world's population remained in the bottom decile by the end of the 1980s. Of course, Table 16.1 does not actually say that, but, regardless, we also know that the increase in within-country inequality in China did not stop hundreds of millions of Chinese from becoming markedly better off over this 25-year period. In a simple accounting sense, China's growth in per capita income *did* remove a significant fraction of the world's population from poverty. On this, therefore, Table 16.1 does not mislead.

Calculations show that the flavour of this conclusion carries more generally.[4] Inequality within countries has certainly changed through time. But the magnitude of those variations is dwarfed by that of changes in per capita incomes due to aggregate economic growth. Thus, to understand the distribution dynamics of worldwide individual incomes, not just of cross-country economic performance, Table 16.1 does a pretty good job representing the salient facts.

The final two rows of the table show a progressive narrowing of income distance between the ten percentile points centred on the 10th and 90th percentiles respectively. This indicates a clustering of observations around those two distinct points on the cross-country income distribution.

An alternative depiction of the message of Table 16.1 is shown in the *emerging twin peaks* of Figure 16.1. The figure illustrates the evolution of the cross-country per capita income distribution, using an estimated model of distribution dynamics. Figure 16.2 shows the actual cross-country distributions in 1960 and 1988, with the incipient rise of the two modes. To understand the mechanics of the emerging twin peaks in Figure 16.1, turn to Figure 16.3: This shows likelihoods of transiting over time from one part of the income distribution to another. Contour plots of the graph on the left of Figure 16.3 show probability mass clustering around distinct parts of the diagonal, and thus greater likelihoods, relatively, of remaining in those parts of the income space upon entry there. Trace through the dynamics of the system by repeatedly applying

Figure 16.1 Emerging twin peaks in the cross-country income distribution

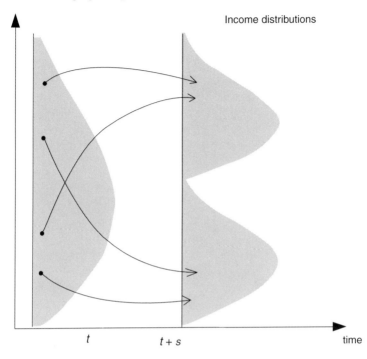

Income distributions

t   *t* + *s*   time

Note: Post-1960 experiences projected over 40 years are drawn to scale, relative to historical cross-country distributions.

the estimated stochastic kernel in Figure 16.3 to Figure 16.2. (Quah, 1997, gives details on this procedure).

16.3 Growth theory and empirics

What do growth models say about Figures 16.1 to 16.3?

The answer I want to give is an unsatisfactory combination of 'a great deal' and 'not a lot' simultaneously. To see why, it suffices to consider the simplest version of the Solow (1956) growth model. The conclusions I will draw relevant for Figures 16.1–16.3 will follow from many other models as well.

The model is standard, and the very brief exposition that follows is mostly to establish notation. Let Y be total output, N be the workforce, and K be the total capital stock. Denote per worker quantities in lower case:

$$y \stackrel{\text{def}}{=} Y/N \quad k \stackrel{\text{def}}{=} K/N \tag{1}$$

Figure 16.2 Actual income distributions across 98 countries (densities of relative output per worker)

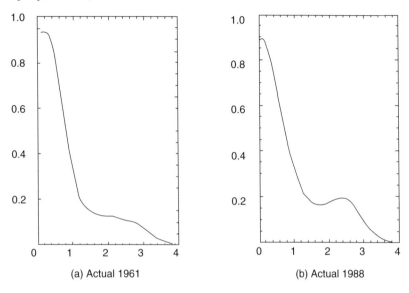

(a) Actual 1961   (b) Actual 1988

Output depends on K, N, and technology A through a standard smooth neoclassical production function. Assume technology A enters the production function multiplicatively in N so that output per worker can then be written as

$$y = Af(k/A), \ f' > 0, \ f'' < 0, \ \lim_{k \to \infty} f(k)k^{-1} = 0 \tag{2}$$

Technology and the workforce evolve exogenously at constant growth rates

$$\dot{A}/A = \xi \geq 0, \ A(0) > 0 \tag{3}$$

$$\dot{N}/N = \vartheta \geq 0, \ N(0) > 0 \tag{4}$$

Capital depreciates at a constant rate δ and accumulates through savings equal to fraction τ of total income Y:

$$\dot{K} = \tau Y - \delta K, \ \tau \text{ in } (0, 1) \text{ and } \delta > 0 \tag{5}$$

Combining (1) through (5) gives the dynamic equation for capital per worker:

$$\dot{k}/k - \dot{A}/A = \tau \frac{-f(k/A)}{k/A} (\delta + \vartheta + \xi) \tag{6}$$

Figure 16.3 Distribution dynamics across countries (relative output per worker)

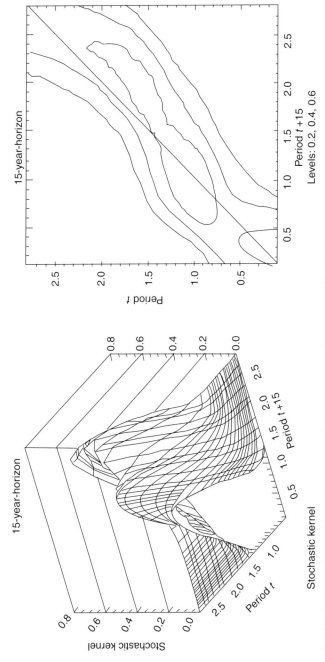

Note: The right panel contains contour plots of the 15-year stochastic kernel in the left panel.

The right side of this equation has the graph given in Figure 16.4. Under the standard curvature assumptions on *f* given in (2), equation (6) has a unique steady-state value [k/A]*.

Taking together equations (2), (3), and (6) then gives observable dynamics for labour productivity:

$$\log y(t) = \Gamma_0 + \xi \cdot t + [\log y(0) - \Gamma_0]e^{\lambda t} \tag{7}$$

where

$$
\begin{aligned}
\Gamma_0 &= \log f([k/A]^\star) + \log A(0) \\
&= g([\delta + \vartheta + \xi]^{-1}\tau) + \log A(0) \quad \text{with } g' > 0 \\
\text{and } \lambda &= \lambda(f_{\prime}(\delta + \vartheta + \xi),\tau) < 0
\end{aligned}
$$

These dynamics are illustrated in Figure 16.5. For any single economy, say with output per worker y_1, economic history is the transition from its initial level to a specific steady-state path. However, the figure also shows that the cross-section of economies, having different underlying steady-state paths varying with Γ_0, displays a wide range of possible behaviours. Economies 2 and 3 diverge away from each other, criss-crossing along the way although they began close together at a middle-income level.

Figure 16.4   k/A dynamics

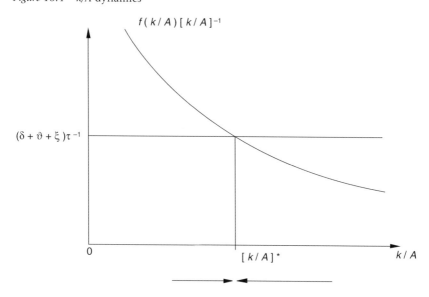

Note: Convergence to steady state [k/A]* occurs for all initial values [k/A].

Figure 16.5   Time paths across countries

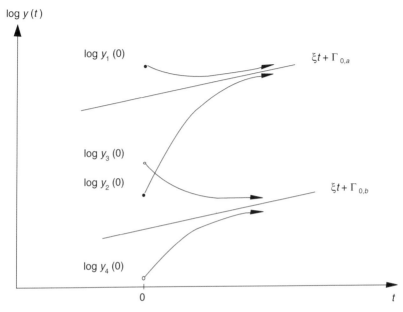

log $y(t)$

log $y_1(0)$

$\xi t + \Gamma_{0,a}$

log $y_3(0)$

log $y_2(0)$

$\xi t + \Gamma_{0,b}$

log $y_4(0)$

0

t

Note: Each economy shows transition from its initial level to a specific steady-state path. But a cross-section of economies, having different underlying steady-state paths varying with Γ_0, shows a range of possible behaviours.

Economies like 1 begin and remain rich; those like 4 begin and remain poor. If the number of countries exceeds that of underlying steady-state paths, then a clustering in the cross-section distribution, as in the emerging twin peaks in Figure 16.1 could well arise.[5]

The cross-section therefore shows great diversity. Despite that, the average economy (or, for that matter, *each* economy taken in isolation) shows a straightforward relentless monotone convergence to its unique underlying steady-state growth path. The behaviour of the cross-section distribution and that of the individual, while each consistent with the other, send markedly different messages about what is quantitatively important. Indeed, a researcher might well conclude he has a good understanding of economic growth after successfully calibrating the dynamic performance of a single economy, but, at the same time, leaving completely at odds the situation for the entire cross-section.

In this accounting, understanding the behaviour of a representative economy entails understanding the economics in ξ and λ. Understanding the disparities in the cross-section means clarifying the sources of differences in Γ_0. Of course, the economics in equations (2) to (5) does not separate cleanly these two sets of factors. Any single economic analysis will usually have implications for both. Knowledge on and guesses about the magnitudes of different elasticities will be needed to isolate what matters more for which.

Here I will pursue technology A, as the key force underlying Γ_0. That technology matters, even within a single economy and for the first fifty years of the twentieth century (much less now), is a point already made as early as Solow (1957): the increase in output per worker from $0.62 per worker-hour in 1900 to $1.28 in 1949 has only 12.6 per cent explained by k; the rest, an overwhelming 87.4 per cent, is due to A.

(I mention these earliest growth-accounting estimates here, rather than later ones that, say, correct for changes in quality of the factors of production. It might well be that upon proper quality-adjustment, these Solow (1957) results can be amended until nothing remains in A. However, my hunch is that that economic reasoning used for understanding A is also the best reasoning available for understanding the economics of the new ideas that improve quality in factors of production. Put another way, what else is it but technology that improves factors of production?)

We can assess A's cross-section importance by asking what we should observe if it were absent or, equivalently for our purposes, identical across countries. A US/India comparison is instructive here. In the Summers-Heston data, for the forty years from 1950 to 1990, the ratio of US to Indian output per worker averaged 14.6. Over the same period, US output per worker grew at 1.5 per cent per year while Indian output per worker grew at 2.3 per cent per year. Output per worker varies from year to year, and while long-run growth rates in the two countries have differed – so that a trend change has occurred – the variation is certainly not monotone.

If we assume that in equation (2), f is derived from a Cobb-Douglas production function,

$$y = A \times (k/A)^\alpha$$

and capital's income share α is taken to be 0.4 – roughly what it is calculated to be in many countries – then the ratio of physical capital's rate of return in India to that in the US should be 56! That worldwide capital flows do not wipe out this huge differential means something other than just differences in k must be responsible for the variation in income levels across the rich and poor countries.

Noting that India, while poorer, is also growing faster, we can perform one further calculation. Maintaining the just-used assumptions, we obtain from equations (2) and (6) an explicit expression for how growth rates, in the transition to steady state, vary as a function of observable variables:

$$\dot{y}/y = \left| \xi - (\delta + \nu + \xi)\alpha \right| + \left(\alpha A^{\frac{1}{\alpha}-1} \right) \times \tau y^{1-\frac{1}{\alpha}}$$

If the term in square brackets on the right of this equation is approximately equal across countries, then to explain how growth rates and income levels differ across US and India, the savings rate in the US must be more than 35 times that in India!

These calculations, where I have simply replicated arguments in Lucas (1990) and Romer (1994), show, in my estimation, the importance of technology A in explaining the large cross-sectional variation in economic performance across countries. This can be put alternatively as follows. Suppose one uses as organizing framework the growth model (1)–(5). How much of the plight of poor countries is due to shortage of material resources like physical capital? The answer suggested by the calculations just presented is: very little.

There are a range of possibilities how one proceeds from here. A researcher might calculate regressions with measured per capita income growth on the left side and a variety of *ad hoc* conditioning variables on the right. This is done with the view that that wide range of conditioning variables can then potentially explain growth in A. Ideally, these regressions should describe the steady-state paths in Figure 16.5 while *convergence* regressions describe transitions to those steady states. A large literature, following a line of reasoning given in Barro (1997), has taken exactly this route. Some of these regressions can be informative, others not easily interpretable, most fragile, and a considerable fraction what some have called 'a blaze of mediocre sociology' – Durlauf and Quah (1999) tabulate over one hundred such equations estimated in the literature.[6]

The empirical analysis can also adopt more intricate methods. An argument is sometimes made that because the data studied in cross-country growth comparisons vary in both cross-section and time-series dimensions, a panel-data analysis is appropriate and informative. Figure 16.5 suggests the opposite. To appreciate this, recall that panel-data analysis typically conditions out (or 'corrects for') individual heterogeneities – the so-called *fixed effects* or *random effects*. Being able to do this, in many microeconometric panel-data studies, is a virtue. In cross-country growth comparisons, however, it is a defect. As represented in Figure 16.5, the variation we are concerned with is precisely that in the underlying country-specific heterogeneities. This variation occupies centre stage in interest – it is exactly what underlies why some countries are rich and others poor. Conditioning it out as statistical nuisance parameters – fixed or random effects, or more generally as unobservable individual heterogeneities – is, in my view, exactly the opposite of what one should do.[7]

A reasoned view on these growth regressions – cross-section or panel – is that the researchers concerned have simply given up on the idea that A represents technology. Instead, A could be anything or everything in a list that includes income inequality, political stability, democracy, property rights regimes, climate, geography, openness of the economy, financial depth, ethno-linguistic fractionalization, and many others. No theory exists that says these variables should *not* affect economic performance somehow. Casual observation suggests that they probably do. However, once we step outside a technology interpretation for A, all these different alternatives amount to believing that societies act in such a way that the resulting outcome falls strictly inside the production possibilities frontier.

On the other hand, even hewing (over-conservatively perhaps but with a scientific discipline) to the simple growth theory laid out in (1)–(5), it remains that one has not yet completely exhausted understanding of the possibilities when A is technology. Why flit to another lode of ore when so much is still to be clarified? Moreover, a technology-based approach is firmly both old growth theory and new growth theory: the extremes agree on the importance of technology; it's those in the middle that diverge.

To be sure, some might argue that the partition between k and A in my discussion is artificial, and that the two, in reality, develop in tandem. This is doubtless true, and interesting research (e.g. Howitt and Aghion (1996)) has formalized this argument further.

In this chapter I want to abstract from such conceptual multicollinearity in k and A. I ask instead, 'What determines the distribution of A across countries?' This is a question in the economics of technology and knowledge dissemination. Analysing it reveals a discipline for what would otherwise simply be behaviour leading to outcomes strictly within the production possibilities frontier.

16.4 Technology across countries

To motivate the theoretical and empirical modelling choices here, a useful first observation is that the important interactions leading to A's dissemination have to lie outside conventional market exchange. Because A is infinitely expansible or non-rival, its free trade would lead to the zero-price, market-failure outcome identified in Arrow (1962). Even if regimes for intellectual property rights (IPRs – patents, copyrights, trade secrets – putatively enforce monopolistic outcomes in the development and provision of A, such systems are contrivances that societies have come to construct and that natural competitive forces seek to circumvent.[8] IPRs are neither primitive nor intrinsic to the problem of technology and idea dissemination (David (1993)).

We can organize relevant analysis into two broad categories, as described by the duality in Figure 16.6. The figure's left panel represents one category, by far the larger in the literature. This analysis takes as given the set of possible follower and leader countries: it then models the rate – fast or slow – of possible catch-up in technology levels, and considers the possibility of overtaking. Empirical examples of such analyses include Coe and Helpman (1995), Bernard and Jones (1996), and Cameron, Proudman and

Figure 16.6 Duality

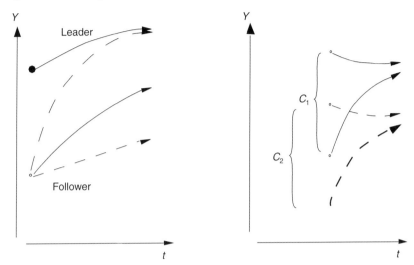

Note: Modelling issue that underlies the left panel: What is the rate – fast or slow – of Follower convergence to Leader? Right panel: Which are the economies that converge, one to the other? What glue binds and separates different clusters like C_1 and C_2.

Redding (1998). The right panel of Figure 16.6 shows the other category, much smaller, that takes the set of economy identities not as given but as objects to be determined. It asks, 'Which are the economies that turn out to be followers and leaders in which (joint) subgroups; what forces determine who gets included in what clusters?' This analysis is relatively new, and includes Quah (1997, 1999b) and Keely (1999) in cross-country growth, although the theoretical ideas and tools useful here are also only seeing recent development (e.g. Bloch (1996), Ray and Vohra (1997, 1999), Yi (1997)).

The analysis in Cameron, Proudman and Redding (1998) well represents the concepts and results in the first strand of literature.

Consider two economies 0 and j, where 0 indexes the initial leader and j a representative follower. Write A dissemination as:

$$\dot{A}_j / A_j = \xi_j - \beta_j \times \left(\frac{A_j - \psi_j A_0}{A_0} \right)$$

$$A_j(0),\ \beta_j,\ \xi_j \geq 0;\ \psi_j \in [0, 1] \tag{8}$$

This adds a layer of complication over the leader country's assumed behaviour, taken from equation (3):

$$\dot{A}_0/A_0 = \xi_0 = \xi \geq 0 \qquad A_0(0) > 0$$

In (8), the constants ξ_j, β_j, and ψ_j are interpreted, respectively, as j's own natural growth rate, j's rate of technology catch-up, and the fraction of A_0 potentially transferable to j.

To clarify what a specification like (8) delivers, define *relative technology* $a_j \overset{\text{def}}{=} A_j/A_0$. Then (8) implies a steady state value a_j^* and transition dynamics:

$$a_j^* = (\xi_j - \xi_0)\beta^{-1}_j + \psi_j$$

$$\dot{a}_j/a_j = -\beta_j \times (a_j - a_j^*)$$

These relations deliver a simple quantification of convergence, divergence, or persistent stagnation, depending on where the value a_j^* lies relative to 1, and on the value of β_j. Except when ξ_j is the same as ξ_0, steady-state relative technology depends on more than just ψ_j.

It is easy in concept, moreover, to justify and estimate the dependence of ξ_j, β_j, and ψ_j on variables such as openness, R&D expenditure or human capital. As just one empirical example, the estimates in Cameron, Proudman and Redding (1998), combining a range of such indicators, suggest that for the UK relative to the US, a_j^* is, for different industries, between 53 per cent and 92 per cent.

Such empirical analyses are useful for pointing the way forwards and establishing what matters empirically. However, the authors themselves have no illusion about the reduced-form nature of the work thus far. It remains unclear, also, whether such analyses can lead usefully to conclusions about the dynamics of the entire cross-section, or will be restricted to pairwise comparisons.

Empirical analysis in the second category is in even earlier stages. Calculations in Quah (1997) suggested that patterns of trade – who trades with whom – rather than just openness, say, matters importantly for the patterns of clusterings that emerge in the cross-section of countries. The theoretical counterparts to that empirical work remain to be studied: a reasonable conjecture is that theories of coalition formation – for idea- and technology-sharing clusters, implicit or explicit – will figure prominently. The key economic consideration is, How does it serve the self-interest of the putative leader – the source of the frontier technology – to have specific hangers-on taking advantage of and learning that technology? What do potential followers bring to the interaction between them that benefits the economy having the current technological lead?

16.5 Conclusions

In their lecture to the Tenth IEA World Congress in Moscow in 1992, Aghion and Howitt (1995) reviewed the issues and content in new growth theory. They observed economics was 'experiencing the second post-war wave of neoclassical growth theory'.

At the same time, however, they noted that much of the substance and many of the ideas in the theory of economic growth had, for decades if not longer, already seen serious work by the most penetrating, analytical minds in the profession. For Aghion and Howitt, no 'grand new insights into the workings of market economies' could explain the remarkable rapid development of endogenous growth theory. They were, therefore, led to ask (Aghion and Howitt (1995, p. 102)):

> What, then, accounts for the phenomenal success of a theory with no fundamentally new ideas on a subject that has been studied for centuries?

We know their question had to be in part rhetorical if not downright disingenuous and mischievous (especially the 'no fundamentally new ideas' phrasing) as Aghion and Howitt have been among the new theory's most prolific developers.

Their answer, similar to that given in Romer (1994), is the technical progress in tools and concepts that economists can now apply in equilibrium analysis. In particular, dynamic general equilibrium analysis with increasing returns – of which endogenous technology is a special case – is now routine.

Among other things, my goal in this chapter has been to suggest how Aghion and Howitt (1995) and Romer (1994) have been too modest. A more complete explanation, in my view, includes at least the following:

1. Cross-country focus on development and growth, more broadly construed;
2. Improvement in data availability;
3. The topicality of high technology, now taken out of R&D labs and the narrow domain of scientists and engineers.

These points are not entirely distinct. The first two of these obviously interact with each other. And, they feed directly into this paper's main topic: what is the cross-country growth record, and how has economic theory helped design its empirical analysis? This chapter has described how looking across countries is important and how doing so signals which models – theoretical and empirical – should be the ones to provide further quantitatively important insights.

Items 1–3, in my view, temper Aghion and Howitt's suggestion that the accomplishments of recent research in endogenous growth have been 'more a matter of form than substance', that 'endogenous growth theory has succeeded mainly because of its technical progress' (i.e. in the tools that equilibrium theory now affords), and that 'technique has come to dominate new ideas as the determinant of professional success'.

In this lecture, I have argued the opposite. The professional success of the theory has not arisen solely from technological change in practitioners. While it is true that ever more intricate models have now become tractable to analysis, that itself is an endogenous outcome that is explained by or jointly emergent with yet other developments. Successful development of growth theory has only proceeded in step and simultaneously with the concerns of empirical research and topical policy.

By the last, I mean simply acknowledging the increasingly important roles of information, knowledge and high technology in everyday economic life, and government responses to that growing recognition.[9] Those changes are highlighted by much-debated and economically significant legal decisions being made on internet and operating system technology – words that had no meaning in the 1950s and 1960s, but are now common currency among consumers.

Before the early 1990s, the demands of empirical research and topical policy – in their current forms – were never as visible nor as pressing. And it is this, in my estimation, that accounts for the resonance and appeal of recent research in both theoretical and empirical analyses of economic growth. At the same time, however, this shift also comes with a warning: 'traditional' growth models that emphasize endogenous technology on the production side of the economy might not provide the sharpest insights for how technology matters in the economy now.

Notes

1. According to the Social Science Citation Index, by May 1999 these two papers had been cited 840 times. This is, moreover, almost surely an undercount as the Summers-Heston data have reached a notoriety where they are sometimes referred to and used without explicit citation.
2. Arrow (1962) provides an early formalization and technical discussion of these properties. That many empirical studies have found knowledge spillovers geographically localized presents a puzzle to resolve, not a fundamental shift of principle. Those findings might suggest, say, that in certain economic activities, tacit knowledge transmitted only through specific kinds of interactions matter more than do generally broadcasted codifiable knowledge. Nonetheless, the latter can remain the more important and significant for understanding cross-country patterns of growth.
3. Composite indexes for, say, 'physical quality of life' or 'human development' might take into account indicators such as infant mortality, life expectancy, educational attainment, per capita incomes downweighting higher values, literacy rates, and so on.

4. For further details, the reader might wish to consult Heston and Summers (1999), Milanovic (1999) and Quah (1999a).
5. More subtle analysis on this same point, within a representative economy framework, appear in Azariadis and Drazen (1990), Durlauf and Johnson (1995), Solow (1997) and de Castro (1999).
6. The informativeness of such regressions been discussed many times elsewere; see, e.g., Durlauf (1996), Quah (1996) and Sala-i-Martin (1996).
7. In some cases (e.g. fixed-effects averaging), a researcher can recover what might appear to be estimates of the underlying individual heterogeneities. It is, however, unclear whether those are useful for the current cross-country growth application. To see this, recall that most sophisticated panel-data techniques are specifically designed to estimate a low-dimensional parameter vector, without requiring or achieving consistent estimation of the individual heterogeneities. This is why such methods are so remarkable – doing the last-mentioned is typically impossible as the dimensionality of individual effects is comparable to sample size. But then it is almost accidental (and perhaps unfortunate) that things looking like estimates of individual effects can be obtained, even when statistically meaningless.
8. Software and internet development provide powerful real-world examples of how the forces Arrow (1962) identified will re-route around artificial barriers like intellectual property rights.
9. Obvious expressions of this include Industry Canada (1994), UK Department of Trade and Industry (1998), and World Bank (1998). Elsewhere, government policies in Australia, Finland, India and Singapore – among others – are notable examples where knowledge and technology have come explicitly to the fore.

References

Aghion, P. and Howitt, P. (1992) 'A Model of Growth through Creative Destruction', *Econometrica*, vol. 60 (2), pp. 323–51.

Aghion, P. and Howitt, P. (1995) 'Technical Progress in the Theory of Economic Growth', in Fitoussi, J.-P. (ed.) *Economics in a Changing World*, vol. 5 of *Proceedings of the Tenth World Congress of the International Economic Association, Moscow* (London: St Martin's Press) ch. 5, pp. 101–22.

Arrow, K.J. (1962) 'Economic Welfare and the Allocation of Resources for Inventions', in Nelson, R.J. (ed.) *The Rate and Direction of Inventive Activity* (Princeton, NJ: Princeton University Press and NBER) pp. 609–25.

Azariadis, C. and Drazen, A. (1990) 'Threshold Externalities in Economic Development', *Quarterly Journal of Economics*, vol. 105 (2), pp. 501–26.

Barro, R.J. (1997) *Determinants of Economic Growth* (Cambridge MASS: MIT Press).

Bernard, A.B., and Jones, C.I. (1996) 'Productivity across Industries and Countries: Time Series Theory and Evidence', *Review of Economics and Statistics*, vol. 78 (1), pp. 135–46.

Bloch, F. (1996) 'Sequential Formation of Coalitions in Games with Externalities and Fixed Payoff Division', *Games and Economic Behavior*, vol. 14 (1), pp. 90–123.

Cameron, G., Proudman, J. and Redding, S. (1998) 'Productivity Convergence and International Openness', in Proudman, J. and Redding, S. (eds) *Openness and Growth* (London: Bank of England) ch. 6, pp. 221–60.

Coe, D.T. and Helpman, E. (1995) 'International R&D spillovers', *European Economic Review* vol. 39 (5), pp. 859–87.

David, P.A. (1993) 'Intellectual Property Institutions and the Panda's Thumb: Patents, Copyrights, and Trade Secrets in Economic Theory and History', In Wallerstein, M.B., Mogee, M.E. and Schoen, R.A. (eds) *Global Dimensions of Intellectual Property Rights in Science and Technology* (Washington, DC: National Academy Press) ch. 2, pp. 19–61.

de Castro, S. (1999) 'Endogenous Consumer-Culture Resistance to Creative Destruction can Explain Convergence Clubs', Working Paper, Universidade de Brasilia, September.

Durlauf, S.N. (1996) 'On the Convergence and Divergence of Growth Rates: An Introduction', *Economic Journal*, vol. 106 (436), pp. 1016–17.

Durlauf, S.N. and Johnson, P.A. (1995) 'Multiple Regimes and Cross-Country Growth Behavior', *Journal of Applied Econometrics*, vol. 10 (4), pp. 365–84.

Durlauf, S.N. and Quah, D. (1999) 'The New Empirics of Economic Growth', in Taylor, J.B. and Woodford, M. (eds) *Handbook of Macroeconomics* vol. 1A (Amsterdam: North Holland/Elsevier Science) ch. 4, pp. 231–304.

Grossman, G.M. and Helpman, E. (1991) *Innovation and Growth in the Global Economy* (Cambridge, Mass: MIT Press)

Heston, A. and Summers, R. (1999) 'The World Distribution of Income: A Synthesis of Intercountry and Intracountry Data to Measure Worldwide Material Well-Being', Working Paper, Economics Department, University of Pennsylvania, August.

Howitt, P. and Aghion, P. (1996) 'Capital Accumulation and Innovation as Complementary Factors in Long-Run Growth', *Journal of Economic Growth*, vol. 3 (2), pp. 111–30.

Industry Canada (1994) *Building a More Innovative Economy* (Ottawa: Industry Canada).

Kaldor, N. (1961) 'Capital Accumulation and Economic Growth', in Lutz, F.A. and Hague, D.C. (eds) in *The Theory of Capital: Proceedings of a Conference Held by the International Economic Association* (London: Macmillan), ch. 10, pp. 177–222.

Keely, L.C. (1999) 'Exchanging Good Ideas', Working Paper, LSE, November.

Lucas, R.E. (1988) 'On the Mechanics of Economic Development', *Journal of Monetary Economics*, vol. 22 (1), pp. 3–42.

Lucas, R.E. (1990) 'Why Doesn't Capital Flow from Rich to Poor Countries?' *American Economic Association Papers and Proceedings*, vol. 80 (2), pp. 92–96.

Milanovic, B. (1999) 'True World Income Distribution, 1988 and 1993: First Calculation based on Household Surveys Alone', Working Paper, World Bank, Washington DC, May.

Quah, D. (1996) 'Empirics for Economic Growth and Convergence', *European Economic Review*, vol. 40 (6), pp. 1353–75.

Quah, D. (1997) 'Empirics for Growth and Distribution: Polarization, Stratification, and Convergence Clubs', *Journal of Economic Growth*, vol. 2 (1), pp. 27–59.

Quah, D. (1999a) '6 × 10^9: Some Dynamics of Global Inequality and Growth', Working Paper, Economics Department, LSE, London, September.

Quah, D. (1999b) 'Ideas Determining Convergence Clubs', Working Paper, Economics Department, LSE, London, July.

Quah, D. (1999c) 'The Weightless Economy in Economic Development', Working Paper no. 155, United Nations University World Institute for Development Economics Research, Helsinki, January.

Ray, D. (1998) *Development Economics* (Princeton, NJ: Princeton University Press)

Ray, D. (1999) 'A Theory of Endogenous Coalition Structures', *Games and Economic Behavior*, vol. 26 (2), pp. 286–336.

Ray, D. and Vohra, R. (1997) 'Equilibrium Binding Agreements', *Journal of Economic Theory*, vol. 73 (1), pp. 30–78.

Romer, P.M. (1990) 'Endogenous Technological Change', *Journal of Political Economy*, vol. 98 (5, part 2), S71–S102.

Romer, P.M. (1994) 'The Origins of Endogenous Growth', *Journal of Economic Perspectives*, vol. 8 (1) pp. 3–22.

Sala-i-Martin, X. (1996) 'The Classical Approach to Convergence Analysis', *Economic Journal*, vol. 106 (437), pp. 1019–36.

Solow, R.M. (1956) 'A Contribution to the Theory of Economic Growth', *Quarterly Journal of Economics*, vol. 70 (1), pp. 65–94.

Solow, R.M. (1957) 'Technical Change and the Aggregate Production Function', *Review of Economics and Statistics*, vol. 39 (3), pp. 312–20.

Solow, R.M. (1997) *Learning from 'Learning by Doing': Lessons for Economic Growth*, Kenneth J. Arrow Lectures (Stanford, CA: Stanford University Press).

Stiglitz, J.E. and Uzawa, H. (eds) (1969) *Readings in the Modern Theory of Economic Growth* (Cambridge, MA: MIT Press).

Summers, R. and Heston, A. (1988) 'A New Set of International Comparisons of Real Product and Price Levels Estimates for 130 Countries, 1950–1985', *Review of Income and Wealth*, vol. 34 (1), pp. 1–25.

Summers, R. and Heston, A. (1991) 'The Penn World Table (Mark 5): An Expanded Set of International Comparisons, 1950–1988', *Quarterly Journal of Economics*, vol. 106 (2), pp. 327–68.

UK Department of Trade and Industry (1998) *Our Competitive Future: Building the Knowledge-Driven Economy* (London: DTI).

World Bank (1998) *World Development Report: Knowledge in Development* (Oxford: Oxford University Press).

Yi, S.-S. (1997) 'Stable Coalition Structures with Externalities', *Games and Economic Behavior*, vol. 20 (2), pp. 201–37.

17
Volatility and Macroeconomic Paradigms for Rich and Poor

William Easterly
Roumeen Islam
The World Bank, Washington DC
and
Joseph E. Stiglitz
Stanford University, USA

Michael Bruno Memorial Lecture: Dedication

Michael Bruno has left us with legacies that include an empiricism free of ideology, a curiosity about what the real facts are, a scepticism about the conventional wisdom, and a willingness to listen to a wide range of opinions. His interest in macroeconomics resulted in one of the most influential books of the 1980s, *The Economics of Worldwide Stagflation*, which examined why the conventional Phillips curve had been turned on its head by institutional mechanisms. His interest in macroeconomic policy was applied to real life when he led the successful Israeli heterodox inflation stabilization effort of 1985, first as adviser and then as central bank governor. As Chief Economist of the World Bank, he emphasized research and economic and sector work relative to lending activities and external relations. In research, while Chief Economist, he showed how high inflation was robustly and negatively related to economic growth, while there was little evidence of a robust relationship between inflation and growth at low rates of inflation (say below 40 per cent a year). Michael Bruno's legacy lives on in the many people whom he inspired by being a good and curious listener and a thoughtful and non-ideological researcher. While inflation was the central macroeconomic issue of the 1980s, the central issue of the late 1990s has been economic instability. This chapter, a lecture dedicated to Michael Bruno's memory, is an attempt to understand the basic determinants of that instability, partly by looking at the institutional structures that affect that instability, just as Michael Bruno tried to understand inflation by looking at the institutional structures that had so affected the processes of wage and price dynamics. We hope that it lives up to the standards that Michael has set for all of us.

17.1 Introduction

The recessions and depressions that have spread around the world in the past two years, beginning in Thailand, moving on to other countries in East Asia, then on to Russia, and now plaguing much of Latin America, are but the most recent of the economic and financial crises which have afflicted the developing world with increasing frequency and severity over the past quarter-century. The most recent crises are markedly different from those that characterized the debt crises of the 1980s: they were not precipitated by profligate governments with large cash deficits and uncontrolled monetary policies. They also occurred in countries which, for the most part, were following prudent macroeconomic policies, and some of which had quite sophisticated institutional arrangements. And while economic fluctuations in all countries have a disproportionate effect on the poor (see Furman and Stiglitz (1999)), in the case of less developed countries (LDCs), their impacts on increased poverty may be especially marked, leaving scars behind in the form of interrupted school and malnutrition, given the limited safety nets and the large impacts on real wages.[1] Even with more extensive safety nets if there is a large enough fluctuation, governments may not be able to cope adequately. Moreover, in contrast to most developed countries, many developing countries exhibit pro-cyclical fiscal policies. In many cases, the expenditure contractions include reductions in social expenditures (even if the share of these expenditures in total government expenditures does not fall); and these social expenditures are often of disproportionate importance to the poor.[2]

Economic volatility is of importance to developing countries not just because of the short-run adverse effects on the poor. It has been shown to also have adverse effects on economic growth. There are thus ample reasons for trying to understand better the determinants of economic volatility. The marked differences in the downturns in Latin America in the early 1980s and in East Asia in the late 1990s means that we need a general framework for thinking about macroeconomic fluctuations – one that can encompass the marked differences among countries.

This chapter attempts to set forth such a general framework. It is a framework which applies both to developed and LDCs. It is general enough to incorporate the important structural, institutional and policy differences between developed and LDCs, which might account for differences in their macroeconomic performance. Creating such a framework is important: the failures in predicting the course of evolution of the economies in East Asia played an important role in shaping policies which, it is now generally agreed, served to exacerbate the downturn in those countries. We shall argue that certain developments in macroeconomics for more advanced countries have provided the intellectual framework around which a *set* of macroeconomic models for LDCs can be constructed. At the same time, the stark outcomes of recent crises in developing countries help us see more clearly some of the underlying structural issues in developed-country macro-economics. As has been the case in the past, for example in the labour market, where efficiency wage theories, first formulated for developing countries, have become central to understanding real wage rigidities in developed countries, there are strong synergies between developed country macroeconomics and macroeconomics for developing countries.

The paper is divided into two sections. The first puts the issue of macro-economic paradigms within a broader setting. The second looks more carefully at a range of short-run dynamic effects, which to date have not been incorporated in traditional macroeconomic analysis. A sequel (Easterly, Islam and Stiglitz (2000)) explores in greater detail the empirical evidence on the determinants of volatility in general and recessions in particular. The conclusion includes some remarks about the policy implications of the analysis.

17.2   Dynamics, macroeconomic equilibrium and the standard competitive model

The starting point of modern macroeconomics is the competitive equilibrium model, in which not only are all resources fully employed, but they are deployed efficiently. Fluctuations in output therefore reflect changes in inputs (say the desire of workers to work) or changes in technology, the relationship between inputs and output. While these real business cycle theories provide plausible explanations for variability in the rate of growth, they have a hard time providing persuasive explanations of economic downturns in a large, closed economy such as the United States: does one really believe that the Great Depression, or even the Reagan recession, was caused by these factors? That the reduced employment was a sudden desire of workers to enjoy more leisure, which quickly changed once again a couple of years later? And that to the extent that the reduction in output exceeded the reduction in labour, it was due to a sudden attack of Alzheimer's disease, technical regress, a forgetting of efficient production technologies? To be sure, for small *open* economies, adverse terms-of-trade shocks can have much the same effect as a negative technology shock, and this is one of the important differences between macroeconomics in these economies and that which underlies some of the traditional closed economy models.

17.2.1   New views of economic fluctuations versus old business cycle theories

Thus employment and output fluctuations inevitably relate to shocks and the manner in which the economy copes with those shocks – the extent to which the individually rational actions of firms and households, and the policy interventions of governments,[3] add up to collective behaviour which either brings the economy quickly back to full employment and efficient resource utilization or not. Thus, analyses attempt to understand the sources of the shocks, and the structures of the economy and policy interventions which either amplify or dampen those shocks, and either make their impacts short or long lived.

The modern perspective on these issues makes the analysis particularly complicated, because what is viewed to be individually rational on the part of households and firms depends on their beliefs both about the behaviour of each other and the policy regime of the government – which in turn may depend on its beliefs about their behaviour. And the shocks themselves are, to some extent at least, endogenous, determined by outsiders' beliefs about the economic structures. Thus macroeconomics is concerned with the dynamics of quite complex systems, and, inevitably, simple models focus on one malfunction or another.

This perspective is markedly different from classical business cycle theory, which saw the economy as described by a set of difference or differential equations, which exhibited cyclicality – the most famous examples of which are Samuelson's multiplier accelerator model and Hicks's business cycle theory. The fundamental objection to these mechanistic approaches – beyond the unpersuasiveness of some of the underlying technological assumptions (e.g. the accelerator) – is that if they were true, downturns would be predictable, and then government, through monetary and fiscal policy, could and should take countervailing measures. In fact, at least for the United States, there is no evidence that the longer the expansion, the higher the probability of a downturn: that is, there is no evidence of a regular cycle (though, to be sure, there are fluctuations).[4]

Wage rigidities versus more general deviations from the competitive model

For nearly half a century, attention was centred on the downward rigidity in money wages and prices. It was, in effect, the price of labour and goods, relative to money, which impeded the adjustment of the economy. Rigid real wages provided an easy explanation of unemployment – a leftward shift in the demand curve for labour immediately turned into unemployment. And the leftward shift in the demand for labour could be explained by the falling demand for goods, itself explained by rigidities in inter-temporal prices – in the interest rate, which monetary policy seemingly could not bring down, or bring down enough to stimulate consumption and investment.

Subsequent work has focused on amplifying the reasons for nominal and real wage rigidities (menu costs, efficiency wage theory, portfolio theories of adjustment) and finding deeper explanations for the failure of monetary policy to bring down interest rates, beyond the liquidity trap (e.g. risk-averse behaviour of banks, especially when confronted with excessively tight regulatory oversight).

More recent strands of research – some reviving strands that pre-dated Keynes (and which actually exist within Keynes) – have focused, for instance, on *differences* in adjustment speeds (see Stiglitz (1999)), as well as on distributive effects that arise from price changes, especially those against which individuals cannot be insured (reflecting incomplete contracts). Economists are increasingly aware that income effects arising from distribution changes can often overwhelm substitution effects arising from price changes; and this is especially so when there are asymmetries in the adjustments of real variables. For example, it is easier, less risky, or less costly to contract the utilization of some inputs than to expand them. (Note that traditional Keynesian theory focused on asymmetries in adjustment of wages and prices; here we argue that asymmetries in adjustments of real variables are every bit as important.)

There has thus been a growing recognition that wage (and price) rigidities may not be the only, or even the most important departure from the standard competitive equilibrium model relevant for explaining the nature of economic fluctuations. Moreover, as we have argued, modern macroeconomics emphasizes the dynamic reactions of market economies to shocks, the *failure* of wages to adjust may not be the most interesting, or most important, part of these dynamics. Traditional macroeconomics incorporates only a few of the relevant rigidities and dynamics. In particular, two important sets of dynamics and rigidities have been underemphasized: real interest rate constraints and dynamics, and balance-sheet dynamics of firms, financial institutions and government, an extreme case of which is illustrated by the dynamics of corporate distress and bankruptcy.

Below, we explain the various channels through which the dynamic forces operate. Such a taxonomy is important, because adjustment processes may differ among countries.

Comparative static analyses versus dynamic analyses

There are several important aspects of this change in perspective that should be stressed. The first is that, in the past, what passed as dynamic analysis was little more than comparative statics. The difference is not just a matter of exposition: the dynamics of adjustment may have the opposite effect from that predicted by a comparative static analysis. For instance, a fall in prices would, it was asserted, raise consumption through the real balance effect. What should have been said is, 'a lower level of prices would be associated with a higher level of consumption'. But for the economy to go from one level of wages and prices to a lower level requires adjustment – typically, there is not an instantaneous jump in prices. The adjustment process has its own consequences: falling prices mean that, at any level of the nominal interest rate, real interest rates are increased. If nominal interest rates cannot be pushed below zero, then the faster prices fall, the higher is the real interest rate – and presumably the lower is investment. As a second example, consider the effect of lowering wages. *Lower* wages might normally be thought of as inducing employers to hire more workers. But if *falling* wages induce increased uncertainty on the part of consumers, they may cut back consumption, and the reduction in aggregate demand (if not offset by some other countervailing government policy) may reduce employment – more than offsetting the direct effect of lower wages.

The importance of institutions

A second difference between the new perspective and traditional macro-analyses is that in the latter, institutions (other than labour market institutions which give rise to wage rigidities) play no role. By contrast, in the new perspective, financial market *institutions* (banks, securities markets, and the governmental authorities that regulate them), in particular, are central. Financial market institutions, in turn, have profound effects on firm behaviour (on how, for instance, firms cope with shocks). Differences in these institutions between developed and less-developed countries provide some of the key insights into the marked differences in macro-behaviour. Another important difference between developed and less-developed countries is the nature of fiscal policy: governments seem to pursue pro-cyclical rather than counter-cyclical policies. There are a number of possible explanations for this pattern, including imperfections in capital markets which put constraints on government's ability to finance deficits in recessions.

Endogeneity of institutions and shocks

The new views emphasize the *endogeneity* of many factors that were previously taken to be exogenous – including institutions and 'shocks'. Thus, East Asia may have had deeper debt financial institutions partly because it had experienced fewer shocks. Had it faced the level of shocks experienced elsewhere, firms would not have been willing to undertake the risks associated with the high-debt strategy, households would not have been willing to save in financial assets, and governments might not have been willing to provide the implicit or explicit insurance which made those risks that much more bearable. But countries in which firms have sufficiently high debt/equity ratios and in which financial institutions are sufficiently leveraged may themselves 'invite' shocks: that is, for instance, they may be highly susceptible to changes in perceptions, for example of the country's economic future. Under conditions of high leverage, slight changes in those perceptions can be amplified into large differences in expected returns, and thus into large changes in capital flows; and these large and swift changes in capital flows (given open capital markets) can induce an economic downturn, or even a crisis.

But clearly, not everything can be endogenous – or at least cannot be perceived that way by the policy economist. Governments can be thought of as adopting a *policy regime*,[5] for instance, whether to open up the capital account (on the short end) or to engage in trade liberalization. While the level of trade or capital flows may be endogenous, the regulatory regime – the rules of the game – can at least be thought of as exogenous. Governments can decide whether to deregulate financial institutions. They may be able to decide – within constraints – on the macroeconomic regime.

17.2.2   Anomalies: further problems with the standard paradigm

In formulating macroeconomic models, we need to look carefully at the data. Models based on, say, price and wage rigidities become unpersuasive if the evidence suggests that wages and prices are highly flexible. The data show that LDCs which have both more flexible wages and prices *still* exhibit high volatility (Easterly, Islam and Stiglitz (2000)). We need to ask: can this high level of volatility be explained simply by the fact that the countries are exposed to more shocks (or have a less diversified economy), or are there other aspects of their structure or policy regimes which explain this volatility?

A model that has a clear prediction which is contravened by the evidence should be viewed with suspicion, particularly if the prediction is 'central' to the theory. For instance, a clear prediction of the standard competitive model is that a small country should face an essentially horizontal demand curve for its exports. Thus, aggregate demand should not be a central problem for a small open economy, assuming that it does not try to set its exchange rate at an inappropriate level. A standard Keynesian model cannot provide a good explanation of unemployment in a small open economy. Yet many small open economies do face serious economic downturns. Similarly, if a country engages in a significant devaluation, output in the tradable sector should only be limited by supply concerns, and unemployment should only be related to the costs and pace of labour mobility – moving from the non-tradable to the tradable sector. The fact that the large devaluations in East Asia (and elsewhere) did not have the predicted result – many firms in the export sectors seemed to have excess capacity – thus suggests that that model may leave out something important, at least as far as a description of those economies is concerned. We call such a deviation, a discrepancy between the prediction of a widely accepted model and 'reality', an *anomaly*.

Anomalies force one to re-examine the assumptions of the model, to look for alternative models which are consistent with the observed behaviour. We argue that many of the seeming anomalies (which we shall shortly describe) can be explained by a model that incorporates a variety of market imperfections and institutions into the analysis; in particular, we shall focus on the role of financial markets, institutions and constraints.

For instance, consider the seeming anomaly just described, the marked fluctuations in output in small open economies and the failure of exports to expand in the predicted manner in East Asia in response to the large devaluation. We can explain both of these phenomena by focusing on supply: there were disturbances to the economy that affect firms' supply curves. In the case of East Asia, the source of the supply disturbance is not hard to find: the interruption in the flow of credit, and the high interest rates that those with access to credit had to pay. The lack of credit availability and the high interest rates combined to force many firms into bankruptcy, further shifting the market supply curve to the left.[6]

Impacts of recent crises on real wages are equally troublesome. Assume, for simplicity, that the trade and non-tradable sectors have production functions of constant elasticity; in the obvious notation:

$$Ln\ Q_T = \alpha \ln L_T, \text{ and}$$
$$Ln\ Q_{NT} = \beta \ln L_{NT}$$

Then in competitive markets, a 20 per cent increase in the labour force in the traded sector results in an $\alpha \times 20$ per cent increase in output of tradables, and a $1 - \alpha \times 20$ per cent fall in real product wages. For instance, with the elasticity of output of 0.8, output increases by 16 per cent and real product wages fall by 4 per cent. But while output in the non-tradable sector contracts, real product wages in that sector rise. Since real wages – measured by consumption – will be disproportionately weighted by non-tradables (if the country imports investment goods), average real consumption wages will fall by less than 4 per cent, and may even rise. For instance, if β also equals 0.8, and half the workforce was initially employed in each sector, and if individuals only consumed non-tradables, then real consumption wages would have (in the neoclassical model) risen by 4 per cent.

Anomalies in the financial market – deviations from what we would predict if financial markets worked perfectly – are perhaps even more telling. Investors in a perfect capital market do not care about own-risk, only about covariances; and a market, such as that of Thailand, is sufficiently small that the covariance with global financial markets is likely to be small. Thus, to a first order approximation, investors will not respond to an increase in the riskiness of the market, only to a change in expected returns. Similarly, changes in overall risk premia should have little effect on the terms at which funds are made available to individual countries.

Earlier literature has called attention to a number of other seeming anomalies: the fact that inventories do not act to stabilize the economy (low marginal costs in a recession should induce firms to produce then, to sell in the boom); the fact that real product wages do not rise in a recession (if firms were moving along a fixed production function/supply curve, as output/employment falls, the marginal product of labour should rise); or the fact that most investment regressions show that nominal interest rate as, or more, important than real interest rates, and that cash flow variables matter. To be sure, each of these anomalies can be explained by Ptolemaic exercises; the point, however, is that there are central predictions of the standard models which seem at odds with the evidence. Analyses focusing on imperfections arising in the capital market provide coherent and plausible explanations for *all* of these phenomena. While we cannot go so far as to suggest that these capital market imperfections fully explain the observed differences in macroeconomic behaviour across regions, models which incorporate these financial-market effects at least provide interesting interpretations of those differences. As we comment in the final section, policies based on neoclassical models – which ignore these and other constraints, market imperfections and dynamic considerations – are not only likely to be ineffective, but they may be counterproductive, as they arguably were in East Asia.

17.3   A taxonomy of effects

As we have already suggested, there is more to macro-dynamics than just the observation that wages and prices fail to adjust to equilibrate markets. But dynamics are complicated. If we are to have a reasonable chance of incorporating all the important dynamic effects, we need to have a systematic way of thinking through these effects. For that, we need a taxonomy of dynamic effects. We can categorize effects in four ways:

1. According to the aspect of aggregate demand which they affect (consumption, investment, exports, imports, government expenditures, taxes).
2. According to the productive sector which they affect (tradables, non-tradables, investment goods, consumption goods, manufacturing, service sector, etc.).
3. According to the *nature* of the effect – that is, substitution (within a period, or inter-temporal substitution effects), income or wealth effects, cash flow (financial constraint) effects, and informational/organizational effects, for example, associated with the bankruptcy of firms and financial institutions;[7] in the case of wealth effects, whether the effects are on households, or firms, whether the effects arise from a changed ability or willingness to bear risk; in the case of financial constraint effects, whether they arise as a result of a reduced cash flow of the firm or household, or because of reduced lending or higher interest rates charged by financial institutions.
4. According to the source of the effect – that is, adjustments in wages, prices, exchange rates, or interest rates, or expectations about changes

in those variables. These variables are, however, often endogenous – though in analysing the dynamics it is often useful to trace out the effects of changes in each of these variables, however they come about (i.e. whether as a result of a changed government policy, such as a change in the exchange rate, or whether as a result of a response to some other change).

Thus, for instance, we can identify the impact of interest rate increases or exchange rate decreases on each component of aggregate demand and on each productive sector of the economy; we can describe, in each case, how those effects operate through substitution effects, through impacts on firms via cash constraints or net worth effects, or through effects on the economy as a result of induced bankruptcies and the resulting weaknesses in financial institutions.

Clearly, meaningful economic analysis needs to select out among this huge array of possible effects those that are likely to be, or have been, most important. It is one of the central theses of this chapter that previous studies have paid too much attention to the consequences of nominal wage and price rigidities, and too little attention to dynamic effects arising from firm and financial institution wealth and cash flow constraints (which by hypothesis under neoclassical theory simply do not exist). These effects affect both supply and demand – and indeed, one of the central implications of the new theory concerns that intermingling of the two sides of the market – a shock to aggregate demand quickly can become translated into a shift in the aggregate supply curve (and not just a movement along the aggregate supply curve.) Moreover, a key part of the dynamic analysis is tracing out *interaction* effects: how a global financial shock, such as occurred in 1998, affects a country depends on the openness of the capital account, its dependence on international trade, and the degree of leverage of firms and financial institutions. Central to our analysis is thus an attempt to understand how certain aspects of the structure of the economy affect how particular shocks (the source of the dynamic disturbance) work their way through various parts of the economic *system*.

17.3.1 Further aspects of dynamic models

Three of the four elements of this taxonomy are easy to understand: the source of the effect, and the sector or aspect of demand which they affect. The most important and difficult to come to grips with is the category we have labelled 'nature' of the effect. If we had limited ourselves to the simple competitive model, our task would be easy: we would only need to identify income and substitution effects. But, as we shall see, there are a variety of 'channels' and 'institutions' through which the impact of a shock to the economy are mediated.

Expectations

Dynamic effects are complicated because they depend on expectations, on beliefs about what will happen in the future, and often we have scant data to infer those beliefs. This is especially true for the relatively rare events we call crises: how should someone have formed their expectations in the midst of the Great Depression, the worst economic downturn since the beginning of capitalism; or in Indonesia and Thailand today, the worst economic crises these countries have faced since the advent of industrialization in their societies? Moreover, with fixed, sunk costs (and, more generally, irreversibilities) and imperfect information concerning the future, households and firms become sensitive to option values, how actions they take today foreclose or open up new options for the future. And in a world with imperfect information, individuals and firms also become sensitive to how their actions – or changes in their actions – affect others' beliefs, and therefore their future opportunities. Still, while we may not be able to predict with any degree of reliability how expectations will change, the fact is that 'shocks' to the economy do exercise their dynamic influence through changes in expectations.[8]

Public dynamics

In addition, dynamic models need to specify the government's dynamic regime: for example, whether government attempts to set the interest rate, the level or rate of expansion of the nominal or real money supply, and so on, and how it adjusts those policies in responses to changing economic conditions. The empirical analysis reported in Easterly, Islam and Stiglitz (2000) shows convincingly that the macroeconomic behaviour of the public sector in developing countries is markedly different from that in developed countries: in particular, there is evidence of pro-cyclical fiscal policy in the latter and counter-cyclical behaviour in the former.[9] Ongoing research is attempting to identify the explanation for these differences; one obvious hypothesis is that developing-country governments typically face more binding capital constraints in downturns, so that while they might like to engage in counter-cyclical policies, declining revenues in a recession and reduced access to funds force a contraction in the (full-employment) deficit[10] and in expenditures.

Balance sheet effects

Firm wealth effects. Theory[11] and evidence[12] both support the hypothesis that firms act in a risk-averse manner, and that the effective degree of risk aversion is affected by their wealth: for example how close the firm is to bankruptcy.[13] Large (unanticipated) increases in interest rates for a firm with a heavy level of short-term indebtedness decrease the firm's net worth. An unanticipated decrease in exchange rates increases the net worth of an exporting firm (measured in local currency), even if it has foreign-denominated debts, so long as it is not overexposed – which, by hypothesis (for a risk-averse firm), it will not normally be.[14] Other firms may have gambled (or had 'irrational expectations'), inducing them to have uncovered positions, such that a decrease in the exchange rate lowers their net worth.[15]

Changes in firm wealth (regardless of source) induce both demand and supply responses, and responses in goods, labour and finance markets. Except when production is to order or there are good forward markets, all production involves risk-taking (since firms must expend resources on inputs before they have assured markets and prices); hence risk-averse firms will cut back on production, and 'liquefy' – reduce inventories (or the pace of inventory accumulation); if the net wealth shock is large enough, a firm may even discharge workers.[16]

There is a particular group of firms which play a pivotal role in the economy – financial institutions. Their 'risky' activity is lending – based on screening and monitoring loan applicants. Adverse net-worth shocks to these institutions lower their ability and willingness to bear risk – that is, lower the amount that they are willing to lend at any interest rate. Certain groups of borrowers may actually be excluded from the market.[17]

Effects of distress.   When negative net-worth shocks are large enough, firms may go into distress, that is, be on the verge of, or in, bankruptcy.[18] The actual dissolution of firms results in a loss of potentially enormously valuable informational and social capital (the 'good will of the firm', which in many cases can be substantial, is a measure of the value of this capital). While when bankruptcy is the result of mismanagement of a firm, there may be a presumption that the loss in organizational capital may be minimal, when it is a result of macro-disturbances, the costs are undoubtedly greater. Indeed, Ferri and Kang (1999) have shown that, in the case of Korea, there is little evidence that bankruptcy acted in the recent crisis as an effective sorting mechanism, distinguishing between well and poorly managed firms.

But the fear of bankruptcy of a firm has adverse effects on all those with whom the firm does business. Good workers start to look for other jobs, customers (in the case of goods other than standardized commodities) will insist on a lower price to compensate them for the risk of the failure of a completion of a contract, or will simply switch to suppliers that are viewed to be more reliable. Indeed, there are reports that this effect was important in East Asia: in spite of the huge devaluation, many apparel purchasers shied away from placing critical orders (e.g. for Christmas goods).

Because of the complex credit inter-relationships among firms – most firms supply credit to customers and/or suppliers – bankruptcy of one firm can set off a 'bankruptcy chain', weakening other firms that depend on it, and possibly pushing some into bankruptcy itself. Thus, the likelihood of bankruptcy becomes a variable of systemic concern (see Orszag and Stiglitz (1999), Easterly, Islam and Stiglitz (2000)). There is a particularly important linkage – that between firms and financial institutions. As more firms go into distress, the number of non-performing loans increases, and thus the financial position of financial institutions deteriorates.[19] Hence financial distress converts into reduced 'net worth' and/or 'lending capacity' for financial institutions; with the ability and willingness to lend lowered, firms (even those whose financial position has not deteriorated) will face higher borrowing costs and reduced access to funds.

Cash-flow constraints. In standard economic theory, cash flow (or liquidity) constraints simply do not exist: anyone with good future prospects can get access to funds. There is no such thing as either credit or equity rationing. In practice, however, there is evidence, especially for small firms, that cash flows do have large effects on firm decisions, for example, investment and, in extreme cases, even production.

It has become fashionable to distinguish between liquidity constraints and solvency concerns, say, in financial institutions. This provides the rationale for a lender of last resort. But advocates of this distinction have not taken sufficient note that this distinction fundamentally undermines arguments for perfect markets: it is setting up a government or international bureaucrat to make judgements about future prospects, which seemingly contravene the 'market's' judgement.

Of course, once one admits the central importance of informational imperfections (and enforcement constraints), then the distinction becomes more understandable. For instance, a firm could have from the perspective of its owner's probability judgements a positive net worth, yet lenders might believe that the expected present discounted value (given *their* probability judgement) of what they could extract from the firm is less than the opportunity cost of those funds.

Imperfections in the equity market (whether arising from adverse selection and incentive concerns or enforcement problems, for example, associated with costly state verification) lead to what may be thought of as equity rationing – or at the very least, the costs of issuing new equity may be very high, making firms reluctant to engage in this form of finance, even when they cannot obtain loans (see Myers and Maljuf (1984), Greenwald, Stiglitz and Weiss (1984), and Helmann and Stiglitz (2000)). Equity rationing also implies that firms cannot diversify their risk well – making them act in a more risk-averse manner. The market imperfections which lead to equity rationing (e.g. problems of monitoring profits, problems in corporate governance, of information asymmetries) are often far worse in developing countries than in developed countries. This may be one of the central ways in which the risk absorption capacity of developing countries is weaker than in developed countries.

More generally, an important determinant of the magnitude of this 'financial sector' effect is the extent of integration of the economy into global capital markets. Weaknesses in the country's own financial market institutions may matter little if firms in the country have easy access to banks abroad. In fact, in relatively few countries – even developed countries – do small and medium-size enterprises have access to banks or other sources of finance outside their own country.

Capital outflows

Outside investors (or even domestic wealth-holders) may, observing the weakening condition of firms and financial institutions within the country, decide to pull their (short-term) money out of the country and put it elsewhere, thus further weakening both firms and financial institutions (e.g. by further weakening the currency), and possibly inducing a crisis.

These adverse effects on the *terms at which firms can get access* to funds will be exacerbated by the presence of *credit rationing*. The increased uncertainty about different firms' balance sheets, caused by the economic disturbance, may lead to a greater prevalence of credit rationing. Credit rationing itself, and the fear of credit rationing, leads to further contractions in demand (investment, including inventories), as firms attempt to increase their liquidity. Further, the increases in interest rates charged by banks in response to their increased perception of risks has further adverse effects on firm's balance sheets (to the extent that they are dependent on short term credit). This reinforces the effects noted above, both on supply and demand.

In conclusion, we need to re-emphasize that the volatility of the economy will differ across countries according to the nature of the shocks they face, the structure of the economy and the policy regime of the government. Small open countries, for instance, are more exposed to external shocks arising from abroad; countries that are exporters of commodities may be particularly vulnerable, given the high level of volatility of commodity prices. Short-term capital flows seem particularly volatile – and expose the country to considerable risk. Hence, countries with more open capital accounts (more integrated into the global capital market) may be better insulated from the impacts of shocks to their own financial institutions (since they can more easily turn abroad to a source of funds), but are more at risk to changes in sentiments concerning the relative risk-adjusted returns at home and abroad. Higher degrees of leverage increase the probability of default of a firm; but the degree of leverage itself should adjust to the risk facing the firm. On theoretical grounds alone, it is difficult to say which of the various effects discussed in this paper will dominate. For example, greater wage and price flexibility may or may not reduce volatility in growth and employment. The data indicate that OECD countries have both lower growth volatility and lower wage flexibility than non-OECD countries. In other words, rigid wages are probably not the most important factor affecting growth volatility (Easterly, Islam and Stiglitz (2000)). In fact, the role of the financial sector turns out to be the most important factor affecting growth volatility.

17.4 Concluding comments

This paper can be thought of as a re-examination of the standard paradigms concerning economic stability. As we have repeatedly emphasized, economic stability is important both because of the short run impacts on society, particularly on the most vulnerable (and LDCs typically have weak safety nets to protect the very poor, and inadequate risk mechanisms even to adequately absorb risk for other segments of the population), and because of its long-run impacts on growth. The recent global crisis has clearly shown weaknesses in both the standard views of what is required for macro-stability and how to respond to crises when they occur. It has shown that a country's financial structure could be as important a source of instability as can large government deficits.

This chapter presents three underlying hypotheses: that macro-behaviour of developed and less-developed countries differ significantly; that in understanding those differences one has to look more carefully at a variety of dynamic effects which traditionally have been omitted or underemphasized in standard economic models, and that some of the most important 'omitted' variables are those relating to the financial sector. The sequel (Easterly, Islam and Stiglitz (2000)) largely confirms these hypotheses empirically.

The results of our theoretical analyses, if correct, have strong policy implications, some of which entail markedly different policy prescriptions from those of the conventional model, as illustrated by the following examples:

- In the standard model, countries are told to render labour institutions more flexible, to allow a more rapid lowering of real wages, so that the demand for labour can more rapidly adjust to supply. But there are aggregate demand effects of wage adjustments, and the adverse effects of these may more than offset the positive effects arising from wage flexibility.

- In the standard model, countries are told that opening the capital account will allow risk diversification, stabilizing the economy; in fact, it appears that any benefits on this score can be more than offset by the fact that capital movements are highly variable – and can be highly pro-cyclical, in some cases inducing downturns, in others exacerbating fluctuations that arise from other sources. Policy makers should devise new financial strategies that hedge against these risks while maintaining their access to finance.

- In the standard model, countries are told that raising interest rates draws capital into the country and thereby strengthens the exchange rate, and thereby the economy. In practice, the evidence that raising interest rates strengthens the exchange rate is, at best, ambiguous; in countries with high levels of short-term indebtedness, the adverse net wealth effects – leading to firm and financial institution distress and exacerbating cash constraints – more than offsets the direct effect. It is not surprising then that some countries have wound up not only with a weaker economy, but even a weaker exchange rate. More generally, our analysis suggests that analyses that do not take account of impacts of policy changes on net worth, distress of firms and financial institutions, and financial constraints and institutions are likely to miss the mark.

- In the standard model, weakening of the exchange rate should quickly result in a strengthening of the economy, as exports increase. If firms have large uncovered positions, these beneficial effects may be more than offset by adverse net wealth effects. But even if that does not occur, if there is a belief that the exchange rate may have overshot, and if domestic investment is complementary with imported investment goods, then the impact effect of the devaluation may be negative; the adverse effects on investment may be larger in the short term than the direct stimulus to exports.

- While most developed countries have built-in stabilizers, provided by progressive taxation and welfare programmes, most developing countries lack these, and in some cases are moving to policy regimes that exacerbate fluctuations, for example rigid implementation of capital adequacy standards, the effect of which is to reduce credit supplies in recessions.

- In the standard model, openness enhances economic growth[20] and high economic growth reduces volatility and makes countries less subject to an economic downturn. But openness also contributes significantly to economic volatility.

- Standard models do not take account of the constraints on government policy; our analysis suggests that such constraints may be so important that governments in developing countries have actually been forced to pursue pro-cyclical fiscal policies.

- Standard models give short shrift to financial institutions (often seeming to suggest that the whole sector can be embedded in a money demand equation); our analysis (confirmed in Easterly, Islam and Stiglitz (2000)) argues that financial institutions play a central role in economic volatility in general and downturns in particular.

There has been a growing consensus that at the root of the problem of instability, or at least an important factor contributing to East Asia's difficulties – and to the increasing frequency of financial and currency crises throughout the world – has been the excessive zeal for financial market and capital account liberalization without taking into account the full range of consequences, including increased volatility, and how countries should respond to this riskier environment, for example by availing themselves of hedging mechanisms against financial volatility when these exist. And research inspired by that crisis has shown that the traditional responses – raising interest rates to defend exchange rates – have at best a spotty record of success in terms of the intended goal, though they can force economies into severe recessions when prolonged.

For several decades now, a basic strategy for understanding unemployment, and economic volatility more generally, has been to ask, 'In what ways does the market differ from the competitive ideal?' Traditional Keynesian analysis emphasized only one way in which market economies deviated from the competitive ideal – wages and prices were rigid – and it followed that increasing wage and price flexibility should be expected to bring economies closer to that ideal. Even within that traditional frame, much of the standard analysis seems to have left out some important first order effects, for example, the *dynamic* consequences of wages and prices falling or of exchange-rate overshooting, which may result in short run adverse effects that appear earlier and more dominant than the comparative static effects, which come into play later, and which have until now been the primary focus of attention.

This approach provided clear guidance for policy: try to make the actual economy approximate more closely the Arrow-Debreu ideal, for example, make wages and prices more flexible. Interestingly, many of the standard prescriptions that were commonplace in the 1980s and early 1990s were selective (in ways which could not be justified by economic theory) in which of the postulates of that model that were emphasized – for example, private property over competition. But ironically, in the same period during which that model gained ascendancy in the context of development, its underlying postulates came under severe attack – its assumptions, for instance, concerning information, and its inability to deal with innovation and entrepreneurship, issues which are central to development. Financial markets are important, precisely because of informational issues: they select among competing use of funds and monitor their use.

Thus, there is now increasing recognition that the Arrow-Debreu model provides a fundamentally flawed view of the market economy; if it had provided an accurate description, market socialism would have had a far better record than it did (see Stiglitz, 1994)), and attaining macro-stability would have been a far easier task than has proved to be the case. It is concerns that appear nowhere in that model – issues such as bankruptcy, imperfections in risk markets (equity markets), credit constraints – that may dominate the short-run behaviour of the economy, both in the private and in the public sector. Unless and until these concerns become incorporated into analytic frameworks used for policy responses in developing countries, there can be little confidence in the effectiveness of policy prescriptions. We cannot even be sure of that perhaps-too-often neglected element of the Hippocratic code: do no harm.

Notes

1. For instance, real wages in Korea fell by more than 9 per cent in 1999. At the same time, some developing countries have managed to cope with the crisis remarkably well, in spite of the absence of a social safety net. In Thailand, there appears to have been little interruption in schooling (though the pace of improvement was adversely affected) and little evidence of increased malnutrition (World Bank (1999)).
2. World Bank (1992) found that shares of spending on health and education in countries receiving adjustment lending remained unchanged, while Corbo, Fischer and Webb (1992) found that education shares declined.
3. There has been increasing attention on the political economy of macroeconomic policy; thus, government is not viewed as a single actor, with well-defined preferences and beliefs.
4. President of the United States (1997) and Stiglitz (1997).
5. Though from the perspective of political economy, even the policy regime can be thought of as endogenous.
6. There are often alternative explanations of a seeming anomaly; for instance, if firms even in a small open economy face downward-sloping demand curves for their products, even a large devaluation may generate only a limited increase in the demand for their products. The power of the models to be presented below is that they simultaneously provide explanations for several of the key anomalies.
7. Other information effects are associated with *changes* in firm behaviour, which lead others (e.g. customers, suppliers, or creditors), to change their views about the firm's financial position (e.g. the likelihood of bankruptcy). Similar effects arise in the labour market, where workers may worry that accepting a low-skilled job will stigmatize them. Still other information effects arise from changes in prices which have variable and uncertain effects: for example, on the net worth of firms. Thus, a large increase in interest rates increases the uncertainty about a firm's net worth, unless there is extremely good data concerning each firm's asset structure.
8. Much of the popular discussion of crises focuses on 'confidence', which could mean either an improvement in, say, the expectation concerning mean return and/or a reduction in the variance of return. Many of the failures of the policy prescriptions can be thought of as based on poor models predicting the impact of actions on 'confidence'.
9. For Latin America, see also Hausmann and Gavin (1996).
10. Though the observed deficit may actually increase.

11. This is because imperfections in equity markets (which themselves can be explained by informational imperfections; in the case of most developing countries, few would question the hypothesis of limitations in equity markets) limit the extent to which risks can be shared and shifted; and because agency problems in large corporations lead to incentive schemes which induce risk averse behaviour in managers. See, e.g, Leland and Pyle (1977); Stiglitz (1982); Greenwald and Stiglitz (1991).

12. There is a large catalogue of firm behaviour which is hard to reconcile with the standard neoclassical model with risk-neutral firms but which is consistent with the theory of the risk-averse firm (see the discussion above and Stiglitz (1982) and Greenwald and Stiglitz (1991)).

13. Note that, when there are costs to bankruptcy, firms whose wealth falls below a critical threshold may start to behave in a risk-loving manner; to use Ed Kane's memorable phrase (in the context of financial firms with negative net worth), they are zombies, gambling on resurrection (see Kane (1990)).

14. There is one possible exception: if foreign lenders have provided funds at sufficiently attractive terms, relative to the cost of local funds, even risk-averse firms may be overexposed, in the sense that their net worth declines as the exchange rate increases. Misguided banking regulations (e.g. in more advanced countries, which encourage short-term lending abroad) can lead even rational financial institutions to provide funds at these favourable terms.

15. Easterly (1990) has a model in which devaluation is contractionary via this channel.

16. Such an action illustrates both the importance of option and information effects. If a firm believes that its demand for labour may soon rise, it will retain workers even if it currently does not need them; if it is uncertain about how long an upsurge in demand will last, it will prefer to pay overtime than to incur the fixed costs of hiring additional workers.

17. That is, as is well known, credit markets may be characterized by rationing. Similar problems arise in equity markets as well.

18. Technically, a firm is in bankruptcy only if its creditors have gone to the courts to seek redress, or the firm has gone to the courts to seek protection from creditors. We use the term 'distress' more generically to refer to situations where either the firm's net worth is negative, or its cash flow (including what creditors are 'voluntarily' willing to lend or roll over) is insufficient to meet its debt obligations. Creditors could, in principle, go to the court, but it may be less costly and more effective to do an out-of-court settlement. Even so, bankruptcy law provides the backdrop against which negotiations in these circumstances occur.

19. Note that these unpaid liabilities inhibit both the activities of firms and of their creditors. The debt overhang is a liability to firms, yet it is not really an asset to financial institutions, which necessarily must take a conservative position in discounting the likelihood of being repaid.

20. This is not quite correct: in the standard model, greater openness induces greater efficiency, a one-time gain in productivity, but it does not lead to sustained increases in economic growth. But the conventional wisdom, and much of the econometric literature, argues that openness not only has one-time efficiency effects, but long-term growth benefits, perhaps as a result of the discipline provided by enhanced competition, perhaps as a result of the increased awareness of new technologies, perhaps as a result of the availability of a broader array of intermediate good inputs.

References

Aizenman, J. and Marion, N. (1998) 'Volatility and Investment: Interpreting Evidence from Developing Countries', *Economica*, vol. 66, no. 262, pp. 157–79.

Ball, L., Mankiw, N.G. and Romer, D. (1988) 'The New Keynesian Economics and the Output-Inflation Trade-off', *Brookings Papers on Economic Activity*, no. 1, pp. 1–65.

Bruno, M. and Easterly, W. (1997) 'Inflation Crises and Long-Run Growth', *Journal of Monetary Economics*, vol. 41, pp. 3–26.

Corbo, V., Fischer, S. and Webb, S. (eds) (1992) *Adjustment Lending Revisited: Policies to Restore Growth* (Washington, DC: World Bank).

De Long, J.B. and Summers, L.H. (1988) 'How Does Macroeconomic Policy Affect Output?' *Brookings Papers on Economic Activity*, no. 2, pp. 433–80.

Easterly, William (1990) 'Portfolio Effects in a CGE Model: Devaluation in a Dollarized Economy', in Taylor, L. (ed.) *Structuralist Computable General Equilibrium Models for the Developing World* (Cambridge, Mass: MIT Press), pp. 269–301.

Easterly, W. and Levine, R. (1997) 'Africa's Growth Tragedy: Policies and Ethnic Divisions', *Quarterly Journal of Economics*, vol. 112, pp. 1203–50.

Easterly, W., Islam, R. and Stiglitz, J. (2000) 'Shaken and Stirred: Volatility and Macroeconomic Paradigms for Rich and Poor Countries', forthcoming.

Ferri, G. and Kang, T.S. (1999) 'The Credit Channel at Work: Lessons from the Financial Crisis in Korea', *Economic Notes*, vol. 28 (2), pp. 195–221.

Furman, J. and Stiglitz, J.E. (1999) 'Economic Crises: Evidence and Insights from East Asia', *Brookings Papers on Economic Activity*, no. 2, pp. 1–135.

Gavin, M., Hausmann, R., Perotti, R. and Talvi, E. (1996) 'Managing Fiscal Policy in Latin America and the Caribbean: Volatility, Procyclicality, and Limited Creditworthiness', Working Paper no. 326, Inter-American Development Bank, Office of the Chief Economist, Washington, DC, March.

Greenwald, B.C. and Stiglitz, J.E. (1991) 'Examining Alternative Macroeconomic Theories', in Phelps, E. (ed.) *Recent Developments in Macroeconomics* (Cheltenham: Edward Elgar), pp. 335–88.

Greenwald, B., Stiglitz, J.E. and Weiss, A. (1984) 'Informational Imperfections in the Capital Market and Macroeconomic Fluctuations', *American Economic Review*, vol. 74, no. 2, pp. 194–9.

Guillaumont, P., Jeanneney-Guillaumont, S. and Brun, J.-F. (1999) 'How Instability Lowers African Growth', *Journal of African Economies*, vol. 8, no. 1, pp. 87–107.

Hausmann, R. and Gavin, M. (1996) 'Securing Stability and Growth in a Shock Prone Region: The Policy Challenge for Latin America', Working Paper no. 315, Inter-American Development Bank, Office of the Chief Economist, January.

Helmann, T. and Stiglitz, J.E. (2000) 'Credit and Equity Rationing in Markets with Adverse Selection', *European Economic Review*, vol. 44, pp. 281–304.

Helmann, T., Murdock, K. and Stiglitz, J.E. (1996) 'Deposit Mobilization through Financial Restraint', in Hermes, N. and Lensink, R. (eds) *Financial Development and Economic Growth* (London: Routledge), pp. 219–46.

Inter-American Development Bank (1995) *Economic and Social Progress in Latin America. 1995 Report: Overcoming Volatility* (Washington, DC: Johns Hopkins Press).

Islam, Nazrul (1995) 'Growth Empirics: A Panel Data Approach', *Quarterly Journal of Economics*, vol. 110, November, pp. 1127–70.

Kane, E. (1990) 'Incentive Conflict in the International Regulatory Agreement on Risk-Based Capital', National Bureau of Economic Research Working Paper no. 3308.

Leland, H.E. and Pyle, D.H. (1977) 'Informational Asymmetries, Financial Structure, and Financial Intermediation', *Journal of Finance*, vol. 32, no. 2, pp. 371–87.

Mayer, C. (1988) 'New Issues in Corporate Finance', *European Economic Review*, vol. 32, pp. 1167–89.

Mendoza, E.G. (1994) 'Terms-of-Trade Uncertainty and Economic Growth: Are Risk Indicators Significant in Growth Regressions?' International Finance Discussion Paper no. 491, United States Board of Governors of the Federal Reserve System, International Finance Division, December.

Myers, S.C. and Maljuf, N. (1984) 'Corporate Financing and Investment Decisions When Firms Have Information that Investors Do Not Have', *Journal of Financial Economics*, vol. 13, pp. 187–221.

Newbery, D.M. and Stiglitz, J.E. (1982) 'Risk Aversion, Supply Response, and the Optimality of Random Prices: A Diagrammatic Analysis', *Quarterly Journal of Economics*, vol. 97, no. 1, February, pp. 1–26.

Orszag, P. and Stiglitz, J. (1999) 'Bankruptcy, Credit Constraints, and Economic Policy', unpublished draft, July.

President of the United States (1997) *Economic Report of the President* (Washington, DC: United States Government Printing Office).

Pritchett, L. (1998) 'Patterns of Economic Growth: Hills, Plateaus, Mountains, and Plains', Policy Research Working Paper no. 1947, Development Research Group, World Bank, July.

Ramey, G. and Ramey, V.A. (1995) 'Cross-Country Evidence on the Link Between Volatility and Growth', *American Economic Review*, vol. 85, pp. 1138–51.

Stiglitz, J.E. (1982) 'Information and Capital Markets', in Sharpe, W.F., Cootner, C. and Cootner, P.H. (eds) *Financial Economics: Essays in Honor of Paul Cootner* (Englewood Cliffs, NJ: Prentice Hall), pp. 118–58.

Stiglitz, J.E. (1994) *Whither Socialism?* (Cambridge, MASS: MIT Press).

Stiglitz, J.E. (1997) 'The Long Boom? Business Cycles in the 1980s and 1990s', paper presented to Georgetown Macroeconomics Seminar, Georgetown University, Washington, DC, 4 September and at the CEPR conference 'The Long Boom', Stanford University, 5 September.

Stiglitz, J.E. (1999) 'Toward a General Theory of Wage and Price Rigidities and Economic Fluctuations', *American Economic Review*, vol. 89, no. 2, May, pp. 75–80.

Stiglitz, J.E. (1999) 'Whither Reform?' paper presented at the Annual Bank Conference on Development Economics, World Bank, Washington, DC, 28–30 April.

Stiglitz, J.E. and Uy, M. (1996) 'Financial Markets, Public Policy, and the East Asian Miracle', *World Bank Research Observer*, vol. 11, no. 2, August, pp. 249–76.

Talvi, E. (1995) 'Fiscal Policy and the Business Cycle Associated with Exchange Rate-based Stabilizations: Evidence from Uruguay's 1978 and 1991 Programs', Working Paper no. 313, Office of the Chief Economist, Inter-American Development Bank, Washington, DC.

Talvi, Ernesto (1996) 'Exchange Rate-Based Stabilization with Endogenous Fiscal Response', Working Paper Series no. 324, Office of the Chief Economist, Inter-American Development Bank, Washington, DC.

World Bank (1992) 'Adjustment Lending and Mobilization of Private and Public Resources for Growth', World Bank Policy and Research Series no. 22, Country Economics Department, Washington, DC.

World Bank (1999) 'Coping with the Crisis in Education and Health', *Thailand Social Monitor*, Issue 2, World Bank Office in Bangkok, Thailand, July.